THE OXFORD HISTORY OF THE BRITISH EMPIRE

COMPANION SERIES

THE OXFORD HISTORY OF THE BRITISH EMPIRE

Volume I. *The Origins of Empire*
EDITED BY Nicholas Canny

Volume II. *The Eighteenth Century*
EDITED BY P. J. Marshall

Volume III. *The Nineteenth Century*
EDITED BY Andrew Porter

Volume IV. *The Twentieth Century*
EDITED BY Judith M. Brown and Wm. Roger Louis

Volume V. *Historiography*
EDITED BY Robin W. Winks

THE OXFORD HISTORY OF THE BRITISH EMPIRE

COMPANION SERIES

Wm. Roger Louis, CBE, D. Litt., FBA

*Kerr Professor of English History and Culture, University of Texas, Austin
and Honorary Fellow of St Antony's College, Oxford*

EDITOR-IN-CHIEF

❧

Environment and Empire

❧

William Beinart

*Rhodes Professor of Race Relations
University of Oxford, and
Fellow of St Antony's College*

and

Lotte Hughes

*Lecturer in African Arts and Cultures
The Ferguson Centre for African and Asian Studies
The Open University*

OXFORD
UNIVERSITY PRESS

OXFORD

UNIVERSITY PRESS

Great Clarendon Street, Oxford OX2 6DP

Oxford University Press is a department of the University of Oxford.
It furthers the University's objective of excellence in research, scholarship,
and education by publishing worldwide in

Oxford New York

Auckland Cape Town Dar es Salaam Hong Kong Karachi
Kuala Lumpur Madrid Melbourne Mexico City Nairobi
New Delhi Shanghai Taipei Toronto

With offices in

Argentina Austria Brazil Chile Czech Republic France Greece
Guatemala Hungary Italy Japan Poland Portugal Singapore
South Korea Switzerland Thailand Turkey Ukraine Vietnam

Oxford is a registered trade mark of Oxford University Press
in the UK and in certain other countries

Published in the United States
by Oxford University Press Inc., New York

British Library Cataloguing in Publication Data

Data available

Library of Congress Cataloging in Publication Data
Beinart, William.
Environment and empire / William Beinart and Lotte Hughes.
p. cm. —(The Oxford history of the British Empire)
Includes bibliographical references and index.
ISBN 978–0–19–926031–7 (alk. paper)
1. Human ecology–Great Britian. 2. Natural resources—Great Britain. 3. Plant ecology—Great
Britain. 4. Great Britain—Colonies—Environmental conditions. I. Hughes, Lotte. II. Title.
GF551.B45 2007
304.209171'241—dc22
2007020652

Typeset by Laserwords Private Limited, Chennai, India
Printed in Great Britain
on acid-free paper by
Biddles Ltd, King's Lynn, Norfolk

ISBN 978–0–19–926031–7

1 3 5 7 9 10 8 6 4 2

FOREWORD

The purpose of the five volumes of the Oxford History of the British Empire was to provide a comprehensive survey of the Empire from its beginning to end, to explore the meaning of British imperialism for the ruled as well as the rulers, and to study the significance of the British Empire as a theme in world history. The volumes in the Companion Series carry forward this purpose. They pursue themes that could not be covered adequately in the main series while incorporating recent research and providing fresh interpretations of significant topics.

Wm. Roger Louis

PREFACE AND ACKNOWLEDGEMENTS

Imperialism has been inseparable from the history of global environmental change. Our aim is to illustrate diverse environmental themes in the history of the British Empire. In the first half of the book we concentrate on the material factors that shaped the relationship between imperial expansion and the extra-European natural world. We explore the way in which British consumers and manufacturers sucked in resources that were gathered, hunted, fished, mined, and farmed in a great profusion of extractive and agrarian systems. Our discussion is based on case studies of environmental and social change, driven by imperial forces, whose legacy is still apparent today. We are particularly concerned to compare the impact of different commodity frontiers on colonized people.

We argue, however, that British settler and colonial states sought to regulate the use of natural resources as well as commodify them. India needed to protect forests for its railways; Australia required pastures for its sheep. We examine the rise of conservation, which aimed to guarantee efficient use of soil, vegetation, and water, or to preserve resources by exclusion. The linked themes of exploitation and conservation provide an essential tension in our narrative. We also explore attempts by scientists to come to terms with complex diseases and their prevention. Our final chapters, which link directly with those at the start of the book, focus on political reassertions by colonized peoples in respect of their environments. In the process of decolonization, and in a post-imperial age, they found a new voice, reformulating ideas about nature and landscape, and challenging views about who had the right to regulate nature.

Environment and Empire is a synthesis, exploring commodity frontiers, environmental change, diseases, conservationist ideas, urban environments, visual images of nature, and political ecology over the long term. Most single-volume histories of empire tend to downplay environmental issues; these are also subdued in the five main volumes of the *Oxford History of the British Empire*. This contribution to the companion series is designed to supplement and expand on the core texts and to implant neglected debates closer to the heart of the historiography of empire.

Unlike other volumes in this series, *Environment and Empire* is not an edited collection with chapters by specialists in particular fields. Inevitably we are straying into geographic zones and topics that lie outside our principle research expertise. We are specialists, respectively, on Southern and Eastern Africa and our understanding of these regions, together with India, has helped to shape our perspectives. Our home ground has provided useful reference points, around which we have built a sequence of linked examples, and India offers itself as a linchpin of empire, demographically preponderant, with a rich historiography. Nevertheless, we have scrambled to learn about other places, to place them centre stage in key chapters, and give them due weight in comparative analysis. Some parts of the empire receive limited coverage and readers for the publishers were perturbed about omissions. We have explained these in the introduction, and trust that our choices will not dissatisfy too many readers. Chapters range from the seventeenth century to the present, but the core of the book addresses the period from 1850 to 1950, when the British Empire was at its geographical and political apex. *Environment and Empire* is written as an introductory text in an accessible style and we hope that it will be useful for students of History, Geography, and Environmental Studies as well as for general readers. The chapters are thematic but cross-referenced. Each aims to include both a strong narrative and historiographical discussion. Rather than attempt encyclopaedic coverage, we use graphic examples, pegged to specific places or interesting individuals. In this way we hope to provide hooks for comparison and discussion. Names of places and peoples have sometimes changed in the post-colonial world and we have tried to use the most recent terminology; the difficult problem of naming peoples is addressed in the introduction.

The book was written between 2002 and 2005 when Lotte Hughes worked as a Research Officer with William Beinart at St Antony's College, and the African Studies Centre, University of Oxford. We discussed each chapter together in some detail before one or the other wrote a draft. We made extensive comments on each other's work, and hammered out the final version in front of a screen together. We have decided not to identify original authorship of each chapter as the final result is often an amalgam. It is probably true to say that Beinart has been more preoccupied and fascinated by the environmental and cultural issues raised in our reading, and Hughes more by the social and political. But we do not conceive environmental history as a tightly bounded field and have tried to straddle all of these approaches. We have some differences in interpretation and emphasis and hope that the discussion is all the stronger for this internal debate.

While the text relies largely on secondary material, we have tried to provide colour and detail from contemporary reports and sources. In addition to our frequent visits to South Africa and Kenya, trips to India, Malaysia, Canada, and Botswana have fed into the book, and enriched our sense of different experiences of empire. Specialists on any of the themes and countries we cover will no doubt be frustrated with the level of generality, but we hope that they are at least stimulated, once they have weathered their annoyance, to think about other places and comparative processes, just as we have been.

Our thanks go to the following people who generously shared information, answered queries, read chapters, or assisted in other ways in the production of this book: Ahmed Al-Shahi, P. P. Bhojvaid and other staff of the Forest Research Institute, Dehra Dun, Maitseo Bolaane, Dan Brockington, Tom Brooking, Karen Brown, Jane Carruthers, Dawn Chatty, staff at the Consumers Association of Penang, Myron Echenberg, Wayne Ellwood, Anwar Fazal, Lindsey Gillson, Mark Harrison, Mary Hickman, Bengt Karlsson, Roger Louis, Duleep Matthai, Jim Miller, Deborah Nightingale, Sunita Narain and colleagues at the Centre for Science and Environment, Delhi, Sunita Puri, Ravi Rajan, Mahesh Rangarajan, Daniel Rycroft, Maui Solomon, Helen Tilley, Troth Wells, David Western, Luvuyo Wotshela, and Graeme Wynn. Staff at the Geography, History, Indian Institute, Middle East Centre, Rhodes House, and Social Sciences libraries, Oxford, have been very helpful. Many of the early drafts were given as lectures to support optional papers in masters courses at the University of Oxford between 2003 and 2005. We must thank the small but very engaged groups of students who provided especially useful feedback.

William Beinart
Lotte Hughes
St Antony's College, University of Oxford, 2006

CONTENTS

ILLUSTRATIONS

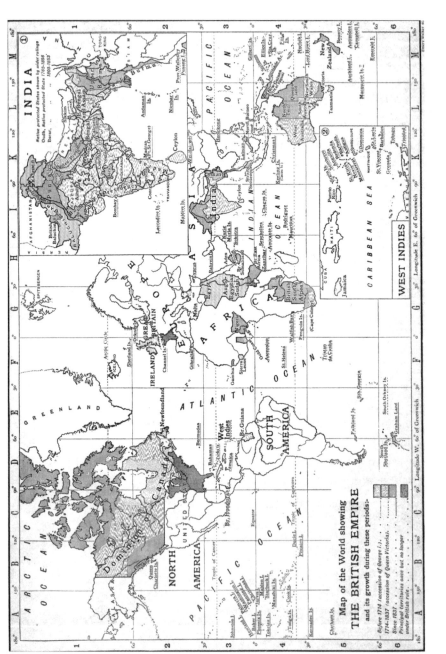

1. The British Empire in the early twentieth century, showing its expansion since 1714.

Credit: The *Encyclopaedia Britannica* (13th edition, 1926).

1

Introduction

European imperialism was extraordinarily far-reaching: a key global historical process of the last 500 years. It locked disparate societies together over a
wider area than any previous imperial expansion; it precipitated the repop-
ulation of the Americas and Australasia (but not of Africa and Asia); it was
the precursor of globalization as we now understand it—and arguably also
recent global asymmetries in wealth and power. European empires helped
to produce the multiple states that are the basis of the world order, and
influenced many of their key institutions. Imperial legacies have contributed
to some of the world's major recent conflicts.

European imperialism was also inseparable from the history of global
environmental change. Metropolitan countries sought raw materials of all
kinds, from timber and furs to rubber and oil. They established plantations
that transformed island ecologies. Settlers introduced new methods of
farming; some displaced indigenous peoples and their methods of managing
the land. Colonial cities, many of which have become great conurbations,
fundamentally changed relationships between people and nature. Consumer
cultures, the internal combustion engine, and pollution are now ubiquitous.
By contrast, while natural resources have been intensely exploited, a related
process, the rise of conservationist practices and ideas, was also deeply
rooted in imperial history. Large tracts of land have been reserved for forests,
national parks, or wildlife.

Most environmental histories deal with reciprocal interactions between
people and other elements in the natural world. Few see humans as entirely
'super-natural'—or above nature.[1] Our book on the British Empire emerges
from these concerns. It is not an environmental interpretation of empire, nor
do we have sufficient space or knowledge to write a definitive environmental
history of the British Empire as a whole. Our aim is to illustrate diverse

---

[1] Donald Worster, 'Appendix: Doing Environmental History' in Donald Worster (ed.), *The Ends of the Earth* (New York: Cambridge University Press, 1989), 290.

environmental themes in the history of that empire. In the first half of the book we concentrate on the material factors that shaped environmental change. We discuss the way in which an expanding capitalist economy devoured natural resources and transformed them into commodities. British and other European consumers and manufacturers sucked in resources that were gathered, hunted, fished, mined, and farmed in a great profusion of extractive and agrarian systems: sugar from the Caribbean; furs and cod from North America; ivory and cocoa from Africa; spices, cotton, tea, and timber from India; wool from the sheep of the Antipodes; rubber from South-East Asia; gold from South Africa; oil from the Middle East. It is remarkable how much space and labour it took to fuel European consumption. These modes of extraction underpinned deep structures in the architecture of the British Empire. They were a feature of specifically imperial environmental relationships, though not exclusive to them.

In many ways, such commodity frontiers and commodity chains gave the Empire its character and unity, and this is where we would like to start. We use the term 'commodity frontier' to suggest meanings that are spatial, environmental, and socio-economic.[2] It refers to the results of expanding European commercial activity, productive enterprises, and sometimes settlement, which targeted raw materials and land in overseas territories. W. K. Hancock, writing in the 1930s, distinguished many different moving, imperial economic frontiers: a frontier of settlement, of imperial trade, a planters' frontier, and an investors' frontier.[3] While each of these activities had its own dynamic, they were often linked and we find it more useful to consider them together. The notion of frontier can also be problematic because it suggests constant, restless, expansion. Many of these operations stabilized spatially, not least because colonized societies increasingly participated in them. Nevertheless, the idea of a frontier is ubiquitous in the literature on empire, and retains a value and resonance.

---

[2] The term commodity frontier has been used in many different contexts. One that comes close to our idea is Jason W. Moore, 'Sugar and the Expansion of the Early Modern World-Economy: Commodity Frontiers, Ecological Transformation', *Review*, 23/3 (2000), 409–33, although we do not share all his views on environmental degradation. For comparative environmental frontiers, John F. Richards, *The Unending Frontier: An Environmental History of the Early Modern World* (Berkeley: University of California Press, 2003), although he focuses more on frontiers of settlement.

[3] W. K. Hancock, *Survey of British Commonwealth Affairs, Volume II, Problems of Economic Policy 1918–1939, Part 1* (London: Oxford University Press, 1940), 6–28.

Some of the natural resources swallowed in the spreading Empire lay unexploited; some were central to indigenous, pre-capitalist economies. In other cases, new species such as sugar were introduced and provided an essential ingredient for the commodification of land. These networks of trade and production intensified the human exploitation of nature. All had a profound impact on natural environments. Yet it is also clear, with reference to the rise of conservation, that both settler and non-settler colonial states sought to regulate the natural environment as well as commodify it. These concerns were formulated over a long period, initially in order to bolster and protect capitalist accumulation and colonial production systems more generally—whether the producers were European settlers, or indigenous peasants. India needed forests for its railways; Australia required pastures for its sheep; soil erosion was seen to undermine African agriculture. Overexploitation threatened resources. Scientists and other imperial servants developed sophisticated arguments about the risk that this posed to nature, food supplies, exports, and economic enterprise. Conservation, as it was often called, aimed both to preserve natural assets by exclusion, and to devise controls that might guarantee long-term, efficient use. Conservationist policies were sometimes imposed by colonial states on colonized people. In this sense they were also an intrinsic part of imperial practices and reflected the asymmetries in power which were the hallmark of empire. The linked themes of exploitation and conservation provide an essential tension in our narrative.

The British Empire as a Unit of Study

The British Empire and Commonwealth is a problematic unit of study, not least for authors in pursuit of environmental history. Britain took over territories that had previously been dominated or influenced by other imperial powers, such as parts of the Spanish Caribbean, French Canada and Mauritius, the Dutch Cape, and German East Africa. When it did so, processes of transformation were already in motion. Imperial expansion was a fragmented and uneven process. Some parts of the Empire were being lost in the eighteenth century (United States) while others were being gained (India). Informal influence through trade in the nineteenth century (Argentina) was contemporaneous with direct colonization or political rule (Australia and South Africa). Settler colonialisms, as opposed to metropolitan British power, were a very significant factor in expansion. The period of direct colonial rule varied greatly—in the Caribbean it lasted more than three centuries, while in some parts of Africa it was barely more than fifty years. Moreover, the indigenous societies into which British power intruded, and which continued to influence socio-environmental processes, were hugely different. No single or typical set of relationships was established: Australian Aboriginal people were displaced and marginalized; West Africans held their land, adopted new plants, and adapted to imperial markets; Middle Eastern societies established considerable control—over the longer term—of oil exploitation. All these factors affected environmental outcomes. By the early 1960s, when the majority of former colonies had achieved independence, the metropolitan ties that bound the Commonwealth were loosening in the face of new regional geopolitical priorities.

Whatever the problems presented by focusing on a specific empire, our book must follow this route, because it is part of the *Oxford History of the British Empire* series—one of the 'companion', follow-on studies to the first five core volumes. And there are certain advantages in doing so. Expanding the scale would require even greater levels of generalization. Conversely, reducing it—for example to the parts of Africa annexed by Britain—would preclude the possibility of interesting comparisons and differing timescales. Moreover, there is a large and exciting historiography on British imperialism and the areas it penetrated, which provides a rich resource for us to draw on and bounce off.

There are also certain unifying features. Ultimately, as suggested above, many of our key themes are rooted in discussion of specifically imperial power relations and stem from the processes of conquest, resistance, and the emergence of hybrid colonial societies. British power, markets, trade, and shipping knitted the Empire together. British military authority, political domination, and institutions provided a common framework for the exercise of colonial power. British scientific networks accumulated knowledge of the extra-European natural world, and experience of managing it. Ideas about nature in the settler submetropoles were to some degree interconnected, as Thomas Dunlap argues in *Nature and the English Diaspora*.[4] The anglophone indigenous elites in South Asia, the Caribbean, Africa, and elsewhere to some extent shared intellectual worlds. The Empire was blurred at the edges, and open to many different influences, but the English language remained one uniting medium.

---

[4] Thomas Dunlap, *Nature and the English Diaspora: Environment and History in the United States, Canada, Australia, and New Zealand* (Cambridge: Cambridge University Press, 1999).

This is an overview covering four centuries and many different countries. We have very limited space and have to work in generalities, drawing heavily on the research of others. Even so we cannot aspire to cover all periods and places equally or evenly. The readers for the publisher have been struck by some of our omissions and we should explain briefly, at the outset, a few of them. One of the virtues of environmental history, as some of its protagonists argue, is that it has the potential to prompt work both across disciplines, and across recently established political boundaries. While it is probably true to say that most environmental history has been written with reference to national units, ecological zones can often make more sense as units of study. We cannot, in general, take this path and are largely limited to the area that came under direct British domination. For example, we focus on parts of the British Caribbean, rather than adjacent islands that remained under Spanish or French authority. North America as a whole might be a useful reference point, but we focus largely on Canada and have decided to exclude any detailed treatment of the United States. It ceased to be a British-controlled territory in the eighteenth century, it is extensively covered elsewhere, and one of us has co-authored a short comparative book which includes it.[5] We make references to the US throughout, and its shadow hovers over this text as a key centre for the writing of environmental history, but it is not central to the discussion in any chapter.

We have also excluded Britain and Ireland as discrete foci for chapters. While British people feature in every chapter, they do so largely as agents in settler and colonial countries. Environmental processes and technological changes in Britain that impacted on the rest of the Empire, such as early deforestation, steam power, and photography, provide reference points. So do particular intellectual and policy frameworks, such as the rise of eco-logical thinking and the developmental state in the twentieth century. But we have decided to focus largely on an extra-European part of the Empire in most chapters. A sequential analysis of British environmental history would have altered the nature of the book, and weighted it even further towards a metropolitan coverage. We have excluded Ireland for the same reason. Although it was colonized, and formed part of the British Empire for a long time, although Irish industrialization was retarded by British rule, and its agrarian economy shaped by subservience to the needs of England,

[5] William Beinart and Peter Coates, *Environment and History: The Taming of Nature in the United States and South Africa* (London: Routledge, 1995).

we see Irish environmental history as essentially European in character.[6] Exceptional Irish events with both imperial and environmental dimensions, such as the 1840s famine, could certainly have formed the basis of a chapter. An analysis would include many core themes in the environmental history of empire: plant transfers, diseases, climate, agrarian change, and distributional issues. Radcliffe Salaman's plant-focused history of the potato long ago pointed the way to such an approach.[7] Moreover, analysis of the famine and environmental change would fill a gap in *The Oxford History of the British Empire* series in that it largely omits, so far, such aspects of Irish history.[8] But we have decided to concentrate on extra-European case studies and touch on famine in the Indian rather than Irish context.

There has been much debate as to whether the empire is best understood from the vantage point of the centre or the periphery.[9] Our overarching themes demand that some of our narrative explores the expansive forces of empire generated within Britain. But while we frequently discuss the demands and influences of British society, our view is on the colonized world. The problems of inclusion and exclusion matter less because our approach cannot, and does not, aim to be encyclopaedic. We are aware that West Africa, the Caribbean, New Zealand, Sri Lanka, and the Mediterranean Empire are under-represented, and some small islands barely surface in the discussion. We considered and proposed a number of additional chapters but had to operate under tight word constraints. In short, rather than aim at representative coverage, we have decided to build upon selected narratives in order to illustrate key processes and themes in the environmental history of empire.

Given the potential for centrifugal fragmentation of the subject matter, as we go spinning off to far-flung zones of the world, one way of binding the volume together would be to adopt the unifying vantage point of

---

[6] For an environmental approach that begins to transcend political boundaries within the British Isles, see T. C. Smout, *Nature Contested: Environmental History in Scotland and Northern England since 1600* (Edinburgh: Edinburgh University Press, 2000).

[7] Radcliffe Salaman, *The History and Social Influence of the Potato* (Cambridge: Cambridge University Press, 1949: revised edn., 1985).

[8] Andrew Porter (ed.), *Oxford History of the British Empire*, vol. III *The Nineteenth Century* (Oxford: Oxford University Press, 1999); Kevin Kenny (ed.), *Ireland and the British Empire*, *Oxford History of the British Empire Companion Series* (Oxford: Oxford University Press, 2004).

[9] P. J. Cain and A. G. Hopkins, *British Imperialism: Innovation and Expansion, 1688–1914* (London: Longman, 1993); and essays in Porter (ed.), *Oxford History of the British Empire*, vol. III and Robin W. Winks, (ed.), *Oxford History of the British Empire*, vol. V *Historiography* (Oxford: Oxford University Press, 1999).

British travellers, officials, and scientists. Most overarching studies of the environmental history of empire have tended to adopt this approach. Lucille Brockway's *Science and Empire* and Richard Drayton's *Nature's Government* use Kew Gardens, and the botanical networks it generated, to explore aspects of imperial expansion, notably the transfer of plant species, and agricultural improvement, in the eighteenth and nineteenth centuries.[10] Richard Grove's *Green Imperialism* traces the early rise of conservationist ideas and policies, especially in connection with forests, in India, the Caribbean, and the Cape.[11] The history of imperial forestry has attracted interest as a major strand in the origins of scientific regulation of natural resources.[12] Dunlap illustrates changing settler ideas about nature in the anglophone world.[13] Studies of Geography and Ecology as academic disciplines point to their intricate links with empire.[14]

These approaches feed into the discussion, but we do not restrict ourselves to ideas, officials, and policies.[15] We also decided against writing comparatively in every chapter about the commodification and regulation of particular natural resources—for example, wildlife, water, forests, pastures, and mineral wealth—throughout the Empire. This would have made it difficult to generate a narrative thrust because of the constant need to compare and contrast. We have chosen an alternative route, especially for the first half of the book, focusing on particular regions as case studies, in order to highlight

[10] L. H. Brockway, *Science and Colonial Expansion: The Role of the British Royal Botanical Gardens* (New York: Academic Press, 1979); Richard Drayton, *Nature's Government: Science, Imperial Britain, and the 'Improvement' of the World* (New Haven: Yale University Press, 2000).

[11] Richard H. Grove, *Green Imperialism: Colonial Expansion, Tropical Island Edens and the Origins of Environmentalism* (Cambridge: Cambridge University Press, 1995) and *Ecology, Climate and Empire: Colonialism and Global Environmental History, 1400–1940* (Cambridge: White Horse Press, 1997).

[12] Ravi Rajan, 'Imperial Environmentalism or Environmental Imperialism? European Forestry, Colonial Foresters and the Agendas of Forest Management in British India 1800–1900' in Richard H. Grove, Vinita Damodoran and Satpal Sangwan (eds.), *Nature and the Orient: The Environmental History of South and Southeast Asia* (Delhi: Oxford University Press, 1998), 324–71; Gregory Allen Barton, *Empire Forestry and the Origins of Environmentalism* (Cambridge: Cambridge University Press, 2002).

[13] Dunlap, *Nature and the English Diaspora*.

[14] Anne Godlewska and Neil Smith (eds.), *Geography and Empire* (Oxford: Blackwell, 1994); Tom Griffiths and Libby Robin (eds.), *Ecology and Empire: Environmental History of Settler Societies* (Edinburgh: Keele University Press, 1997); Peder Anker, *Imperial Ecology: Environmental Order in the British Empire, 1895–1945* (Cambridge, MA: Harvard University Press, 2001).

[15] William Beinart, *The Rise of Conservation in South Africa: Settlers, Livestock and the Environment, 1770–1950* (Oxford: Oxford University Press, 2003) explores the history of conservationist ideas in South Africa.

some important patterns of commodity extraction, dramatic environmental changes, or advances in conservation. It makes sense to explore environmental aspects of the slave trade and sugar in the Caribbean, specifically Barbados, because this was an early site of intense production and profound change. It makes sense to discuss wildlife in southern Africa, because this is an important example of a hunting frontier. A similar logic guided us to furs in northern North America, forestry in India, settler pastoralism in Australia, rubber in Malaysia, and oil in the Middle East. This does lead to arbitrary exclusions. We could have discussed timber in Canada and Burma; wool was critical to the South African, as well as Australian, economy. Sugar was produced under different conditions in many sub-tropical sites from Queensland to Natal, and Trinidad to Fiji. Resources such as cod and guano, diamonds and gold largely escape our grasp. But by restricting ourselves in this way we hope to be able to tell coherent stories, with particular arguments, that give examples of wider processes, and of historiographical debates. We also aim to provide a window on distinctive elements in the environmental history of some countries. In the second half of the book, where conservation, resistance, and indigenous reassertions become more central, there is a stronger comparative approach.

Environmental Themes in the History of Empire

ENVIRONMENTAL CAUSATION

A multitude of forces drove European expansion: economic growth and the development of capitalism; new patterns of consumption; population explosion; the technology for military conquest and transport—especially shipping in the early seaborne empires; the competitive quest for territory and overseas political domination; Christianity, visions of improvement, and a sense of racial superiority. As the historiography grows, it is increasingly difficult to understand imperialism without reference to environmental factors: climate, disease, water, natural resources, or the transfer of plants and animals. Alfred Crosby's *Ecological Imperialism* has been the most influential analysis.[16] He draws on histories of disease in order to explain the colonization of the Americas and Australasia, and argues for the importance of non-human auxiliaries, especially plants and domesticated animals, in facilitating the process. The susceptibility of isolated societies to smallpox

---

[16] Alfred Crosby, *Ecological Imperialism: The Biological Expansion of Europe, 900–1900* (Cambridge: Cambridge University Press, 1986).

in particular, and the relative immunity of European colonizers, gave the latter, he suggests, an enormous advantage in the struggle for power and land. Animals and plant species domesticated in the 'Old World' spread and acclimatized easily. Crosby contrasts 'New World' regions that were suited to European expansion by their climate, ecology, and benign disease environments with zones, such as West Africa, where tropical diseases inhibited settler colonialism and indigenous people shared European immunities to smallpox. He argues that these differences profoundly affected patterns of colonization. His propositions can be set alongside texts that try to explore the impact of soils or climate on the evolution of society and environmental change.[17] There is also a growing literature, some of it aimed at a popular market, which deals with the environmental impact of particular events such as El Ninos, droughts, earthquakes, volcanoes, and tsunamis.[18]

Environmental causation is illustrated in the first few chapters, for example, in discussing the spatial and demographic dimensions of the Atlantic slave trade and plantations. These issues have hardly penetrated into mainstream historiography of empire, if the volumes of the *Oxford History of the British Empire* are an indication. Yet an explanation of this extraordinary system requires discussion of disease patterns, plant transfers, climate, and wind for shipping, as well as the character of European colonial forces, and the relative power of indigenous societies in Africa and the Americas. More broadly. the historical impact of disease, demography, and ecological imperialism, illustrated by Crosby and others, does help to distinguish the history of the settler states of the United States, Canada, Australia, New Zealand, and South Africa from other parts of the British Empire. There are many problems with Crosby's model. Demographic outcomes were not always clear-cut. South Africa, as Crosby recognizes, was a hybrid. It once appeared to be a settler state, but African demographic strength paved the way for political resistance and reassertion. The other neo-Europes in which British settlers once seemed so dominant, have become more culturally diverse. But for all its problems, it is difficult to escape the logic of Crosby's

---

[17] For example, H. H. Lamb, *Climate, History and the Modern World* (London: Routledge, 1997).

[18] Ross Couper-Johnson, *El Nino: The Weather Phenomenon that Changed the World* (London: Hodder & Stoughton, 2000); Mike Davis, *Late Victorian Holocausts: El Nino Famines and the Making of the Third World* (London: Verso, 2001); Simon Winchester, *Krakatoa: The Day the World Exploded, 27 August 1883* (London: Viking, 2003).

model. We attempt, in a number of chapters, to compare disease histories, demographic outcomes, and their implications.

Environmental factors also contributed to shape commodity frontiers and patterns of emigration in fundamental ways. These influences have tended to slip beneath the gaze of most authors in the *Oxford History of the British Empire*, or at least they are generally subsumed in economic analyses.[19] The location of colonial extraction and production was mediated by many social and economic processes such as advances in transport, the adaptation of indigenous technologies, increasing amounts of imperial capital, and the appliance of science. But environmental factors influenced where natural products were found, the routes by which they could be exploited, the location of indigenous populations whose labour, skills, or knowledge were required for their extraction, and the trajectory of European intrusion.

In the early phases of imperial expansion, commodities that could not be produced in Britain, such as spices, sugar, tobacco, cotton, and tea were particular objects of desire. By the beginning of the nineteenth century, sufficient sugar and tea were being imported into Britain for an average of one sweet cup per person per day (Chapter 2). These crops could only be grown in frost-free subtropical and tropical environments, and this pattern of demand framed the spatial configuration of empire. It is true that the first British colonial settlements in the Americas predated production of major tropical crops so that this form of commodity frontier was not always the origin of imperial expansion. But if Britain had wanted only wheat, it would hardly have bothered with the Caribbean. Subsequent imperial impulses were in part driven by the demand for pastoral productions such as wool and meat. Although transferred domesticated animals were more adaptable than tropical plants—and they could survive in the heat of Africa and India as well as the cold of Canada—they required space and pastures. The spread of pastoralism was equally fundamental in shaping routes of imperial expansion. There were no empty lands in colonized zones, but it proved more possible to carve out space in the Americas and the southern hemisphere.

Concurrently, we need to keep in mind the influence on colonial territories of environmental change in Britain: for example, the complex implications of timber shortages, resulting from gradual domestic deforestation.[20] This hastened dependence on coal for energy, which helped to drive the industrial

[19] B. R. Tomlinson, 'Economics and Empire: The Periphery and the Imperial Economy', in Porter (ed.), *Oxford History of the British Empire*, vol. III, 53–74, is an exception.
[20] Smout, *Nature Contested*.

revolution in the second half of the eighteenth century. By 1800, Wrigley notes, 'Britain was already producing and consuming 15 millions tons of coal a year, several times the combined coal production of the continent of Europe ... and the equivalent in energy terms of the annual produce of about 6 million hectares of woodland.'[21] To supply this amount would have required more than a quarter of Britain's surface area to be exploitable forest. Deforestation also created a large demand for timber and, by the late nineteenth century, Britain was importing roughly 90 per cent of its needs at the height of an urban house-building boom.[22] In turn the gradual switch from wood fuel, and human and animal power, to machine power based on fossil fuels such as coal and oil, enormously expanded the possibilities of metropolitan production and consumption. It facilitated a new surge in imperial expansion, carried by steamships, railways, and motor vehicles. With the rise of the internal combustion engine, massive demand for rubber and oil drove commodity frontiers in new directions.

By the late nineteenth century, new sources of capital, new technology, and the mobility of workers facilitated the spread of plantations and factories. In some cases, producers were freed from environmental constraints. However, raw material extraction and plantation production often remained site-specific or subject to environmental opportunities. Sugar, for example, though widely transposed, was still restricted to subtropical climates. Forest plantations, using exotic trees, marched up mountain slopes throughout the Empire, but they required moisture. Strikingly, production of three of the most important commodities in the twentieth-century Empire was tightly bound to specific locations by geology or climate: oil in the Middle East; gold in southern Africa; and rubber in South-East Asia. These were critical resources, viewed as essential in the metropolitan, industrialized world as the British Empire reached its apogee and their extraction had a profound effect on the societies of these zones.

An exploration of environmental causation offers exciting opportunities for interdisciplinary thinking and research. However, this is not our central concern and we do not offer an environmental interpretation of the causes and development of imperialism. We are particularly cautious about environmental determinism: that is, trying to explain human cultures, or

---

[21] E. A. Wrigley, 'Meeting Human Energy Needs: Constraints, Opportunities, and Effects', in Paul Slack (ed.), *Environments and Historical Change: The Linacre Lectures* (Oxford: Oxford University Press, 1999), 86.

[22] R. S. Troup, *Colonial Forest Administration* (London: Oxford University Press, 1940).

the rise and fall of states, or empires, or conflict and rebellions, or even sometimes famines, by recourse to immediate environmental influences. Environmental factors are often predisposing, background influences on historical processes. Historical actions and events are usually shaped more immediately by the dictates of economic survival, material benefit, political contingency, or particular patterns of consciousness. Braudel, in his classic work on the Mediterranean, distinguished between these layers of historical time and process: on the one hand, a history of people's relations with the environment 'in which all change is slow' and, on the other, a political history 'of brief, rapid, nervous fluctuations'.[23] Environmental change was not always slow, and in many places it was hastened by empire. But environmental and epidemiological influences cannot directly explain political, economic, and social outcomes; rather they can frame these processes. That said, environmental history is a relatively new field; while there is a growing literature, there are also many gaps in understanding. Environmental influences deserve further exploration. Crosby may overemphasize the significance of environmental causation in imperialism, but *Ecological Imperialism* is a corrective intervention, aimed at illustrating impulses that had been neglected in the historiography of European settler expansion.

Environmental Impacts

The writing of environmental history has been profoundly influenced by late twentieth-century environmentalism and some of the most fascinating texts chart the destructive impact of human society: Worster on the American Dust Bowl; MacKenzie on hunting in southern Africa; Cronon on Chicago's hungry industries; Kurlansky on the exhaustion of cod fisheries; Isenberg on the demise of the American bison; and Lines on the taming of Australia.[24] While some authors see all human societies as capable of wreaking destruction on nature, most focus on capitalism, industrialization, and empire

[23] Fernand Braudel, *The Mediterranean and the Mediterranean World in the Age of Philip II*, Vol. 1 (London: Fontana/Collins, 1975), 20–1.

[24] Donald Worster, *Dust Bowl: The Southern Plains in the 1930s* (New York: Oxford University Press, 1979); John M. MacKenzie, *The Empire of Nature: Hunting, Conservation and British Imperialism* (Manchester: Manchester University Press, 1988); William Cronon, *Nature's Metropolis: Chicago and the Great West* (New York: W. W. Norton, 1991); William J. Lines, *Taming the Great South Land: A History of the Conquest of Nature in Australia* (Berkeley: University of California Press, 1991); Mark Kurlansky, *Cod: A Biography of the Fish that Changed the World* (London: Jonathan Cape, 1998); Andrew Isenberg, *The Destruction of the Bison: An Environmental History* (Cambidge: Cambridge University Press, 2000).

as the key forces. According to this view, European or settler industrial society ransacked the world for resources, with limited concern for their renewability, or installed productive systems that degraded environments, diminished biodiversity, and polluted the atmosphere. 'Nowhere', wrote Donald Worster of a Mid-West agricultural community, 'is there much sense of living in the presence of nature; the land ... is by and large as sterile and uninteresting as a shopping center's parking lot; the soil has become a dead, inert, brown flatness.'[25] MacKenzie detects an apocalyptic view of generalized, continuous degradation of natural resources and ecology, as each new zone or product was engulfed in the tidal waves of empire.[26]

Such arguments draw upon an older moral and economic unease—going back to Marxist theory—about imperialism. They emphasize that Britain gained most of the economic benefits. In the 1930s, Harold Innis saw imperial systems as creating a staples trap and retarding the development of peripheral economies; more recently strands of this argument have informed underdevelopment theory.[27] By adding an environmental dimension, a parallel set of historiographical concerns have been raised—notably the evaluation of environmental loss. Alier is exploring the idea of an environmental audit that would entail calculating the historic value of natural resources, or environmental assets, transferred over time to the imperial centre.[28] It may be an impossibly complex task, but the balance sheet was clearly highly asymmetrical. Historiographical discussion of colonized land provides an analogy. In British imperial thinking, more intensive utilization of land was often thought of as improvement and progress: it had both an economic and moral purpose.[29] In economic history written about empire, land is often referred to as under-utilized. By adding an environmental dimension, the terms of historiographical debate can be shifted to include a curiosity or concern about the ecological consequences of improvement. Economic gains could result in environmental degradation.

[25] Worster, *Dust Bowl*, 238.

[26] John M. MacKenzie, 'Empire and the Ecological Apocalypse: the Historiography of the Imperial Environment', in Tom Griffiths and Libby Robin (eds.), *Ecology and Empire: Environmental History of Settler Societies* (Edinburgh: Keele University Press, 1997), 215–28.

[27] Harald A. Innis, *The Fur Trade in Canada: An Introduction to Canadian Economic History* (First pub. 1930; Toronto: University of Toronto Press, 1999).

[28] Juan Martinez Alier, 'The Andean Case', paper presented to a conference on 'The Environmental Dimensions of European Colonialism: A Comparative Perspective', Centre for Brazilian Studies and African Studies Centre, St Antony's College, University of Oxford (2004).

[29] Drayton, *Nature's Government*.

As noted above, commodity frontiers and their diverse impacts are major themes, especially in the first half of the book. But we want to explore a less unilinear analysis, and to introduce countervailing tendencies. All human survival necessitates disturbance of nature; population increase has required, and been intricately related to, intensification of production and trade. To judge all change as degradation is not, conceptually, very useful. We need a concept of degradation, but also a more neutral set of terms to examine the complexity of environmental transformations. This includes the reordering of relationships between human beings and nature in order to ensure that resources can sustain larger numbers of people over long periods. Intensification of production has been fundamentally linked to global population growth, enhanced overall food security, and in some cases improved standards of living. Moreover, the cutting edge of exploitation could move on, and in certain cases, environmental restoration was possible. Technological advances could rapidly change modes of extraction. Human occupation and investment could 'green' as well as destroy, by planting, channelling water, and enriching local diversity; more people do not always mean more erosion.[30] Regulatory and conservationist strategies and policies have also reshaped resource use.

CONSERVATIONISM

Pioneering American historians who wrote about the rise of conservationist ideas tended to place their national experience at the heart of modern environmental concerns. But environmental regulation lies deep in the history of many societies, and takes a multitude of forms, more or less explicit. Historians of Britain have discussed the evolution of a more benign view of nature by the end of the early modern era.[31] Richard Grove sees global conservationism as not least rooted in the imperial periphery, borne out of the knowledge generated in Dutch, British, and French botanical gardens, and maturing when colonizing powers began to count the cost of degraded small islands which serviced ships in their maritime empires.[32] By the eighteenth century this had evolved into a multifaceted critique of overexploitation. Botanists and foresters wrote about the links between

[30] Mary Tiffen, Michael Mortimore, and Francis Gichuki, *More People, Less Erosion: Environmental Recovery in Kenya* (Chichester: Wiley, 1994).

[31] Keith Thomas, *Man and the Natural World: Changing Attitudes in England, 1500–1800* (Harmondsworth: Penguin, 1984); Smout, *Nature Contested*.

[32] Grove, *Green Imperialism*.

vegetation, soils, water flows, and degradation. Conservationist modes of thought were well established among specialist officials in India by the mid-nineteenth century. Afforestation promised to restore both water and timber supplies, and to combat desiccation, disease, and famine. By the late nineteenth century, conservationist concern was frequently accompanied by a discourse blaming some settlers, and especially indigenous people, for environmental degradation.

Distinctive positions are emerging on the provenance of imperial conservationism, challenging the significance of the periphery. Agrarian improvement in eighteenth-century Britain, Drayton argues, emphasized scientific management of natural resources, as well as enclosure of the commons.[33] These ideas radiated out to colonial territories and also fed into the growth of natural sciences—a vehicle for increasingly complex environmental understanding. Agricultural improvement could run in tandem with conservation though the priority of harnessing nature, and enjoying its bounty, outstripped still weakly developed notions of wise usage. Rajan would agree about the importance of European rather than American origins for forestry as an important early manifestation of scientific conservationism. He locates the key impetus in German and French practice at the time of the eighteenth-century Enlightenment rather than on imperial peripheries.[34] From there systematic forestry spread to the United States, India, and the rest of the Empire. The arguments put forward by Rajan and Grove have different emphases, but both stress the significance of natural scientists in formulating conservationist ideas, and are not necessarily mutually exclusive.

While scientific disciplines evolved in metropolitan institutions, there were multiple nodes of conservationist innovation and intervention in different parts of the colonized world—in response to local crises of subsistence and overexploitation, or as a result of a moving metropolis of scientific priorities.[35] These are evident over a long period. For example, Grove cites eighteenth-century officials in Mauritius and the Caribbean as key environmental innovators, who were well aware of intellectual developments in Europe. From the nineteenth century, the United States became an increasingly important pole of conservationist initiative such as

---

[33] Drayton, *Nature's Government*; Richard Drayton, 'Science, Medicine, and the British Empire' in Winks (ed.), *Oxford History of the British Empire:* vol. V: *Historiography*, 264–76.

[34] Rajan, 'Imperial Environmentalism'.

[35] The term is from R. MacLeod, 'On Visiting the Moving Metropolis: Reflections on the Architecture of Imperial Science', *Historical Records of Australian Science*, 5/3 (1982), 1–16.

the demarcation of national parks, as well as the celebration of wilderness. Imperial officials in India developed distinctive approaches to forestry and water management and in the twentieth century Australia and South Africa were significant sites for debates about pasture and wildlife conservation. In many different parts of the Empire, local knowledge fed into discussions about appropriate use.

Some analyses are highly critical of science and conservationism in the Empire, seeing mechanistic male science as essentially geared to the exploitation of nature.[36] They regard science as having been at the heart of the intensely anthropocentric orientation of Western modernity. An equally fundamental critique dominates much recent analysis of the history of Indian forestry (Chapter 7), as well as colonial regulation of peasant economies and African wildlife management (Chapters 16 and 17). Imperial power enabled forest reserves in India and wildlife reserves in Africa to be imposed in ways that would have been far more difficult in Britain itself. In some cases conservation excluded the colonized from access to natural resources, or established regimes of regulation that cut across indigenous agrarian systems and knowledge. This strand of literature often argues for the salience of indigenous or local knowledge.

In parts of the British Empire, land was not only appropriated from indigenous people, but racially based legislation restricted them to reserves or limited their capacity to purchase in areas that had been privatized. Conservationist controls could be linked to the management of reserved areas, and where this was the case, they exacerbated political tensions over dispossession. In African countries, some of the most intense conflicts had their origins in the assertion of local rights to land and natural resources, in the face of colonial conservationism. After the Second World War, when colonial states became more assertive in respect of development, and as intervention escalated, environmentally linked protests began to feed into mass anticolonial movements.

We will explore science and conflicts of knowledge about environments and disease in a group of chapters in the middle of the book on forestry in India, on plague, on trypanosomiasis in Africa, and on water management in India and Egypt. They are followed by overarching discussions of

---

[36] Vandana Shiva, *Staying Alive: Women, Ecology and Development* (London: Zed, 1988); Vandana Shiva and Maria Mies, *Ecofeminism* (London: Zed, 1993); Carolyn Merchant, *The Death of Nature: Women, Ecology, and the Scientific Revolution* (San Francisco, CA: Harper & Row, 1990).

colonial science and environmental contestation. Our argument certainly highlights the potential for authoritarian interventions, intrusive regimes of environmental control, and associated conflicts. But we will depart somewhat from the recent polarized understandings of these histories, suggesting that scientific knowledge was often intricately imbricated with the ideas and practices of both settlers and indigenous people. Scientists such as Albert Howard admired eastern agricultural systems that maintained soil fertility by recycling and manuring. He spent much of his career researching and improving such practices in India, and brought his ideas back to Britain where he became one of the founders of the organic farming movement. William Willcocks, the imperial dam-builder who played a major role in Punjab irrigation projects and the Aswan dam, developed a self-critique, admired the strengths of indigenous irrigation schemes, and advised his British superiors to emulate them. In the settler colonies, and in South Asia, scientists were increasingly nationals, rather than imperials, which influenced their orientation and research agendas. We wish to restore the salience of science in the empire, as an exciting field of practice and research, which has left historians a legacy of concepts, and documentation, for the exploration of environmental change.

Conservationist concerns could also be stimulated by the visual imagination (Chapter 13). The rise of photography and printing enabled the British public to picture the natural resources of empire. From the early twentieth century, artists in the dominions consciously projected and celebrated their country's nature.[37] Local plants and animals became national symbols for European settlers, while outdoor recreation and appreciation of nature became important leisure pursuits. Game-viewing is one case in point. White South Africans, many of whom had no direct experience of an earlier hunting frontier, absorbed a sense that they had a special relationship with wildlife in the new national parks, and learnt, through visits and photography, how to take pleasure from viewing animals.[38] In *Idleness, Water and a Canoe*, Benidickson describes how indigenous technology, adapted for the fur trade, was transformed into a ubiquitous symbol in modern Canada, as well as the vehicle for 'paddling for pleasure'.[39] After the Second World War, wildlife

[37] Dunlap, *Nature and the English Diaspora*, 96.

[38] David Bunn, 'An Unnatural State: Tourism, Water and Wildlife Photography in the Early Kruger National Park', in William Beinart and JoAnn McGregor (eds.), *Social History and African Environments* (Oxford: James Currey, 2003), 199–218.

[39] Jamie Benidickson, *Idleness, Water, and a Canoe: Reflections on Paddling for Pleasure* (Toronto: University of Toronto Press, 1997).

documentary films—seen by millions of British television viewers—were intentionally aimed at increasing sympathy for wild animals. In the cinema, they reached an apogee in the feature film *Born Free*, set in Kenya, which helped to shape British attitudes towards conservation. However, growing conservationist concerns did not in themselves stop exploitation.

Indigenous Societies and Local Knowledge

The character of the Empire was profoundly affected by those subjected to British political authority. Imperial expansion set up a sequence of asymmetrical relations of power and domination, yet these differed greatly and in some cases, such as in West Africa, India, and Malaysia, the exercise of colonial power was highly constrained. We try to maintain a consistent comparative focus on the impact of specific commodity frontiers, and diseases, on colonized people. But dealing adequately with those who became imperial subjects is a major dilemma for us. Although our focus is on extra-European territories, our unifying themes are ultimately provided by imperial expansion and natural resource management. It has been difficult to capture the diversity and specificity of experiences among the colonized within the space available.

It is also difficult to find an acceptable terminology to describe all imperial subjects. The term 'settlers' is problematic enough and collapses together people of many backgrounds; even more so the term 'indigenous'. The latter is sometimes convenient shorthand when talking collectively about those descended from long-established communities in colonized territories. But many do not self-identify as indigenous, nor conform to United Nations-inspired definitions—generally speaking the descendants of those, such as Australian Aboriginal people or Canadian First Nations, who previously occupied the areas that became settler states. This narrower usage also includes tribal people in India, and indeed it is uncomfortable to use 'indigenous' of the Indian population as a whole. Similarly, the term is now applied to Khoisan/BaSarwa people in southern Africa, although it is also sometimes used to refer to the dominant black African population. 'Native' is unacceptable, except with reference to North America.

We have not found a consistent way around these problems but we try to avoid conceptualizing indigenous peoples, or the colonized, as one category or field of analysis. They comprised different societies with different ideas of nature, religions, systems of production, and different capacities to resist disease and domination. Analysing empire as a polarity between Europe, or the West, and the rest, is also sometimes an inescapable shorthand, useful for certain points. But it obscures the changing balance of power between Britain and different parts of the Empire and simplifies the complexity and multi-polarity of many relationships. By dealing with specific commodity frontiers in different regions, and with people's differing capacities to resist, we hope that some of this diversity, as well as some comparative discussion, can be suggested.

The power and skills of indigenous peoples shaped the nature and location of imperial systems of production. Power was in turn closely related to demographic outcomes. West Africa, for example, was suitable climatically for growing many of the tropical commodities that Britain wanted, yet it proved very difficult to establish plantations there, not only because of problems of disease and soil, but also because local populations could not be displaced and local political authorities prevented the alienation of land. Export commodities, largely based on new crops, were later produced by local people, and without their displacement. Trade with India largely drew on the intensification of existing patterns of production. In the case of Canada, the supply of furs from the sixteenth century depended initially on the trapping, hunting, and canoeing skills of First Nation people. In turn, the nature of these relations influenced colonial policy. In order to protect their fur supply lines, the Hudson's Bay Company was uneasy about European settlement for a long time. In South Africa, settlers attempted to shoulder aside African people but their capacity to do so was limited by demographic realities. By contrast, indigenous people were rapidly swept aside by the plantation economy of the British Caribbean and the pastoral frontier of Australia. One of the sub-themes of the book is to explore the influence of particular commodity frontiers, as well as diseases, on the relationship between colonizer and colonized.

Indigenous peoples engaged with, bargained, deflected, or resisted the demands of colonial power and traders. Their practices also changed. Whatever their prior attitudes to wildlife, Africans adopted firearms and became suppliers of ivory when opportunities arose, just as Native Americans contributed to the demise of beaver and bison. Innovation by cash-cropping peasant producers throughout the Empire, attuned to imperial demand or local markets, had a major impact on their environments. Local knowledge was not static, and many people adopted new plants, animals, and techniques.

In certain cases indigenous societies drew on and reasserted alternative traditions of knowledge or claims to natural resources. It is important to distinguish between colonies in Asia and Africa, where most colonized populations held onto their land, and settler societies where British and other immigrants became demographically dominant. Decolonization provided the opportunity for the former to gain national control over natural resources, although the legacies of imperial land use and planning could remain powerful. In the latter, indigenous communities made more limited gains, although many have found a new voice, reformulating ideas about nature and heritage. In turn, such understandings have fed into modern environmentalism. We will explore their influence on popular struggles and environmental thinking, especially in Canada, Australia, and New Zealand over the last few decades (Chapter 19). Indigenous peoples are challenging, at a local and global level, views of who has the right to regulate nature, and asserting the value of community management of natural resources.

Our major theme in the final chapters on the post-colonial period concerns political ecology and conflicts over resources, urban as well as rural.[40] The end of formal British colonial control did not usually signal a significant change in the pace of exploitation. New consumer demands, new ruling groups, and civil conflict could hasten extraction of natural resources. Rapid urbanization in developing countries, coupled with global migration has shifted the location of consumption with unpredictable results. The British Empire was unusual in that its former subjects did not migrate to its core in the United Kingdom at the apex of empire, but they did so subsequently. Europe has quickly become more socially diverse and the demand for commodities reflects this—from spices for Indian restaurants to bushmeat for West Africans in London. The spice trade, a driving force of early European expansion, is booming again. Movement in the other direction, such as mass tourism to former colonial countries, has an equally complex impact. On the one hand, it has reinforced efforts to protect nature, such as wildlife, which is a major attraction for tourists. On the other, it can create pressures to exclude local people from land and scarce natural resources. New global environmental problems of pollution, climate change and global warming have become key issues, displacing the anxieties of conservationists in the colonial era about regulating agrarian societies and

---

[40] Raymond L. Bryant and Sinead Bailey, *Third World Political Ecology* (London: Routledge, 1997); William M. Adams and Martin Mulligan, *Decolonizing Nature: Strategies for Conservation in a Post-Colonial Era* (London: Earthscan, 2003).

extractive industries.[41] The politics of conservation have changed but the arguments for both global and local environmental regulation, whose roots lie partly in the imperial era, remain.[42]

Historical writing on environmental themes sometimes evinces a restorationist element—a yearning after a greener and more balanced world. Environmental history can carry a powerful critique of imperial and global capitalism, those restless vehicles for the transformation of nature, in their many historic forms. We hope that we have been able to reflect some of these strands in the literature. But we are not convinced that equilibrium will ever be found, nor that society can achieve the elusive goal of sustainability. We are equally interested in change, unpredictability, and uncertainty. We do not judge all change as degradation. And our discussion is concerned throughout to illustrate social as well as environmental issues, to ask questions about access to natural resources, as well as environmental change.

[41] John McNeill, *Something New Under the Sun: An Environmental History of the Twentieth Century* (London: Allen Lane, 2000).

[42] T. C. Smout, 'Review Article: Problems for Global Environmental Historians', *Environment and History*, 8 (2002), 107–16.

2

Environmental Aspects of the Atlantic Slave Trade and Caribbean Plantations

African Slavery and European Consumption

The Atlantic world became Britain's main early imperial arena in the seventeenth century. Subsequent to Ireland, North America and the Caribbean were the most important zones of British settler colonialism. At the northern limits of settlement, around the Atlantic coast, the St Lawrence River, the Great Lakes and on the shores of the Hudson Bay, cod fisheries and fur-trading networks were established in competition with the French. This intrusion, while it had profound effects on the indigenous population, was comparatively constrained. Secondly, British settlements were founded in colonial New England from 1620. Expanding agrarian communities, based largely on family farms, displaced Native Americans, while the ports thrived on trade and fisheries. In the hotter zones to the south, both in the Caribbean and on the mainland, slave plantations growing tropical products became central to British expansion. Following in Spanish footsteps, coastal Virginia was occupied in 1607 and various Caribbean islands were captured from the 1620s: Barbados in 1627, and Jamaica in 1655.

The Atlantic plantation system was shaped in part by environment and disease. But these forces cannot be explored in isolation from European capital and consumption, or the balance of political power between societies in Europe, Africa, and America. An increase in European consumer demand for relatively few agricultural commodities—sugar, tobacco, cotton, and to a lesser extent ginger, coffee, indigo, arrowroot, nutmeg, and lime—drove plantation production and the slave trade. The possibility of providing these largely non-essential additions for British consumption arose from a 'constellation' of factors 'welded in the seventeenth century' and surviving until the mid-nineteenth century, aided by trade protectionism.[1] This chapter analyses some of these factors and addresses the problem of how much weight can be given to environmental explanations.

Plantations concentrated capital and large numbers of people in profoundly hierarchical institutions that occupied relatively little space in the newly emerging Atlantic order. In contrast to the extractive enterprise of the fur trade, this was a frontier of agricultural production, which required little involvement from indigenous people. On some islands, such as Barbados, Spanish intrusions had already decimated the Native American population before the British arrived; there was little resistance. Shipping was by far the cheapest way of moving goods so that proximity to the sea or navigable rivers minimized the costs and difficulty of moving heavy commodities. Islands, and mainland littorals, some of which proved to have fertile soil, were ideal locations for plantations.

The plantation system depended upon the import of slaves from Africa. Perhaps 11–12 million Africans were transported to the Americas in a period of over four centuries from 1450.[2] (Millions were also exported to the Muslim states of North Africa and the Middle East.) Between 1450 and 1600, average exports across the Atlantic were about 2,700 annually and in the sixteenth century the number rose gradually to a height of about 5,000 per year. In the seventeenth century, the average was about 13,500 and numbers rose to about 20,000 per year; in the eighteenth century, the average was perhaps 60,000 and numbers rose to over 80,000 a year. At the height of the trade, an estimated 400 ships would be required to carry this number. British ships and merchants did not initially dominate the trade, but by the eighteenth century they were by far the biggest carriers, transporting something like 2.5 million slaves—about 40 per cent of the total.[3] It was an extraordinary system, imposing a brutal labour regime and causing a great deal of human misery and death. Its impact straddled continents thousands of miles apart.

---

[1] Sidney W. Mintz, *Sweetness and Power: The Place of Sugar in Modern History* (Harmondsworth: Penguin, 1985), 61; Sidney W. Mintz, *Caribbean Transformations* (New York: Columbia University Press, 1989).

[2] Paul Lovejoy, *Transformations in Slavery: A History of Slavery in Africa* (Cambridge: Cambridge University Press, 2000), 19 and *passim*.

[3] Lovejoy, *Transformations in Slavery*, 48.

Plant transfers lay at the heart of imperial expansion and the Atlantic slave trade.[4] Sugar cane was a New Guinea cultivar that spread along migration routes to India, where it hybridized, and improved by crossing with local wild species.[5] The sweet moist interior of its bamboo-like stalks could be eaten raw, or the whole cane could be crushed to yield a juice. When boiled and cooled, a practice apparently developed in India, the juice forms crystals, which provide an intense, concentrated sweetener that could be stored. The product was known as a luxury in the Mediterranean by the time of the Greek and Roman Empires and the crop was spread to the warmer parts of this area via the Arab world, in early medieval times, if not before. Effective sugar production requires processing on the spot because cane, once cut, loses its sucrose content rapidly, after a few days. Sugar mills were therefore established on, or close to, the fields. Although there was a seasonal pattern of harvesting, a more permanent labour force was needed for a wide range of other agricultural tasks and for work in the mills. This combined requirement for agriculture and manufacture leant itself to plantation production.

While the key tropical commodities were known in Britain in the sixteenth century, most were curiosities or luxuries for the rich—sugar was used as a spice and medicine. The context for increasing consumption of sugar, Carole Shammas argues, was a sharp rise in incomes during the seventeenth century, followed by a steady fall in prices in the eighteenth, both of imported goods and of domestic foodstuffs.[6] Thus British consumers as a whole did not have to sacrifice staple foods for sugar, or foods containing sugar. But expanding consumption cannot simply be related to incomes and prices. Consumption required a new imagination about material life, and opened up new ways of living. It was bound up with the growth of social classes 'whose expectations, whose hopes and fears, whose prospects of integration … increasingly depended upon … continued expansion of the system of goods'.[7] Changes

---

[4] William Beinart and Karen Middleton, 'Plant Transfers in Historical Perspective: a Review Article', *Environment and History*, 10/1 (2004), 3–29.

[5] Jared Diamond, *Guns, Germs and Steel: A Short History of Everybody for the Last 13,000 Years* (London: Vintage, London: 1998), 148; Mintz, *Sweetness and Power*.

[6] Carole Shammas, 'Changes in English and Anglo-American Consumption from 1550 to 1800' in John Brewer and Roy Porter (eds.), *Consumption and the World of Goods* (London: Routledge, 1994), 182.

[7] Brewer and Porter, *Consumption and the World of Goods*, 2; Simon Schama, *The Embarrassment of Riches: An Interpretation of Dutch Culture in the Golden Age* (Berkeley: University of California Press, 1987).

in diet could entail alterations in people's self-image.[8] Social desires in turn stimulated demand, markets, and technologies. Leisure, together with wealth, expanded social possibilities; innovation sometimes began with luxury goods, which then became more generalized.[9]

Sugar replaced honey as a sweetener and proved effective as a preserver of fruit. It was quickly soluble and consumption was closely linked with new sweetened beverages, coffee and tea.[10] Initially grown in the Middle East, coffee was spread to Indonesia by the Dutch, to Brazil by the Portuguese, and to Jamaica by the British. By the early nineteenth century, Jamaica exported 30 per cent of world coffee. Up to that time, tea was imported from China. Coffee consumption spread from the Ottoman empire, and by the late seventeenth century, 'many prosperous middle-class Londoners spent part of every day in a particular coffee house'.[11] James Walvin begins his book on British slavery by telling us that London had 550 coffee houses in 1740. Coffee was therefore significant in the Atlantic economy both as a crop and as a solvent for sugar.[12]

Cacao played a similar dual role, on a smaller scale. An American plant, used by indigenous people to make a drink, it was adopted by the Spanish and cultivated in slave plantations. When the British captured Jamaica in 1655, they found cacao being grown; Dutch and British pirates enjoyed this chocolate drink as well as their rum.[13] Jamaican crops were wiped out by blight and the drink was more favoured in southern Europe than in England. But plants established in Trinidad, which Britain captured in 1802, hybridized and were spread very widely as a successful commercial crop. London boasted chocolate as well as coffee houses; some, like White's, became fashionable and exclusive clubs.

While coffee and chocolate were initially drinks for the wealthy, in private as well as public contexts, tea was increasingly imbibed in the British workplace. Taken with sugar, it became a significant source of calories for those whose diets were, on average, only just beginning to include sufficient energy to sustain them through a day of heavy labour. Tea was usually

[8] Mintz, *Sweetness and Power*, 13.

[9] Maxine Berg, 'In Pursuit of Luxury: Global History and British Consumer Goods in the Eighteenth Century', *Past and Present*, 182 (2004), 85–142.

[10] James Walvin, *Black Ivory: Slavery in the British Empire* (Oxford: Blackwell, 2001), 3.

[11] John E. Wills, Jr., 'European Consumption and Asian Production in the Seventeenth and Eighteenth Centuries' in Brewer and Porter, *Consumption and the World of Goods*, 141.

[12] A. N. Porter, *Atlas of British Overseas Expansion* (London: Routledge, 1991), 63.

[13] Sophie D. Coe and Michael D. Coe, *The True History of Chocolate* (London: Thames & Hudson, 2000), 197.

served hot, and perceived as a valuable warming drink in a cold climate.[14] Sweet tea was an important indicator of rising standards of living. As food manufacturing expanded, sugar's adaptability as a preservative in jam and an ingredient in popular wheat-based sweet delights such as cakes, pastries, and biscuits cemented its position. 'Soon enough', Sidney Mintz writes, its 'absence from daily life would become virtually unimaginable.'[15]

Annual average consumption of sugar (based on imports divided by population for England and Wales) was about 2 lb (0.8 kg) per capita in the 1660s, 6 lb in 1700, 17 lb in 1750, and 24 lb by 1800. Rum was a popular by-product. Tea imports increased from very little in 1700 to at least 2 lb per person per year by 1800—roughly sufficient for each person to have a sugared cup a day. The price fell perhaps fourfold over the century. Annual average per capita imports of tobacco, grown largely on the American mainland, into England increased to over 2 lb per person in the seventeenth century.[16] Tobacco was even more important in Holland and social intercourse in the Dutch Empire, when it was at the height of its economic predominance in this century, was wreathed in smoke. Food crops, including rice from Africa, were also grown in coastal American plantations to supply largely local markets.[17]

Environmental Factors in the Location of Plantations

The evolution of the Atlantic system was the outcome of a series of opportunities, and localized decisions, in part shaped and facilitated by environmental factors. Most key plantations crops could not be grown in Europe. Northern Europe was unsuited to the cultivation of cane sugar. While it was grown as a plantation crop on Mediterranean islands in the medieval period, these had too great a temperature variation to be ideal. The balmy Canary Islands, further south off the Saharan coast, were colonized from the fourteenth century, and became part of Spain. Sugar thrived there and they provided a model for the later transformation of the Americas. The indigenous Guanche people were largely wiped out or enslaved, and the islands rapidly deforested

---

[14] Mintz, *Sweetness and Power*, and Mintz, 'The Changing Roles of Food in the Study of Consumption' in Brewer and Porter, *Consumption and the World of Goods*, 261–73.

[15] Mintz, 'Changing Roles of Food', 264.

[16] Shammas, 'English and Anglo-American Consumption', 180.

[17] Judith Carney, *Black Rice: The African Origins of Rice Cultivation in the Americas* (Cambridge, MA: Harvard University Press, 2001).

to make space for new crops.[18] But of the seven main islands, some were too mountainous and others too dry, so that suitable terrain was limited. Tobacco, an American domesticate, proved a little more adaptable. It was grown in limited quantities in England and the Netherlands and later became a significant crop in southern Europe, although never on a sufficient scale to displace tropical plantation production. Cotton also required warmth.

Portuguese colonizers transplanted sugar to the previously uninhabited Cape Verde, Madeira, Azores, and São Tomé islands, the latter close to Africa, in the fifteenth century, and in part used African slaves to work the plantations.[19] Madeiran sugar reached Britain as early as the 1450s. One of the founding myths recalled by Madeira colonists was a fire that burned for seven years—a powerful metaphor for deforestation.[20] The neighbouring island of Porto Santo was invaded by European rabbits—a precursor for the Australian experience—which bred so successfully that they initially precluded human settlement. In the sixteenth century, São Tomé, in the Gulf of Guinea directly south of the mouth of the Niger, had an African slave workforce of 5,000–6,000 people. The area of suitable soil on these Atlantic islands, however, was again too small.

Plantations could have been established in West Africa and colonial powers made a number of attempts to do so. If they had succeeded, the Atlantic system—and possibly the history of parts of Africa—would have been significantly different. As Eltis notes: 'the geographic movement of the plantation complex in the fifteenth and sixteenth centuries was toward Africa rather than the Americas ... what happened in the Americas was what Europeans wanted to happen in Africa but could not bring about'.[21] São Tomé could have provided the stepping-stone. The Portuguese started settlements in the Kongo kingdom and Angola from the sixteenth century and they kept slaves, some of whom were used for agriculture. Most of their farms, however, supplied foodstuffs for the slave trade and ports. English adventurers hoped to find riches in the soil of West Africa. The British Royal African Company, founded in 1660, was primarily interested in West African precious metals, especially gold, and slaves. But it also experimented

---

[18] Crosby, *Ecological Imperialism*; Felipe Fernandez-Armesto, *The Canary Islands after the Conquest: The Making of a Colonial Society in the Early Sixteenth Century* (Oxford: Clarendon Press, 1982).

[19] Herbert S. Klein, *The Atlantic Slave Trade* (Cambridge: Cambridge University Press, 1999).

[20] Crosby, *Ecological Imperialism*, 76.

[21] David Eltis, *The Rise of African Slavery in the Americas* (Cambridge: Cambridge University Press, 2000), 139.

in agricultural crops, especially cotton and indigo, and introduced cotton machinery into Gambia from Barbados.[22] Sierra Leone was thought suitable for sugar and rice was well established locally.[23] Sugar, cotton, indigo, and ginger were planted around Cape Coast Castle on the Gold Coast. The Dutch also made sustained efforts to establish sugar around their West African trading forts, using slaves, and the French hoped to establish tropical crops for export in Senegal.

Few of these African plantations succeeded in the longer term. Environmentally related diseases have been invoked as an explanation for this failure and for the transposition of plantations to the Americas.[24] One pillar of the argument rests on West Africa as the white man's grave. European settlement or even supervision was greatly hampered by high rates of death, largely from the mosquito-borne diseases yellow fever and malaria—a 'deadly barricade just beyond the beaches'.[25] In his influential overview of disease in Atlantic history, Crosby accepts this proposition: from the earliest Portuguese incursions, Europeans in West Africa faced a 'striking angel with a flaming sword of deadly fevers', and they 'tended to sizzle and die'.[26]

Such dangers were all too evident during the key period for British establishment of sugar plantations in the second half of the seventeenth century. The Royal African Company, for example, accumulated considerable experience of operating in tropical climates. It was a major slave-trading operation, selling by auction about 90,000 slaves in the Caribbean between 1672 and 1711.[27] Its major centre of activity was the fort at Cape Coast, acquired in 1664; between 1683 and 1713 it maintained a garrison of about 60–90.[28] At its largest, the company's West African service employed about 300 white men. Recruitment of Europeans was always difficult and rates of death were very high. In one five-month period in 1684–5, one-quarter of the white men on the Gold Coast succumbed, about one every ten days: 'for most men, West Africa was a place to get away from or to die in'.[29] During the early eighteenth century, the Company lost half the Europeans it sent to West

---

[22] K. G. Davies, *The Royal African Company* (New York: Atheneum, 1970).

[23] Eltis, *African Slavery*, 143.

[24] Philip D. Curtin, 'Epidemiology and the Slave Trade', *Political Science Quarterly*, 83 (1967), 190–216; Philip D. Curtin, *The Rise and Fall of the Plantation Complex: Essays in Atlantic History* (Cambridge: Cambridge University Press, 1990).

[25] Kenneth F. Kiple, *The Caribbean Slave: A Biological History* (Cambridge: Cambridge University Press, 1984), 4.

[26] Crosby, *Ecological Imperialism*, 138–9.   [27] Davies, *Royal African Company*, 299

[28] *Ibid.*, 240, 251.   [29] *Ibid.*, 257.

Africa within a year. Only one in ten of those Englishmen who worked in this region prior to the mid-nineteenth century returned home alive.[30] The Company thus retained the minimum presence necessary for the operation of the slave trade. Some of the artisans were African and locally employed slaves did most of the manual work.

Philip Curtin has calculated death rates among British troops in various colonies in the early nineteenth century. Although these figures are from a later period, they confirm the dangers of coastal West Africa for newly arrived Europeans during the slave trade era. An average of about half of the troops garrisoned in Sierra Leone between 1819 and 1838 died annually.[31] By contrast, death rates of British troops in the Cape Colony at the time were 1.5 per cent per year. Even in India, where many stations were in tropical climates, rates were about 6 per cent. African troops in the same West African garrisons sustained death rates of about 3 per cent per annum. West Africans could weather endemic mosquito-borne tropical diseases, because of partial immunities. Yellow fever was less devastating for children than adults, and those that survived childhood infection acquired immunity.

Africans also shared many diseases with European and Middle Eastern populations through trade, migration, and shipping across the Sahara, down the Nile, and around the Indian Ocean. From the fifteenth century they were participants in Atlantic maritime links. They were thus not as susceptible as Native Americans to newly introduced strains of smallpox. Some African societies adopted inoculation against smallpox, as practised in Muslim societies.[32] Inoculation, as opposed to vaccination based on cowpox, was a risky method of prevention in that it could spread the disease, but it could give immunity. West African coastal land, in contrast to parts of the Caribbean, was not made empty by conquest and introduced disease.[33] Although slave captures may have reduced populations in restricted zones

---

[30] Kiple, *The Caribbean Slave*, 13–14.

[31] Philip D. Curtin, *Death by Migration: Europe's Encounter with the Tropical World in the Nineteenth Century* (Cambridge: Cambridge University Press, 1989). It should be noted, however, that French troops in Senegal had lower death rates of about 16 per cent at this time.

[32] Eugenia W. Herbert, 'Smallpox Inoculation in Africa', *Journal of African History*, 16 (1975), 539–59.

[33] Joseph Inikori (ed.), *Forced Migration: The Impact of the Export Slave Trade on African Societies* (London: Hutchinson, 1982), makes the strongest argument in connection with the demographic impact of the slave trade in West Africa; Joseph E. Inikori and Stanley L. Engerman (eds.), *The Atlantic Slave Trade: Effects on Economies, Societies, and Peoples in Africa, the Americas, and Europe* (Durham NC: Duke University Press, 1992).

at particular times, there was no demographic collapse that opened land for settlers or plantations.

Curtin is nevertheless cautious in using environmentally related diseases as the major explanation of the failure of a European-controlled plantation economy in West Africa.[34] David Eltis directly disputes the idea that disease entirely disabled the European impact suggesting, for example, that the 'five hundred to one thousand Europeans living on the Gold Coast in the early seventeenth century could have just as easily supervised plantations as trading posts'.[35] He stresses the importance of African agency and the political balance in this early modern era.[36] Europeans lacked the power to carve out land in the densely occupied West African coastal areas. African political systems were strongly developed and they were not easy to dislodge militarily; European military power seldom penetrated 'beyond a cannon shot from the coast' before the nineteenth century. Neither was it possible to transform African internal social relations except, ironically, by facilitating the expansion of the existing slave supply and further commodifying it.[37] Europeans were restricted to islands and coastal forts and economic activity depended on negotiation. When slaves were acquired for local plantations in Africa, it was difficult to stop them from escaping. By contrast, slaves were trapped especially on the smaller Caribbean islands, where full colonial political control was established. Whereas Spanish adventurers captured the silver mines of South America in the sixteenth century, the gold mines of West Africa remained beyond the European grasp.

Eltis poses a direct challenge to explanations relying upon environmentally related diseases. Can we salvage these? A first response would be, as noted in the Introduction, that environmental factors are often predisposing, background influences on historical processes rather than direct explanations for historical events. Secondly, Eltis does not directly compare the positions in West Africa and the Caribbean, nor ask about the scale of European management and settlement required for plantations in the latter. Thirdly, with respect to West Africa's role in the Atlantic economy, environmental explanations in some respects reinforce the political. African political and military capacities must clearly be brought centrally into the equation. But the fact that Africans shared most of the diseases brought by Europeans underpinned their demographic and political security. At the

---

[34] For example in Philip Curtin et al., *African History* (London: Longman, 1978), ch. 7.

[35] Eltis, *The Rise of African Slavery*, 146, n. 44.

[36] *Ibid.*, 138–47.   [37] Lovejoy, *Transformations in Slavery*.

same time, African diseases of animals, as well as humans, greatly constrained the possibility of European conquest or intrusion in the seventeenth and eighteenth centuries. On the coast, trypanosomiasis, carried by tsetse flies, made it very difficult to keep cattle or horses in any number. African horse-sickness compounded the problem. Horses were often, along with firearms, vital in underwriting European military superiority elsewhere. The Asante of Ghana's forest zone built their kingdom, probably the largest and most powerful in West Africa by the eighteenth century, on the back of foot soldiers with muskets.[38]

A subsidiary environmental argument suggests that low soil fertility, high acidity, and problems with rainfall distribution in West Africa discouraged plantation production.[39] But plantations required relatively small, favourably located enclaves, and in the Americas they initially took up relatively little land. Soil quality did not prevent successful cultivation of a wide variety of cash crops in different parts of West Africa from the mid-nineteenth century, including cotton, coffee, and cocoa. Nor did soil preclude the adoption of American maize in the forested heartland of the Asante kingdom, before the nineteenth century.[40] Over the long term, this crop and other introductions made a significant difference to food supplies and possibly demography.

More puzzling, perhaps, is the failure of West Africans themselves to establish plantations in association with colonial companies. Some of the building blocks were in place in the seventeenth century. In addition to maize, the people of the region adopted a wide range of new, especially American, plants: sweet potatoes, cocoa, chili, cassava, tomatoes, groundnuts, and some types of beans and pumpkins. Internal slavery was also widespread and while much of this was domestic, there are records of slaves working the fields of kings, as well as mining the gold of Asante, in the seventeenth century.[41] Gold and other commodities were a more important export than slaves till the early eighteenth century, so that the rulers of this major kingdom certainly conceived of organizing coerced labour for the production of exports. In the early nineteenth century, after the British abolition of the slave trade (1807), African rulers in Dahomey and elsewhere set slaves to work on palm-oil

---

[38] Ivor Wilks, *Asante in the Nineteenth Century: The Structure and Evolution of a Political Order* (Cambridge: Cambridge University Press, 1975).

[39] Henry A. Gemery and Jan S. Hogendorn, 'Comparative Disadvantage: The Case of Sugar Cultivation in West Africa', *Journal of Interdisciplinary History*, 9 (1979), 429–49.

[40] James McCann, *Maize and Grace: Africa's Encounter with a New World Crop, 1500–2000* (Cambridge, MA: Harvard University Press, 2005).

[41] Lovejoy, *Transformations in Slavery*; Wilks, *Asante*.

plantations; much of the product was exported to Europe for soap manufacture and machine oil. It was difficult for African rulers to override strong
local rights over land and to set up large-scale intensive production. But in
some kingdoms, practices and values with regard to land and labour were
changing through this period, and cannot in themselves explain the absence
of plantations.[42] Ultimately, some Africans rulers—whose power was based
around conquest and tributary authority—and traders chose to engage with
the Atlantic economy through the slave trade, rather than by organizing agriculture. They captured and supplied the great bulk of slaves for the external
trade, and this enterprise became far more than a by-product of war: in some
kingdoms, such as Dahomey, it became their priority. Ironically, their capacity to resist colonial intrusion gave them the power to make these decisions.

Once the potential for sugar plantations in the Americas had been demonstrated by the Portuguese in Brazil in the sixteenth century, and a supply of
slaves became accessible in Africa, these two poles of the triangular Atlantic
trade gradually became established—and their growth was not undermined
by an alternative geographic location for plantations. In an age of sail, the
prevailing winds across the Atlantic reinforced this pattern, and provided
another predisposing, rather than immediately causative, environmental
force that underpinned the Atlantic system. The predominantly easterly
trade winds in the South Atlantic favoured a crossing westwards, south of
the Canaries, or via Africa, and the eastward crossing was best across the
North Atlantic.[43] Winds facilitated the triangular trade in which European
goods—firearms, textiles, iron, and copper bars—were taken to Africa and
traded for slaves, who were shipped on the southerly routes to the Americas.
Plantation commodities were then loaded for the return northerly voyage to
Europe. Maximum economic benefits could be gained from keeping ships
fully laden, although this triangular trade was by no means always the rule.

American Depopulation and African Immunities

Environmental factors and diseases, as well as political power and the
economic strategies of rulers, help to explain why tropical plantations did
not spread on the West Africa coast. We should now switch attention to the
Americas and especially to the Caribbean. Major studies emphasize Native

---

[42] John Thornton, *Africa and Africans in the Making of the Atlantic World, 1400–1600*
(Cambridge: Cambridge University Press, 1992).

[43] Crosby, *Ecological Imperialism*, 118.

American susceptibility to diseases introduced by Europeans. At the core of the argument, vividly summarized by Crosby, is the idea that plant and animal domestications, in the Eurasian (and, it should be added, African) landmass during the ten thousand years before Columbus's voyage, fostered both population growth and a range of parasites and germs. Domesticated animals were a particularly important source of new diseases. Exposure to infection in turn stimulated immunity. Europeans moving to the Americas were 'supermen' and 'superwomen' not primarily because of their size and technology, though the latter helped, but because of the pathogens they brought. These fellow travellers were a major component in ecological imperialism.

The Americas had been colonized, probably 12–15,000 years ago, during a cold period, across the northerly land and ice bridge from Asia. But global warming, Crosby continues, resulted in the flooding of that bridge soon afterwards and cut the flow of Asian migrants as well as contact with Asia. Native Americans also domesticated plants, but not many animals, and they did not develop immunities against highly infectious new diseases such as smallpox, measles, tuberculosis, and pneumonia. Up to a third of populations could succumb in epidemics among communities with no immunity. Death and sickness undermined subsistence production during epidemics, so that starvation killed some who survived disease. Demographic devastation helps to explain the rapidity of land clearance in the Americas, and the limits of the local labour force.

Kiple argues that the indigenous Carib and Arawak populations of the Caribbean were hit by a double scourge.[44] Their islands became a corridor for European shipping and some were early recipients of African slaves. In addition to smallpox and other infectious diseases, Africans or shipping from Africa brought tropical diseases with them, notably falciparum malaria (the most severe strain), yaws, hookworm, and, later, yellow fever. Whereas mainland indigenous populations, especially in isolated or elevated areas, were shielded from diseases, and some were able to acquire immunities or retreat, this was more difficult in the Caribbean. Carib populations survived the early Spanish onslaughts on some islands, such as St Lucia and Barbuda, where, in the seventeenth century, they tried to fight off British settlers. Barbados, by contrast, occupied by British settlers from the 1620s, and the first significant sugar producer, had largely been cleared by the Spanish by

---

[44] Kiple, *The Caribbean Slave.*

this time. The Caribbean was not vacant. It was made so by the cultural and biological hurricane of colonizers and their diseases.

Millions of Native Americans survived on the mainland. Portuguese sugar planters in sixteenth-century Brazil enslaved indigenous people—as many as 40,000 in Bahia—but disease decimated them, and from the 1550s they were largely replaced by Africans.[45] By 1650, the black population there had reached 150,000, despite high death rates. Spanish slave imports were authorized in 1518. On the Mexican highlands, where four million merino sheep had been established by the end of the sixteenth century for wool exports, Africans provided much of the labour and their relationship with indigenous people could be fraught.[46] African skills, for example in managing livestock, or in pearl fishing, were initially valued highly.[47] Slaves were imported to Virginia, the first British tropical settlement, in 1619.

Barbados, bigger and flatter than the other small Caribbean islands initially captured by Britain, became the hothouse for the British American plantation economy. Within two decades, by 1645, 24,000 people had settled there. Of these, 75 per cent were Europeans—many of them initially indentured workers.[48] Barbados then housed nearly as many Europeans as mainland New England, and considerably more than Virginia and Maryland. Settlers soon established cotton and indigo plantations. A few Arawaks were transported from the mainland to demonstrate the cultivation of American plants for food; they were then enslaved. Food crops grew all year round in the fertile soil, and matured quickly. Pigs, left intentionally by the Spanish, both as a meat supply and to disrupt Indian settlement, had run feral and also had to be killed because they devoured crops. Hog hunts with dogs were an early island sport.

Portuguese sugar estates in Pernambuco, northern Brazil, provided a model for the switch to sugar in Barbados from the 1640s. The British authorities ensured that this potentially lucrative trade was tied to the imperial centre. Cromwell sent a fleet to Barbados in 1651 to subdue a rebel royalist faction. His forces conquered Spanish Jamaica in 1655. In 1660, the Navigation Act effectively bound the island economy closely to

---

[45] Richards, *The Unending Frontier*, 391–2.

[46] Elinor G. K. Melville, *A Plague of Sheep: Environmental Consequences of the Conquest of Mexico* (Cambridge: Cambridge University Press, 1997), 83, 122.

[47] Thornton, *Africa and Africans*.

[48] David Watts, *The West Indies: Patterns of Development, Culture and Environmental Change since 1492* (Cambridge: Cambridge University Press, 1987), 148–51, 173.

England, restricting sales to Britain alone, but ensuring a steady market. By 1650, sugar made up the bulk of exports from the island and Barbados became Britain's most valuable colony. Rum, derived from sugar, added to the island's revenue. It was not invented in Barbados but apparently so named on the island, and exported widely through British trading networks, including to West Africa.

Sugar required more skill and labour than the earlier crops grown on Barbados. The workforce accounted for over a third of the annual costs. Barbados imported about 12,000 indentured prisoners of war, largely from Ireland and Scotland, during the Cromwellian period but this supply diminished rapidly after the English Civil War ended in 1660. Although African slaves were initially more expensive, they were purchased for life, had fewer rights, were more exploitable, and had proved effective elsewhere. It was an 'unthinking' decision to choose slaves—there was not a moral issue.[49] And while Africans were resistant to European diseases, European indentured workers were susceptible to African diseases that gradually penetrated into the Caribbean. The rise of sugar plantations in the Caribbean facilitated the spread of yellow fever to the Americas.[50] Its carrier, the mosquito *Aedes aegyptii*, had probably crossed the Atlantic by 1640, and the use of huge quantities of clay pots on the plantations to drain molasses created ideal conditions for their breeding. The Caribbean's increasingly dense human population provided human hosts for the mosquitoes.

Barbados experienced its first recorded yellow fever epidemic in 1647. Nearly half the English troops that conquered Jamaica (1655) died soon afterwards. Slaves born in West Africa were generally immune through childhood exposure—some may have carried partial genetic immunity. So were those people who contracted the disease as children in the Caribbean, and survived. The most susceptible group were non-immune adult men—such as newly arrived European soldiers, sailors, and indentured workers. Yellow fever helped to make Barbados uncomfortable for them and the white population reached its peak in 1655 at about 30,000. Many of the landless then left for Jamaica and the mainland and were not replaced. The advantages presented to landowners by African slaves were increasingly evident and by 1665 over 30,000 worked the plantations. This new disease,

---

[49] *Ibid.*, 202.

[50] Kiple, *The Caribbean Slave*; J. R. McNeill, 'Ecology, Epidemics and Empires: Environmental Change and the Geopolitics of Tropical America, 1600–1825', *Environment and History* 5 (1999), 175–84.

coupled with the economic advantages of slaves, helped to transform the racial demography of Barbados. Kiple argues that Africans, with exposure and partial immunities to both European and African diseases, were 'inexorably selected' as the key Caribbean workforce. By the end of the eighteenth century, over three-quarters of the population were slaves, and 3 per cent freed blacks. Barbados set the pattern for the British Caribbean, especially Jamaica, which—because of its size—soon became the empire's major sugar island. In 1675, 50 per cent of Jamaica's population was white, in 1700 about 15 per cent, and by 1800 less than 10 per cent—despite the overall growth in the white population.

Disease patterns, linked to ecological transformations, helped to shape the conquest and peopling of the Americas, but, John McNeill argues, they also constrained British expansion in tropical zones. As their power expanded, British interests were keen to control further areas for sugar production.[51] They were constrained by the death rates of soldiers in the Caribbean, and in Spanish-controlled areas of the mainland. While British forces did invade some of these areas during the eighteenth century, including Cuba and Nicaragua, disease sometimes constrained their capacity to establish a lasting hegemony. By contrast, Spanish Creole communities, born in the Americas, achieved a higher degree of resistance. The spread of yellow fever may not have been a fundamental factor in conquest, but McNeill suggests it favoured a geopolitical stability.

Environmental Consequences of Plantations in the Caribbean

The establishment of plantations necessitated destroying the forests on Barbados with a combination of ring-barking and burning in the dry season. Much of the work for 'The Great Clearing' was done first by indentured workers and then by African slaves.[52] West Indian cedar was felled and used for building and carpentry, as was the locust tree. Limited amounts of *Lignum vitae*, a highly durable wood for bowls and furniture, were exported.[53] But felling was primarily done to clear land, initially for tobacco, ginger, and sea-island cotton. By 1650 half of the island was cleared of forest, and almost all by the end of that century. At least one tree species, mastick, eventually

---

[51] McNeill, 'Ecology, Epidemics and Empires'.

[52] Bonham C. Richardson, *The Caribbean in the Wider World, 1492–1992: A Regional Geography* (Cambridge: Cambridge University Press, 1992), 30.

[53] Watts, *The West Indies*, 155.

became extinct. Cleared ground provided advantages for other species, such as the edible native guava.

Over the longer term, sugar cultivation took its toll on the soils. In his influential book *Capitalism and Slavery* (1944), Eric Williams—later Prime Minister of Trinidad—drew attention to falling yields and the environmental collapse on the older sugar islands in the late eighteenth century, and saw this as a contributory factor to the abolition of slavery.[54] It supported his argument that capitalists were no longer economically interested in the perpetuation of slavery. Drescher, in *Econocide*, took issue with Williams: the plantation economy, he maintained, was still profitable on many islands; slave imports increased in the late eighteenth century; and there was still new land to be brought within the system. As one Jamaican planter argued, he would accept abolition 'but not until every acre in the islands was cultivated'.[55] Jamaican sugar production was still increasing and coffee, which could be grown on higher slopes, took off in the late eighteenth century. The French-controlled islands, especially St Domingue, and Spanish Cuba were booming at this time. British Guiana and Trinidad had hardly been exploited for sugar, and promised major new frontiers.

Drescher's argument does not, however, preclude the possibility of severe environmental damage on longer-exploited islands. Concerns about the decline in soil fertility were articulated in Barbados in the 1660s, and even before in relation to tobacco. Silting and soil wash were exacerbated by the practice of planting cane in trenches which sometimes followed the slopes downwards. Yields on some land were perceived to be declining by the end of the seventeenth century; fields were becoming 'barren, rocky gullies, runaway land, waste land, and all the rest much worn out and not so fertile as it was'.[56] However, despite massive deforestation, Barbados was to some extent protected from the worst effects of soil erosion over the long term by the predominance of flat land and gentle slopes. Its porous rock absorbed rain, and the sugar itself provided a cover of vegetation.[57] More mountainous islands in the Windwards, such as Grenada, experienced more severe erosion

---

[54] Eric Williams, *Capitalism and Slavery* (London: Andre Deutsch, 1944).

[55] Seymour Drescher, *Econocide: British Slavery in the Era of Abolition* (Pittsburgh, PA: University of Pittsburgh Press, 1977), 93.

[56] Watts, *The West Indies*, 397.

[57] Bonham C. Richardson, *Economy and Environment in the Caribbean: Barbados and the Windwards in the late 1800s* (Barbados: University of the West Indies Press, 1997), 102–3.

over a shorter period.[58] Even in Barbados, and especially elsewhere, planters retained forest patches on steeper elevations and some land was given over to livestock farming.[59] Cattle were essential for food supply and for traction to power the sugar mills.

Planters responded to declining fertility by altering the system of cultivation. Walls and weirs were built to stop soil-washing, and soil was carted by slaves back to the fields. Intensive manuring regimes were introduced, using both animal dung and plant waste. Ginger-growers with smaller estates turned to dung farming; the renewing fertilizer was carried to the sugar estates by slaves in baskets on their heads. From the early eighteenth century, planters began to use a system of 'cane holing'—or planting between earth ridges along the contour that stopped water flow across the lands. Little waste was allowed from the sugar plants. Barbados was short of space on which to graze cattle; baggasse from the mills and cane tops were used as fodder. Although some estates allowed slaves access to small subsistence plots, food was also imported in considerable quantities, thus relieving some pressure on the land. These innovations could only partly offset environmental losses, and food imports, as well as intensifying workloads, increased costs. By the mid-eighteenth century, average sugar output per slave in Barbados was less than half that in Jamaica.[60] By 1775 Barbadian sugar production was one third of its peak in the late seventeenth century. In 1780, the island was flattened by a hurricane; over 2,000 slaves were killed 'and the most beautiful island in the world [had] the appearance of a country laid waste'.[61] In the 1790s, insect pests attacked the sugar. Undoubtedly, environmental pressures contributed to this decline: 'the old sugar colonies had served their purpose. Their sun had set.'[62] Sugar crushed an earlier landscape as well as hundreds of thousands of lives. For some, however, the new landscapes created for economic crops were aesthetically attractive as well as productive.

Not all islands were so profoundly affected. Barbados, deforested for a century, imported wood from Tobago, which was relatively unexploited, in the late eighteenth century. Richard Grove details the development of

---

[58] Richardson, *Economy and Environment*, 102.

[59] Richards, *Unending Frontier*, chs 11 and 12, emphasizes the significance of livestock farming interspersed with plantations in Brazil and the Caribbean.

[60] Watts, *The West Indies*, 276.   [61] Carrington, *Sugar Industry*, 59.

[62] Selwyn H. H. Carrington, *The Sugar Industry and the Abolition of the Slave Trade, 1775–1810* (Gainesville: University of Florida Press, 2002).

forest protection on St Vincent and Tobago, which Britain acquired in the 1763 Peace of Paris. A botanical garden was founded on the former in 1765. One consequence of deforestation, regularly cited at the time, was declining water supply and this became all the more obvious on smaller islands. When an ordinance protecting the remaining woodlands in Barbados was promulgated, the reason cited was not only the supply of timber but also 'to prevent that drought which in these climates is the usual consequence of a total removal of the woods'.[63]

Despite the beginnings of conservationist interventions, the environmental consequences of the Atlantic system on the Caribbean islands were profound. Kiple concludes that 'only the limestone, coral, volcanic rock, and underlying mountain ranges upon which they rest', remained entirely indigenous, while 'most of the flora that adorn them, and the fauna that inhabit them, are imported. So are the men who dominate them'.[64]

[63] Grove, *Green Imperialism*, 271.   [64] Kiple, *The Caribbean Slave*, 3.

3

The Fur Trade in Canada

In the tropical zones of mainland America and the Caribbean islands, plantations became a key vehicle for imperial expansion—an early hothouse of intensive production which boosted Caribbean populations from 200,000 to two million over a couple of centuries. The indigenous population, as noted in the last chapter, had no place in this system and was largely destroyed or its remnants absorbed. But the labour requirements of the plantation system, its location, and the diseases it engendered also shaped a demography weighted against white settlers, especially in the Caribbean. At the northern limits of European intrusion, on the Atlantic coast, down the St Lawrence River, and on the shores of the Hudson Bay, the imperial frontier was extended more by trade than by agrarian settlement. In this chapter, we illustrate how the natural environment of this region, as well as economic and political forces, influenced the routes of intrusion and patterns of interaction. In contrast to the Caribbean, Native Americans had a major role in supplying imperial markets.

Coastal settler society in the Americas, from Boston north, grew partly around the cod fisheries. The Grand Banks off the Canadian coast were a particularly rich source of cod and had been fished by the Spanish, Portuguese, and Basques since the sixteenth century or before.[1] By the early seventeenth century, as many as 300 French and 150 British ships were recorded at one time on what became the Canadian coast. Cod fisheries were largely run by Europeans and based on European technology. They became the basis for an important export trade in dried and salted cod, bacalhau, to Europe and the Caribbean, where sources of protein were in short supply. On the sugar islands, especially, there were severe constraints on keeping livestock, and a lack of indigenous species to hunt. Dried cod, traded from North to Central America, to some degree filled this dietary gap; not only did it last well but it was also light to transport.

---

[1] Harold A. Innis, *The Cod Fisheries: The History of an International Economy* (New Haven: Yale University Press, 1940); Kurlansky, *Cod*; Phillip A. Buckner and John G. Reid, *The Atlantic Region to Confederation: A History* (Toronto: University of Toronto Press, 1994).

Crosby has argued that North America was particularly porous with respect to the absorption of Eurasian animal and plant species and that these greatly facilitated settler colonialism. However, Crosby's argument applies more cogently to relatively small pockets of land around New England, the southern plantation states, and California. On the northerly Atlantic seaboard, and the area north of the Great Lakes and Missouri Basin, long cold winters presented problems for acclimatizing imported animals and plants. While no particular disease disabled settler farming, environmental conditions, as well as First Nations power and isolation from markets, helped to constrain it in the early centuries of colonial intrusion.

In these vast northern reaches, pockmarked by lakes and waterways, the key commodity frontier developed around fur trapping and trading. As in the case of sugar, tobacco, and cod, fur served very specific demands within European societies. But whereas sugar created a world that was in most ways imported, and cod fishing, although dependent on a local resource, mostly relied on European skills, the commodification of fur drew deeply on local knowledge. The fur trade gave rise to a different sort of commodity frontier, shaped both by the product, its provenance, and the environment. To a greater extent than indigenous peoples further south, and for a longer period, First Nations people in what became Canada were able to work with and influence the European intrusion.[2]

Animals in colder landmasses tend to have thicker fur, coveted for the warmth it gave to people and, in respect of some species, for its richness and colour. Many were hunted for their coats. Beavers (*Castor canadensis*) could withstand the freezing temperatures of the northern winters. Their fur consists of an outer layer of longer, thicker hair and a thick inner layer of finer, downy hair. Whole furs, sewn together, were used for garments but this was not their major value in British markets. The inner fur of the beaver has tiny barbs that proved ideal for the process of felting in order to produce hats. The fibres could be matted and beaten, and then stiffened and shaped into soft, durable felt that was warm and waterproof. Old established techniques of felting were perfected in France in the sixteenth century. When the Huguenots were expelled in 1585, they transported their felting skills to Britain, which then became a major production centre. Beaver hats were at a certain level functional. More significantly, they became a mark both of rank

---

[2] In writing on African history, the colonial term 'native' has long been unacceptable. It is still, however, widely used in writing sympathetic to Native Americans. The preferred Canadian term is First Nations, though this does not include Métis and Inuit peoples.

and style. In Stuart England, during the reign of Charles I (1625–49), the wide-brimmed Spanish style, which required a large amount of felt, became popular. Hats were expensive and beaver skin could fetch a high value for its weight; as much as 20 shillings for a pound at times on the London market. Castorium from the beaver's anal scent glands proved a valuable by-product, used as a treatment for fever, headaches, spasms, epilepsy, mental illness, and many other ailments. The sticky substance was sold as pear-shaped Beaver Stones. Beaver meat was consumed both by Native Americans and settlers. Catholics declared beaver tails to be fish, and ate them on Fridays.

Environmental Influences and Indigenous Responses

While beaver habitat stretched across much of northern North America, straddling political boundaries, the fur trade has been seen as especially significant in Canadian history. Harold Innis, doyen of early Canadian economic historians, argued in 1930 that 'Canada emerged as a political entity with boundaries largely determined by the fur trade'.[3] He added that the 'northern half of North America remained British because of the importance of fur as a staple product'.[4] Innis was distilling an insight, and did not argue for beavers as the sole determinant of complex political processes. But his proposition is valuable in suggesting the links between ecology, economics, and state formation. It also provides scope for recognizing the role of the First Nations of Canada, as much as the settlers, in the construction of this new society—and its colonially imposed boundaries—through their involvement in trapping and trading.

Beavers survive largely on bark, stems, and twigs of the softer deciduous trees such as birch, poplar, and willow. The limits of their northern range were thus set by that of the deciduous forests. Their tree diet is low in nutrition and they have to gnaw continuously. If they do not use their four large incisors in this way, these grow too long and blunt. This is one reason why beavers were very difficult to domesticate: they chewed their way out of any wooden enclosure. Beavers are also semi-aquatic and require water. They create a suitable environment for themselves by damming streams with felled logs. They live in lodges built of this timber, cemented with mud, just above the water level. Beavers were therefore concentrated around ponds, lakes, and associated river systems.

---

[3] Innis, *The Furx Trade in Canada*, 393; Peter C. Newman, *Company of Adventurers*, vol. 1 (Toronto: Penguin, 1986), 55.

[4] Innis, *Fur Trade*, 396.

Beaver furs tended to be darker, and thicker, in more northerly terrain. These were favoured for the fur trade. Prime fur territory was a vast sweep of land, from coast to coast, north of the St Lawrence and the Great Lakes, south and west of Hudson Bay. Much of this area is called the Canadian shield, bared during the retreat of the last Ice Age, about 10,000 years ago, and shaved of its soil by glacial movements. The rocks ground down by the retreating ice were deposited as soil and silt around the Great Lakes and St Lawrence lowlands—and this became a fertile area. But further north, the land is much rockier, interspersed with myriad lakes and channels, draining vast amounts of fresh water. Even where valleys offered deeper soil, and good drainage, the shortness of the growing season discouraged agriculture.

Beavers did not migrate and their lodges were easy to find. Once iron implements were introduced for breaking them open, and survival in their terrain was mastered, they were relatively easy to hunt and trap. Beavers also took some time to reproduce and as soon as the trade achieved any volume, the demand could not be met from renewable resources. The fur trade therefore produced a continually moving boundary of exploitation. Its direction was shaped by the sequential involvement of First Nation communities, by the location of prime beaver habitats, by constraints and opportunities for transport, and by the competitive strategies of fur-trading companies. The routes of the trade were along internal watercourses; as in the case of the oceans, these greatly reduced the costs of transport.

From the sixteenth century, cod fishermen bartered for furs at their shore-based settlements. When Jacques Cartier arrived to explore the Gulf of the St Lawrence in 1534, Mi'kmaq people were prepared to trade.[5] They used beaver skins for clothing, five to eight sewn together with moose-skin thread. They treated the skins by scraping, which loosened the longer hairs, and rubbing the downy inner surface with bone marrow. The felted side, facing inwards, became softer with use. This supple, worn garment-fur was initially most in demand for hat making and First Nations communities were, in a sense, involved in its manufacture.[6] Europeans exchanged knives, hatchets, and firearms, which increased Native American capacity to hunt and fight. They also traded iron kettles, currency, and beads.

It was difficult for Europeans to command First Nations people directly in a fur-trapping enterprise because colonial authority was weak, the sites

[5] Innis, *Fur Trade*.

[6] Jim R. Miller, *Skyscrapers Hide the Heavens: A History of Indian–White Relations in Canada* (Toronto: University of Toronto Press, 2000), 37–9.

of hunting were so dispersed, and trade depended upon local knowledge.[7] Some French and Métis people did hunt and trap, but most traders relied on indigenous labour. The question arises as to why indigenous peoples were prepared to service this trade. Graeme Wynn, drawing on well-established literature, argued that a fundamental starting point in Canadian environmental history is that they saw nature and animals in a different way from Europeans, who were intent upon exploiting 'a collection of things to be used'.[8] First Nations people exchanged goods not because they shared the same economic imperatives but because the new commodities fitted into their models of exchange, status, accumulation, and political alliances. Early trade could be contained by aboriginal societies. Trade goods were often conceptualized as gifts; transactions were framed within elaborate ceremonial, and extended personal interaction, rather than quick depersonalized exchanges. Understanding their response requires reading beyond the words of European sources—the only ones available for this period—to discover the meaning of such trade to indigenous people.[9]

Arthur Ray, whose research elaborated on indigenous participation in the trade, emphasized, by contrast, cultural transformation, arguing both for differential responses by First Nations societies and for a careful periodization of change. He suggests that economic considerations became increasingly dominant at a relatively early phase of interaction.[10] Richard White explores 'the middle ground', in two senses.[11] He focuses largely on the settler borderlands south of the Great Lakes, home of the Algonquin peoples, much of which was absorbed into the United States rather than Canada. His middle ground was a contact zone of cultural interaction in which neither society was dominant: 'the Algonquian and French worlds melted at the edges and merged'.[12] His approach also lays greater stress on social context

    [7] Arthur J. Ray, *Indians in the Fur Trade: Their Role as Trappers, Hunters and Middlemen in the Lands Southwest of the Hudson Bay, 1660–1870* (Toronto: University of Toronto Press, 1974).

    [8] Graeme Wynn, *Remaking the Land God Gave to Cain: A Brief Environmental History of Canada*, lecture series no. 62 (London: Canada House, 1998), 6. For a historiographical summary, Arthur J. Ray and Donald B. Freeman, *'Give Us Good Measure': An Economic Analysis of Relations between the Indians and the Hudson's Bay Company before 1763* (Toronto: University of Toronto Press, 1978).

    [9] Jennifer S. H. Brown and Elizabeth Vibert (eds.), *Reading Beyond Words: Contexts for Native History* (Peterborough, Ontario: Broadview Press, 1996).

    [10] Ray and Freeman, *'Give Us Good Measure'*, 236.

    [11] Richard White, *The Middle Ground: Indians, Empires, and Republics in the Great Lakes Region, 1650–1815* (Cambridge: Cambridge University Press, 1991).

    [12] White, *Middle Ground*, 50.

and continuity. It is true that early seventeenth-century sources can suggest indigenous awareness of shared interests. A Jesuit missionary amongst the Montaignais reported in 1606: 'I heard my host say one day, jokingly … "The Beaver does everything perfectly well, it makes kettles, hatchets, swords, knives, bread; and, in short, it makes everything"'.[13] This source is often quoted to illustrate that indigenous people recognized the utility and practical importance of exchange commodities. However, there is a clear suggestion in the humour, and in the text as a whole, that the informant distinguished between Native values and those of Europeans. Ray and Freeman also recognized the longevity of trading protocols and practices that were drawn not least from First Nations ceremonial. At least for larger transactions, negotiations were preceded by gift exchanges and silent smoking of four-foot pipes carved with animal motifs—a ritual affirmation of peace. News and praise was swopped in lengthy speeches. Alexander Graham of the Hudson's Bay Company noted in the late eighteenth century that 'the ceremony of smoking the calumet is necessary to establish confidence, it is conducted with the greatest solemnity'.[14]

Such debates are central to understanding many colonial encounters and have environmental implications. In the Canadian context, Ray's analysis is particularly interesting. We need to be cautious about assuming the sustainability of pre-colonial relations between people and nature, particularly after colonial intrusions. Most pre-industrial, pre-urban people lived close to animals and the rhythms of indigenous life in North America were not least structured around the movement and behaviour of wild animals. This also implied knowledge of habitats, and animals featured strongly in folk-lore. But in the pre-colonial period, Native Americans were almost certainly implicated in the extinction of large mammals such as the mammoth and the giant bison, after the Ice Age.[15] The fur trade provided access to new technology that facilitated more intense exploitation. Metal implements were soon turned against the beaver and saved time and energy in hunting, fishing, chopping, and household manufacture. Horses provided new options for buffalo hunting. In the longer run, neither First Nations nor the traders allowed concerns about renewability to constrain their activities as they drove, metaphorically speaking, their hatchets further into the

---

[13] Reuben Gold Thwaites (ed.), *The Jesuit Relations and Allied Documents*, 73 vols. (Cleveland, Ohio: Burrows Brothers, 1896–1901), vol. 6, 297.

[14] Ray and Freeman, *'Give Us Good Measure'*, 57.

[15] Diamond, *Guns, Germs and Steel*.

interior. In Canada especially, resources seemed to be inexhaustible, because the frontier seemed so boundless. And prosperity flowed directly from the natural resource, rather than investment in agriculture or industry.

The Fur Trade and Colonization

Fur trading drew the French into the interior and underpinned early settlements in Quebec and Acadia (later Nova Scotia). Champlain tried to foster a more diverse French community at Quebec City, but by the time of his death in 1635, the bulk of the 150 settlers were still involved in the fur trade.[16] Dutch traders worked rival networks from Fort Orange (Albany) exporting through New Amsterdam (New York). Champlain formed alliances with the Huron and Algonkin, while the Iroquois supplied the Dutch. Better-armed Iroquois hunters, who had depleted the beaver in their zones, moved northwards, and attacked Huron canoe traffic making the long journey from the Ottawa river to Quebec. By 1650, the Huron had been conquered, killed by disease and famine, or absorbed by the Iroquois. The fur trade indirectly destroyed an indigenous society very early in its history. Iroquois power also extended the range of their Dutch and English allies. Closer to the Atlantic coast, Mi'kmaq numbers had declined from perhaps 35,000 in 1500 to 2,000 in 1700.[17]

Some of the traders learnt aboriginal languages and lived for long periods within First Nations societies. Radisson and Groseilliers have become legendary figures in early Canadian colonial history. Pierre-Esprit (Peter) Radisson (c.1638–1710) wrote a journal of which a copy survives in the Bodleian Library, Oxford. Born in a French Canadian settlement, he was captured at the age of fifteen by Mohawks while shooting ducks. After living with them, and learning their language, he escaped and returned to the French settlement at Trois-Riviers. There he met Groseilliers, who later married his half sister, and from 1659 they made increasingly ambitious trading trips north into Cree territory, penetrating beyond existing European trading networks. They heard from the Sioux and the Cree about even richer beaver stocks to the north, as well as rivers flowing north into an inland sea. Radisson was a crosser of boundaries, not only between European and First Nations, but also between French and British society. The French governor of Quebec, concerned about losing a monopoly of trade, refused to give

---

[16] Margaret Conrad, Alvin Finkel, and Cornelius Jaenen, *History of the Canadian Peoples: Beginnings to 1867* (London: Copp Clark Pitman, 1993), 100.

[17] Conrad, Finkel, and Jaenen, *History of the Canadian Peoples*, 99.

permission for them to explore or trade in the north. They travelled instead to Britain in 1665, to seek royal patronage.

Charles II and Prince Rupert, Duke of Cumberland, royalist hero in the recent English Civil War, were attracted by the promise of mineral wealth as well as fur, and keen to limit French expansion. Rupert had previously visited Gambia in 1652, interested the court in the African trade, and helped to secure a charter for the forerunner of the Royal African Company (1660).[18] The coast of the Hudson Bay had been explored in an attempt to find a north-west passage to Asia in the 1610s. After sponsoring a preliminary trading voyage via this route, with Radisson as agent, Rupert and his co-financiers were awarded a royal charter in 1670 giving them rights—in British eyes—to the sea and lands around Hudson Bay. In that era of concessions and mercantilism, they were also given a monopoly of trade and administration of the area. Their capitalization was much smaller than the contemporaneous Royal African Company, involved in trading slaves (Chapter 2).

The Hudson's Bay Company established small forts, or factories, near the mouths of the larger rivers flowing into the bay. Its southernmost posts were vulnerable to French attack and confiscation, and in the 1680s, the largest factories were established on the west coast of the bay at the Churchill and Nelson Rivers. Hat makers ranked the rich Hudson Bay furs above those from New England or the St Lawrence. The company started to make large profits within a decade, and survived, with access to some of the best furs, for nearly two centuries. British control of Hudson Bay was confirmed in 1713 when it also secured the cession of Newfoundland and Acadia. Cree and Assiniboine traders, whose networks penetrated deep into the interior, supplied the company and worked hard to exclude Europeans from intruding on their position as middlemen.

The value of this trade was initially small compared to the sugar plantations.[19] But after a century, by the 1770s, up to 100,000 furs were exported annually.[20] In 1854, at the last peak of exports, over 500,000 Hudson's Bay pelts were auctioned in London alone. At prices of about 20 shillings a pound, the value sold by the company in London may have been around £500,000, and there were other skins sold, as well as other companies and manufacturing

[18] Davies, *Royal Africa Society*, 41.

[19] Nuala Zahedieh, 'Overseas Expansion and Trade in the seventeenth century', in N. Cholas Canny (ed.), *Oxford History of the British Empire*, vol. 1 *The Origins of Empire*, (Oxford: Oxford University Press, 1998), 415.

[20] Innis, *Fur Trade*, 142. He gives figures of about 90,000 for 1770.

centres. This was not a trade on the scale of the tropical plantation crops, but it assumed transcontinental dimensions and drew in many First Nations communities.

Just as the products of the trade were shaped by the environment, so too the cycle of trade was determined by the seasons. Life at the forts was hierarchical, harsh, isolated, and bone-chillingly cold in the winters. Summers were relatively brief, and plagued by insects. Ice constantly threatened ships. They could not leave England before May because Hudson Bay took so long to melt; turnaround time had to be minimized because ships could be trapped in frozen seas after September. Only a couple of ships sailed every year and there was little other reason for vessels to venture into Hudson Bay. Traffic was small compared to that bound for the British colonies on the North American coast or Caribbean where, by the end of the seventeenth century, about 150 and 275 English-based ships called annually.[21] Trading with First Nations peoples took place especially in June and July, before the ships arrived. Fur-trading captains headed downriver to the forts in large canoe flotillas.

French and Métis fur traders operating overland, as well as Hudson's Bay employees, minimized costs by living off the land. Radisson set the tone for the northern frontiersmen—the coureurs des bois. He was

apparelled more like a savage than a Christian. His black hair ... hung in a wild profusion about his bare neck and shoulders. He showed a swart complexion, seamed and pitted by frost and exposure in a rigorous climate. A huge scar, wrought by the tomahawk of a drunken Indian, disfigured his left cheek. His whole costume was surmounted by a wide collar of marten's skin; his feet were adorned by buckskin moccasins. In his leather belt was sheathed a long knife.[22]

Although he retained an assured sense of cultural superiority, and the 'ruthlessness of the exploiter', he appreciated the 'sagacity of the Native' and their modes of living.[23]

First Nations provided Europeans with many of the technologies they required—snowshoes, canoes, moccasins, toboggans—and identified edible plants such as wild rice. They helped provision trading posts and factories over a long period. As early as 1535, Cartier described using the indigenous bark tea to cure his men of scurvy.

---

[21] Zahedieh, 'Overseas Expansion and Trade', 402.

[22] Newman, *Company of Adventurers*, vol. 1, 150.

[23] Germaine Warkentin, 'Discovering Radisson: A Renaissance Adventurer between Two Worlds' in Brown and Vibert, *Reading Beyond Words*, 49.

After this medicine was found ... there was such strife about it, who should be the first to take of it, that they were ready to kill one another, so that a tree as big as any Oake in France was spoiled and lopped bare ... if all the phisicians of Montpelier and Louvain had been there with all the drugs of Alexandria, they would not have done so much in one yere, as that tree did in six days.[24]

Hudson's Bay employees built from, and burnt, abundant local timber; they hunted, fished, and caught birds for food; they wore coats of moose-skin and beaver, and trousers of deerskin. They were also allowed to trap and hunt for skins and to keep half the proceeds. Even more than in South Africa (Chapter 4), hunting subsidized journeys to the interior. David Thompson, who worked for the company in the early nineteenth century before moving to the rival North West Company, explored extensively along little-travelled northern and western Canadian routes, mapping and trading.[25] He and his canoe teams often lived off the land, or exchanged goods for food from local people. They also employed local hunters. Food supplies were a frequent preoccupation and he vividly details the range of meat eaten, including beaver, buffalo, many deer, and in an extremity, wild felines, horses, and dogs.[26] A fictional account of a nineteenth-century Hudson's Bay factory banquet included also dried moose nose, whitefish fried in buffalo marrow, and 'a buffalo calf removed from its dam by Caesarean operation'.[27] A little fresh food was also grown in the short summer season as an anti-scorbutic.

Many of the company employees were recruited from the poorest rural communities in Scotland and the Orkneys, where ships passed en route from London. Men at all levels developed relations with local Cree women.[28] Beyond sex and comfort, women offered material skills, access to indigenous society, and linguistic interpretation. Cree leaders generally accepted or encouraged such liaisons for the connections they provided to information and goods from the factories. For women, it could be a dislocating experience. Some went through public marriage rites, but many company employees left them behind when they departed. There were exceptions. Thompson married

[24] Jacques Cartier, *Principal Navigations, Voyages, Traffiques and Discoveries* (New York: Macmillan, 1904), 250–1, cited in Lee Miller (ed.), *From the Heart: Voices of the American Indian* (New York: Pimlico, 1997).

[25] D'Arcy Jenish, *Epic Wanderer: David Thompson and the Mapping of the Canadian West* (Toronto: Anchor Canada, 2004).

[26] Jenish, *Epic Wanderer*, 139, 141.

[27] Guy Vanderhaeghe, *The Last Crossing* (London: Abacus, 2005), 342.

[28] Sylvia Van Kirk, *Many Tender Ties: Women in Fur-Trade Society, 1670–1870* (Norman: University of Oklahoma Press, 1983).

a half Cree woman, first by native custom, and fifteen years later by Christian rites; although he was frequently away, the relationship lasted. Some of the Métis families later settled in the south of Canada, at the Red River.

The Hudson's Bay Company was able to make links further into the interior, and closer to the main sources of fur, than those trading on more southerly routes overland from Quebec. The latter had to penetrate by canoe down the river systems and across the lakes, in an area where furs were generally poorer and competition stronger. But the conquest of New France by Britain in 1758–60 marked a turning point in the company's fortunes. British traders moved into Montreal, and there was a major migration northwards by loyalists during the American War of Independence. They took over and expanded French networks, forming the Canadian-based North West Company. Both organizations used liquor in the trade—the North West probably more freely.

By the 1770s, trading companies working from Montreal and Ottawa had found their way overland to the Hudson Bay watersheds, and as far as the rich beaver grounds of Lake Athabasca. The North West Company was dependent upon traders over-wintering in the interior and negotiating with First Nations

2. Europeans and Native Americans trading beaver pelts, 1777.

Credit: Getty Images.

middlemen. Their canoes were run by French-speaking Canadian-born voyageurs who improved indigenous construction in producing larger, freight-bearing vessels made from the bark of yellow birch.[29] Weighing less than 300 lb dry, or twice that wet, the canoes carried up to four tons of people and cargo. The birch bark was held together by spruce gum, around a cedar frame, with ash or spruce ribs; they could be repaired on the move from local materials with simple tools. The voyageurs performed extraordinary feats of endurance, paddling at forty-five dips a minute, twenty-five miles a day or more. Leaving Montreal in May, they rendezvoused at Grand Portage and exchanged cargoes with teams who then paddled as far as Lake Athabasca, 2,000 miles away. At the peak of its activities, the North West Company employed 1,100, many dressed distinctively in moose-skin moccasins, corduroy trousers tied by crimson sashes, and blue or buckskin coats.

The steersmen were highly skilled in navigating large canoes, heavily laden, in difficult waters. Where rapids were impassable or lakes ended, they would have to portage, carrying both the canoes and individual loads of up to 180 pounds (80 kg). 'Les hommes du nord' were the elite, wintering in the fur country, and they also struck up relations with local women. But they were ruled by industrial time and fed by complex supply chains. Pemmican made by indigenous people was an important food source along the canoe routes. They pounded buffalo meat, mixed and preserved with fat and saskatoon berries that helped to prevent scurvy. For First Nations, the pemmican trade was as valuable as fur itself and they hunted buffalo for supplies.

By the 1790s the North West Company controlled over 75 per cent of the northern fur trade.[30] The Hudson's Bay Company, faced with intense competition and declining prices, cut corners on its servicing both of staff and of First Nations traders. Competition prompted further exploration as the frontiers of overland expansion were being reached at the Rocky Mountains. Alexander MacKenzie, who explored the Athabasca area for the North West Company, was the first to cross the continent, in 1793, well before Lewis and Clark did so to the South. Simon Fraser followed him and showed that it was impossible to send freight canoes over the Rockies: the 'geographic limits of the trade with the canoe were reached'.[31] David Thompson, however, organized an expedition down the Columbia River to the west coast. In the process, the western side of the continent was linked to the east.

[29] Peter C. Newman, *Caesars of the Wilderness* (Toronto: Penguin, 1988), 35.
[30] White, *Middle Ground*, 478.
[31] Innis, *Fur Trade*, 365.

Birch bark was thinner on the milder, western side of the mountains and less suitable for canoe construction. But fur was sufficiently valuable to sustain an expansion of the trade to the west coast. Astor, a German-American immigrant in New York, who began by trading with the Iroquois, developed a port on the Pacific at the mouth of the Columbia River around 1800. His ships exported furs to China, brought tea back to New York, and then—in a round-the-world journey via Cape Horn—transported trade goods to the Pacific. His enterprise threatened the North West Company's western interests and in 1812 they took over these sites.

Environmental Exhaustion, Indigenous People, and Settlement

In order to compete, the Hudson's Bay Company had to move into the interior from its coastal factories. Their new inland posts also required canoe teams and supplies, so that even greater pressure was placed on the buffalo and moose for pemmican, and caribou for venison. By the early nineteenth century, an official wrote, 'The buffalo have receded so far from the forts, and the quantity of white fish from the lakes ... has decreased so greatly, that now a winter rarely passes without serious suffering from want of food.'[32] By mid-century, one post stocked 12,000 lb of dried meat, mostly caribou, as well as 2,000 tongues, a delicacy.[33] As the posts desperately needed food of low bulk and high nutritional value, indigenous hunting increased in intensity. Beaver trapping also intensified from the late eighteenth century with the introduction of a more effective steel trap.[34] The disappearance of beaver forced indigenous hunting communities, especially the most skilled Iroquois, to move westwards with that frontier. Other species were also being hunted. In the late eighteenth and early nineteenth centuries, beaver only constituted about one-third of the value of skins exported. Deer, martin, otter, bear, and racoon were all in demand, with prices generally rising.

Both the Hudson's Bay and North West Companies had long been uneasy about European settlement that might disturb the fur trade. But the former supported the establishment of farm settlements in Red River, south of Lakes Winnipeg and Manitoba, from the 1810s. Aside from asserting the company's land claims, these promised to provide recruits as activities moved inland, and a home for those who had taken indigenous wives, and also much needed supplies. The Red River valley was a major source of pemmican, and by the early nineteenth century much of the hunting was done by the

---

[32] Innis, *Fur Trade*, 302.   [33] *Ibid.*, 300.   [34] *Ibid.*, 264–5.

Métis communities who were settled there. At their height, these hunts were semi-military operations, involving hundreds of men, reloading their muzzle-loaders on horseback.[35] Women would follow to skin the carcasses, and wheeled carts were used to transport the meat.

The rapid expansion of the fur trade from the 1770s had a major impact on First Nations populations. Great Lakes nations, such as the Sioux and Assiniboine, had supplied furs to French, North West, and Hudson's Bay networks. As the supplies diminished, the Sioux adopted horses and moved to the Upper Missouri and adjacent plains to hunt bison for pemmican.[36] They first used arrows tipped with metal, then firearms. Their increasingly mobile society was reconstructed around a more effective form of natural resource exploitation. Smallpox had been an occasional visitor to Canada, but its impact was cushioned, compared with areas to the south, by the relative isolation of First Nations groups in the interior. The quickening of trade and contact facilitated the spread of smallpox, triggering a major epidemic in 1780–2, which probably killed more than half of the sedentary agriculturalists on the upper Missouri river, including many Assiniboine. The Sioux were less susceptible. 'Equestrian bison hunting', Isenberg argues, 'saved the nomads from greater mortality', because they remained more isolated and more dispersed.[37]

The 'Indians' that became stereotypes in depictions of the northern plains of the American West were in part a product of 'the horse, the fur trade, and epidemic disease'.[38] With beaver exhausted in the upper Missouri and agricultural communities devastated by smallpox, many headed towards the bison herds. For a few decades the hunters traded north, to more settled communities, supplying meat to be made into pemmican for the canoe routes. This was not a secure lifestyle and necessitated major adaptations in social organization and diet, which now included locusts and horsemeat. In 1837–8 another smallpox epidemic decimated many of these Plains communities.[39] Some Cree intermediaries were inoculated, which helped them weather the icy fingers of disease. By the mid-nineteenth century, intruding settlers and the demise of the fur trade further destabilized indigenous society. The geographic scale of Canada, however, ensured that both First Nations and the hunting frontier survived beyond this period. The 'middle ground' could still be found in accounts of the late

[35] Newman, *Caesars of the Wilderness*, 214.
[36] Isenberg, *The Destruction of the Bison*, 50.   [37] *Ibid.*, 58.   [38] *Ibid.*, 61.
[39] Conrad, Finkel, and Jaenen, *History of the Canadian Peoples*, 459.

nineteenth century, such as Vanderhaeghe's fictional evocation of southern Saskatchewan society, in which a central character, the half-Blackfoot Jerry Potts, evinced a deep knowledge of the natural world, and translated between cultures.[40] The eventual destruction of buffalo by this time, however, spelt disaster and starvation for Plains people.

By the mid-nineteenth century, the country of Canada was being locked together by the Hudson's Bay Company. George Simpson, sent in 1820 to head the operations, amalgamated with the North West Company, which reduced competition and staff. As 'the Birchbark Napoleon', he ran the Hudson's Bay conglomerate for four decades. He also acquired the North West's Pacific operation, which moved up the coast to Vancouver Island under James Douglas. In the absence of state authority, the fur trade again required the construction of interior forts and a degree of negotiation, up to the mid-nineteenth century.[41] But First Nations communities around the Straits of Georgia had been assailed and weakened by smallpox since 1782. The time frame of intrusion was quicker, and the balance of power tilted to the company. The British government initially extended rights of governance over the island to the company and, when a Crown Colony was established on mainland British Columbia, Douglas was appointed first governor in 1858.

The beaver was to some degree saved by changes in fashion in Europe and the use of other materials for hats, but not before the trade came close to destroying commercial supplies of fur. The Hudson's Bay Company did become more aware of exhausting its resources in the nineteenth century. And there is evidence that indigenous North Americans, initially at the cutting edge of new commodity frontiers, did so too. We should not expect to see static attitudes. By the early nineteenth century, restorationist ideology, or nativism, was bubbling up among indigenous societies in the northern United States. Tecumseh, the Shawnee leader, used his brother's reconstructed vision of the traditional past to advocate political unity and a defence of land rights. He fought with the British in Canada against the Americans in the war of 1812 in the hope of winning back resources. First Nations spokesmen felt that they were being excluded from access to natural

---

[40] Vanderhaeghe, *The Last Crossing*, and Guy Vanderhaeghe, *The Englishman's Boy* (London: Anchor, 1998).

[41] Cole Harris, 'Voices of Smallpox around the Strait of Georgia' and 'Strategies of Power in the Cordilleran Fur Trade', in C. Harris, *The Resettlement of British Columbia: Essays on Colonialism and Geographic Change* (Vancouver: UBC Press, 1998).

resources: 'now if a poor Indian attempts to take a little bark from a tree to cover him from the rain, up comes a white man and threatens to shoot him, claiming the tree as his own'.[42] An Ottawan prophet 'conveyed a message from the Great Spirit' to his people (1807).

You complain that the animals of the Forest are few and scattered. How should it be otherwise? You destroy them yourselves for their skins only and leave their bodies to rot or give the best pieces to the Whites. I am displeased when I see this, and take them back to the Earth that they may not come to you again. You must kill no more animals than are necessary to feed and clothe you.[43]

Such statements were subsequently taken up, and reworked, in indigenous ideologies of reassertion, and in western environmentalism (Chapter 19).

Beaver numbers did recover, as the frontier of exploitation moved on. While European settlement spread through the Great Lakes area in the second half of the nineteenth century, and some areas of the Canadian shield were deforested by commercial logging, the scale of the country and lack of fertile land provided zones of protection. National parks, demarcated from the late nineteenth century, ensured that beaver populations would not be endangered. It is interesting, however, that beaver farming does not seem to have succeeded on a significant scale. They were difficult to domesticate, required specialized conditions, and destroyed cages. Ostrich farming, begun in the 1860s in the Cape, was one of the few examples of nineteenth-century domestication. It depended on controlling reproduction by incubating eggs, as well as specialist feeding regimes based on lucerne. Such controls were more difficult to impose on a wild mammal.

More sustained concerns about renewability emerged in the twentieth century when the fur trade had lost its central economic importance. In 1925 the Hudson's Bay Company employed Charles Elton, the British ecologist, to investigate fluctuations in the population of fur-bearing animals in order to improve the management of this resource and help control prices.[44] He drew on the knowledge of local employees to compile a history of population dynamics. In an echo of colonial regulation elsewhere, he suggested ways in which resource use by the indigenous population could be monitored.[45] When fur sales declined in the Great Depression, the company curtailed the research.

---

[42] White, *Middle Ground*, 502, quoting Gomo, a Potawatomi chief in Illinois.
[43] *Ibid.*, 486.   [44] Anker, *Imperial Ecology*, 98–9.   [45] *Ibid.*, 108.

Harold Innis analysed the way in which staple production shaped economic growth, as well as the political map, in the 'open' colonial economy of Canada.[46] Innis was critical of such staple extraction and the lack of processing within Canada. However, his analysis of the staples trap is seen from the vantage point of the European settlers, and the capitalist economy of Canada as a whole. From the vantage point of the First Nations, there may have been some temporary advantages in the structure of the early colonial economy. Arguably, the limited development of agriculture and manufacturing reduced settler inflows. Climate, technological difficulties, and the lack of markets helped to douse the stimulus for an agrarian economy. The export of primary products procured largely by indigenous people gave them some power to negotiate. They experienced fewer pressures than Native Americans further south on the frontier of European settlement. The First Nations of Canada were temporarily protected by their own skills in hunting and in weathering an extreme environment. In the earlier centuries of colonization, their experience diverged sharply from that of indigenous people in the Caribbean, and some other zones of plantation production. The Hudson's Bay Company for a long time discouraged settlement in its areas of influence, because this would disturb the fur supply. The cost was to some degree a less diversified economy.

We should not exaggerate these benefits to indigenous people. Alcohol, including Caribbean rum, washed across the continent as an increasingly significant element in the trade, and caused major social dislocation. Few communities escaped the demographic and social devastation caused by smallpox and other introduced diseases. By the mid-nineteenth century, as settlers moved onto the cultivable Plains, even the company changed direction, focussing on land development, and participating in the railway construction that opened up the interior; it also branched out into financial institutions and the retail trade, servicing settlers. Canadian First Nations retained relatively more land than Native Americans to the south, but often in areas on the margins of European settlement that were unsuitable for agriculture. While the northern environment and the nature of the commodity frontier in Canada gave them a relative advantage in the British-colonized parts of America, ultimately, they too were decimated by disease. Unlike indigenous people in African and Asian colonies, they became a

[46] Innis, *Fur Trade*; Harold A. Innis, *Problems of Staple Production in Canada* (Toronto: Ryerson Press, 1933).

demographically marginal group within a settler nation. By 1900, about 130,000 people were classified as aboriginal, or 2.4 per cent of the total population of nearly 5.4 million.

In this chapter, we have chosen an American case that directly contrasted with that of the Caribbean. We have tried to illustrate some of the ways in which the natural environment shaped commodity frontiers, and in turn the interaction between First Nations and colonial forces. We will touch on these legacies in subsequent chapters.[47]

[47] Benidickson, *Idleness, Water, and a Canoe.*

4

Hunting, Wildlife, and Imperialism
in Southern Africa

Imperial networks in northern North America flowed initially along the waterways that gave access to the trade-associated hunting, trapping, timber extraction, and related activities. Hunting was essential to many indigenous societies, and required relatively little investment for the first wave of traders and settlers. It generated valuable resources in a number of colonized zones. But hunting frontiers in the British Empire differed. In part, the reasons were environmental. The assemblage of species in North America and Africa were possibly more similar 15,000 years ago 'when the American West looked much as [the] Serengeti plains do today'.[1] Large mammals including mammoths, big cats, and wild horses roamed the northern hemisphere prairies. Climate change, combined with the impact of rapid human migration through the Americas 10–12,000 years ago, resulted in many extinctions so that the wildlife of the two areas had become distinctive by the onset of European colonization. This opened up divergent opportunities for consumption and trade.

Southern Africa was a frontier of heat rather than cold. There were no animals with the thick glossy fur favoured by Europeans for outer garments or for felt. Southern Africa's most prized hunted commodity—aside from meat—was equally unpredictable. While mammoths had been exterminated in North America, an elephant species with large tusks survived into the modern era in Africa. Environmental factors also shaped the technology of hunting and carriage. Southern Africa lacked navigable rivers and lakes; Canada's abundance of water was matched by South Africa's dearth. Although the spread of firearms and horses was common to both regions, South Africa's transport sinews were dusty, rutted ox-wagon tracks across the veld rather than the cool, wooded lakes and streams along which canoes could be paddled.

---

[1] Diamond, *Guns, Germs and Steel*, 46.

In part, differences resulted from the chance value of particular animal products. Southern Africa was home to an extraordinary range of large mammals. The richness of wildlife can be judged by the variety of predators at the top of the food chain—lions, leopards, cheetahs, caracals, hyenas, wild dogs, jackals, as well as smaller cats. The antelope population was unparalleled in the diversity of its species. But variety did not in itself translate into value. There was no product that could rival beaver skins. Ivory was exported over a long period from various parts of Africa; the value from Cape ports rose to a peak of about £60,000 in 1875. Skins and ostrich feathers were also exported at various times: Clarks shoe company experimented with wild animal leather, including lion, in the nineteenth century. But wildlife in southern Africa did not underpin a colonial export economy on the scale of the fur trade in Canada in the seventeenth and eighteenth centuries, much less sugar in the Caribbean.

The social contexts were as diverse as the environmental. Settler hunting in southern African, as in Canada, depended to some degree on the skills and knowledge of indigenous people, but it was probably more important for the export trade. Despite this, and paradoxically, indigenous southern African people were far better able to challenge and contain imperial and settler incursions. They were less susceptible to disease than Native Americans, and, with the exception of the Khoisan, experienced no demographic disasters. By 1904, when Canadian censuses registered about 130,000 First Nation people, South Africa recorded 3.5 million Africans out of a similar total of 5 million. Together with other long-term historical processes, which we cannot cover here, this gave them relative strength in the colonial encounter. Socially, as well as environmentally, these became sharply contrasting extractive frontiers.

Despite these differences, there are intriguing parallels. In both cases, indigenous and settler knowledge became intermingled; in both, wildlife provided a significant subsidy, in the shape of meat, to early colonial penetration and imperial expeditions. In both cases, wildlife, hunting, and related transport systems, by ox-wagon and canoe respectively, left deep cultural legacies in settler society. In both Canada and South Africa, the value of hunted commodities was eclipsed by economic development after the early decades of the nineteenth century. Extractive hunting was a means of exploiting nature's bounty for those on the peripheries of imperial expansion with little capital at their disposal. But hunting on this scale exhausted the resource on which it depended. Hunting frontiers can be contrasted with colonial agrarian systems (Chapters 2, 6, 8, and 14), and mining, which demanded greater investment and produced greater value for the imperial economy.

Southern African colonization cannot be analysed through the lens of hunting alone. Agriculture, and especially the pastoral economy, was more central for most white and black societies from the beginnings of colonization in the seventeenth century. Nevertheless, the hunting of wildlife is a fascinating route into the environmental history of the region. We have chosen southern Africa as an example, not only because of the significance of wildlife, and the scale of devastation, but because this region became a touchstone in the empire for preservation and conservation. It also helped to fuel another major market in Britain for the imaginative recreation of exotic places and adventures, largely in the shape of hunting sagas and travel literature (Chapter 5).

Varieties of Hunting

When the Dutch colonists landed at the Cape in 1652, there were three main African societies in the region. The San, or Bushmen as they were called by the colonists, who did not cultivate or keep livestock, depended on hunting, gathering plants, and foraging. Lee found that the remnant groups surviving in the Kalahari desert in the 1960s ate fifty-five different animal species.[2] The Khoikhoi, closely linked to the San, kept livestock and developed a life of transhumant pastoralism. They were frequent hunters, motivated by the need to protect their herds and flocks from predators as well as to procure meat and animal products.

Most Khoisan peoples had been pushed into the drier, western half of southern Africa by Bantu-speaking black Africans, who gradually populated the region from the north about 2,000 years ago, bringing crops as well as livestock. Their settlements were largely restricted to the wetter, eastern and highveld zones, with a rainfall of over 500 mm, sufficient for dryland crops. In the eighteenth century, the Khoisan were conquered, decimated, and elbowed aside by Afrikaner settlers. While some groups maintained an independent identity in what became Botswana, Namibia, and the Northern Cape, most survived only as workers and servants on colonial farms. Diseases of the kind that facilitated European conquest in the Americas devastated the

[2] Richard B. Lee, *The !Kung San: Men, Women, and Work in a Foraging Society* (Cambridge: Cambridge University Press, 1979).

Khoisan and eased the settler occupation of the western and central Cape; there were major smallpox epidemics in 1713 and 1752. The susceptibility of Khoisan to smallpox has not been adequately explained in South African historiography. They traded and intermarried with Africans, who carried immunities, but clearly some groups were too isolated to experience regular contact and they were highly vulnerable to exclusion from key natural resources such as water sources.

By the late eighteenth century, the expanding settler pastoral farmers encountered African people with more centralized political systems, and more effective military power. African links with societies to the north also gave them some immunity to introduced diseases. While they lost a great deal of land to both Boer and British settlers, African populations were rising by the mid-nineteenth century and they were always in the demographic majority. Africans in the region were organized into chiefdoms or kingdoms; in the eighteenth century most chiefs counted their followers in the tens of thousands, some less. By the early nineteenth century a process of centralization culminated in the emergence of powerful leaders. The Zulu kingdom was the largest, reaching its early apogee under Shaka (1818–28) who ruled over perhaps 2–300,000 people.

Africans hunted predators in order to protect their herds, they hunted antelope and small mammals to eat, and also targeted animals, such as the omnivorous baboon, which scavenged their crops. Until the widespread introduction of maize, which had a covered cob, all standing crops of sorghum and millet had to be guarded daily against birds, which were trapped and snared. There were further reasons for large-scale hunting. In one of the most densely settled areas of the east coast, the Zulu kings tried to clear zones around the centre of the kingdom to fend off the tsetse fly which they associated with wildlife and bush (Chapter 11). Shaka organized at least one huge hunt around 1819, using his regiments to drive animals into the fork of the white and black Umfolozi rivers.

Positioned in a favourable spot to which the game was driven, [he] himself participated in hamstringing and killing elephants, rhinoceros and buffaloes. Eland, wildebeest, sable, roan, giraffe, zebra, kudu, waterbuck, impala and bushbuck were all trapped and speared ... There were a number of human fatalities, but vast quantities of meat resulted from the drive and it was followed by a great feast.[3]

---

[3] MacKenzie, *The Empire of Nature*, 62.

In many African chiefdoms, a complex symbolic world developed around hunting and its products. Praise singers attributed the powers of wild animals to their kings.[4] Chiefs wore the products of the hunt: blue crane feathers, ivory bangles, or cloaks made of leopard skin. Wherever possible, they claimed the most valuable items as their prerogative. In the 1840s, the Mpondo king Faku, south of the Zulu, made overtures to the British government via missionaries to protect his chiefdom against the expanding Boers. He called for his *induna* (councillor) Diko.

Diko my son, [he said], go and hunt elephants so that I may send government a present of ivory ... Diko assembled the Bushmen who were employed by Faku as hunters in those days ... The Bushmen hunted elephants for a month and then returned bringing the tusks. They handed these to Diko saying 'Diko here are your things'. Diko placed the tusks at Faku's feet saying 'My chief here are your things'.[5]

This tradition asserted the chief's right to ivory. Oral tradition in Mpondoland also records that Christianity was bought with an elephant tusk.

As in North America, settlers and imperial markets rapidly transformed the nature of hunting by indigenous societies. The intensification and commercialization of hunting enmeshed all southern African peoples and hastened the destruction of wildlife in the region. African people changed their hunting strategies. One of the striking features of nineteenth-century southern African history was the rapidity with which some of the chiefdoms turned their armies from foot soldiers wielding spears and shields, into mounted cavalrymen with rifles. The Sotho and the Xhosa, on the northern and eastern boundaries of the expanding Cape colony led the way from the 1830s. The acquisition of firearms was initially intended for defence but it also had a major impact on wildlife. Most of the damage was done, by both settlers and Africans, with muzzle-loaders and before the introduction of breech-loading rifles and revolvers in the 1870s.

From 1660 to 1860 Afrikaner settler livestock farmers gradually spread out through much of the semi-arid and temperate areas of South Africa. They destroyed Khoisan life but also learnt from them about the location of water, and the routes and behaviour of wildlife. Khoisan tracking skills were

    [4] MacKenzie, *The Empire of Nature*, 66.

    [5] William Beinart, 'Production and the Material Basis of Chieftainship in Pondoland, c.1830–1880', in Shula Marks and Anthony Atmore (eds.), *Economy and Society in Pre-Industrial South Africa* (London: Longman, 1980), 129.

legion, and their ability to read the signs on the earth construed almost as a form of literacy.[6] They were often recruited as guides for expeditions in the eighteenth and nineteenth centuries. Frontier graziers were sometimes able to avoid slaughtering their own animals for food, because they could use venison. Servants were also effectively fed and paid in this way. In one Boer homestead: 'The whole roof in the kitchen was hung with thick slices of buffalo's flesh, which, being dried and smoked, they ate as hung beef ... Buffaloes were shot ... by a Hottentot who had been trained to this business by a farmer, and in this manner found the whole family in meat, without having recourse to the herd.'[7]

Wildlife were free goods, not owned by anyone, at least in colonial law. Afrikaners organized hunting expeditions both as part of the process of settlement and as a way of making money to invest in land and livestock. Some claimed land and settled on the hunting frontier, which was always mobile. In the drier districts of the interior, many adopted transhumant practices, or trekking, for part of the year in order to find water and grazing for their cattle and sheep. Much of this movement initially took place incrementally in family groups. In the 1830s tens of thousands of 'voortrekkers' moved as a phalanx out of the colony in what became called the Great Trek. They wished to escape British rule, imposed in 1806, but environmental forces were also operating. The eastern Cape frontier, from which the majority of trekkers came, was closing and they required new grazing land. Drought and locust plagues were particularly severe at the time. And their movement was initially facilitated by the richness of antelope populations in the interior in what became the Boer republics of the Free State and Transvaal.

Hunting became 'intrinsic to Boer culture' in the nineteenth-century Transvaal. It was 'a preferred occupation among the whole male section of the white immigrant population of the highveld' and the 'jagtersgemeenskap' (hunting fellowship) helped bind together trekker groups.[8] Paul Kruger, Transvaal President, wrote that 'every Boer took an active part in this work, and the rising youth ... did a great deal in this way to make the

[6] William J. Burchell, *Travels in the Interior of Southern Africa* (London: Batchworth Press, 1953, reprint of 1822–4th edn.), ii, 66; Louis Liebenberg, *The Art of Tracking: The Origin of Science* (Cape Town: David Philip, 1990).

[7] This was the Cape buffalo *Syncerus caffer*, a different species from the American.

[8] Roger Wagner, 'Zoutpansberg: The Dynamics of a Hunting Frontier, 1848–1867', in Marks and Atmore (eds.), *Economy and Society*, 329, 336.

country habitable'.[9] Men showed their prowess through hunting: Kruger is said to have killed between thirty and forty elephants. Carruthers suggests, following Nash's argument about settlers in the United States, that Calvinist ideas played a part because they laid such great stress on man's separation from, and ascendancy over, nature.[10]

Britain assumed control over the Cape in 1806 and a wave of British settlers followed, notably in 1820; in 1844 British authority was declared over Natal. Southern Africa became increasingly attractive to British people seeking hunting adventures. They included officers of the Indian army and civil service, stopping en route to the East or taking paid leave in an area with a salubrious climate. Some of them were hunters more predatory and profligate than in the wildest dreams of African chiefs, or even Afrikaner frontiersmen. R. G. Cumming, who published *Five Years' Adventures in the Far Interior of South Africa* in the 1850s was from the Scots nobility, an old Etonian, Indian Lancer, and scourge of at least 105 African elephants.[11] He joined the Cape Mounted Riflemen briefly in 1843 and, after participating in a military expedition to Mpondoland, left to indulge his 'passion' for five years. Cumming was in search of 'sport' and the 'freedom of nature' but he also needed to supply his party with meat and tried to finance himself from ivory.[12] He traded with Africans as well as shot, bartering muskets and gunpowder that were in short supply for the interior Tswana chiefdoms. By his own admission, he made extortionate profits, selling rifles that cost him less than a pound for ivory worth £30.[13] (In turn the Tswana chiefs were able to secure ivory from Bushmen hunters.) He claimed to make £1,000 from one of his trips.

Much of Cumming's book is a report of what he shot and where—shocking to our sensibilities in its detail and the lack of constraint. His party travelled with a supply of baked elephant foot and trunk for the road. He saw social benefit as well as personal gratification in his expedition: 'it was always to me a source of great pleasure to reflect that, while enriching myself in following my favourite pursuit of elephant-hunting, I was frequently feeding and making happy the starving families of hundreds of Bechuanas and Bakalahari tribes, who invariably followed my wagons, and assisted me in

---

[9] Jane Carruthers, 'Game Protection in the Transvaal 1846 to 1926', unpublished Ph.D. thesis, University of Cape Town (1988), 41.

[10] Carruthers, 'Game Protection in the Transvaal', 40.

[11] Roualeyn George Cumming, *Five Years' Adventures in the Far Interior of South Africa* (London: John Murray, 1856).

[12] *Ibid.*, iv.   [13] *Ibid.*, 193.

3. A hunter and his horse are startled by lions.

Credit: R. G. Cumming, *Five Years' Adventures in the Far Interior of South Africa* (London: John Murray, 1856).

hunting, in numbers varying from fifty to two hundred'.[14] If we read beyond his mid-Victorian extravagance, Cumming provides insight into African hunting and trade, as well as the insecure but skilled world of the servants and auxiliaries on colonial expeditions. He was well aware of their value to him and noted, for example, that a Khoikhoi assistant called Carolus was one of the finest horsemen he had ever seen. He was occasionally aware of the sensitivities of his readers, as well as their thirst for vicarious adventure and the chase. When he experimented on where best to shoot an elephant, he assured them 'my object was *not* to torture the animal, but to put an end to its life and pain in the quickest manner possible'.[15] But Cumming was an unabashed self-publicist about his hunting prowess and he won considerable renown touring Britain in the 1850s as 'lion of the season', showing his trophies and spoils.[16]

The ivory frontier moved northwards quickly during the years following Cumming's expeditions.[17] The last elephants were shot in the coastal

[14] *Ibid.*, 187.   [15] *Ibid.*, 228.

[16] Harriet Ritvo, *The Animal Estate: The English and Other Creatures in the Victorian Age* (Harmondsworth: Penguin, 1990), 249–51.

[17] MacKenzie, *Empire of Nature*, 107–9.

Transkei in the early 1860s.[18] Ivory was important in the economy of the settler Transvaal for its first thirty years, from 1840–70, and was initially perhaps its largest export.[19] Attempts were made by the Transvaal authorities to restrict hunting and protect closed seasons from the 1850s in order to conserve stocks.[20] But the right to hunt was deeply embedded in Boer social ideas, and government authority was never sufficient to enforce these regulations. As the hunting frontier penetrated malaria and tsetse belts, where whites, their horses, and ox-wagons were more at risk, so African employees and servants, the 'swart skuts' (black shots) did the majority of the hunting.[21] As in Canada, indigenous people, combining old skills and new technologies, became absorbed in a colonial commodity frontier.

By the 1870s, both British and Boer hunters moved north to present-day Zimbabwe, northern Botswana, around Chobe, and eastern Zambia, where they found rich fields. Karl Mauch, the German explorer, hunter, and prospector, who came upon the Zimbabwe ruins in 1871, found Afrikaners in the vicinity. Henry Hartley, who worked with him, and was among the first new prospectors to notice gold—long mined by Africans in Zimbabwe—was a prolific ivory trader.[22] By the 1880s, elephants had largely been cleared from these areas. Khama, the Tswana king, who raised revenue by levying half the value of tusks from elephants shot in his territory, tried to introduce controls over hunting. Wildlife survived in reasonable numbers in northern Botswana partly because of such regulation, and partly because the Okavango swamp and tsetse belt gave elephants a retreat.

This chronology is reflected in the Cape ivory export figures. Recorded quantities at the ports continued to increase from 58,000 lb, worth £15,000 (5.2 shillings a lb), in 1861 to a peak of 160,000 lb, worth £60,000 (8.4 shillings a lb), in 1875. At an average of perhaps 50 lb of ivory per animal, this would imply the killing of 3,200 elephants. (The average weight of Mauch's ivory from 91 elephants shot in 1867 was about 44 lb per animal.)[23]

---

[18] C. J. Skead, *Historical Mammal Incidence in the Cape Province, vol. 2: The Eastern Half of the Cape Province, including the Ciskei, Transkei and East Griqualand* (Cape Town: Provincial Administration of the Cape of Good Hope, 1987).

[19] Wagner, 'Zoutpansberg'; Peter Delius, *The Land Belongs to Us: The Pedi Polity under Sekwati and Sekhukhune* (Johannesburg: Ravan Press, 1983).

[20] Carruthers, 'Game Protection in the Transvaal'.   [21] Wagner, 'Zoutpansberg'.

[22] MacKenzie, *Empire of Nature*, 122.   [23] Ibid., 124.

Ivory exports, Cape ports[24]

	Quantity	Value	Price in shillings
1861	58,330	14,731	
1862	113,379	24,813	4.4
1870	52,945		
1871	37,406		
1872	87,389	23,976	5.5
1873	90,872	32,339	7
1874	73,747	26,667	7
1875	143,682	60,402	8.4
1876	161,234	58,626	7.2
1877	137,660	50,711	7.4
1878	149,701	50,155	6.7
1879	79,225	23,769	6
1880	56,779	16,982	6
1881	50,442	17,081	6.8
1882	10,263	4,019	8.2
1883	11,915	5,746	9.6

Exports then fell, never to recover. Some ivory was also exported via Durban and Delagoa Bay. The value was not very significant to the Cape's export economy, by then dominated by wool, diamonds, and ostrich feathers. Income from ivory did not even match that of goatskins. But the limited overall value of tusks should not disguise the impact of commercial hunting on elephants; ivory sold through Cape ports alone perhaps required the slaughter of 25,000 over twenty years and they could not renew their populations.

The African elephant was butchered to provide knife handles, combs, and carved ornaments. Billiard ball manufacture expanded in the late nineteenth century and required soft young ivory from east and southern African elephants; only a certain section of the tusk could be used. From the mid-nineteenth century the major demand was probably for piano keys, by then manufactured industrially with metal frames and metal strings. Pianos were a symbol of middle-class values in many Victorian British homes, an indispensable tool for entertainment in working-class bars and music halls, and a sign of domestication for the newly settled farming population of the

[24] Figures compiled from *Cape Statistical Registers*.

American Plains. In the later decades of the nineteenth century, the biggest importers of ivory globally were probably the piano-key manufacturers Pratt, Read and Co., and Comstock, Cheney and Co., in Ivoryton, Connecticut.[25]

Mackenzie sees a transition, in the late nineteenth century, from commercial hunting to The Hunt in southern Africa, which became a marker of white dominance, manliness, and sportsmanship.[26] He distinguishes this hunting as a largely non-utilitarian pursuit for pleasure or excitement—all the more attractive in Africa because it was free from some of the restrictive hierarchies and social customs which characterized it in Britain. The British notion of sport clearly had a specific cultural content, which included the separation of leisure from subsistence pursuits, and the term sport was often applied to hunting in the nineteenth century. But it is not easy to distinguish between sport, economic gain, and necessity. On the one hand, many Africans who had to hunt for survival also found it pleasurable. Amongst Xhosa men, it was described as a 'favourite pursuit'.[27] On the other hand, even British Indian army officers sought some income from wildlife. Like Africans and Afrikaners before them, British settlers in South Africa and Zimbabwe partook in much the same regime of predator extermination, land clearance, and tsetse eradication well into the twentieth century. While we can accept, with Mackenzie, that exotic trophies played a fascinating role in the Victorian symbolic world, as emblems and prizes of sport, it is analytically problematic to suggest that there was a sharp transition in the nature of hunting.

Literary Accounts of Hunting

Accounts of hunting and adventure in far-flung corners of the world were well established as a literary genre in the Victorian era. Some of the earliest books by British settlers in South Africa set this tone. Thomas Pringle is known for his defence of freedom of the press and for writing among the first liberal texts on South Africa. He became secretary of the British Aborigines Protection Society on his return home in the late 1820s. But the first volume of his *Narrative of a Residence in South Africa* (1834) was not least about 'our

---

[25] Don Malcarne, Edith DeForest, and Robbi Storms, *Deep River and Ivoryton* (Charleston: Arcadia Publishing, 2002); Don Malcarne, 'Ivory Cutting in the Valley' (Ivoryton Library Association) on <http://www.ivoryton.com/articles>.

[26] John M. MacKenzie, 'Chivalry, Social Darwinism and Ritualised Killing: The Hunting Ethos in Central Africa up to 1914', in David Anderson and Richard Grove (eds.), *Conservation in Africa: People, Policies and Practice* (Cambridge: Cambridge University Press, 1987), 41–62.

[27] Stephen Kay, *Travels and Researches in Caffraria* (New York: Harper, 1834), 122.

wars with the beasts of prey'.[28] He gave detailed descriptions of three lion hunts. The bravery and power of the beast was stressed. Hounds were sent in first and a 'poor dog was destroyed in a moment' by 'a single blow from the lion's paw'. Chaos overcame the party as the lion threatened and pounced.

In a twinkling he was upon them; and with one stroke of his paw, dashed John Rennie (my brother in law) to the ground. The Scene was terrific! There stood the lion with his foot upon his prostrate foe, looking around in conscious power and pride upon the band of his assailants, and with a port the most noble and imposing that can be conceived. It was the most magnificent thing I ever witnessed.[29]

As in most of these texts, the lion was then dispatched with a volley of fire or a single accurate shot in the nick of time. Wild animals could indeed be dangerous, especially when hunted, and predators attacked livestock of all kinds, including horses. But these accounts increasingly emphasized dominance as much as risk. By the time of Cumming's publication, which went into multiple editions and at one time outsold Dickens, the presentation tended to be more prosaic—a celebration of plenty as much as peril.

Predatory slaughter in foreign parts was widely acceptable in print as well as in practice, and literature greatly encouraged this form of adventure. Literacy created the market and to some extent fuelled that imagination. By the beginning of the Victorian era, 66 per cent of men and 50 per cent of women in Britain were literate, and by the end the proportion was significantly higher.[30] Ritvo suggests that 'the hunter emerged as both the ideal and the definitive type of the empire builder', and 'that narratives written by the potent protagonists fanned public appreciation'.[31] While some early texts in this mode were limited subscription editions, illustrated sporting reminiscences streamed from publishers by the mid-nineteenth century and were 'written to be read by the masses'.[32]

Authors of hunting sagas sometimes saw the written word as serving a further purpose: to record and increase general knowledge about the natural world of the Empire. In the self-deprecatory words of Pringle, 'these zoological scraps are intended for the general reader merely, and without

---

[28] T. Pringle, *Narrative of a Residence in South Africa*, vol. 1 (first pub. 1834; repr. Brentwood, Essex: Empire Book Association, 1986), 105.

[29] *Ibid.*

[30] David Cressey, 'Literacy in Context: Meaning and Measurement in Early Modern England', in Brewer and Porter (eds.), *Consumption and the World of Goods*, 305–19; D. Vincent, *Literacy and Popular Culture: England' 1750–1914* (Cambridge: Cambridge University Press, 1989).

[31] Ritvo, *The Animal Estate*, 254–5.   [32] *Ibid.*, 256.

pretension to add any gleanings of natural history worthy of the particular attention of men of science'.[33] Some writers justified their actions as being in the interests of science. Discovering a new species was an exciting possibility or at the least they could add to the understanding of animal incidence and behaviour. They kept detailed records and a few started private museums or shot for natural history museums.

This is a large body of literature that has often been used by historians attempting to reconstruct pre-colonial African societies. Some hunters in southern Africa were in the vanguard of colonial penetration. Mackenzie, Ritvo, and others have rediscovered and excavated these texts for what they have to say about the imperial ethos and its popular expressions. The hunters have, in a sense, been awaiting their sentence. The attribution of blame for the slaughter of game, and environmental destruction more generally, in southern Africa has long been a politicized issue. There was a tendency in the colonial period to blame Africans for the destruction of nature on their continent. Africans were characterized as being cruel to animals and disposed to cut down trees, whereas colonials saw themselves as kind to animals and planters of trees. Thus African hunting methods which used snares and traps were condemned as wasteful—as were the techniques of the landless 'poacher' in Britain[34]—whereas it is clear that firearms were far more significant in the overall destruction and probably led to quite as many animals being injured. These hunting texts have increasingly been used as evidence of the British and settler role in the destruction of animals.[35] It is also clear that the animal kingdom was far richer prior to colonialism.

Hunting, Ecological Change, and Conservation

There is a macabre fascination in this literature, and elements of it survive in the construction of Africa by Europeans. But we should hesitate before allowing British men to occupy centre stage, which they undoubtedly wished to claim. Literacy as well as firearms gave them that power. We need to see British hunters in perspective as reinforcing processes of ecological change set in train initially by Africans and Boers, and to see all of them in the

---

[33] Pringle, *Narrative of a Residence*, 105.

[34] D. Hay, 'Poaching and the Game Laws on Cannock Chase', in D. Hay *et al.*, *Albion's Fatal Tree: Crime and Society in Eighteenth Century England* (Harmondsworth: Penguin, 1975), 189–253.

[35] Stephen Gray, 'The Rise and Fall of the Colonial Hunter', in *Southern African Literature: An Introduction* (Cape Town: David Philip, 1979).

context of changes in habitat and ecology—especially those resulting from new types of land use.

By the time the British took over the Cape in 1806, the blue buck had been exterminated and the quagga, a lesser-striped zebra, was soon to succumb. Different animals were vulnerable for specific reasons: the urgency with which they were hunted, which in turn could be shaped by some quirk of international markets or some chance characteristic. The impact of intensified hunting also depended partly on the terrain, the geographic range, and the adaptability of particular species. The quagga was exterminated because it was restricted to open plains, easily seen, and had so narrow a range in the Cape. Eland, the largest antelope, were favoured for their meat; elephants were a prime target because of their tusks. Despite their portrayal as the most formidable of beasts, lions were often the first to be killed off in any area of settlement because they were an immediate danger to people, horses, and livestock. Leopards, and smaller feline predators such as caracal, survived far better in the colonial environment because their favoured habitat was in mountainous areas. If the ranges of the eland, elephant, or lion had been smaller, they may also have been exterminated.

Intensified farming deeply influenced ecology, usually to the detriment of biodiversity and of indigenous animals. Hippos were widespread even in drier parts of the Cape, as is indicated by the frequent occurrence of Dutch place names including *zeekoei*. But they were restricted to riverine and *vlei* (shallow pool) environments, which also attracted people, livestock, and crops. Intensification of livestock farming and desiccation of *vleis* helped to destroy their habitats. Perhaps it would be possible to generalize that plains and riverine animals, in more direct competition with people and livestock for grazing and water, were usually more vulnerable than those on desert peripheries, or in mountain and forested areas. Even the latter zones were not, however, exempt from fire used both by whites and Africans as a means of clearing land and renewing pastures.

The impact of agrarian change was sometimes unpredictable. From the 1830s, the numbers of merino, wool-bearing sheep (Chapter 6), expanded rapidly in the Karoo, the Eastern Cape and the Free State.[36] By 1890 there were about 12 million merinos in the Cape alone and by 1930, 24 million. The national figure was then nearly double this. The great seasonal migratory treks of springbok from the arid northern Cape and southern Kalahari

---

[36] Beinart, *Rise of Conservation.*

into wetter parts of the Karoo shuddered to a halt.[37] They were shot in their hundreds of thousands, to protect the pastures, and hamstrung by fences. Wild dogs, initially a scourge of sheep, and energetically hunted, rapidly dwindled. Sheep farms became, in a sense, a monocrop world. But while intensive agriculture clearly worked against most wildlife species, there were some animal beneficiaries in this dynamic, if ecologically diminished, agrarian environment. The black-backed jackal (*Canis mesomelas*) thrived on the rising number of merinos. A secretive scavenger of lamb, increasingly nocturnal in its habits, the jackal found a niche in the interstices of the colonial agrarian world. For over a century, from the 1850s, it was the main object of vermin extermination campaigns and hunting clubs. Jackals were poisoned and chased on horseback with dogs; these hunts became social sporting events—another example of the links between pleasure and necessity. The dassie (rock hyrax) prospered because of the destruction of their predators, such as the black eagle, colloquially called the lammervanger and thought to catch lambs. Baboons and monkeys adapted to the fruit of Mexican prickly pear, initially introduced for hedging and to supplement fodder supplies for livestock, but soon a rampant invader in some districts. They also spread the plant through their seed-filled droppings, thus unintentionally expanding their food supply.

Attempts were made to domesticate wildlife species in southern Africa. The only significant success was the ostrich—one of few new domestications of animals to take place in the nineteenth century. There had long been a small market for their feathers for use in fans and hats, met by hunting ostriches. In the 1860s, Dr William Atherstone, Eastern Cape physician and scientific polymath, and others found a way of incubating the eggs, which allowed for more rapid and controlled reproduction and breeding. Intensive rearing was made possible by large-scale planting of lucerne as fodder, together with dam construction necessary in order to irrigate the crop. Since this big heavy bird could not fly, it was more easily farmed in small enclosures. The number of farmed ostriches climbed steadily to a peak of about 800,000 in 1910.[38] At their peak around 1910, ostrich feathers sold from the Cape fetched £2 million annually.[39] In this context perhaps, a product from a South African wild animal did rival the beaver skin. Feathers were used largely for decorative boas and hats. It is interesting that this exotic,

---

[37] Chris Roche, ' "Ornaments of the Desert": Springbok Treks in the Cape Colony, 1774–1908', unpublished MA thesis, University of Cape Town (2004).

[38] Beinart, *Rise of Conservation*.   [39] *Ibid.*, 13–14.

dangerous snake gave its name to the scarves draped by women around their necks and shoulders.

Commercial livestock production had unpredictable outcomes for wildlife in other ways. Some wealthier landowners with large farms kept limited numbers of antelope for hunting, venison supplies, and aesthetic reasons. By the early twentieth century, springbok numbers were probably increasing on pastoral farms, where they grazed alongside sheep. The rare bontebok and mountain zebra had also, like the quagga, been threatened with extermination because of the narrowness of their range. These species were nurtured on private farms for nearly a century before the state stepped in with national parks to protect them around 1930.

Hunters were also involved in early preservationist initiatives in that some took on the role of penitent butchers (see Chapter 17).[40] By the late nineteenth century, alarms were being raised about the decline in wildlife throughout southern Africa. Game laws had long been promulgated in the colonial states in an attempt to control hunting, restrict hunting seasons, and protect vulnerable species. They were difficult to apply because so much land was privately owned, or beyond effective policing. An Act passed in 1886 stiffened the game laws in the Cape; there was already some protection for the small remnant elephant herd at Addo—probably one of the last two in South Africa.[41] From 1890, the colonial states and Boer republics began to reserve protected areas, partly because of the failure of game laws. The largest of these was in the Transvaal around Sabi, which later became the geographic core of the Kruger National Park. These drew on the model provided by state and national parks in the United States, such as Yosemite and Yellowstone; there were also local precedents in the shape of forest reservations where hunting was restricted.

The US parks were reserved more for scenery or landscapes, while the South Africans focused on wildlife.[42] However, the colony of Natal did try to reserve spectacular sections of the Drakensberg range. Wildlife preservation and national parks became particularly important to southern African colonial societies, and were increasingly justified by strict scientific

[40] Carruthers, 'Game Protection'; Jane Carruthers, *The Kruger National Park: A Social and Political History* (Pietermaritzburg: University of Natal Press, 1995).

[41] Karen Brown, 'Cultural Constructions of the Wild: The Rhetoric and Practice of Wildlife Conservation in the Cape Colony at the Turn of the Twentieth Century', *South African Historical Journal*, 47 (2002), 75–95.

[42] Beinart and Coates, *Environment and History*, ch. 5.

preservationism. James Stevenson-Hamilton, the first warden of Sabi and later Kruger, prohibited sports hunting and tried to restore what he believed to be the natural balance of species.[43] Representations of wildlife continued to find an audience in Britain, but increasingly in photographs and film, rather than as trophies or in hunting books (Chapter 13). By the early twentieth century, the beginnings of an alternative relationship with wildlife was discernable within the empire. Conservationists in southern Africa played a leading role in forging it, though for some decades the hunting ethos remained a powerful rival.

Such partial transitions can be seen in individual lives. Frederick Selous, from a well-off British family, with a public school education, was inspired by literature to seek the 'free-and-easy' life in Africa.[44] On arrival in 1871, he found little to hunt around Kimberley, but was just in time to help shoot and export perhaps 100,000 pounds of ivory from Zimbabwe between 1872 and 1874. As he explains in his first book, A Hunter's Wanderings in Africa, he never found another field so rich. Selous was incorporated into the heart of the colonial endeavour, striking treaties with African chiefs and leading Rhodes's pioneer column into Zimbabwe in 1890. He continued to hunt, and extended his range to America; he later acted as partner and guide to Theodore Roosevelt in his post-presidential hunting extravaganza in Kenya in 1909. But his experience also alerted him to the vulnerability of wildlife, and Selous began to shoot in a more constrained way, supplied the Kensington Natural History museum with choice specimens, advocated wildlife reserves, and joined the prestigious Society for the Protection of the Wild Fauna of the Empire, launched in 1903.

Hunting in southern Africa was not of great economic significance to Britain; this was not a commodity frontier that could rival the export economies of the Americas or South Asia, or the later agricultural and mineral exports from this region. Rather, its importance lies in its contribution to

---

[43] Carruthers, Kruger National Park; Jane Carruthers, Wildlife and Warfare: The Life of James Stevenson-Hamilton (Pietermaritzburg: University of Natal Press, 2001); James Stevenson-Hamilton, South African Eden: The Kruger National Park, 1902–1946 (first pub. 1937; Cape Town: Struik, 1993).

[44] Ritvo, Animal Estate; MacKenzie, Empire of Nature; Stephen Taylor, The Mighty Nimrod: A Life of Frederick Courteney Selous, African Hunter and Adventurer, 1851–1917 (London: Collins, 1989); Frederick Courteney Selous, A Hunter's Wanderings in Africa (first pub. 1881; London: Macmillan, 1928).

shaping early settler colonialism, the literary representation of empire, and in its impact on wildlife and ecology. Over the longer term, the gradual emergence of an alternative view of wildlife, as a response to its destruction, became a key feature of southern African states and a bedrock of the tourist industry.

5

Imperial Travellers

In a global maritime empire, travel was intrinsic. As sailors and slavers, traders and hunters, Europeans traversed colonized space and literacy gave them the power to record what they saw and found. In their mapping and classification of lands and peoples, many of these travellers helped to commodify and package the resources of empire. In their fulsome descriptions of the riches of overseas territories, they made these lands and all that they contained desirable to prospective hunters, settlers, speculators, and administrators. The direct uses that imperial powers made of traveller's accounts were hinted at in 1887 by British explorer and geologist Joseph Thomson, in a note to the second edition of his best-selling *Through Masai Land*.[1] 'Then [1885] Masai land was for the first time made known to the world; now it has come within the "sphere of British influence"—a delicate way, I suppose, of saying that it now practically forms a part of our imperial possessions.'[2]

In fact British East Africa, of which Maasailand formed a large part, was not established for another eight years, in 1895. But Thomson anticipated accurately: having 'discovered' and mapped a direct route from the coast to Lake Victoria, which cut right across Maasailand to Uganda, and described the rich pickings (including fertile land, valuable pastures, water sources, timber, and game animals) that lay along the route, he had paved the way for European trade and takeover. Sir John Kirk, British agent and consul at Zanzibar, wrote that Thomson's 'admirable description is the only reliable one we yet possess of the region thus secured to us, if we choose to avail ourselves of the opportunity'.[3] Britain, anxious about Germany's competitive ambitions, duly took it.

From the mid-eighteenth century a particular kind of traveller did more than most to promote the natural potential of empire: those who combined

---

[1] Joseph Thomson, *Through Masai Land* (London: Sampson Low, Marston, Searle, & Rivington, 1885). Maasai is the correct spelling, but Masai will be used when quoting early sources.

[2] 'Note to the new edition', Thomson, *Masai Land*, 2nd edn. (1887), xi.

[3] Sir John Kirk, 'Britain and Germany in East Africa: Note', postscript to Thomson, *Masai Land* (1887), 357–9.

touring with botany and other scientific, or quasi-scientific, enquiries. The avid collection of specimens—from fauna and flora through, in some cases, to human body parts—had become an adjunct to the European adventurer's taxonomy of the natural world. Since European expansion coincided with the development of print, as illustrated in our chapter on hunting, the production and publication of texts became a by-product of travel. One of the people responsible for the new vogue (though there were earlier precedents, and he cannot be blamed for encouraging the collection of human body parts) was the Swede Carl Linnaeus, whose *Systema Naturae* (published in 1735) was the first classificatory system for categorizing all plant forms according to their reproductive parts. A Lutheran pastor and doctor who became Professor of Medicine at the University of Uppsala, Linneaus boasted that his 'new "Language of Flowers" was ... so straightforward that even women could understand it'. His terminology was controversial at the time for its sexual innuendo, but Joseph Banks, President of the Royal Society, became an enthusiast and 'made Linnaean botany central to British science'.[4]

All the ensuing note-taking and collecting of species was an even greater curiosity to the local people who greeted European travellers. When an African chief first came on board Irishman Captain James Tuckey's ship in 1816, somewhere off West Africa (it is not clear where), he had expected to learn that the visitors had come to buy slaves, which he was happy to provide. Wrote Tuckey: 'He was very inquisitive to know, whether the ships came to make trade, or make war; and when he was distinctly told that the object was neither the one or the other, he asked, "what then come for; only to take walk and make book?" '[5] It is a lovely riposte to the learned. As travellers interrogated the curiosities of new worlds, those in the prospective empire sometimes stared back and quizzed the visitors. A Norwegian botanist/geologist, a Kew gardener, and an anatomist were all on Tuckey's ill-fated expedition, which claimed the lives of everyone but gardener David Lockhart. The botanist's specimen collection, containing 620 plants of which 250 were described as 'absolutely new', and copious notes on fauna and flora, survived him.

---

[4] Patricia Fara, *Sex, Botany, and Empire: The Story of Carl Linnaeus and Joseph Banks* (Duxford: Icon Books UK, 2003), 3, 19–20, 95; Londa Schiebinger, *Plants and Empire: Colonial Bioprospecting in the Atlantic World* (Cambridge, MA: Harvard University Press, 2004).

[5] J. H. Tuckey, *Narrative of an Expedition to Explore the River Zaire, Usually Called the Congo, in South Africa in 1816* (London: John Murray, 1818), 36.

The Taxonomy of Travelogues

Mary Louise Pratt has classified imperial travellers operating in the 'contact zone' or 'space of colonial encounters'.[6] Her starting point is the mid-eighteenth century, when natural history emerged as a 'structure of knowledge' and explorers' attentions turned from maritime adventures to the so-called interior of continents. She claims that classificatory systems of natural history sought to displace 'vernacular peasant knowledges'. After the 'Linnaean watershed', Pratt argues, travellers focussed on nature and generally took far less notice of people. 'Where, one asks, is everybody? The landscape is written as uninhabited, unpossessed, unhistoricized, unoccupied even by the travellers themselves.'[7] As for indigenous voices, they are almost never quoted, and even Africans in the travellers' own party are not named or personalized in other ways. Recognizing that not all travellers were conquerors, Pratt labels certain of them 'anti-conquest', meaning that they had 'a utopian, innocent vision of European global authority'.[8] Nevertheless they were invariably male, secular, urban, and lettered. In their travelogues they indulged both in science and sentiment. Their writings on natural history tried to produce an order out of nature, by classifying what they saw.

Pratt claims such writers paved the way for colonial appropriation, even though some were ostensibly anti-conquest. Cheryl McEwan, writing on women travellers in West Africa from 1830, follows a similar line—'representing West African forests as commodity demanded that they were also represented devoid of people'.[9] Pratt provides useful benchmarks against which to measure scientific travel texts, but by looking at a different range of texts, we aim to question some of her arguments and suggest other dynamics of the contact zone. The travellers we have chosen are not necessarily typical, but their approach is distinctive. Such writings can be used to illustrate, and support the views of, historians who are critical of the idea that there was any consistency in the stereotypes created by Europeans about non-European nature and people. Certain European travellers defy facile stereotyping.

For example, an illustration from naturalist Anders Sparrman's 1775 work, reproduced in Pratt's text, contradicts her main claim. His frontispiece

---

[6] Mary Louise Pratt, *Imperial Eyes: Travel Writing and Transculturation* (London: Routledge, 1992), 5–7.

[7] *Ibid.*, 51.   [8] *Ibid.*, 39.

[9] Cheryl McEwan, 'Representing West African Forests in British Imperial Discourse c. 1830–1900', in Reginald Cline-Cole and Clare Madge, (eds.), *Contesting Forestry in West Africa* (Aldershot, VT: Ashgate, 2000), 19.

shows a 'Hottentot' family in the foreground, outside their home, looking for all the world like European landowners asserting their right to property in a late eighteenth-century portrait.[10] A group of Boers with ox-wagons and horses trek by in the far background; this is a significant spatial relegation of European colonists to marginal brushstrokes. Sparrman (a student of Linnaeus) and later travellers in southern Africa such as William Burchell (published 1822–4), can be read another way—as intensively interacting with people at all levels of colonial society, not least the bilingual Khoisan guides upon whom they depended.

Tuckey's book, which includes a journal written by the ship's botanist, also contradicts this 'empty landscapes' argument. Local people were frequently described as getting in the way of the scientific enterprise—by creating too much noise, making constant demands, drinking all the brandy, being haughty and bullying. They were very much active, present, and personalized. One African man introduced himself in English as Tom Liverpool—clearly after some generic English slaver. His mix of European and local dress, as well as his fetish adornment, was described in detail, and his hostile views on the abolition of slavery quoted at length.[11] This is only one of many similar descriptions, in which local people are quoted and descriptions of them are (as in Wallace and Darwin's work) integrated comfortably with descriptions of landscape, fauna, and flora. Unusually, Tuckey advocated a non-interventionist approach to local communities and their environments: 'it will be highly improper to interrupt, in any manner, the ceremonies of the natives, however they may shock humanity or create disgust; and it is equally necessary, in the pursuits of the different Naturalists, to avoid offending the superstitions of the natives in any of their venerated objects'. He counselled other 'Officers and Naturalists' to do likewise.[12] We shall look at three travel experiences in the nineteenth century, and illustrate the variety of texts that were produced.

Wallace in Malaysia

British interests in Malaysia were established from 1786, with the leasing of Penang island as a base for East India Company trade with China. More Straits settlements followed, at Malacca and Singapore, which united in 1826

---

[10] William Beinart, 'Men, Science, Travel and Nature in the Eighteenth and Nineteenth-Century Cape', *Journal of Southern African Studies*, 24/4 (December 1998), 775–99.

[11] Tuckey, *Narrative*, 61–3, 265–6.   [12] *Ibid.*, 71.

to become the fourth presidency of British India. In 1867, five years after Wallace visited the Malay archipelago, they were converted to a Crown colony. These ports, powered largely by Chinese immigrants, were a vital hinge in the seaborne trade between Britain, India, and China. Through the Straits flowed gold, tin, spices, opium, timber, tea, Sumatran coffee, sugar, arms, and many other valuable commodities.[13]

Alfred Russel Wallace was one of the greatest of the Victorian traveller-naturalists. He and Darwin made history by almost simultaneously putting forward theories about natural selection and evolution, though Darwin is better remembered as the discoverer of nature's primary law.[14] Unfortunately for Wallace, who sent an outline of his theory to Darwin for comment, Darwin—who had been working on the same subject for twenty years—was able to rush into print in Britain while Wallace was still ensconced in eastern jungles, bagging his beloved butterflies. While in Sarawak, he had written an important paper 'On the Law Which Has Regulated the Introduction of New Species', but its publication in 1855 went largely unnoticed, while a paper sent to the Royal Geographical Society from Malaysia was never printed.[15] It was on his 14,000-mile journey (1854–62) that Wallace formulated his version of the theory of natural selection; the resulting work on *The Malay Archipelago*, first published in 1869, was dedicated to Darwin.[16]

Poor and virtually self-taught, Wallace financed his working trips by selling specimens to an agent who disposed of duplicates to museums and wealthy collectors. On this journey he collected more than 125,000 specimens, largely beetles, butterflies, and birds, many of them new to Europeans. He was driven by a desire to learn how the world came to contain such an amazing variety of species, why certain species occupied some environments and

[13] C. M. Turnbull, *The Straits Settlements, 1826–67: Indian Presidency to Crown Colony* (London: Athlone Press, 1972).

[14] It is said they 'co-authored' the theory. The story is told in Tim Severin, *The Spice Islands Voyage: In Search of Wallace* (London: Abacus, 1998); Peter Raby, *Alfred Russel Wallace: A Life* (London: Pimlico, 2003); Michael Shermer, *In Darwin's Shadow: The Life and Science of Alfred Russel Wallace* (Oxford: Oxford University Press, 2002); R. A. Slotten, *The Heretic in Darwin's Court: The Life of Alfred Russel Wallace* (New York and Chichester: Columbia University Press, 2004).

[15] The first paper was published in *The Annals and Magazine of Natural History*, second series, 16 (1855), 84–96. The Linnaean Society published a second in 1858, 'On the Tendency of Varieties to Depart Indefinitely from the Original Type'.

[16] A. R. Wallace, *The Malay Archipelago: The Land of the Orang-utan, and the Bird of Paradise: A Narrative of Travel, With Studies of Man and Nature* (London: Macmillan, 1869). North read it in preparation for her own journey to Borneo and Java.

4. Natives of Aru shooting the great bird of paradise.

Credit: A. R. Wallace, *The Malay Archipelago* (London: Macmillan, 1869).

not others, and what universal laws could be applied to explain (among other things) individual variations in species. On the Malay voyage he correctly discovered that Indonesia was the meeting point between species that had spread from Asia and Australia. He drew a line through the string of islands he visited—which came to be known as Wallace's Line—and divided them into Indo-Malayan and Austro-Malayan faunal regions. Most of the islands, apart from Timor and its neighbours, were richly clad in forest. They teemed with unique varieties of fauna and flora, while scores of volcanoes, active and passive, swept through the islands in a splendid curve. He could see they formed 'a connected whole' that had broken off from their adjacent continents. The telltale signs were in the bird species found there: barbets, fruit-thrushes, and woodpeckers on Bali, yet none of these just a few miles away on Lombock, which had cockatoos, honeysuckers, and brush-turkeys—all unknown on Bali or any other island further west. He remarked: 'we may pass in two hours from one great division of the earth to another, differing as essentially in their animal life as Europe does from America'.[17]

Wallace is hailed as a pioneer environmentalist for his foresight in prophesying that human interference would lead to the extinction of species and loss of habitat, though this did not deter him from frequent kills for scientific purposes. While Darwin's style was relatively dry, and his position aloof (always that of an observer, rarely a participant), Wallace immersed himself in the nature he was reporting—largely because he needed to acquire specimens in their natural habitat. One of his main reasons for going to Borneo was to observe orang-utan in this way. Sometimes the immersion was literal; while chasing one orang-utan in thick jungle he 'got into the water, which was nearly up to my waist, and waded on till I was near enough for a shot'. He thrashed his way through creepers, leeches, and thorns. He also did his best to provide a soundtrack in words, vividly describing the cacophony of jungle sounds from the distinctive noise that monkeys made when scampering through dead palm-leaves, to the extraordinary 'booming voice' of pigeons, 'more like the roar of a wild beast than the note of a bird'.[18]

The television naturalist David Attenborough has acknowledged Wallace as his professional inspiration and hero. One can almost hear Wallace's voice in Attenborough's awed descriptions of the natural world—in his excitement at finding a rare species, chasing a butterfly, or proving a theory. Without the

[17] A. R. Wallace, *The Malay Archipelago: The Land of the Orang-utan, and the Bird of Paradise: A Narrative of Travel, With Studies of Man and Nature*, 25–6.
[18] *Ibid.*, 67, 59, 64, 168–9.

benefit of TV or other technical props, Wallace created word paintings that
thrilled and educated generations of readers. This best-seller went into many
reprints and translations, including a children's edition in Dutch in 1873–4.[19]
His tone always resembled that of a friendly teacher, though he never talked
down, and took his readers on a collective journey of discovery. Also, unlike
some explorers of Africa in the same period, Wallace did not depict Europeans
and other human beings as necessarily top of nature's pecking order.

He had unusual attitudes to local people, as did Darwin. Here was a
naturalist as interested in humans as in the rest of the natural world—'and
interested, moreover, in the improvement of the condition of man by a radical
change in the social and economic order'[20] The use of 'man' is inappropriate,
since Wallace primarily advocated the advancement of indigenous women
and wanted to see them relieved of their hard labour, which he believed
had a direct impact on women's fertility, mother and child health, and
mortality. His views were reformist without being religious, and inspired
by the Welsh social reformer Robert Owen. Far from seeking to displace
'peasant knowledge', in Pratt's terms, Wallace valued people's knowledge and
skills, collecting vocabularies from fifty-seven regional languages, listening
admiringly to their music, noting ingenious designs for houses, bamboo
bridges, and aqueducts. And he tended to live among local people, at
the heart of the community, rather than disdainfully removed in superior
quarters. Ever willing to try what everyone else was eating and doing, he
threw himself with relish into local habits. Unlike many explorers of Africa
he did not have hundreds of porters trailing behind, carrying their masters'
support system of European foods and luxuries. He used porters, but largely
to carry his specimens, chemicals, and instruments; his personal baggage
was comparatively small. He depended upon a few assistants, principally
the young Englishman Charles Allen and a Malay lad called Ali, who taught
Wallace Malay and stayed with him for seven years. He never portrayed
himself as a 'lone' adventurer surviving without staff.

Wallace was mostly admiring of the landscape and the peoples living
in it. On Bali he was 'astonished and delighted' to find cultivation and
elaborate irrigation 'that would be the pride of the best cultivated parts of
Europe'. Houses 'marked out by dense clumps of coconut palms, tamarind
and other fruit-trees, were dotted about in every direction', while handsome

[19] John Bastin, Introduction to Wallace, *Malay* (Oxford and Singapore: Oxford University
Press, 1989).
[20] *Ibid.*, xxi.

indigenous cattle were tethered in the pastures. On Borneo, he admired Dyak longhouses (up to 300 feet long by 50 feet wide) and the many uses to which Dyaks put bamboo.[21] He downplayed the dangers. Referring to the threat from tigers and tiger-pits while insect hunting, he commented: 'It was rather nervous work'. He was more bothered by leeches than big cats. As for local customs, he mentioned staying in a house containing baskets full of dried, shrunken human heads, but did not elaborate—the reference is dismissed in one line. (Thomson would have spun this into a major melodrama.) He often failed, and was frank about his failings. Like Sparrman and North, he told stories against himself and often acknowledged superior local knowledge. He challenged racial stereotypes: for example, by refuting the idea that Dyaks were still headhunters and pirates.[22]

Wallace was not asserting European hegemony except by his very presence as a white European male in the East. His vision was utopian, but resolutely anti-sentimental or sensationalist. His fascination with small insects above all other creatures was also distinctive—though Darwin, and later Attenborough, shared this interest in the minutiae of nature. Though he shot larger creatures for specimens, he seems to have derived little pleasure from this form of conquest. He fostered a baby orang-utan whose mother he had killed, noting how much it behaved like a human infant, and cared for it day and night until it died of fever. There was a hint of regret that he had caused its demise. The harmful side-effects to nature of European contact were not lost on him, here and elsewhere.

This is above all a 'moral' tract. Wallace specifically hoped to appeal to 'the moralist and the politician who want to solve the problem of how man may be best governed under new and varied conditions'.[23] He concluded, from his observation of many peoples, that the morals of so-called civilized man had in many cases sunk lower than those of 'savages', as his damning postscript makes clear. He talked about the need to develop local resources for the benefit of local people, not primarily European resource extractors, although he did hope that increased prosperity would lead to greater local consumption of European manufactured goods. However, as Bastin points out, there were serious anomalies in his attitudes, which contradicted his reformist principles. He approved of the Dutch plantation system that used slaves. He believed that absolute freedom did not work; only a firm hand and a touch of 'paternal despotism' would raise the uncivilized from barbarism.[24]

---

[21] Wallace, *Malay*, 135, 161–2, 87–90.   [22] *Ibid.*, 35, 65, 99.
[23] *Ibid.*, 110.   [24] *Ibid.*, 261–4.

This view is only understandable in the context of his obsession with the idea of natural stages through which all living organisms advanced or went to the wall. Struggle bred strength and ultimate survival. He was simply applying what he saw as natural law to humans, too. Yet there was a visible tussle going on between Wallace the determinist and Wallace the reformer, who dreamt of human advancement through social betterment and equitable justice. Improvement of nature formed part of his notion of betterment, but he warned that the ultimate goal of all kinds of betterment should not be to increase wealth and commerce, for many 'evils ... necessarily accompany these when too eagerly pursued'.[25]

Marianne North, a Painter in Eden

The Victorian botanical painter, Marianne North (1830–90), broke the mould in many ways. A number of women had established themselves as travellers, collectors, and botanical illustrators.[26] North distinctively described herself as 'heathen' (and objected to Christian missionaries), was non-metropolitan by upbringing, had little formal education, no scientific pretensions, and wrote in a sentimental but non-sensationalist style, playing down the dangers she faced while journeying. In 1871 at the age of 39, after the death of her remaining parent, North set off on the first of several lone expeditions round the world to paint tropical plants. The fruits of these travels—more than 830 paintings—were later offered to Kew Gardens, where she built a gallery to house them. Darwin advised her and encouraged her to visit Australia, a suggestion which she followed as if it were 'a royal command'.[27]

She painted nearly 1,000 tropical species, and four plants previously unknown to scientists were named after her. She does not appear to have preserved any specimens, confining her captures to paint, and specifically acknowledged the impossibility of human domination of nature. Writing of Brazil, she recalled:

The great blue and opal Morpho butterflies came flopping their wide wings down the narrow lanes close over our heads, moving slowly and with a kind of

[25] *Ibid.*, 598.

[26] Schiebinger, *Plants and Empire*; N. Jardine, J. A. Secord, and E. C. Spary (eds.) *Cultures of Natural History* (Cambridge: Cambridge University Press, 1996).

[27] Marianne North and Graham Bateman, *A Vision of Eden: The Life and Work of Marianne North* (Exeter: Webb & Bower, 1980), 68. This is an abridged version of her autobiography, *Recollections of a Happy Life*, edited by her sister Mrs J. A. Symonds (London: Macmillan, 1892).

see-saw motion, so as to let the light catch their glorious metallic colours, entirely perplexing any holder of nets. Gorgeous flowers grew close, but just out of reach, and every now and then I caught sight of some tiny nest, hanging inside a sheltering and prickly screen of brambles. All these wonders seeming to taunt us mortals for trespassing on fairies' grounds, and to tell us they were unapproachable.[28]

While she is remembered solely as a botanical artist, she also depicted local people and planted them firmly (though diminutively) in the landscape. Her text was more graphic than her art in its portrayal of people. In Australia, she similarly foresaw the fate of Aboriginal people and how this connected with the European exploitation of forests: 'Great piles of sawdust and chip, with some huge logs, told that the work of destruction had begun, and civilised man would soon drive out not only the aborigines but their food and shelter'.[29] She wrote of the Californian redwoods: 'It broke one's heart to think of man, the civiliser, wasting treasures in a few years to which savages and animals had done no harm for centuries.'[30] She clearly despised the idle class of wealthy European women (though she was rich and leisured herself), and often either escaped into solitude or jumped on her horse and fled (usually with an indigenous escort) in search of new places to see and subjects to paint.

The frustrations of being an adventurous, single woman in a constricting Victorian world are palpable, and she clearly saw the colonies as offering European women certain freedoms. For example, she wrote enviously of the sister of the Attorney General of Jamaica, 'the person I liked best in Jamaica', that as a girl she had gone to live in Australia 'where she had had no so-called "education", but had ridden wild horses and driven in the cattle with her brothers'.[31] If she could learn from an experience, she welcomed it regardless of physical hardships. She took risks, and shrugged off scaremongers: 'I landed entirely alone and friendless, but at once fell into kind helpful hands ... It was thought rather shocking and dangerous for me to wander over the hills alone; wild stories were told about runaway slaves, etc.'[32]

As for the attractions of the tropics *per se*, she declared: 'I had long had the dream of going to some tropical country to paint its peculiar vegetation on the spot in natural abundant luxuriance'.[33] She clearly relished the difference, immediacy, sensuality, and fecundity of the natural tropical

---

[28] North and Bateman, *Vision*, 68.   [29] *Ibid.*, 160.   [30] *Ibid.*, 13 (introduction).

[31] *Ibid.*, 50.   [32] *Ibid.*, 47 (Jamaica), 78 (Brazil).

[33] North and Bateman, *Vision*, 31; *Recollections*, 39; for other views F. Driver and L. Martins (eds.), *Tropical Visions in an Age of Empire* (Chicago: University of Chicago Press, 2005).

world, all of which contrasted with her relatively dull social life in England. Reading Charles Kingsley's book *At Last* 'added fuel to the burning of my rage for seeing the Tropics'. There she found everything 'intensely exciting' and 'too good to be real'.[34] The natural world was pulsatingly colourful, three-dimensional, intensely rich. She drew from it the energy to work around the clock.

Unlike those travellers who sought to make order out of perceived chaos, North was actively drawn to confusion in nature—entanglements, weeds, and plants running wild—and wanted it left that way. The word 'tangle' crops up constantly in her prose.[35] She revelled in the chaos of the Fern Walk, Jamaica, where ferns grew 'piled on one another ... it was like a scene in a pantomime, too good to be real, the tree-fern fronds crossing and recrossing each other like network' [*sic*].[36] Her paintings also reflect this: creepers strangle their host trees, colours and plants are entwined in glorious embrace, writhing over and under each other. The orderly still life is represented, too, but it is very much in the minority.

In other respects, Marianne North also stands out from the crowd in the contact zone. She chose to travel slowly, and savoured her surroundings. Typical are her remarks on Borneo: 'I resolved to stay quiet for a month or more, and learn a little Malay before I went anywhere else ... it was a real joy to sit still and look at [the garden] ... I enjoyed going slowly and stopping to rest often, when I could sketch the people in the little wayside places.'[37] This is the total opposite of the perpetual motion—and grand claims for that motion, as if there was something inherently admirable in forward movement—of someone like Thomson, who in reality often went backwards or round in circles. (Fabian claims that expeditionary caravans in Central Africa—including one jointly led by Thomson in 1878–80—were stationary much of the time, delayed for reasons such as ill health, disputes, camp chores, and attacks by wild animals. This forced idleness was rarely admitted.)[38] She never killed a wild animal for science or sporting trophy, and despised those who did, remarking: 'What a killing race the British are!' She applied the same attitude to plants, according to her sister: 'Her feeling for plants in their beautiful living personality was more like that which we

---

[34] North and Bateman, *Vision*, respectively 31, 47, 50 (Jamaica); 94 (Singapore).

[35] For example, North, *Recollections*, vol. 1, 83, 101, 127. [36] *Ibid.*, vol. 1, 89.

[37] North and Bateman, *Vision*, 103, 108.

[38] Johannes Fabian, *Out of Our Minds: Reason and Madness in the Exploration of Central Africa* (Berkeley, CA: University of California Press, 2000), 44.

all have for human friends. She could never bear to see flowers uselessly gathered—their harmless lives destroyed.'[39] While in Australia, someone shot 'a poor little sloth-bear ... before I could say "don't"—so soft and harmless ... I felt so sorry for the useless murder'. She asked more questions than provided answers.[40] North tried to conquer nothing but her own sense of inadequacy, travelling on and off for sixteen years before her health collapsed.

An African Explorer

Thomson is credited with being the first European to cross northern Maasailand, East Africa, in 1883. He wrote about his journey in a celebrated and racy travelogue. By the age of 26, the Edinburgh graduate had led three major expeditions to 'the interior of Africa' and was hailed as a hero in Europe.[41] He made treaties with local rulers, drew maps, 'discovered' natural wonders, and opened up trade routes. Likened to Livingstone, he is still written about in unequivocally glowing and largely uncritical terms; for instance, one biographer, Rotberg, claims: 'Unlike so many other explorers and the men of advancing empires, Thomson ostensibly approached Africa and Africans with methods worthy of admiration.'[42] Thomson did not, in the manner of German explorer Carl Peters, for example, shoot his way through encounters with local people, but this is still too easy an appraisal.

Thomson was an overt imperial expansionist, and he paved the way for trade and colonial takeover in 1895. It is no coincidence that the Imperial British East Africa Company was formed by Scottish ship-owner William Mackinnon in 1888, just five years after Thomson had proved it was possible to reach Lake Victoria safely from the coast—despite the 'dreaded' Maasai, to use German missionary Ludwig Krapf's term (1860). His descriptions of landscape and peoples were sentimental and sensationalist in the extreme, overlaid with scientific pretension. He was self-consciously one of those 'essential mediators between the scientific network and a larger European public', equally at home describing his travels to his sponsors, the Royal Geographic Society, or to the public at large.[43] He wrote as if he were conquering the landscape. In his naming and claiming of waterfalls and other wonders, he clearly aimed to place his stamp on territory. He declared large areas

---

[39] Preface to North, *Recollections*, Vol. 1, vi.   [40] North and Bateman, *Vision*, 115, 160, 68.
[41] See Robert I. Rotberg, *Joseph Thomson and the Exploration of Africa* (London: Chatto & Windus, 1971) for Thomson's other journeys and publications.
[42] *Ibid.*, preface, 9.   [43] Pratt, *Imperial Eyes*, 29.

of Maasailand were uninhabited, which ignored seasonal transhumance by the Maasai migrating with their livestock. This myth was used to justify the alienation of Maasailand (which straddled British and German East Africa) by the British and Germans in the 1900s. His depictions of humans and nature were painterly, sometimes overtly so. Above all, he used the printed word to capture the public imagination, and his Maasai travelogue probably reached hundreds of thousands of people through being co-published in the United States and translated into German and French.

But Thomson also upsets and defies neat categorization. His landscapes were very much inhabited, and he was disquieted by the nature of that occupation. The Maasai in particular refused to be framed in his word paintings, but leapt out, stared insolently back, dominated the conversation, laughed uproariously at him, physically fingered him, and forced him to perform for their entertainment. They controlled the territory and he had to negotiate every step forward. From these encounters, Thomson emerged frustrated and psychologically bruised. This is apparent in the travelogue, but more so in a lesser-known work, the novel *Ulu* which he co-wrote with a former female classmate.[44] In *Ulu*, he rehashed the expedition story to make his Scottish hero Gilmour emerge triumphant from his brush with the Maasai. Gilmour is also described as 'passing through some great mental and moral crisis' in which his contempt for Western society, and his desire for the African girl Ulu (half Chagga, half Maasai), are central.

Thomson condemned the Maasai for their apparently aimless wandering—a label that stuck, and fatally influenced the colonial administration's view of transhumant pastoralists—yet they rightly saw *him* as the aimless rover of the piece. He showed great ambivalence towards them; admiration and attraction (not least sexual) mingled with repugnance, and the latter intensified as the journey advanced. The Maasai never attacked Thomson, despite his worst fears, yet his text confirmed and amplified a nineteenth-century stereotype of their essentially bloodthirsty nature. Maasai ferocity *à la* Thomson became the primary image, with their alleged sexual promiscuity a close second. Both stereotypes were used and embellished upon by his friend Rider Haggard in the novel *Allan Quatermain*.

---

44 J. Thomson and Miss E. Harris-Smith, *Ulu: An African Romance* (London: Sampson Low, Marston & Co., 1888). For a deconstruction of this novel and comparison with the travelogue, see Lotte Hughes's chapter in G. de Vos, L. Romanucci-Ross, and Takeyuki Tsuda (eds.), *Ethnic Identity: Problems and Prospects for the Twenty-first Century*, 4th edn. (Lanham, NY: AltaMira Press, 2006).

Most importantly, in his rural scene-setting Thomson painted a bucolic landscape that attracted at least two generations of European settlers to the highlands of what became Kenya. His sentences were textured, onomatopoeic, alliterative, and he always drew mouth-watering parallels with home. He seemed to be deliberately appealing to landed stock farmers, seeking pastures new. For example, plains were 'covered with a close and succulent coating of grass quite indistinguishable from the pasture of more temperate climates'.[45] He made the timber appear equally attractive to potential extractors. While depicting the rich diversity of African environments, he also underscored likeness to Europe through simile and metaphor. Winds were 'suggestive of an early spring in Scotland'; he was 'enveloped in an unmistakable Scotch mist'; and one view 'embraced the head of the glen'.[46] 'Park-like country' and 'fragrant flowering shrubs' jostled with buffalo, elephant, and rhino, and Laikipia was the most 'charming' area of all. 'There is little in the aspect of the country to suggest the popular idea of the Tropics. The eye rests upon coniferous trees, forming pine-like woods, and you can gather sprigs of heath, sweet-scented clover, anemone and other familiar forms.'[47]

Unlike North and Wallace, Thomson emphasized the frontier-busting nature of his journey (calculated to rouse armchair adventurers) by repeating statements such as 'we proceeded to take the important step of crossing the threshold of the dangerous [Maasai] region'. Thomson never simply travelled, but injected maximum drama into every move. 'Let us now hurry forward, for the day is big with fate!'[48] The future was typically tinged with the threat of Maasai attack, which never came.

The aesthete in him was a product of the Scottish Enlightenment, and Victorian romanticism. In one sense there was nothing innately imperial in his attitude to nature; he saw the Scottish countryside in much the same way as he saw the East African landscape, and praised the latter precisely because it reminded him of his beloved home country—while also promising health and tropical fecundity to settlers. He was consciously promoting the key resources of pasture, water, timber, and big game to Europeans. But according to his brother, Thomson had loved nature from an early age—long before his imperial ambitions formed. Over time 'Nature became his religion' and some of his beliefs were practically pagan.[49]

---

[45] Thomson, *Masai Land*, 91.   [46] *Ibid.*, 204, 92, 270.   [47] *Ibid.*, 170, 237.
[48] *Ibid.*, 91, 93.
[49] J. B. Thomson, *Joseph Thomson, African Explorer: A Biography by his Brother* (London: Sampson Low, 1896), 10.

Finally, there is a striking contrast between his anthropomorphic descriptions of wild animals and his later, harsher depiction of the Maasai after his 'magic' had failed. He had pretended to be a great *laibon* or medicine man, and performed various stunts to impress the locals, but they tired of this and stopped showing him any respect. When he wrote of animals it was almost as if wild beasts were exhibiting the responses he craved from humans to his 'harmless, though phenomenal' person. For instance, 'buffaloes turned up their noses and snorted astonishment' on seeing him and his party.[50] Unlike Wallace and Darwin, his favourite animals were all big and usually dangerous—lion, elephant, rhino, and buffalo. In common with other imperial hunters, he invariably described large game in such class terms as noble, stately, aristocratic, the implication being that he was rendered noble by killing them (see Chapter 4). He had no time for insects.

This ostensibly scientific expedition and text has a paucity of scientific observations of nature. Rotberg concedes that Thomson's scientific accomplishments were 'sketchy'.[51] He confirmed the existence of Mount Kenya but failed to climb it and placed it too far west on the map; gave up his attempt on Kilimanjaro and failed to take a precise barometric reading of the altitude; and never used a microscope.[52] Apart from 140 species of plant specimens, dealt with in an appendix, the travelogue only offers interesting but fairly inexact descriptions of fauna, flora, and rock formations. His obsession with classifying, and condemning, the Maasai ultimately took precedence over nature notes. Furthermore, much of his environmental information was clearly not gained empirically but came both from his coastal guides and the obliging residents of Maasailand, a fact he acknowledged: 'They had an admirable knowledge of the geography of an enormous area. This they had acquired by their continuous war raids and their nomadic habits, and they imparted their information without reserve'.[53]

Nature is central to these Victorian travelogues, but the diversity of approaches and consumption of nature is remarkable. North marvelled at it, and painted it, but had little specifically scientific interest. Wallace voraciously collected nature, and strove to form an overview. Thomson wished to lay claim to East African landscapes on behalf of his scientific sponsors, although his keen appreciation of the spiritual and aesthetic

---

[50] Thomson, *Masai Land*, 204, 227.
[51] Rotberg, Introduction to the Third Edition, in Thomson, *Masai Land*, xi–xiii.
[52] Rotberg, *Thomson*, 158, 195, 198, and elsewhere.
[53] Thomson, *Masai Land*, 195.

qualities of nature were also evident in his writing. Each revealed an aspect of imperial interactions with the natural worlds that British power came to dominate. They all peopled the landscapes, but represented those people differently—more so than is suggested in the categories of conquest and 'anti-conquest'. Thomson saw the potential for expropriation. In North and Wallace particularly, strands of conservationist thinking are apparent. We shall pursue some of these elements in subsequent chapters.

6

Sheep, Pastures, and Demography in Australia

The Pastoral Economy and Dispossession

Succeeding phases of British economic growth prompted strikingly different imperatives for expansion, for natural resource exploitation, and for the social organization of extra-European production. In the eighteenth century, sugar, African slaves, and shipping in the Atlantic world provided one major dynamic of empire. But in the nineteenth century, antipodean settlement and trade, especially that resulting from expanding settler pastoral frontiers, was responsible for some of the most dramatic social and environmental transformations.

Plantations occupied relatively little space in the new social geography of world production. By contrast, commercial pastoralism, which took root most energetically in the temperate and semi-arid regions of the newly conquered world, was land-hungry but relatively light in its demands for labour. The Spanish Empire based in Mexico can be considered a forerunner. By the 1580s, within fifty years of their introduction, there were an estimated 4.5 million merino sheep in the Mexican highlands.[1] The livestock economy, incorporating cattle as well as sheep, spread northwards through Mexico to what became California by the eighteenth century. Settler intrusions followed in the vast landmasses of southern Latin America, southern Africa, Australia, and New Zealand. Australia was one of the last-invaded of these territories, and, in respect of the issues that we are exploring, was in some senses distinctive. Unlike Canada and South Africa, there was no long, slow period of trade and interaction with the indigenous population; like the Caribbean, the Aboriginal people were quickly displaced by disease and conquest. The relative scale of the pastoral economy was greater than in any other British colony.

Supply of meat and dairy products to rapidly growing ports and urban centres was one priority for livestock farmers. Cattle ranching remained a major feature of livestock production in Australia. Bullock-carts, not

---

[1] Mellville, *A Plague of Sheep.*

dissimilar to South African ox-wagons, were essential for Australian transport up to the 1870s. But for well over a century, from the 1820s to the 1950s and beyond, sheep flooded the southern lands. Although mutton became a significant export from New Zealand and South America, wool was probably the major product of these pastoral hinterlands—and a key focus of production in Australia and South Africa. The growth in antipodean sheep numbers was staggering. Sheep were first introduced to Australia in 1797. By the 1890s, Australia carried perhaps half of southern-hemisphere sheep, over 100 million in all. By the 1930s, the sheep population of Argentina, Uruguay, South Africa, Australia, and New Zealand reached about 300 million.[2]

Some historians writing in the interwar years of the twentieth century, such as W. K. Hancock, emphasized the centrality of sheep to Australian development: 'from wool came the economic impulse which opened up the Australian continent. The history of Australian exploration is inseparable from the history of the pastoral industry'. Elsewhere he claimed 'wool made Australia a solvent nation, and in the end, a free one'.[3] There are strong echoes of Harold Innis, writing at the same time, on Canada. Roberts put the rural squatters at the heart of Australian history, though he did not romanticize frontier existence.[4] Barnard argued that 'wool was an important source of political influence ... and the focus for a large part of government legislation and administrative action; wool was the chief means of the successful spread of colonial settlement'.[5] A focus on the history of wool production and exports highlighted a rural, male, settler world, and a specifically colonial export economy. This is a more muted theme in later twentieth-century historiography, which tends to focus more on dispossession, on race, and on urban, nationalist, and gendered perspectives. The squatter came to be seen as 'frontier tyrant, in the light of Aboriginal and frontier conflict studies'.[6] Australian historiography has rightly incorporated the Aboriginal

[2] Rough numbers, drawn from B. R. Mitchell, *International Historical Statistics: Africa, Asia and Oceania, 1750–2000* (Basingstoke: Palgrave Macmillan, 2003); Union of South Africa *Yearbooks* for the 1920s and 1930s, which give comparative sheep numbers; M. L. Ryder, *Sheep and Man* (London: Duckworth, London, 1983).

[3] W. K. Hancock, *Australia* (London: Ernest Benn, 1930), 12.

[4] Stephen Roberts, *History of Australian Land Settlement, 1788–1920* (Melbourne: Macmillan, 1924) and *The Squatting Age in Australia, 1835–1847* (Melbourne: Melbourne University Press, 1935, reprinted by Cambridge University Press, 1964).

[5] Alan Barnard, *The Australian Wool Market, 1840–1900* (Carlton, Victoria: Melbourne University Press, 1958), xv.

[6] Anne Allingham, *Taming the Wilderness: The First Decade of Pastoral Settlement in the Kennedy District* (Townsville: James Cook University of Northern Queensland, 1977), xi.

past, recognized the long demographic predominance of urban society, and escaped relegation to an economic and cultural footnote of British history. Yet in discussing environmental aspects of the nineteenth century, it is difficult to escape the significance of the commercial pastoral economy.

Sheep were deeply implicated in the displacement of indigenous people as well as in bringing about environmental change: 'pastoralism enabled the conquest of the indigenous populations and the domination of vast areas of rural space'.[7] But in Australia, as in the Americas, it was not only settler power and commercial impulses that shaped the outcome of this intrusion. Disease must be set alongside conquest as facilitating domination.[8] Smallpox, transmitted through northern Aboriginal contacts with Indonesia, may have preceded British contact and weakened indigenous resistance.[9] Certainly within a year of the 1788 settlement at Botany Bay (Sydney), a disease that was probably smallpox afflicted nearby Aboriginal communities. Perhaps half the population died, and more deaths were reported in the interior. Soon afterwards, the Murray River valley, one of the best watered and most fertile, was said to be depopulated.[10] Measles, tuberculosis, and venereal diseases took a toll and there were further smallpox epidemics in the nineteenth century, notably from 1828 to 1832. While some argue that warfare and violence were limited on the Australian frontier up to the 1830s, everyday settler violence, and retributive police expeditions, as opposed to organized warfare, was in the longer term among the worst on British colonial frontiers.[11] The British monopoly of horses and firearms certainly gave them an overwhelming advantage. Aboriginal societies, by contrast, were highly decentralized, with little military capacity to resist the incursion. Unlike indigenous Canadians, they had no immediately attractive commodity to offer, and few communities could create the space to adapt to colonialism.

There were few other places in the British Empire where the indigenous population was so quickly dehumanized, and so systematically dispossessed and displaced. This is more striking because the period of conquest of

---

[7] Mellville, *A Plague of Sheep*, xi.

[8] David Day, *Claiming a Continent: A New History of Australia* (Sydney: HarperCollins, 2001) Robert Hughes, *The Fatal Shore: The Epic of Australia's Founding* (New York: Knopf, 1986); Lines, *Taming the Great South Land*.

[9] Judy Campbell, *Invisible Invaders: Smallpox and Other Diseases in Aboriginal Australia, 1780–1880* (Carlton, Victoria: Melbourne University Press, 2002).

[10] Crosby, *Ecological Imperialism*, 206, 308–9.

[11] John Connor, *The Australian Frontier Wars, 1788–1838* (Sydney: University of New South Wales Press, 2002).

Australia was not that of the conquistadors, or slave traders, but when evangelical, abolitionist, and liberal forces were at their strongest in the British Empire. Australia was not empty, although the Aboriginal system of subsistence necessitated dispersed, low-density settlement. Pre-colonial Aboriginal population estimates vary greatly: 300,000 was once commonly given for 1788; more recently, one million is often quoted, while Eric Rolls hazards 'at least 1.5 million'.[12] It was reduced to perhaps 60,000 in 1900 and census counts in the 1930s gave 77–80,000.[13] The demographic transformation of Australia was not as complete as that in the British Caribbean. Nor did Australia import slave labour. But the destruction of the Aboriginal population was quicker than in Canada, and the demographic outcome was of a completely different order from South Africa.

Wool was a truly colonial commodity in that the bulk of Australian produce was exported to Britain and Europe in the nineteenth century. Industrial manufacture of woollen yarn and textiles from the late eighteenth century enabled far larger quantities of cloth to be produced, creating a 'soaring demand' for wool.[14] As in the case of other colonial products, such as sugar and beaver skins, wool consumption in the nineteenth century was intimately linked to changing consumer tastes. With growing populations and rising incomes, more Europeans purchased a wider range of garments—effectively a wardrobe. Military demand was important; red was a popular dye for woollen coats because it was cheap. British wool tended to be of shorter staple and produced a weave increasingly considered too coarse for clothes. Merinos provided a finer wool and lengthier staple, suitable for smoother, lighter, worsted textile weaves. Improved woollen materials could be used for 'a vast variety of new descriptions of goods, light, beautiful, cheap, and adapted both for dress and furniture'.[15] Worsted production tended to be on a larger scale, more highly mechanized and specialized.[16]

[12] Eric Rolls, 'The Nature of Australia' in Tom Griffiths and Libby Robin (eds.), *Ecology and Empire: Environmental History of Settler Societies* (Edinburgh: Keele University Press, 1997), 38.

[13] Russell McGregor, *Imagined Destinies: Aboriginal Australians and the Doomed Race Theory, 1880–1939* (Carlton, Victoria: Melbourne University Press, 1997), 123.

[14] D. T. Jenkins and K. G. Ponting, *The British Wool Textile Industry, 1770–1914* (London: Heinemann, 1982), 22, 27.

[15] Edward Baines, 'On the Woollen Manufacture of England, with special reference to Leeds Clothing District', *Report of the Proceedings of the British Association for the Advancement of Science, Transactions of the Sections* (London, 1858), 159.

[16] Barnard, *Australian Wool Market*, 26.

Merino sheep were first bred in Spain, but when Spanish production and export was disrupted by the Napoleonic Wars, Saxony supplanted it in British markets. Joseph Banks, botanist, farmer, and President of the Royal Society, supervised an experimental merino flock in Britain—without longer-term success.[17] By 1830, 27 million pounds of imported wool, out of the total of around 32 million, came from Germany. By 1870, this source of supply was displaced by rocketing colonial production. Australia provided 175 million and South Africa 33 million of the 260 million pounds of wool imported. Two decades later, when Australian and South African sheep numbers first peaked, this had increased 2.5 times.[18] British farmers continued to produce wool, but by the 1930s output had slipped to about 120 million pounds annually whereas Australia and South Africa, the two biggest merino wool producers, accounted for ten times that amount. From the late nineteenth century Australian wool was increasingly sold within the country and exported to European buyers.

Wool manufacturers were increasingly concentrated in Yorkshire, which had the advantages of specialized technology, skilled workers, plentiful soft water, cheap coal, and easy access to ports. British producers were now supplying a global market, including blankets to indigenous people in South Africa and Canada. There too changing fashions—reinvented 'tribal dress'—were driving the market. The mills of Leeds and Bradford spun their links extraordinarily wide, helping to bind the southern hemisphere to the north. The great majority of sheep farmers and workers in Australia were British. Indigenous communities did sometimes adapt to the new breeds of sheep, where they could retain sufficient land to do so. The Navaho in the United States, who did not previously rear sheep, adopted them. In southern Africa alone, of all the southern hemisphere zones mentioned, there had been a pre-colonial pastoral economy, although the sheep were fat-tailed varieties with hair rather than wool. Africans switched breeds as they adapted to colonial markets.[19] In Australia, some people of Aboriginal origin were absorbed as a pastoral working class, like the remnant Khoisan of South Africa and gauchos in South America.

[17] Patrick O'Brian, *Joseph Banks: A Life* (London: Collins Harvill 1987).

[18] Barnard, *Australian Wool Market*, 218.

[19] Colin Bundy, *The Rise and Fall of the South African Peasantry* (London: Heinemann, 1979); Beinart and Coates, *Environment and History*.

Australian Natural Resources and the Impact of Sheep

Tim Flannery, in his ecological history of Australia, poses the question as to which are Old and which are New Worlds.[20] Australia was often seen as part of the historical New World, but its surface is, geologically, one of the world's oldest; by contrast the surface of the so-called Old World, and especially northern Europe, is mostly much newer. Australia escaped glaciation and hence lacked rich pulverized soils; age and weathering compounded their poverty. Nitrogen-fixing leguminous plants struggled in this low-phosphorous environment. Australia's poor, old soils, Flannery notes, had limited capacity to sustain vegetable and hence animal life. A high percentage of land—over two-thirds—can be classified as arid and semi-arid, with less than 500 mm (20 inches) of rainfall. Precipitation is unpredictable, and highly susceptible to El Nino cycles. As one consequence, the megafauna of Australia, most now extinct, were smaller than those of Africa. The climate and soils 'forced some unusual adaptions in its plants and animals', such as 'parsimony born of resource poverty, low rates of reproduction and strict obedience in following and exploiting brief windows of opportunity as they open erratically over the land'.[21]

Flannery argues that Aboriginal people remade the landscape; they used fire to hunt and clear vegetation, and were in part responsible for exterminating some large mammal species. But he goes further to suggest that, conversely, the old and relatively resource-poor world of Australia shaped its colonizers.[22] The Aboriginal population, which arrived at least 50,000 years ago, remained small, and relied on complex networks of reciprocal obligation, over extensive areas, to tide them over natural disasters or dearth. More controversially, he argues that this 'low-nutrient' natural world also helps to explain why Australia's settler population remained small. There is a nationalist streak to his book, which stresses continuities in the way that all Australians, Aboriginal and settler, were shaped by their environment. He tries to root Australian identity in a material landscape, echoes environmentalist concerns with ecological safety, and, from the vantage

---

[20] Timothy F. Flannery, *The Future Eaters: An Ecological History of the Australian Lands and People* (London: Secker & Warburg, 1996).

[21] *Ibid.*, 85.

[22] Flannery, 'The Fate of Empire in Low- and High-Energy Ecosystems' in Griffiths and Robin (eds.), *Ecology and Empire*, 46–59.

point of a scientist, reflects a broader shift in Australian historiography that incorporates the Aboriginal past.[23]

Debates about the poverty of, and limits to, Australian natural resources began in the nineteenth century and have been energetically canvassed since the 1920s.[24] In that decade, champions of immigration promoted an 'Australia Unlimited' where irrigation would make the deserts bloom and open the way to rapidly increasing settlement. Griffith Taylor, a leading geographer at the University of Sydney, was deeply critical of these views and popularized the idea of environmental limits to settlement.[25] The challenge for Australia, he argued, was not to perpetuate 'romantic nineteenth-century frontiering' but to develop efficient and conservationist resource use. He predicted (with uncanny accuracy) a population of about 20 million by 2000 and 'saturation' of perhaps 65 million. More recently, the very high percentage of population in Australian cities, and their location around the wetter fringes of the continent in eight major concentrations, is often deployed in arguments about resource poverty in much of the interior.

Taylor's opponents at the time were pro-settler and pro-empire advocates of white Australia. Some accused him of environmental determinism. The same point could be made with respect to Flannery's perspective. We may now find Taylor's position more comfortable both politically and environmentally, but there are still difficulties with his approach. The notion of limited natural resources presents problems in understanding nineteenth-century Australian history. While the percentage of land in Australia with rainfall over 500 mm (*c*.30 per cent) may have been low compared to North America, the total of this area was huge, nearly a million square miles. This was more than twice the size of South Africa—which itself had nearly as much semi-arid and arid land (55–60 per cent) and was equally susceptible to drought.

Despite a 136-year head start, the South African settler population was outstripped by the Australian within a few decades; disease was not a significant constraint. Australia also had rich mineral resources, which underpinned a demographic expansion in Victoria, from 1850 to 1861, more rapid than that

[23] Bain Attwood (ed.), *In the Age of Mabo: History, Aborigines and Australia* (St Leonards, NSW: Allen & Unwin, 1996).

[24] Dunlap, *Nature and the English Diaspora*; Tim Bonyhady, *The Colonial Earth* (Carlton, Victoria: Miegunyah Press, Melbourne University Press, 2000).

[25] J. M. Powell, *An Historical Geography of Modern Australia: The Restive Fringe* (Cambridge: Cambridge University Press, 1988), 129–41; Flannery, *Future Eaters*, 363–7.

experienced later on the South Africa goldmines. Of the one million settlers by 1861, the majority were urban. Until 1869, when the Suez Canal was opened, settlers travelling to Australia all went by ship via South Africa and—excepting the limited number of convicts—many had, in theory, the option to disembark en route. The great majority continued their arduous journey, drawn by reports of resource plenty and opportunity. It is true that Australian colonial governments put far more public money into subsidized immigration, especially from the 1860s, than their South African counter-parts, but before this, and overall, voluntary immigration was the most important source. By the time that the unified Commonwealth of Australia was formed in 1901, the population had reached 3.4 million. While South Africa, with 5 million, had a larger overall population, South Africa's white society numbered little more than 1.1 million.[26] These different demographic trajectories had a profound effect on the histories of the two countries.

For nineteenth-century settlers, the comparative richness of Australian grasslands, especially nearer the coast in New South Wales and Victoria, was more apparent than resource poverty. Australia was relatively free of indigenous parasites such as ticks and tsetse, so damaging in southern Africa. Australia's hunting was less rich in that there were no antelopes—although kangaroo were eaten. But, as a corollary, Australia also had a far smaller range of predators that fed on sheep—only bird raptors and the dingo, a feral dog introduced by the Aborigines. Heat and drought proved much less of a barrier to livestock than the cold of Canada. Sheep and goats were probably the most adaptable of the big five domesticated animals, more so than cattle, horses, and pigs, and particularly so in drier environments. As in Mexico and South Africa, merino adapted well to the semi-arid Australian terrain.[27]

Cape sheep farmers greatly envied Australians for the fecundity of their environment. Moreover, the costs of land were initially very low—both in monetary terms and because the cost of coercion required to empty it was far less. During the nineteenth century, South African settlers and colonial states fought frequent, draining, and expensive wars against indigenous African people to carve out a smaller area of land, and Africans held onto significant sections of the wetter, eastern half of the subcontinent. Usable space became abundant for colonists in Australia, as it did in Argentina, and

---

[26] The first complete South African census of 1904 returned 1.1 million whites.

[27] E. W. Cox, *The Evolution of the Australian Merino* (Sydney: Angus & Robertson, 1936). He was wrong, however, to see Australia as the only other place where the merino was environmentally at home.

commercial ranching—dependent on natural pastures—above all needed space. Australia, even more than North America, fits closely to Crosby's model of a neo-Europe in the nineteenth century. The limits to natural resources had by no means been reached.

Australia was not initially colonized because of its promise for sheep. But by the late eighteenth century, when the first small penal settlement was established, British people were skilled at unlocking the potential of newly available lands in the Empire. They transferred and experimented with a number of familiar animals and plants. This took place well before the formation of dedicated 'acclimatization' societies in the 1850s and 1860s.[28] In the early decades, Sydney traders were 'desperately' trying to find an export product that would free them from the restricted market of government orders for the penal colony.[29] Sealing and whaling provided one option. A trade in pork and sandalwood obtained from Fiji and Tahiti was pursued energetically. The traders shipped wood as far as China, and these small islands' timber supplies were quickly exhausted. The Australian colony had far-reaching environmental impacts, beyond its own territory, from its earliest years.

Twenty fine-wooled merino sheep were taken from the Cape, when Britain first took control there in 1797, to Australia. Official and landowner John MacArthur, and his wife Elizabeth, pioneered wool production; they had brought with them a good knowledge of livestock breeding. One of the wettest parts of Australia, around Sydney, was initially the key zone of expansion for sheep farming and after a decade, 20,000 merinos were recorded. In the 1820s, Britain removed the duty from imported wool. As the market for Australian wool grew, colonial horizons expanded beyond the coastal land, east of the Blue Mountains, and squatters moved out to occupy much of New South Wales between 1830 and 1840. (In southern Africa, the term 'squatter' was used to refer to Africans, usually small-scale tenant and peasant farmers settled on white-owned land; in Australia it referred to white landholders on what could be large estates.) Sheep did well not only on grass pastures but also on shrubs such as Australian saltbush (atriplex species), which was highly nutritious, drought resistant, and helped to control animal diseases.

Private land tenure was soon introduced and the best coastal land alienated to individuals, especially in Victoria and New South Wales. Some of the drier interior was retained as state-owned public land—notably in

[28] Dunlap, *Nature and the English Diaspora*, 54.
[29] D. R. Hainsworth, *The Sydney Traders: Simon Lord and his Contemporaries, 1788–1821* (Melbourne: Cassell, 1971), 114.

Queensland and South Australia—and distributed in leasehold. The sheep runs were largely unfenced before the 1860s, so the system depended on shepherds—usually poorer whites—who brought the animals back nightly to central corrals. Estates, called stations, could be huge; the British author Trollope recorded 200,000 sheep at a station on the Darling Downs in the early 1870s.[30] Landholding was highly concentrated. Powell notes that 'even in the case of the Americas, it is difficult to find a comparable example of frontier expansion in which so few people rapidly assumed control of such immense tracts'.[31] Anxiety about underutilization of land suffused public debate in the late nineteenth century.

In 1843 an Act made sheep and their wool legal security for loans, greatly increasing farmers' ability to raise money. In 1847 the property rights of squatters who had moved beyond the authorized limits of settlement were recognized. The pace at which sheep numbers grew was extraordinary: in New South Wales alone, there were 12 million by 1853. From then on, national figures are available: in 1860–4, an average 24 million were enumerated, by 1890–4 over 100 million. New South Wales accounted for about half the sheep, followed by Victoria, and Queensland.

As sheep farming penetrated drought-prone semi-arid zones by mid-century, transport links were stretched. While animals could be driven to market, wool had to be carried. It was light in relation to its value, compared to grain, but the costs of transport put a premium on reducing weights by washing wool on the stations. Bullock carts were essential for transport, and their mobility was facilitated by investment in roads. Clearing the Murray and Darling rivers for navigation in the 1850s and 1860s helped to open up further areas. South Africa, by contrast, had no such navigable routes. Rail transport expanded quickly from the 1860s. Once the wool had reached the coast, transport was less costly. In an empire where trade and movement were seaborne, the 'tyranny of distance' did not strangle economic growth.[32]

In the later decades of the nineteenth century, the expansion of sheep farming based on natural pastures was reaching its boundaries and a process of intensification began. Water supplies for livestock were always a problem and dependence on natural sources such as springs and streams often

[30] Anthony Trollope, *Australia and New Zealand*, Vol. 2 (London: Chapman & Hall, 1873), 121.
[31] J. M. Powell, *The Emergence of Bioregionalism in the Murray-Darling Basin* (Canberra: Murray Darling Basin Commission, 1993), 20.
[32] G. Blainey, *The Tyranny of Distance: How Distance Shaped Australia's History* (London: Macmillan, 1975).

required driving animals long distances. Farmers sank boreholes to provide drinking water for stock. Scientific understanding enabled destructive animal diseases such as scab, fluke, and bovine-pleuropneumonia to be controlled. Dipping against scab was made compulsory—a major undertaking in view of the millions of animals involved. Fencing of farms and paddocks diminished the need for shepherds; labour costs in Australia were relatively high. It also helped to keep out grass-eating kangaroos and rabbits, which were more easily shot as vermin, and to protect sheep against dingos. Sheep could now run free, saved from the long daily trek to and from the corrals. Pastures benefited in that they were not 'tramped' by sheep on the same scale. Lambing rates, carrying capacities, and wool quality increased. Systematic stud breeding, facilitated by the control of flocks in paddocks, helped yields to improve from about two pounds weight of wool per sheep in 1860 to nearly seven by the end of the century. Higher yields also made it worth investing in improvements. In one respect, however, rural investment subsided: wool-washing on the farms, and scouring—or commercial cleaning—in the towns declined. While this benefited the rural water supplies, it spelled the demise of a significant rural industry.

Wool prices fell from the mid-1870s until the end of the century. Where there was sufficient rainfall, farmers diversified into crops in order to secure their incomes, serving the growing urban, rather than export, markets. Diversification was not usually at the expense of sheep, which grazed on wheat stubble and manured the land for future plantings. By contrast, the carrying capacity of the semi-arid lands—where crops could not be grown—was much lower, and the costs associated with improvement and transport higher. The biggest operators owned or leased a number of stations and moved their animals between them to beat the droughts. For some, however, 'overgrazing was the only way to stay solvent'.[33]

Environmental Degradation

Eric Rolls pictures pre-colonial Australia as a land where only padded feet, whether of animals or humans, trod.[34] There were no hoofed livestock, nor boots, nor metal implements to break the soil. However, the pre-colonial environment was not static. Australia was a land of hard fires as well as

[33] Geoffrey Bolton, *Spoils and Spoilers: A History of Australians Shaping their Environment* (Sydney: Allan & Unwin, 1992), 17.
[34] Rolls, 'The Nature of Australia'.

soft soles. Natural wildfires were frequent and had shaped the landscape; some vegetation, such as eucalyptus trees, was partly adapted to them.[35] Aboriginal people used fire to stimulate new growth, which attracted wildlife for hunting. Even so the British intrusion and introduction of livestock precipitated an ecological revolution. Comments on degradation arose very early in the period of settler expansion. In 1827 New South Wales colonists understood something of their impact.

Overpasturing certainly seems to do considerable injury, and the old residents will still smile to hear the new-comers extol the pastoral richness of the newly discovered county: 'Wait, wait', they will say, 'till they have been as long and as heavily pastured as the old country'.[36]

Sheep concentrated around water sources, devoured the best grasses, and ate plants close to the soil. They were more aggressive grazers than native animals and the grasses were not adapted to their voracious appetites. Their large numbers and sharp hooves compacted the soil—so much so that sheep farming was declining in coastal New South Wales by 1850. The Hunter Valley, north of Sydney, so rich for early settlers, was 'worn out' and 'abandoned by the sheep farmer'.[37]

Fire was intensified in some areas for clearing brush and promoting grass growth; trees were killed by ring-barking and then burnt. The sheep farmers, Bolton maintains, were 'enemies of Australia's trees'.[38] Tall, annual, and highly nutritious grasses such as kangaroo grass (*Themeda australis*) were replaced by shorter, perennial species and bare ground, resulting in torrential run-off and soil erosion. Kangaroo grass was adapted to the spongy absorbent soil of the pre-sheep era; it could not respond as well to quick run-off from compacted soils. Shrub growth intensified in some areas. Aboriginal spokesmen observed 'the European people are very good at managing cattle and sheep but not so good at managing land'.[39]

The process of environmental change was evident across all of the sheep zones of Australia, over a long period, not least when the pastoral economy penetrated more marginal inland zones. The Kimberleys, a semi-arid area in the north of Western Australia, was a late-colonized frontier, little settled until about 1880, and rich in wildlife:

[35] Stephen J. Pyne, *Burning Bush: A Fire History of Australia* (New York: Holt, 1991).

[36] Neil Barr and John Cary, *Greening a Brown Land: The Australian Search for Sustainable Land Use* (Melbourne: Macmillan, 1992), 13.

[37] Mellville, *Plague of Sheep*, 67.   [38] Bolton, *Spoils and Spoilers,* 42.

[39] Barr and Cary, *Greening a Brown Land,* 101.

on all sides one could hear the rustling of wings, and could trace the dark plumage of the wild pheasants as they flew noisily from tree to tree; or one could see the grey, uncanny looking frilled lizards scrambling up the trunks or along the branches … as we disturbed them by our passage. Small red kangaroos would bound across the path, wombats and other small game starting up almost under our horses' feet … while all around us overhead, immense flocks of multi-coloured cockatoos shrieked discordantly.[40]

Twenty years and quarter of a million sheep later the fragile environment had been denuded, and by 1924, sheep numbers were halved and severe soil erosion ensued.[41]

The rapidity of Australia's transformation also opened it to invasion by alien species. Many useful new plants, as well as animals, were deliberately introduced, and clearly economic growth depended largely on exotic species. But sheep farming also facilitated the spread of weeds. The term 'weed' is a cultural rather than a botanical construct referring to unwanted, useless plants, out of human control, or those conceived to be in the wrong place.[42] Cape tulips (*Homeria breyniana*), burrweed (*Xanthium spinosum*), and prickly pear (*Opuntia* species) all invaded the pastures, elbowing aside indigenous plants that had generally been better for fodder, such as saltbush.[43] The Scotch thistle was a 'particular menace' and Victoria's colonial government attempted to enforce annual thistle cutting, before flowering ended, and appointed thistle inspectors as enforcers.[44] Blackberries were introduced for their fruit and valued for much of the nineteenth century but, spread by people and birds, became a major pest. St John's wort came from Europe, apparently imported by a midwife who wished to use it to induce abortion. The plant displaced natural pastures degraded by heavy grazing and was a major irritant to cattle. As in the case of scab in sheep, a great deal of effort in eradication of weeds could be negated by reinvasion from small pockets of land.

Rabbits were introduced to Australia by sailors and settlers as a source of food.[45] In 1859 Thomas Austin of Geelong, near Melbourne, notoriously started breeding and distributing wild Scottish and domestic brown English rabbits for hunting. They quickly multiplied.[46] By 1865, he claimed to have

---

[40] Lines, *Taming the Great South Land*, 105.   [41] Barr and Cary, *Greening a Brown Land*.
[42] Crosby, *Ecological Imperialism*; William Beinart and Karen Middleton, 'Plant Transfers in Historical Perspective: A Review Article', *Environment and History*, 10/1 (2004), 3–29.
[43] Lines, *Taming the Great South Land*, 59.   [44] Barr and Cary, *Greening a Brown Land*, 22.
[45] Eric Rolls, *They All Ran Wild: The Story of Pests on the Land in Australia* (Sydney: Angus & Robertson, 1969); Lines, *Taming the Great South Land*.
[46] Barr and Cary, *Greening a Brown Land*, 25.

killed 20,000 on his property alone with a further 10,000 estimated alive. Rabbits thrived on the indigenous grasses, shortened and made more accessible by millions of sheep. They contributed further to deforestation by eating saplings, including eucalyptus, and they inhibited tree planting. In a symbiosis with plant invaders, they found shelter in blackberry bushes. Potential predators, such as dingos and raptors, were being killed to protect sheep. Rabbits exposed soil and their burrows opened the way to tunnel erosion where water flowed into fragile subsoil before collapsing the surface into gulleys.

Rabbits were classified as vermin and bounties placed on their heads. By the 1870s they were eating so much that they drove some graziers out of business in Victoria. Rabbit meat was canned, first for human and later for pet food, and a hat-making industry developed using the felt.[47] New South Wales reported 10 million rabbits destroyed in 1887 and the costs to landowners and government were very high. Individual owners attempted to protect themselves with wire net fences; Queensland and Western Australia tried to fence themselves off completely. They were briefly successful as thousands of dead rabbits piled up against the wire, with bare ground around them. But a few open gates could provide a thoroughfare, and itinerant swagmen deliberately distributed rabbits as a source of food. In 1887 New South Wales offered a £25,000 reward for a successful eradication strategy and Pasteur, who had worked on Australian anthrax, offered chicken cholera for this purpose. This early experiment in biological control was not pursued because of the potential costs to other animals. Foxes were also introduced. William Lines argued that the rabbits' 'contribution to the biological pauperization of Australia [was] incalculable'.[48] They did, however, help temporarily to diminish the number of sheep from about 100 million in 1891 to 50 million soon after the turn of the century. Australia's wool clip greatly diminished, although its value, peaking at £24 million in 1891, was only temporarily affected and had recovered by 1906.[49] The initial fall coincided with lower wool prices and serious droughts in the 1890s.

Prickly pear or *opuntia* cactus species, originally from Mexico, were introduced with the first fleet for a cochineal dye industry and later for hedging in the Hunter Valley, probably in the 1830s. These plants had proved very useful, especially for poorer people, in a wide range of environments,

[47] Dunlap, *Nature and the English Diaspora*, 81.
[48] Lines, *Taming the Great South Land*, 120.
[49] Bolton, *Spoils and Spoilers*, 92–3; N. G. Butlin, *Australian Domestic Product, Investment and Foreign Borrowing, 1861–1938/39* (Cambridge: Cambridge University Press, 1962), 66.

from the Canary Islands and the Mediterranean coastlands, to the Cape, Madagascar, and India. Some species, particularly *Opuntia ficus-indica*, yielded a sweet fruit and the cladodes, or leaves, could be used as a fodder if the spines were burnt. But prickly pear ran wild in Queensland by the 1860s. It invaded most effectively down watercourses, carried by storm torrents, or where other vegetation was diminished. Livestock, wild animals, and birds ate its fruits and deposited seeds in the most inaccessible places. The wild, spiny varieties could seriously damage livestock, which nibbled at their moisture-rich cladodes in droughts. Fruits, including fallen fruits, were attractive, and their tiny glochids or spicules stuck in the mouths of animals, causing sepsis. For an economy based on increasingly valuable animals, any advantages from the plant were offset by the damage it caused. By 1925, an estimated 25 million hectares were infested, reducing the area available for farming. After some years of experimentation with mechanical and chemical means of clearance, Australian scientists imported and bred large numbers of cactoblastis moths whose larvae were natural predators of prickly pear in the Americas. These were released in the mid-1920s in a major biological campaign that proved largely successful.[50]

Prickly pear controls were just one aspect of multifaceted scientific work, coupled with increasing investment and environmental regulation. Research and policy were developed on controlling locusts—an important issue also in the mid-western United States—sheep blowfly, and weeds. Water storage, more systematic grazing management through rotation, and fodder increased the capacity of rangelands and sheep numbers recovered. In 1928, immediately prior to the Great Depression, sheep numbers were again over 100 million and proceeds from wool peaked at £75 million.[51] Australia became an important submetropole for pasture and ecological research (Chapter 13). Investment and disease control pushed back ecological limits. This was increasingly a managed landscape, although in the short term environmental degradation was not contained. The environmental nadir was probably reached in the 'erosion decades' of the 1930s and 1940s.[52] To the weight of sheep was added more intensive cropping

[50] Ian Tyrrell, *True Gardens of the Gods: Californian–Australian Environmental Reform, 1860–1930* (Berkeley, CA: University of California Press, 1999).

[51] Butlin, *Australian Domestic Product.*

[52] Barr and Cary, *Greening a Brown Land.* Ann R. M. Young, *Environmental Change in Australia since 1788* (Melbourne: Oxford University Press, 1996) places greater weight on natural processes.

with American-style dry-farming, or bare fallow, methods that left the earth exposed to the elements for long periods.[53] But environmental understanding, stronger regulation, and conservationist strategies were simultaneously gaining ground.[54]

Resources and Demography

Except during the 1850s and 1860s gold rush around Ballarat, wool was Australia's most valuable export for over a century.[55] Australian settlers enjoyed, on average, one of the highest standards of living in the world by the late nineteenth century.[56] The pattern of pastoral farming, together with the demise of the indigenous population, contributed to the formation of a specifically settler society. Owner-occupied farms with largely white workers, as opposed to plantations with coerced labour forces or indigenous migrant workers, helped shape the nineteenth-century demography. The federally administered Northern Territory was the last frontier for Australia, less populated by settlers, where Aboriginal people were drawn to a greater extent into the pastoral economy. But even here indigenous people were marginalized and as late as the 1920s, it 'was the scene of countless massacres and individual killings'.[57] As the Protector of Aborigines commented in 1938, they had become intruders in a white man's country. This is the great irony of settler societies. Those that were most successful at displacing the indigenous inhabitants were for a long time the most self-confident, the best protected against indigenous political reassertion, and received the least opprobrium.

Crosby's model of *Ecological Imperialism* is useful in discussing Australian history, where disease and the introduction of exotic species played a major role in displacing indigenous society, as well as sustaining a British settler population. Some reservations should, however, be made. The traffic in plant

---

[53] Barr and Cary, *Greening a Brown Land*, 129–34; Beinart, *Rise of Conservation*, ch. 7; Mary W. M. Hargreaves, *Dry Farming in the Northern Great Plains, 1900–1925* (Cambridge, MA: Harvard University Press, 1957); Jonathan Raban, *Bad Land: An American Romance* (New York: Vintage, 1997).

[54] Dunlap, *Nature and the English Diaspora*; Bonyhady, *The Colonial Earth*; Warwick Frost, 'Australia Unlimited? Environmental Debate in the Age of Catastrophe, 1910–1939', *Environment and History*, 10/3 (2004), 285–303.

[55] Butlin, *Australian Domestic Product*; 1903 was another exception.

[56] Simon Ville, *The Rural Entrepreneurs: A History of the Stock and Station Agent Industry in Australia and New Zealand* (Cambridge: Cambridge University Press, 2000).

[57] Day, *Claiming a Continent*, 182.

species was not all one way. The value of quick-growing Australian eucalypts was quickly realized and they were transferred around the world—to India, South Africa, California, and beyond—in the first half of the nineteenth century, where they became the basis of plantation forestry. We also need to be cautious in seeing the nineteenth-century anglophone dominance as setting an unbreakable mould.[58] Other European populations increasingly joined the migration, supplemented by Asian communities when racial restrictions on immigration were lifted. Australia is increasingly diverse, rather than simply a neo-Europe. After the Second World War, the Aboriginal population increased again, partly because of broadening self-definition (Chapters 18 and 19).[59] It is, however, difficult to imagine indigenous societies asserting political control, as they have been able to do in the former settler-controlled states of southern Africa.

We have argued against the idea that Australia's environment set specific limits to settlement, at least in the period discussed here. Nevertheless, the gap between the population of Australia (20 million) and the continental United States minus Alaska (280 million), which both occupy a similar area, is striking. Flannery points to richer soil—'youthful, fertile and deep'—and resources in North America.[60] Australia's demographic experience was more similar to Canada's, where cold, rather than aridity, and poor soils similarly limited the population.

Yet we should be cautious about an environmentally determinist analysis of Australian demography. It is possible to picture a different scenario. If Aboriginal people had weathered colonization more successfully, or if an African agrarian society with its disease resistance, its cattle, sorghum, and American maize had colonized Australia, and then experienced the same population growth as Africa's indigenous population, the demographic outcome may have been different. The same might have applied if, as Taylor conjectured, Australia was settled by Asian people who had been prepared to live in different ways to British immigrants.[61] So also if the Ballarat goldfields had proved deeper, or if Sydney and Melbourne had become leading wool-textile producers, or if they had become major financial centres, or if free immigration had been allowed to all people. Urban capitalist society allows far larger concentrations of people who may not be dependent upon

---

[58] B. R. Tomlinson, 'Empire of the Dandelion: Ecological Imperialism and Economic Expansion, 1860–1914', *Journal of Imperial and Commonwealth History*, 26/2 (1998).

[59] Attwood (ed.), *In the Age of Mabo*; Day, *Claiming a Continent*, 61.

[60] Flannery, 'The Fate of Empire', 56–7.   [61] Flannery, *Future Eaters*, 364.

the natural resources in their immediate hinterland. The only absolute constraint was water, and in this regard decisions about the distribution of water (much of it went to agriculture) rather than the quantity available would have been the key. Comparatively speaking, Australian settlement was rapid and the constraints on settler demographic growth had as much to do with political economy as the availability of resources.

7

Forests and Forestry in India

The Riches of Indian Timber

The 'riches' of provincial India that were shown at the Punjab Exhibition of 1864 were later described in two hefty volumes by B. H. Baden-Powell of the Bengal Civil Service as the *Hand-Book of the Economic Products of the Punjab*.[1] It began simply as a catalogue of all the items exhibited, but mushroomed into something more. Timber and other forest products featured alongside minerals, metals, manufacturing dyes, pottery, salt, and soils. A section was devoted to animal products such as lac (later used to make gramophone records), silk, musk, and wool; opium and 2,038 other drugs were listed, as well as the economic crops tea, cotton, flax, spices, grains, and pulses. Baden-Powell savoured the size, colour, and quality of each specimen, interspersed with grand descriptions of the countryside from which they came. But it was their uses, primarily to empire, and also to local communities, which distinguished these specimens.

'A collection properly grouped together', Baden-Powell wrote in the introduction, 'becomes to the intelligent spectator a perfect history of the social condition of the country it represents'.[2] More particularly, this provided a shopping list of tradable resources and their uses—a detailed breakdown of the natural wealth of India, about which many classical writers had enthused. Indigenous hardwoods were prime riches in this treasure trove; essential to the British army, navy, and railways, they became cogs in the conquest of India. The new demands inevitably led to deforestation.

This chapter explores the debates over exploitation of India's forests, and focuses more specifically on the rise of conservationist concerns, in which forestry played a major role. By conservation, we mean a set of ideas and practices that aimed at efficient and regulated usage of natural resources, so that they would be maintained in the longer term. We also

---

[1] B. H. Baden-Powell, *Hand-Book of the Economic Products of the Punjab*, 2 vols. (Roorkee: Thomason Civil Engineering College Press, 1868–72).

[2] *Ibid.*, vol. 1, i.

consider forests as contested spaces, and the implications of their reservation for access to resources—in particular by local people. We have touched on conservationist views in respect of wildlife (Chapters 4 and 5) but it is important to examine forestry since it had such a major impact upon peoples and landscapes over time, it was a precursor to other forms of scientific environmental management, and the ideas and practices developed in India were exported to other parts of the Empire.

By the mid-nineteenth century, British India's factories, workshops, and recently established railway networks (from 1853) were 'entirely dependent' on deodar cedar, a durable and easily worked wood whose 'huge logs ... are floated down on the great rivers, from the mountain forests that are within reach of their banks'.[3] Deodar (*Cedrus deodara*) could grow to a height of more than 200 feet, hence it made excellent masts, and beams were known to last hundreds of years. Teak (*Tectona grandis*), long prized and protected as a 'royal' tree, was valued above all other woods for its durability, strength, virtual immunity to insect and fungus attack, relatively light weight, and resistance to corrosion on contact with metal. It was valuable for railway sleepers and carriages, shipbuilding (because it did not warp), and other types of construction such as bridges, houses, and furniture. The army also used teak for munitions boxes, shell cases, and horse saddletrees. The timber was even used to make camp furniture and build an army barracks at Bangalore, before it was realized that dwindling supplies were far too good to be wasted. Teak was exported to Europe and America; Burma or 'Admiralty' teak was known to be the strongest. Used for navy frigates, it was said to have saved Britain during the Napoleonic Wars and aided her maritime expansion.[4]

Fast-growing sal trees (*Shorea robusta*) provided a strong, hard, heavy wood for sleepers and all types of construction; the bark was used in tanning. Deodar and the chirpine (chir) also yielded resin, in demand as varnish by the makers of maps and cabinets, oil painters, and carriage builders. From the multi-purpose deodar came an antiseptic wood-oil that preserved timber from insects. Various species of acacia and other trees produced gums, used locally for everything from red ink to medicines and sweetmeats, in calico printing, shoe making, and tanning. Gum Arabic was a mucilage in European medicines, while the bark was the most-used tanning substance in India and its wood was prized for plough

---

[3] Baden-Powell, *Hand-Book of the Economic Products of the Punjab*, vol. 1, xi.

[4] Madhav Gadgil and Ramachandra Guha, *This Fissured Land: An Ecological History of India* (New Delhi and Oxford: Oxford University Press, 1992), 119.

handles and cartwheels. Sandalwood, grown in a belt across Mysore in South India, was valued for carving, inlays, and incense, and like that from Tahiti (Chapter 6), largely exported to China. Red sandalwood yielded a dye for leather and wood, and a pharmacists' colouring agent. The rubber trees of Assam produced exports worth nearly £109,000 in 1881–2.[5]

The depletion of British woodlands was one backdrop to the expanding use of Indian timber in this period. It hastened the shift to fossil fuels, particularly coal, for domestic power and heat and resulted in huge demand for imported wood.[6] Britain had relied on imports from New England and the Baltic, but the latter supplies were cut off temporarily as a result of wartime blockades from the 1790s, and she had to look further afield.[7] The growing crescendo of conflicts in the mid-nineteenth century, including the second Anglo-Burma war (1852–3), the Crimea (1856–7), the Anglo-Iranian War (1856–7), and the Rebellion (formerly called Mutiny) of 1857, also intensified the need. The Rebellion was itself a spur to railway building because it taught the British a lesson about the dangers of isolation and poor communications.[8] Railways were critical for moving troops and thereby controlling territory. Rolling back the forests to make way for cultivation was also seen by the East India Company as a means of extending control.[9]

Railways remained at the heart of domestic timber demand in the years after Baden-Powell wrote. No coal was then being mined in the Punjab, and seaborne coal from Bengal, Britain, and Australia was expensive, so forests largely supplied the fuel until other domestic coalfields became accessible.[10] Each mile of railway devoured between 1,760 and 2,000 sleepers, and by the 1870s more than one million sleepers were needed every year.[11] Most of these did not last more than 12–16 years, and by the 1920s more than four million replacements were required annually, which used up a great deal of teak,

[5] D. Brandis, *Forestry in India* (1897; reprinted, Dehra Dun: Natraj Publishers, 1994), 41.

[6] R. S. Troup, *Colonial Forest Administration* (London: Oxford University Press, 1940), 5.

[7] Mahesh Rangarajan, 'Imperial Agendas and India's Forests: The Early History of Indian Forestry, 1800–1878', *The Indian Economic and Social History Review* 31/2 (1994), 154.

[8] E. P. Stebbing, *The Forests of India*, vol. 1 (London: John Lane, 1922), 295.

[9] Rangarajan, 'Imperial Agendas', 153; Michael Williams, *Deforesting the Earth: From Prehistory to Global Crisis* (Chicago and London: University of Chicago Press, 2003), 355, on loss of forest to cultivation.

[10] Brandis, Forestry, 63, and D. Brandis, *Progress of Forestry in India* (1884, no publisher or place given, reprinted from Transactions of the Scottish Arboricultural Society), 21. D. Arnold, *Science, Technology and Medicine in Colonial India: The New Cambridge History of India III: 5* (Cambridge: Cambridge University Press, 2000), 108–9.

[11] Gadgil and Guha, *Fissured Land*, 122.

sal, deodar, and the cheaper, treated chir pine.[12] Botanist Dietrich Brandis, the country's German-born first Inspector-General of Forests, also wrote of growing prosperity that had triggered new internal demands: 'The peasantry of entire districts, who have hitherto been content to live in miserable huts, desire to build good substantial houses and to use better furniture. Hence there was an increased demand for bamboos, wood, and timber'.[13] Forest products were a glue—sometimes literally—holding together military and naval power, buildings, arts and crafts, and a myriad other goods.

The workable forests were those on slopes near rivers, whose floods carried timber down to the plains. Usually a slide had to be cut so that the logs could tumble to the water below. Elephants, oxen, and buffalo were also used to bring timber out. Once they reached the river, the logs were formed into rafts. Using rivers as conduits was not easy: where narrow and rocky, the rafts had to be kept small. Once the river widened out huge rafts could be made, floated down to depots such as the one at Wazirabad on the river Chenab north of Lahore. The Bombay-Burma Trading Company and other firms with forest leases undertook rock blasting on streams and rivers. Logs were branded to identify them as government or other persons' property, but foresters had to watch out for traders who rustled timber by cutting off marks and adding their own. Logs that became stranded had to be re-launched, logjams cleared, and whirlpools avoided. Baden-Powell complained about trees being 'felled in hundreds and flung down the rocky hill side on the chance of their reaching the river below'. Timber was easily split on the rocks it passed over, and no more than one-tenth of what had been cut ever reached the rivers.[14]

The distribution and character of forest species was governed largely by rainfall, temperature, humidity, and soils. Sal grew predominantly on the slopes of the Himalaya, parts of Bihar, Orissa, and eastern Madhya Pradesh. Deodar was largely to be found in the north-west provinces, the Punjab and Himalaya, while teak's natural range took in Burma, South-Central India, and the peninsula. Teak was first planted in India in 1844, introduced to Bihar and Orissa forty years later, and successfully planted in North Bengal from 1868.[15] By the time conservator Hugh Cleghorn reported on the state

[12] H. Trotter, *The Common Commercial Timbers of India and their Uses* (Calcutta: Government Printer, 1929), 132. Williams, *Deforesting the Earth*, 360.

[13] Brandis, *Forestry,* 30.   [14] Brandis, *Hand-Book*, vol. 1, 527–9.

[15] *The Wealth of India: A Dictionary of Indian Raw Materials and Indian Products,* 10 (New Delhi: Council of Science and Industrial Research, 1976), 141.

of India's forests in 1851 for the British Association for the Advancement of Science (BAAS), exports of teak were running at 11,000 to 18,000 tons a year.[16]

Cleghorn and Conservation

Baden-Powell was concerned to illustrate 'riches', but forests were by then under threat and conservation was becoming a major British preoccupation in India. Cleghorn, who became Conservator of Forests for the Madras Presidency in 1855, has been highlighted by Richard Grove as a key figure in this development. Born in Madras, he was brought up and educated in Scotland. After training as a surgeon, Cleghorn returned to his birthplace in 1841 to study Indian diseases at the city's General Hospital. Scottish medical training included a strong focus on botany, and he became Professor of Botany at Madras before joining the committee appointed by the BAAS to report on forests.[17] As its main author, he saw neither the administration nor the 'community at large' as benefiting sufficiently from what the forests could offer: 'numerous products—valuable to science, and which might be profitably applied to the interests of social life—lay neglected within the depths of the forests.' In particular, he was concerned about 'wastage', the depletion of teak, the clash of interests between private forest resource extractors and the state, and the urgent need for 'maintaining a supply of first-class timber without seriously or permanently interfering with the future prospects of the forest'.[18] Cleghorn wrote in 1861:

It is only of late years, that attention has been drawn to the importance of conserving tropical forests … The matter of complaint was, that throughout the Indian empire large and valuable forest tracts were exposed to the careless rapacity of the native population, and especially unscrupulous contractors and traders, who cut and cleared them without reference to ultimate results, and who did so, moreover, without being in any way under the control or regulation of authority.[19]

---

[16] H. Cleghorn, R. Baird-Smith, and R. Strachey, 'Report of the Committee Appointed by the British Association to Consider the Probable Effects from an Economical and Physical Point of View of the Destruction of Tropical Forests', offprint from *Report of the Meetings: British Association for the Advancement of Science*, 21 (1851).

[17] Grove, *Green Imperialism*, 451–3; M. A. Waheed Khan, 'Dr Cleghorn's Role in Indian Forestry', *The Indian Forester*, 88/6 (1962).

[18] Hugh Cleghorn, *The Forests and Gardens of South India* (London: W. H. Allen, 1861), preface, vi, vii.

[19] *Ibid.*, v.

This excerpt from his classic guide to the forests and gardens of South India contains some key words from the lexicon of imperial forestry: control, regulation, authority, conserve, valuable, juxtaposed with the alleged 'careless rapacity' of local people. He was also concerned with production needs, warning that people ought to be prevented from stripping the forests of teak, which would rob the state of its main source of 'commercial prosperity'. He believed that 'indiscriminate denudation' had made it necessary to 'organise a system of forest administration, which would enable the authorities to economise public property for the public good'.[20]

Together with Brandis, Cleghorn has been called—in literature prior to recent critiques of forestry—the 'father' or 'founder' of Indian forestry, and credited with introducing scientific forest conservancy to the country. Their influence was broader in so far as ideas and practices honed in colonial India were later exported to Britain and other parts of the Empire. Not only did they attempt to control use of existing forests, but they also drew on French and German models to develop single-species plantations with trees in straight lines—even if this was not always achieved in practice. Forest surveyor Thomas Webber was amazed to see, on visiting Germany with Brandis, how different their state forests looked: 'Every row was as straight as a line, vistas running forwards in endless perspective, left and right, as far as the eye could reach. What a revelation to one direct from the Himalayas, where no two trees are of the same kind or the same age'.[21] They introduced fast-growing exotics, such as Australian acacias and eucalypts (from 1843), as part of what Cleghorn called 'this great experiment'. Scientific forestry came to be defined as the systematic planting, cultivation, and sustainable exploitation of woodland. Brandis's goals were effective protection, forest regeneration, good lines of communication, and methodical working plans.[22] His disciple, Webber, later wrote: 'the *Wirthschaft Plan*, or "working plan", is the keystone of forestry, and without this foundation everything is haphazard and futile'.[23]

The BAAS report created a climate in which administrators began to organize systematic forest conservancy in India.[24] Concerns about recurrent

---

[20] Hugh Cleghorn, *The Forests and Gardens of South India*, v–vi, vii.

[21] Thomas W. Webber, *The Forests of Upper India and their Inhabitants* (London: Edward Arnold, 1902), 319. He was describing the Harz forest.

[22] Brandis, *Forestry in India* (1994), 49.   [23] Webber, *Forests of Upper India*, 321.

[24] Grove, *Green Imperialism*, 451.

famine and drought also acted as a spur. When a Forest Department was established in 1864, Britain had few experts of its own.[25] Brandis had been brought in two years previously from Burma, where he was credited with saving the Burmese teak forests from timber traders, for the benefit of British shipbuilders.[26] The total numbers of forest officers grew from 57 in 1869 to 107 by 1885.[27] The Rebellion had resulted in a transfer of power to the Crown, which inherited a financial crisis. The conservators were under pressure to manage the forests effectively, meet the needs of the admiralty and others for large quantities of timber, simultaneously turn a profit, and contain local peoples' claims on the forests.

One of the first tasks facing the department was to work out which forests were state property. This varied from province to province, and depended on approaches to so-called wastelands. The 'waste' that fell within the boundaries of village communities was considered common property, and settlement officers in the Central Provinces, for example, set it aside for the use of villagers, with some prohibitions such as bans on teak cutting.[28] However, wastelands were progressively absorbed into state lands. The British laid claim to territory they considered unoccupied and unclaimed, and regarded princely property as theirs by right of conquest, but this did not solve muddy issues around user rights, both prescriptive and granted. Legislation was needed. Two Indian Forest Acts, of 1865 and 1878, marked the real start of state appropriation of forests—though the laws did not apply to all of British India.[29] Under the first, state control of forests was limited and user rights not totally abolished. The second Act reclassified state-controlled forests as either reserved or protected, and moved away from recognizing local people's access and usufructuary rights to seeing these as privileges. In reserved forests user rights were not recognized, unless explicitly ceded by provincial governments, while in protected forests existing rights were recorded but not settled; it was up to Indians to prove that they had them.

---

[25] Individual presidencies set up forestry departments earlier (e.g., Bombay in 1847) and a Forest Conservation Department was founded in 1857.

[26] See Ajay S. Rawat, 'Brandis: The Father of Organised Forestry in India', in Rawat (ed.), *Indian Forestry: A Perspective* (New Delhi: Indus Publishing, 1993).

[27] B. Ribbentrop, *Forestry in British India* (Calcutta: Government Printer, 1900), 79–80.

[28] D. E. U. Baker, *Colonialism in an Indian Hinterland: The Central Provinces, 1820–1920* (Delhi: Oxford University Press, 1993), 114–15.

[29] The government of Madras resisted the 1878 Act until a separate Forest Act was passed in 1882, and separate acts were also passed for Burma (1881) and Berar (1886); Rangarajan, 'Imperial Agendas', 164.

5. Káders [indigenous people] gathering honey, Anamalai Hills, Madras Presidency.

Credit: Douglas Hamilton, artist, in H. Cleghorn, *The Forests and Gardens of South India* (London: W. H. Allen, 1861).

Administrators tried to convert protected areas into reserved ones, over which they could exercise more control. By the end of 1882 there were 46,213 square miles of reserved and 8,612 square miles of protected forests, and the proportion reserved continued to grow.[30]

Cleghorn believed conservation was 'imperative' in the tropics in particular because water supplies, and consequently food and other produce, depended upon the existence of healthy forests. A series of forest officials' reports and studies fed into departmental concerns about the effects of deforestation on climate, desiccation, landslides, and soil erosion.[31] These were used to justify swingeing forest regulations aimed at curbing practices

[30] Ribbentrop, *Forestry*, 121. By 1900, 81,400 square miles were reserved and 3,300 protected; Gadgil and Guha, *Fissured Land*, 134.

[31] K. Sivaramakrishnan, 'Colonialism and Forestry in India: Imagining the Past in Present Politics', *Comparative Studies in Society and History*, 37 (1995), 6–7.

such as burning and shifting cultivation. Yet conversely, concern for Indian communities also drove initial conservation policy to some extent and the two were not mutually exclusive. An official in southern India, having talked to villagers, told Cleghorn in 1867 that 'the people themselves are unanimous in their wish for conservancy' because of the disastrous effects of deforestation on water supplies.[32] Cleghorn's exhortation to 'economize public property for the public good' seems to have meant commoditizing and realizing the wealth of a common resource for the good of all, both state and subjects, while also protecting it. But the term 'public good' or 'public interest' has been used since the seventeenth century by governments and others to justify a wide range of actions, many of them detrimental to poor and powerless imperial subjects.

Shifting views of Shifting Cultivation

Forests were not only physical domains, but also contested social spaces to which different groups of people attached different meanings. These opposing ideas clashed in the arguments that raged around *kumri*. It is an ancient form of cultivation in forest clearings, known by different names in various regions and prevalent in many agrarian systems outside of South Asia. It is often termed swidden or shifting cultivation, or labelled slash and burn in more condemnatory texts. It took different forms but was generally less labour intensive, and required fewer tools, than sustained arable production on open fields. Trees were felled, left to dry, burned, and seeds then sown in the ashes, which act as a fertilizer. One or more rice varieties were often inter-cropped with vegetables, chillies, gourds, and cotton. Crops could be harvested for between one and five years before the area was left fallow. Cultivators would return after several years, ideally twelve or more, and repeat the process. Shifting cultivators often augmented their food crops with the fruits of forest hunting, gathering, and small-scale pastoralism. Many were tribals or *adivasis*, distinct indigenous peoples who remain among the most marginalized communities in India.

The practice was denounced as a primitive form of agriculture and major cause of deforestation and soil exhaustion. Pre-colonially, it appears the Mughal state was unable to control shifting cultivators. Nineteenth-century mercantile interests in timber were one factor in increasing competition

---

[32] Puckle to Cleghorn, 30 Sept. 1867, in D. Brandis, *Memorandum on the Demarcation of the Public Forests in the Madras Presidency* (Simla: no publisher given, 1878), 3.

with shifting cultivators for forest resources, and their penetration of forests literally and metaphorically rendered *kumri* newly visible to the colonial state.[33] This coincided with more general conservationist concerns. In the late 1840s, while an Assistant Surgeon, Cleghorn had cut a swathe through *kumri* by persuading the authorities to stop shifting cultivation over the greater part of Mysore and Coorg (in the south-western tip of the peninsula). As conservator, he extended bans on *kumri* four years before the Forest Department even came into being. He called it 'wasteful' and 'rude', while acknowledging that it was neither possible nor desirable to ban it altogether since it produced types of nutritious millet. He wanted to see it prohibited in specific places, such as the banks of navigable rivers.[34] Official objections largely focused on the annual firing of the undergrowth, the threat this posed to the rest of the forest, the effects of fire on water supplies and climate, and the perceived waste of good wood.

Cleghorn condemned the indigenous lifestyles dependent on *kumri* as much as the practice itself. It was seen to attract 'vagabonds', those who were 'impatient of control' and 'fond of a wild roving life'. This encouraged 'unsettled habits', irregular cultivation, and crime. These were familiar evolutionary refrains at the time, from officials anxious to expand agricultural production and wage labour. Subjects had to stay in one place if the state was to bring about 'permanent improvements' in their lives and productive capacity.[35]

But some officials also spoke up for local subsistence needs. 'To abolish this species of cultivation would deprive a great number of persons of their accustomed means of support', wrote the Sub-Collector of Canara. The voice of the colonial state was by no means uniform. Brandis had realized the value of *taungya*—the local version—in his Burma days, experimenting in 1856 by encouraging tribals to inter-plant teak with rice. 'Twenty years afterwards this attempt had grown into a regular system, by which areas were being annually stocked with teak at a cost far below that of regular plantations.'[36] Shifting cultivation was fine, in his eyes, so long as the state controlled it and could benefit from the available labour. In Burma, the state

---

[33] Ajay Pratap, *The Hoe and The Axe: An Ethnohistory of Shifting Cultivation in Eastern India* (Delhi: Oxford University Press, 2000), 20, 40.

[34] Cleghorn, *Forests and Gardens*, 126.

[35] Sanjay Nigam, 'Disciplining and Policing the "Criminals by Birth", Part 1: The Making of a Colonial Stereotype—The Criminal Tribes and Castes of North India', *Indian Economic and Social History Review*, 27/2 (1990), 131–64.

[36] Stebbing, *Forest*, 376; Brandis, *Forestry*, 117–20.

claimed the teak plantations after the cultivators had moved on. There were other circumstances in which silviculturalists 'successfully manipulated' customary practices, such as grazing, lopping, and burning, for their own ends.[37] Forester and indigenous forest user were themselves sometimes inter-planted, and could be found working alongside each other in this complex human wood.

Cleghorn's views changed as he confronted the reality of forest protection and he admitted that 'strict conservancy' did not work if it was 'too stringent' and too oriented towards the interests of the state.[38] After the 1865 Forest Act, arguments broke out between one forestry camp, which wanted to see community rights respected, and another, led by Baden-Powell, which pushed for state control. Brandis favoured a middle way, preferring a policy of selective annexation of key areas, while respecting village rights. It has been suggested that this was because he drew on cross-cultural comparisons—'for Brandis the forest history of Europe called for a similar treatment of village rights in India'.[39] He likened Indian peasant rights to those in England's New Forest. Cleghorn suggested it was necessary to draw up forest regulations so that 'the rights of Government ... would be placed on as equitable and sound a basis as the rights of the people themselves', which did at least acknowledge that local people had rights.[40] These included free collection of forest produce such as wood, grass, leaves, compost, and bamboo, and rights to hunt, graze, and practise shifting cultivation. Baden-Powell, by contrast, declared that the colonial state had acquired through conquest sovereign rights over all forests and uncultivated land, and local people's use of them did not signify possession of legal rights but privileges which the state could withdraw at will. He clearly put his stamp on the 1878 Act.[41] This marked the beginning of a process of marginalization and discrimination against indigenous forest users that was to climax in major protest movements.

[37] Guha, *Unquiet Woods*, 50. M. Gadgil and R. Guha, 'State Forestry and Social Conflict', in D. Hardiman (ed.), *Peasant Resistance in India, 1858–1914* (Delhi: Oxford University Press, 1989), 157.

[38] Cleghorn, *Forests and Gardens*, vii.

[39] R. Guha, 'An Early Environmental Debate: The Making of the 1878 Forest Act', *Indian Economic and Social History Review*, 27 (1990), 73–4.

[40] Cleghorn, *Forests and Gardens*, x.

[41] Guha, 'Environmental Debate', 83–4; M. Rangarajan, *Fencing the Forest: Conservation and Ecological Change in India's Central Provinces, 1860–1914* (New Delhi and Oxford: Oxford University Press, 1996), 30–1.

Hunting in Forests

In India, unlike much of Africa, wildlife was concentrated in forested areas. Hunting was the favourite leisure pursuit of foresters—'the standard recreation'—and of all officials, they 'had the best opportunities'.[42] MacKenzie notes that some foresters focused almost entirely on hunting in their memoirs, as if forestry had been a sideline to the main event. When discussing the qualifications of forest officers, Berthold Ribbentrop (Inspector-General of Forests from 1889) simply said that some were naturalists, others sportsmen, as if these were two sides of the same coin.[43]

Leading forester Sainthill Eardley-Wilmot, for example, spent a fortnight of every May in the 1870s in Nepal, when the average bag was fifteen to twenty elephants, twenty tigers, panthers, bears, and as many deer as the party could shoot.[44] When in charge of Kheri Division, he shot forty stags in six weeks; this is redolent of hunters such as Cumming in southern Africa. Though hunting in general clearly gave him enormous pleasure, this future Inspector-General of Forests referred to tiger hunting as defensive of ordinary Indians and their livelihoods, describing how a Gujar tribesman, trembling with rage, had come begging him to despatch a tiger that had killed three of his cows; he was happy to oblige. Eardley-Wilmot, like Cumming, wrote about such episodes as if he was performing a social service. Hunting was also used for information gathering off the beaten track and to build social bridges with Indian aristocrats. From the viceroy down, British hunters 'consciously sought to inherit the mantle of the Mughals through an opulent and highly visible command of the environment, as well as to establish relations with the princely States through an apparently shared enthusiasm'.[45] After the visit of the Prince of Wales in 1875–6, a series of royal trips to India revolved around hunting, particularly tiger-shoots on elephant-back.

It was not until the early twentieth century that the thoughts of both princes and colonizers turned to preserving the big game they had so wantonly slaughtered, because so many species were fast disappearing. The first sanctuary was Kaziranga in Assam, set aside for rhino preservation in 1908—a couple of decades after African precedents.[46] (See Chapter 17.) Ordinary

---

[42] MacKenzie, *Empire of Nature*, 168.   [43] Ribbentrop, *Forestry*, 78.

[44] Sainthill Eardley-Wilmot, *Forest Life and Sport in India* (London: Edward Arnold, 1910).

[45] MacKenzie, *Empire of Nature*, 169.

[46] M. Rangarajan, *India's Wildlife History: An Introduction* (New Delhi: Permanent Black, 2001), 56–7.

Indians were singled out for blame; forest administrator Edward Stebbing accused them of threatening wild animals through poaching.[47] Colonial officials sometimes likened mobile tribals to dangerous and predatory wild animals who required 'watching', 'taming', and 'hunting up'.[48] Forests were often perceived as harbouring dangerous people as well as game, who had to be flushed out, and the language of control over popular hunting ran in parallel with that over shifting cultivation, criminalizing subsistence hunters while elevating the activities of officials and Indian elites. This had environmental consequences; for example, a post-Rebellion clampdown on the annual hunts of the Santal tribals removed an important check on wildlife populations.[49]

However, it is necessary to make two qualifications to this argument. Firstly, as in the British countryside, hunting allowed asymmetrical, but close, relationships across class and colour (Chapters 3 and 4). After waxing lyrical about the dogs, elephants, and horses which had faithfully served him in the jungles, Eardley-Wilmot recorded that 'the natives of India must not be forgotten, those who were lovers of sport for sport's sake … those who enjoyed the success of the hunt after sharing its toil and danger'. Without careful cultivation of such relationships, 'neither the forester nor the solitary sportsman could hope to be successful'.[50] He singled out 'Abdul the shikari', calling him his 'brother-sportsman'. Together, they killed thirty-five tigers and countless panthers and bears. The forest or 'jungle' could be a space of freedom in which cross-class relationships were allowed and even celebrated. In other European hunting memoirs, the focus is similarly on relationships with low-ranking Indian *shikaris*, not aristocrats, and the comments made are respectful.[51] Bertram Beresford ('B. B.') Osmaston, a member of the forest service from 1888–1923, also praised his trackers and the Lepchas of Darjeeling: 'real forest people and well versed in every form of jungle law … They are real naturalists, fond of their jungles and excellent observers'.[52] Despite the prevailing view of forest dwellers as criminals,

[47] MacKenzie, *Empire of Nature*, 173, citing E. P. Stebbing, *The Diary of a Sporting Naturalist in India* (London and New York: John Lane, 1920), 241–567.

[48] Nigam, 'Disciplining and Policing', 149.   [49] Rangarajan, *India's Wildlife History*, 26.

[50] Eardley-Wilmot, *Forest Life*, 39–40.

[51] Jacqueline Toovey (ed.), *Tigers of the Raj: Pages from the Shikar Diaries, 1884 to 1949, of Col. Burton, Sportsman and Conservationist* (Gloucester: Alan Sutton Publishing, 1987); M. Rangarajan, (ed.), *The Oxford Anthology of Indian Wildlife*, vol. 1: *Hunting and Shooting* (New Delhi: Oxford University Press, 1999).

[52] B. B. Osmaston, *Wild Life and Adventures in Indian Forests*, ed. Henry Osmaston (Ulverston, Cumbria: pub. by Henry Osmaston, 1977, 1999).

Eardley-Wilmot found few dangers: 'The forester is often safer from theft and other dangers when dwelling with the jungle tribes than amongst the more settled population.'[53]

Secondly, some members of this elite group of hunters became conservationists. They included Richard Burton, early member of the Bombay Natural History Society, who lobbied the government to establish an Indian Board for Wildlife. A generation later, forester P. D. Stracey, author of *Elephant Gold* (1963), stayed on after independence and became committed to wildlife protection. Osmaston, an expert birdwatcher, became Chief Conservator of the Central Provinces. Jim Corbett—though he never entirely gave up shooting—was among the best known of these 'penitent butchers', while forester turned eminent wildlife photographer F. W. Champion, author of *With a Camera in Tigerland* (1927), never supported hunting except for food. (See Chapters 4 and 17.)[54]

Critiques of Colonial Forestry and their Problems

Gadgil and Guha have led the field in arguing that British colonial rule was the instigator of today's ecological crisis, and in human terms led to 'profound dislocations at various levels of Indian society'.[55] British interference with the Indian environment, they argue, upset social relations in the countryside that were predicated upon different modes of resource use (such as shifting cultivation, hunting-gathering, and pastoralism). The move away from communally held and managed land began during the heyday of colonial forestry, leading to a situation where the state came, after the 1878 Act, to preside over 'a vast government estate' covering over a fifth of India's land surface, most of it reserved forest.[56]

Gadgil and Guha do not go so far as to claim, as some have, that rural precolonial Indian societies were naturally conservationist. They point out, for example, that the restraints that regulated hunter-gatherer behaviour may not have had anything to do with far-sighted conservationist vision. Indeed, hunter-gatherers sometimes destroyed the natural resources upon which their enemies relied. As we have illustrated, external trade and encroachment, competition over natural resources, or human population growth,

---

[53] Eardley-Wilmot, *Forest Life*, 141.

[54] See Rangarajan, *India's Wildlife History*, ch. 7.

[55] Gadgil and Guha, *Fissured Land*, 5. Repeated in 'State Forestry and Social Conflict' (1989), 142.

[56] Gadgil and Guha, *Fissured Land*, 2; 'State Forestry and Social Conflict', 142.

could all push indigenous communities into increasing their demands on natural resources. The authors' most swingeing indictment of colonial scientific forestry may be their claim that there was nothing particularly 'scientific' about it. The faster formal scientific knowledge grew, the faster deforestation accelerated, or where plantations were established, biodiversity was destroyed by introducing monocultures such as teak. Though science greatly enlarged knowledge of physical and chemical processes, they argue, it failed to understand the ecological consequences of human interventions that followed. Unlike religious and customary restraints upon human behaviour, scientific intervention knows 'no social restraints' and is therefore boundless. 'Ironically, therefore, religion and custom as ideologies of resource use are perhaps better adapted to deal with a situation of imperfect knowledge than a supposedly "scientific" resource management.'[57]

They concede that state management of forests was not unknown in the pre-colonial period, but it was restricted in scale and application. There was commercial exploitation, too, of produce such as pepper, cardamom, and ivory, but nothing to match the sheer enormity of colonial timber extraction. Within pre-colonial village societies, it was the task of certain castes to regulate resource extraction on communally held land—for example, by preventing unauthorized woodcutting. These authors argue that such diversification, the territorialism and exclusions that accompanied it, and caste sanctions against profligate use of resources, minimized human competition for these. Some forests were set aside for elephants, others for princely hunting; both represented forms of territorial control by elites who thereby regulated and curbed usage.

More recent literature challenges rosy views of a pre-colonial equilibrium. Rangarajan asserts that 'the pre-British era was not an idyllic one' for 'regimes had often encouraged the clearance of woodlands to augment revenues and secure military control'.[58] Rulers and landed elites in Sindh and Awadh in particular excluded local people from certain areas. Williams concurs: 'The precolonial forest ... was not an untouched, pristine Eden nor a community resource shared equitably'.[59] There is mounting evidence both of the scale of pre-colonial forest use and continuity in the policies pursued by Indian rulers and their British successors.

A further area of intense debate concerns the nature and key imperative of the conservationist impulse. Grove unpicks the assumption that the

---

[57] Gadgil and Guha, *Fissured Land*, 52–3.   [58] Rangarajan, 'Imperial Agendas', 152.
[59] Williams, *Deforesting the Earth*, 342.

destructiveness of the colonial period had its roots in ideologically 'imperialist', extractive attitudes towards the environment. Forest conservation aimed both to enhance production and to restore the basic resource over the longer term. Its goal was efficient—in modern terms sustainable—exploitation. Rajan offers an important shift of focus by suggesting that there was in fact little specifically 'colonial' about Indian colonial scientific forestry, for its roots and influences lay in European traditions and training. Since Indian scientific forestry was in turn the parent of imperial forestry elsewhere, 'there was … nothing unique or imperial about forestry in the British Empire'.

The main lacuna, says Rajan, is that historians of colonial forestry have failed to focus on the scientific communities in question and he challenges the received wisdom that 'politically controversial agendas of resource use promoted by scientists and scientific institutions first emerged and got institutionalised during the colonial era'.[60] Nor were foresters and other colonial officials a homogeneous group, their eyes trained solely on commercial goals, stern administration, and the advancement of the state. We will explore parallels at a later period, and also in colonial Africa, where scientists and doctors sometimes differentiated themselves from the ruling elite and were at odds with their masters. Gadgil and Guha often mention in passing criticisms of state policy by government officials, yet do not ultimately give these due weight. More broadly, Arnold cautions us against going too far in playing down the scientific significance of Indian forestry.[61] Forestry was relatively successful. By 1920, net revenues from state forests had quadrupled since the 1880s. Timber was only a part of this; so-called 'minor produce' such as bamboo and grass could raise as much as one-fifth of revenue.

The implementation of the 1878 Act proved to be far more variable than its protagonists intended. Scholars who have made detailed regional studies question whether Guha and others have not overstated what European power was able to achieve: 'their assertions … grant [Europe] an astonishing capacity to disrupt and colonize peripheral societies and ecologies', writes Sivaramakrishnan, on the basis of forestry research in Bengal.[62] Rules were violated everywhere and after repeated attempts at enforcement, they were relaxed. For example, though *kumri* was largely banned in all reserved forests, communities broke or circumvented the regulations or employed

[60] Rajan, 'Imperial Environmentalism', 3.

[61] Arnold, *Science, Technology and Medicine*, 48.

[62] K. Sivaramakrishnan, *Modern Forests: Statemaking and Environmental Change in Colonial Eastern India* (Stanford: Stanford University Press, 1999), 14–15.

more direct forms of protest that linked with wider opposition to colonial regulation (Chapter 16).[63] Foresters' thinking remained divided, and some official attitudes changed in favour of permitting local usage. Dipping back into Troup's 1940 account of colonial forestry, one finds this glowing appreciation of the role of *kumri* in establishing plantations:

Of the various methods of forming plantations, there is one that deserves special mention owing to its wide applications in the tropics, that is, the system of forest planting with the aid of shifting cultivation, which has been found to be the cheapest and most satisfactory method wherever it could be carried out successfully. The practice ... is in itself an extremely harmful one, but if the cultivators can be induced to plant young trees of valuable species among their crops and keep them weeded until the temporary clearings are abandoned, plantations can be established at a very cheap rate, since the clearing of the forest and the early weeding are carried out free of cost.[64]

The cultivators were either given 'a small reward' or simply allowed to continue practising *kumri* in reserved forest—a quid pro quo which suited everyone. Indian colonial foresters reached some kind of accommodation with *kumri*; it was only regarded as 'extremely harmful' when it produced nothing for the state. It was preferred to other forms of clearing and planting because skilled labour was already present in the forest, and there was no need to import food for workers since they grew it themselves. Troup noted the system had been extended to forests in Africa, and suggested it could 'hold out promise of becoming an important method of regenerating the forests'. Ribbentrop made similar remarks.[65] Stebbing, too, interspersed his condemnation of shifting cultivation with a description of how it had been used since 1920 in India for other species. Grazing was allowed in some areas because it kept the undergrowth down and enabled chir and deodar to grow, helping commercially valuable conifers win their 'struggle' with other species. Regulated burning also came to be accepted.

Criticisms of *kumri* have continued since independence in 1947, and studies show that minimum cultivation cycles of ten to fifteen years are necessary to maintain soil fertility at a reasonable level, not the five or six they are today. The practice is still widely considered to be a major cause of deforestation, soil erosion, loss of soil fertility, reduced crop yield, and

---

[63] Troup, *Forest Administration*, 249.
[64] *Ibid.*, 174.   [65] Ribbentrop, *Forestry*, 73.

lower ground water.[66] But social scientists and subaltern historians have now argued powerfully that it is well adapted to local conditions and may enhance biodiversity.[67] *Kumri* is a way of life, not simply a mode of resource extraction, which may account partly for its longevity. Far from being primitive and inefficient, its supporters maintain that it is an ingenious system of organic multiple cropping well suited to the heavy rainfall of the hill tracts, as well as multiple livelihood strategies by poor people.[68] Large-scale timber logging is more likely to account for deforestation, loss of biodiversity, and other environmental damage. By the late twentieth century, *kumri* was still being practised in an area between 4.35 and 7 million ha of India, and elsewhere in tropic forests.[69]

Another legacy of the imperial Indian Forestry Service is the Research Institute at Dehra Dun, founded in 1906 by Eardley-Wilmot (but preceded by a Forest School established by Brandis in 1878) and still going strong. It aimed to provide a mixture of practical and theoretical training for would-be forest rangers, who were all Indians. Students did practical work in the woods for eight months of the year and spent the other four studying maths, natural sciences, and forestry. Surveying was a core subject—'a mode of knowledge that coexisted with and shaped the cataloguing, managerial, developmental modes of knowledge throughout the nineteenth century'.[70] As the twentieth century advanced, the forest service was increasingly staffed by Indians. Foresters attached to the school produced a host of publications, and were closely associated with *The Indian Forester* journal. Brandis, though committed to 'the study of nature in the forest', saw the school and journal as building blocks in the establishment of scientific forestry in India. The journal was important for the interchange of information with other

---

[66] J. Singh, I. P. Bora, and A. Barnah, 'Changes in the Physico-Chemical Properties of Soil under Shifting Cultivation with Special Reference to Karbi Anglong District of Assam', *Indian Journal of Forestry*, 26/2 (June 2003); A. Agarwal, R. Chopra, and K. Sharma (eds.), *The First Citizens' Report: State of India's Environment* (New Delhi: Centre for Science and Environment, 1982, 1996), 44.

[67] T. R. Shankar Raman, *Jhum: Shifting Opinions*, viewable online at <http://www.india-seminar.com>; Pratap, *The Hoe and the Axe*.

[68] P. S. Ramakrishnan, *Shifting Agriculture and Sustainable Development: An Interdisciplinary Study from North-eastern India*, MAB Series, vol. 10 (Paris: UNESCO, 1992), cited in Shankar Raman, *Jhum*.

[69] Joe Human and Manoj Pattanaik, *Community Forest Management: A Casebook from India* (Oxford: Oxfam, 2000), 29; R. K. Luna, *Plantation Forestry in India* (Dehra Dun: no publisher given, 1989).

[70] Sivaramakrishnan, *Modern Forests*, 80.

colonies, publishing reports from Mauritius, South Africa, New Zealand, and elsewhere.[71]

British imperial control of India had a major impact on its extraordinarily varied range of trees and forest products. It also restricted access to forests by poor people, though not as rigorously as initially envisaged. The later exclusion of humans from wildlife parks was partly rooted in the forest laws of the colonial period, which treated local people as wasteful and destructive.[72] Despite attempts at conservation, loss of forests under the British led to progressively worsening water shortages and soil erosion. Where shifting cultivation did persist, restriction of available areas and population pressure tended to reduce fallow periods, with the potential for dangerous environmental consequences. But pressures on the forest did not end with independence. The current rate of deforestation is said to be well over one million ha every year.[73] Now as then, critics of state policy point the finger at 'contradictory and inconsistent' forest policies that ostensibly aim to protect the environment while also milking it for profit.[74] The tension faced by Cleghorn and his peers continues to resonate in India.

[71] Brandis, *Forestry* (1994), 57–60.

[72] V. Saberwal, M. Rangarajan, and A. Kothari, *People, Parks and Wildlife: Towards Coexistence* (New Delhi: Longman, 2000).

[73] Agarwal, Chopra, and Sharma, *First Citizens' Report*, 33. Unofficial estimate.

[74] Duleep Matthai, 'Report of the Committee on the Ecological Role of Forests, Forest Protection and Meeting the Development Aspirations of the People in and around Forests' (unpublished, commissioned by Government of India, 1990), executive summary, point 9.

8

Water, Irrigation, and Agrarian Society in India and Egypt

Hydraulic Societies and Imperial Engineers

Water drives the world. Without it, our bodies cannot function, settlement is impossible, livestock die, and farmers cannot grow crops that feed millions. Great civilizations have been built upon irrigation, and fallen when the irrigation failed. Water carried armies, navies, commodities and labour across the globe, into places unreachable by land transport, and at far lower cost. When harnessed it produced steam engines and electricity, and helped to power industrial society. This natural resource, both fresh and salt, helped shape the patterns of empire in terms of the location of settlement and routes of communication. Irrigation became a major enterprise in the British Empire. Dammed and channelled water did not become a commodity in quite the same way as sugar, furs, or teak. But direct charges were often made for channelled water, and its value was also materialized in crops and livestock.

In many places, control of water was intimately bound up with command over territory. State-owned irrigation is a highly visible assertion of power, and management of water has sometimes required a centralized and ruthless bureaucracy, not least in order to collect the new revenues generated. As with forestry, colonial states tended to claim that their approach to water involved greater rationality and efficiency, in contrast to existing indigenous practices—though individual engineers did praise the ingenuity of the latter.[1] Some scholars have argued that despotism has followed human attempts to assert authority over water and its products, because it is a very basic way in which one group of people can dominate other, weaker groups. Such controls could also be a bedfellow of capitalist enterprise and empire. Making the link between the control of water and the rise of

---

[1] Robert Burton Buckley, *Irrigation Works in India and Egypt* (London and New York: E. & F. N. Spon, 1893), ch. 1; Satyajit Singh, *Taming the Waters: The Political Economy of Large Dams in India* (Delhi: Oxford University Press, 1997), 37.

empires, Donald Worster has written of the American West: '[It] can best be described as a modern *hydraulic society*, which is to say, a social order based on the intensive, large-scale manipulation of water and its products in an arid setting ... The technological control of water was the basis of a new West'.[2] Ultimately, it helped to make California the leading state in America. But there were far earlier precedents, and the hydraulic engineers of the American West—which Worster calls an empire—learned from older empires in India, Egypt, and Mesopotamia. It is the first two of these, when they came under British authority, that concern us here.

The term hydraulic societies or hydraulic civilizations—together with the idea that they were often despotic—comes from Karl Wittfogel. Inspired by Max Weber and Marx, though highly critical of the latter's view of nature as a passive resource, Wittfogel analysed how bureaucratic elites and ruling classes used irrigation—dams and canals—to gain political power in the ancient world.[3] The drive to dominate nature was instrumental in class formation, including that of what Wittfogel called the working class, without whose blood and sweat hydraulic societies could not have arisen. Giant irrigation projects required great numbers of labourers to build and maintain them; many were slaves, unpaid serfs, or bonded workers, press-ganged into the task of reorganizing nature. Sari-clad women bearing rocks on their heads helped to build the canals of pre-colonial India, and Egyptian peasants were forced to slave unpaid, as they had on the pyramids, to build dams and other works on the Nile. These practices had gone on for thousands of years, and continued in some form under the European powers, although the British abolished the corvée system soon after their arrival in Egypt. A major feature of imperial irrigation projects in these two countries, however, is that they were designed for the benefit of local people, not European settlers—though irrigated land meant higher taxes for the state and the potential of exports.

In our chapter on forestry, we discussed key ideas and practices in the early development of imperial conservationism. Water management was also sometimes called conservation in the late nineteenth and early twentieth centuries, although unlike forestry it did not involve the protection of certain species but was designed primarily to enhance agricultural production systems and improve communications. As with forestry, there was an

---

[2] Donald Worster, *Rivers of Empire: Water, Aridity, and the Growth of the American West* (New York, Oxford: Oxford University Press, 1985), 7, 10.

[3] Karl. A. Wittfogel, *Oriental Despotism: A Comparative Study of Total Power* (New Haven: Yale University Press, 1957).

imperative to boost output, regulate supply, and apply scientific approaches to natural resources. In both scenarios there were also tensions between colonial state management and established local practices. In fact, many communities, including some in India, continued to manage water locally and sometimes communally. Wittfogel's ideas have been challenged by some who argue that although such systems may have been created centrally, their organization and maintenance tended to be undertaken at a local level.[4] We must be aware of the limits of state authority.

Hydraulic engineers could nevertheless wield a great deal of power in the empire. Some, such as Sir William Willcocks (1852–1932) saw themselves as both improving agricultural production and the socio-economic condition of ordinary subjects. The story of imperial irrigation in India and on the Nile can partly be told through his life. Moreover, it has tentacles that reach other parts of empire, since Willcocks also advised on irrigation in Mesopotamia (now Iraq) and South Africa (irrigation departments in the Cape and Transvaal were formed largely as a result of his 1901 report), and lectured in Canada and the United States.[5]

Born in India, in a tent on an irrigation canal at the foot of the Himalaya, Willcocks was immersed in irrigation from the start. His father, an army captain, was then in charge of the head works of the Western Jumna Canal, and he grew up surrounded by water engineers.[6] He studied at Roorkee College—the first engineering college in the British Empire, now a university—graduating top of his year, and his first job involved helping to build the Lower Ganges Canal. He cut his teeth, hydraulically speaking, during eleven years' service in India, where he supervised construction on the Betwa Dam. He went to Egypt in 1883, a year after British forces occupied it, and worked for the irrigation service there until 1896. His professional peers wrote about him in biblical terms, likening the way he travelled through Egypt and acquainted himself with its challenges to 'Joseph of old'.[7]

---

[4] David Hardiman, 'Small-Dam Systems of the Sahyadris' in David Arnold and Ramachandra Guha (eds.), *Nature, Culture, Imperialism: Essays on the Environmental History of South Asia* (Bombay: Oxford University Press, 1995), 188.

[5] William Willcocks, *Report on Irrigation in South Africa* (Johannesburg: Printed by Authority, 1901).

[6] W. Willcocks, *Sixty Years in the East* (Edinburgh and London: William Blackwood & Sons, 1935), 3, and W. Willcocks, *Lectures on the Ancient System of Irrigation in Bengal and its Application to Modern Problems* (Calcutta: University of Calcutta Press, 1930), 2.

[7] Sir Hanbury Brown, Introduction to the 3rd edn., W. Willcocks and J. I. Craig, *Egyptian Irrigation*, vol 1 (London: E. & F. N. Spon; New York: Spon & Chamberlain, 1913), xvii.

(A serious biblical scholar and translator, he probably saw himself in a similar light.) His irrigation achievements included planning and building the first Aswan Dam on the Nile, and the Hindia Dam on the Euphrates. But his importance can also be judged in cultural and environmental terms. For instance, he was very impressed by Bengal's ancient flood or overflow irrigation, and argued in a series of lectures in the 1920s that the system should be restored because it was best suited to the region and the needs of its people. As for the future of India, he foresaw British withdrawal and did not lament its passing: 'Every part of India will gradually be handed back to the native chiefs of the old or of a new creation.'[8]

Irrigation in India

By the time of British conquest, India had networks of canals, small dams, village tanks, and channel-fed terraced fields dating back thousands of years, which allowed crops such as rice to be grown in places where rainfall was scanty, and gave major agrarian systems enough surplus water to thrive. Great rivers fed by Himalayan glaciers flowed through the plains of north India, and though the melt water was seasonal, these guaranteed the availability of water for irrigation. By contrast, south India relied on the monsoon for its water supply. With the monsoon season lasting only three months, people had to develop 'water wisdom' and ingenious rain-harvesting systems to make the dry months liveable. A wide range of hydraulic systems was invented to suit different ecosystems, and vivid references to them abound in the pages of ancient religious texts such as the Mahabharata.[9] Although British administrators sometimes admired the design of ancient dams and watercourses, and claimed they wanted to preserve them, David Hardiman notes that in practice they 'generally ... placed a low value on any irrigation system which the peasantry themselves were responsible for'.[10] Willcocks agreed. After he left India, he condemned his former masters in the strongest terms:

the Government of India never identified itself with the people of India, it acted as though it had no duties and no obligations to poverty-stricken people who

[8] Willcocks, *Sixty Years in the East*, 72.

[9] Traditional water-harvesting systems are described in Anil Agarwal and Sunita Narain (eds.), *Dying Wisdom: Rise, Fall and Potential of India's Traditional Water Harvesting Systems* (New Delhi: Centre for Science and Environment, 1997).

[10] Hardiman, 'Small-Dam Systems', in Arnold and Guha, (eds.), *Nature, Culture, Imperialism*, 1996 edn. (Delhi Oxford University Press), 204.

were often poor owing to the ignorance of the Government itself. It accepted its obligations on rare occasions and on a very small scale. It was for this reason it turned down the most necessary projects for the well-being of those who were most in want of them, and delighted in reclaiming deserts where there were no poor to provide for.[11]

The initial aims of colonial irrigation were to encourage agricultural settlement and political stability, boost production, increase state revenue, and improve communications. Protection against drought, and the prevention of famine, were secondary aims which subsequently became much more important. More subtly, the state wanted to extend its control over the environment, in a centralized and integrated way. Once canals, roads, and railways criss-crossed India, there were few places that government officials and armies could not go. There was also a major epistemological shift. The water engineers, argues David Gilmartin, saw the environment in a very distinctive way: as a 'mathematically modelled system ... of discrete and interlocking parts, knowable (and potentially controllable) by "objective" observers and by the state'.[12] (Willcocks tellingly described a former maths professor, Sir John Eliot, later head of the Indian Meteorological Department, as 'the man who had the most abiding influence on me'.)[13] It was believed ordinary Indians could not know about the environment in the same way. By classifying local people, on occasion, as part of nature, some officials also saw them as objects for moulding and control, just as water was. Furthermore, the fact that a military board was in charge of irrigation policy until 1854, and the majority of water engineers in nineteenth-century India were military men, influenced ideology and methods.

Restoration of existing waterways was the first priority, and this was initially undertaken by the British East India Company. After the Crown took over in 1858 the British built their own systems; by 1892 they had constructed nearly 43,800 miles of main canals and distributaries, irrigating 13.4m acres.[14] The first large-scale irrigation works began in south India, with

[11] Willcocks, *The Restoration of the Ancient Irrigation Works on the Tigris* (Cairo: National Printing Department, 1903), 13.

[12] David Gilmartin, 'Models of the Hydraulic Environment: Colonial Irrigation, State Power and Community in the Indus Basin', in Arnold and Guha (eds.), *Nature, Culture, Imperialism*, 211–12.

[13] Willcocks, *Sixty Years*, 32. They wrote to each other until the day Eliot died.

[14] Elizabeth Whitcombe, 'Irrigation', ch. 8 in D. Kumar and T. Raychaudhuri (eds.), *The Cambridge Economic History of India*, vol. 2: *c.1757–1970* (Hyderabad: Orient Longman with Cambridge University Press, 1983).

Major Cotton's reconstruction of the Grand Anicut Barrage at Trichinopoly from 1836 to 1838. In the next decade, nearly 70 per cent of the entire public works budget was spent repairing, enlarging and, in some places, building from scratch, irrigation works on the plains from Rajahmundry south to Madura. Madras (now Chennai) was the centre of imperial hydraulic activity; the first public works department in British India was created there in 1852, with irrigation its main priority.

The vast cost of this was passed on largely to Indians. Canals had to make money, and they did so in several ways: through water rent or irrigation charges; rent from mills that ran on water power; rent paid for watering cattle; transit duties on rafted timber; sale of wood, grass, and other produce from canal plantations; and fines for breach of canal regulations. The face of the taxman and law enforcer was sometimes that of the water engineer; for example, on the Jumna Canals in north India (reconstructed between 1817 and the 1830s), the executive engineer was also the revenue officer and magistrate responsible for protecting the canals.[15] For many rural Indians, irrigation was a central feature of the colonial state.

Despite these charges, profits did not cover expenditure. In Bengal, plans to run minor channels off the main canals into farmers' fields became mired in problems with local property rights. Poor drainage along the Jumna Canals gave rise to filthy swamps, increased salinity, and outbreaks of swamp fever, which the British had to remedy. A malarial epidemic at Karnal in 1843 was blamed on the Western Jumna, and the government set up a committee of enquiry to explore the links between climate, irrigation, and fever. As a result, parts of the canal were realigned and efforts made to improve the offending swamps. Around this time, connections were also made to forest loss; for example, it was noticed that deforestation in Mysore had reduced the amount of water in the Kavery river and raised summer temperatures in Tanjore and Trichinopoly in 1842.[16] Mounting grievances about state-controlled irrigation, and the fever, salination, and increased charges that resulted, helped to stoke opposition to the East India Company that boiled over in the 1857 Rebellion.[17]

---

[15] *Ibid.*, 682.

[16] C. A. Bayly, *Indian Society and the Making of the British Empire, The New Cambridge History of India II: 1* (Cambridge: Cambridge University Press, 1988), 140.

[17] Whitcombe, 'Irrigation', 691–2; Eric Stokes, *The Peasant Armed: The Indian Revolt of 1857*, ed. C. A. Bayly (Oxford: Clarendon Press, 1986).

The Impetus of Famine

A series of devastating famines, mostly following monsoon failure, forced the British to see irrigation in another light and accelerate what they were doing. An 1833 famine badly affected coastal Andhra, and prompted damming and other works on the Godavari River from 1847. There were 800,000 deaths from famine in the North-Western Provinces, Punjab, and Rajasthan in 1837–8. Ten more major famines between 1837 and 1900, exacerbated by disease, affected millions.[18] Famine induced poverty: people tried to survive by selling all their assets, including oxen and farm implements, and were unable to plant crops when rain fell.[19] 'The end is told', a newspaper reported in 1869, 'by the whitening bones lying round every village, over which pariahs and jackals quarrel with birds of prey … In some instances not a soul remains.'[20] The government was concerned not only about widespread deaths but also loss of revenue from failed crops, riots, growing unemployment, and violent crime.

In the 1837–8 famine only the irrigated districts withstood the worst effects of drought. The lesson was clear: more ambitious irrigation was needed to cover a wider area, with the main aim of protecting local people from drought. The Ganges Canal, opened in 1854, was built to irrigate an area of 1.5m acres in the North-Western Provinces. This gigantic feat of engineering was 900 miles long, and the capital costs of more than £3m were raised from loans in London; this was the first of northern India's major irrigation schemes to be built with borrowed cash. Once the Crown took over from the Company, however, irrigation was classified not as 'State Works' but as 'Works of Internal Improvement', which had to be made to pay. The door was opened to private investors who were expected to contribute serious capital for irrigation and share the profits with government. Some officials, including Governor-General Dalhousie, raised concerns about the welfare of poor cultivators, but the door became a floodgate for private capital. Opponents feared this would mean the 'unprecedented and undesirable

---

[18] Appendix 5.2, *Famines in the Indian Sub-continent during 1750–1947*, in L. and P. Visaria, 'Population (1757–1947)', in Dharma Kumar and Tapan Raychaudhuri, *Cambridge Economic History of India*, vol. 2 (Cambridge University Press, 1983), 463–532.

[19] Davis, *Late Victorian Holocausts*, 33.

[20] *Times of India*, 23 January 1869. Cited in *The Indian Problem Solved: Undeveloped Wealth in India and State Reproductive Works: The Ways to Prevent Famines, and Advance the Material Progress of India*, no author or publication date, preface written 1874 (London: Virtue, Spalding & Co.), 32.

creation of rights to private property in water', regarded as incompatible with community welfare.[21]

After the 1876–8 famine, when 5.25m people died and £9.75m was spent on relief, a Famine Commission was set up to look into the history of famines and analyse the effectiveness of relief and prevention programmes.[22] Was irrigation helping or not? The most profitable cash crops and best-quality rice were benefiting, it seemed, at the expense of poorer-quality rice and millets grown in poor upland areas, whose terrain made irrigation difficult if not impossible. As earlier, there was evidence of waterlogging, increased salinity, and sickness in areas around canals.[23] But the Commission, which exonerated the government of responsibility for the famine deaths, concluded that the benefits of canal irrigation outweighed the deficits. The government expanded perennial irrigation across upper India as fast as finances would allow. Two major 'famine protective' projects, the Betwa Canal and the Swat River Canal in the North-Western Provinces, were given the go-ahead in the 1880s. In the same decade the Indian Famine Codes were drafted—the first modern written policy statements, which were to influence future famine relief in the developing world.[24] The acreage irrigated by canals grew by about 50 per cent between 1879 and 1897.[25]

Cultivators were offered land grants to settle along the canals of the western Punjab. The British had massively rebuilt and extended these Mughal waterworks on the Indus from 1885 onwards. 'Canal colonization' had arrived, creating opportunities as well as greater social division. Settlers in the canal colonies were chosen according to 'a strict hierarchical classification of capitalists, yeomen and peasants'.[26] Punjabis flocked to these farming settlements from far afield, displacing cattle and camel herders. Unlike the pastoral nomads they paid tax; by 1915 the Punjab generated more tax revenue for the Crown than any other district in India.[27] Water was siphoned off

[21] Whitcombe, 'Irrigation', 693–5, 710.

[22] R. Guha (ed.), *Subaltern Studies III: Writings on South Asian History and Society* (Delhi and Oxford: Oxford University Press, 1984), 69.

[23] E. Whitcombe, 'The Environmental Costs of Irrigation in British India: Waterlogging, Salinity, Malaria', in Arnold and Guha, *Nature, Culture, Imperialism*, 237–59; McNeill, *Something New*, 160–1; Stokes, *The Peasant Armed*, 138 and *passim*.

[24] David Hall-Matthews, 'Historical Roots of Famine Relief Paradigms: Ideas on Dependency and Free Trade in India in the 1870s', *Disasters: The Journal of Disaster Studies, Policy and Management*, 20/3 (1996), 216–30.

[25] B. M. Bhatia, *Famines in India, 1850–1945* (London: Asia Publishing House, 1963), 198.

[26] Whitcombe, 'Irrigation', 712.

[27] McNeill, *Something New*, 159–60; Stokes, *The Peasant Armed*, 117.

from old inundation canals for the colonies. The irrigated, most productive areas became richer and the rest, including pastoralists, more marginalized.

Despite all the outlay on preventive works, famine continued to strike with a vengeance. By the turn of the century, the British had realized that irrigation was not the cure-all they had hoped for. To millions of Indians, it was in fact a curse. In the 1920s, the government invited Willcocks to advise it on why India was still facing recurrent famine. The answer was unwelcome: he simply referred officials to Bengal's flood irrigation system, and told them the best thing they could do was to learn from the 'natives'.[28] Despite nineteenth-century restoration, he was concerned about the fact that some irrigation works, such as the 3,000-year-old Bengal canals, had become derelict. Though a modernizer, he was also very aware of the value of indigenous practices and technologies, and the damage done to some of them by imperial development priorities. Willcocks emphasized that 'the decay of both health and wealth is due to the fact that the country has been deprived of its rich red flood water'.[29] Under the old system, flood water was able to enter the fields by inundating the canals, carrying with it rich, organic, silty sediments and fish which swam into the lakes and tanks to feed on the larva of mosquitoes. Now the channels were choked with silt, and neither floods nor fish were anywhere to be seen. Having talked to elderly peasants, he wrote:

I have learnt from these men why the peasantry long for the old days when the rice fields and tanks and pools were full of the fish ... They crave for the fish which were the food of the poor in old days, which the poor so seldom see to-day ... I have already said more than once that overflow irrigation combats malaria, enriches the soil and prevents congestion of the rivers which feed the canals.[30]

Willcocks did not suggest an expensive, technological remedy. All that was needed to restore the canals was to level them down and clear them out, though he also recommended building a barrage. 'They are nature's own masterful and cunning handiwork, and need no time spent on surveying and general levelling.'[31] In his 1920s lectures he emphasized that his role in Egypt and Mesopotamia had been that of a 'resuscitator' of ancient systems, made by 'real giants', not an innovator of new works. As in the

---

[28] Agarwal and Narain, *Dying Wisdom*, 29.   [29] Willcocks, *Restoration*, 8.

[30] Willcocks, *Lectures*, 59. He was influenced by his friend Dr Charles Bentley, Bengal's Director of Public Health, author of *Malaria and Agriculture in Bengal: How to Reduce Malaria in Bengal by Irrigation* (Calcutta: Bengal Secretariat Book Depot, 1925).

[31] Willcocks, *Restoration*, 5.

case of forestry, officials were by no means of one mind. Some became aware of alternative management strategies and questioned the domination of nature by all modern means. Willcocks was concerned about rural people's greater susceptibility to malaria once the decline of overflow irrigation led to more standing water and fewer fish. Denouncing Bengal's irrigation department for never having tried its hand at overflow irrigation, Willcocks made the most swingeing indictment: 'The resulting poverty of soil, congestion of the rivers, and malaria, have stalked the canals and banks, and the country is strewn today with the wrecks of useless and harmful works'.[32]

Irrigation in Egypt

ANCIENT SYSTEM OF IRRIGATION

'Thus they do, sir: They take the flow o' the Nile
By certain scales i'the Pyramid; they know,
By the height, the lowness, or the mean, if dearth
Or foizon follow: The higher Nilus swells,
The more it promises: as it ebbs, the seedsman
Upon the slime and ooze scatters his grain,
And shortly comes to harvest.'

Willcocks, quoting Shakespeare, Antony and Cleopatra, ii. 7

MODERN SYSTEM OF IRRIGATION

'Naturam furcâ expellas, tamen usque recurrit'
('You may drive out nature with a pitchfork, yet she will constantly come back')

Willcocks, quoting Horace[33]

Willcocks prefaced his *Egyptian Irrigation* with the conviction that 'without irrigation there could be no Egyptian people, certainly no civilisation in Egypt'.[34] As his excerpt from Shakespeare explains, the Nile floods seasonally, and as its waters fall farmers plant their crops in the rich alluvial soil of the Nile basin. These floods are both a blessing and a curse, a conundrum which generations of Egyptians have wrestled with: it was to Egypt what the

---

[32] Willcocks, *Lectures*, 27.

[33] Title-page, W. Willcocks, *Egyptian Irrigation*, 2nd edn. (London: E. & F. N. Spon; New York: Spon & Chamberlain, 1899). We have added a translation by David Hughes of the second quote.

[34] Willcocks and Craig, *Egyptian Irrigation*, 3rd edn., vol. 1 (1913), xv.

monsoon was to India, something both relied upon and gambled with by cultivators.[35]

The Blue Nile rises in Ethiopia, and meets the White Nile at Khartoum; together they drain nearly the whole of north-eastern Africa, an area of nearly three million square kilometres. Efforts to control the Nile pitted France and Britain against each other in the Sudan at the end of the nineteenth century, and Britain was forced into lengthy negotiations with the Belgians to stop King Leopold II, Germany, and Italy from muscling in on the river.[36] Desire for such control (and hence access to Suez and Britain's oriental empire) was a major impetus behind the British campaign to re-conquer the Sudan in 1898, an expedition described by Winston Churchill in *The River War*. 'The Nile', he wrote, 'is the great melody that recurs throughout the whole opera ... It is the life of the lands through which it flows. It is the cause of the war: the means by which we fight; the end at which we aim.'[37] Churchill's purple prose was itself flood-like, but he suggested in one swollen line Egypt's dependency on waters that originated somewhere else. Waiting for the annual flood, which reached its peak below Khartoum by early September, was a regional occupation. Its arrival only heightened the tension, as a former Egyptian sanitary physician described:

The period of high water is the crisis for the country. The people are in a state of excitement, and 'How much has the Nile risen to-day?' is the daily question of every one who thinks about the future. For, if the overflow is too scanty, a multitude of fields remain uncultivable and fallow ... and the consequence is scarcity, if not actual famine. If, on the other hand, it is too abundant, then it is almost impossible to keep the element within bounds, and great damage is everywhere caused by the bursting of dykes, the devastation of cultivated land ... and the drowning of cattle and human beings.[38]

Willcocks was among those who boosted Egypt's fortunes, at least in the short term. This was in Europe's interests, because Egypt had gone bankrupt in 1876—partly because it had come to depend on foreign loans—and Britain excused her interventionism by claiming to act as a trustee of

---

[35] Ranabir Chakravarti, 'The Creation and Expansion of Settlements and Management of Hydraulic Resources in Ancient India', in R. H. Grove, V. Damodaran, and S. Sangwan (eds.), *Nature and the Orient: The Environmental History of South and South East Asia* (Delhi: Oxford University Press) 88.

[36] R. O. Collins and Francis M. Deng (eds.), *The British in the Sudan, 1898–1956* (London: Macmillan, 1984) 10.

[37] Winston Churchill, *The River War* (London: Eyre & Spottiswood, 1933), 4.

[38] C. B. Klunzinger, *Upper Egypt: Its People and Products* (London: Blackie & Son, 1878), 127.

European interests in Egypt. The British occupation lasted from 1882 to 1914, but the country was never formally annexed by the Crown; it was initially a 'veiled protectorate', which Egypt's rulers had reason to tolerate (see Chapter 14 for a similar situation in late-nineteenth-century Kuwait).[39] It only became a protectorate between 1914 and 1922. Britain invested heavily in irrigation to boost agricultural production, increase the area of taxable land, and make sure Egypt repaid its European creditors.[40] The waterworks contributed to an economic turnaround: export earnings rose by £11m in the decade after 1889, the value of imports doubled, and revenue rose by £4.5m.[41]

From 1883 to 1896 Willcocks restored the Delta Barrages on the Nile (built between 1843 and 1861 but made so poorly they were barely used), drew up the designs and estimates for the first Aswan Dam and the Assiut Barrage (both completed in 1902), managed the Cairo Waterworks, and planned a major drainage project for the city. The irrigation problems he found in Egypt revolved around soils and climate. Nile mud and Egyptian soil were intimately linked, the latter being mainly Nile deposit. With clay soils, the rise of the Nile did not greatly affect the surface of the surrounding country. But where there were sandy soils, as soon as the Nile had risen about a metre above the level of the country, the surrounding fields became stagnant pools. In Upper Egypt, peasant farmers dug wells for summer irrigation, and their water levels rose and fell with the river. Once saturated, some soils seriously deteriorated, and low-lying lands were 'sacrificed' to those at a higher level. Waterlogged soils killed off the roots of crops, and prevented useful bacteria from working. As in India, salination was also a major problem in some areas. In high flood the Nile scoured out its bed, while in low flood it silted up, and since low floods were more common than high ones, silting was gaining dangerously over scouring.

Willcocks's masterwork includes a host of graphs and tables showing the slopes and velocities of the Nile, its depth, the height of its floods, the effective volume of rain in its catchment basins, the average number of microbes per cubic centimetre, evaporation rates, and so on. He described how more than 1.3m Egyptian landowners depended on the river, on 5.4m

---

[39] John Darwin, *Britain, Egypt and the Middle East: Imperial Policy in the Aftermath of War, 1918–1922* (London: Macmillan, 1981), 54, 56.

[40] Alan K. Bowman and Eugene Rogan, 'Agriculture in Egypt from Pharaonic to Modern Times', in A. K. Bowman and E. Rogan (eds.), *Agriculture in Egypt from Pharaonic to Modern Times* (Oxford: Oxford University Press, 1999), 3.

[41] Brown, Introduction to Willcocks and Craig, *Egyptian Irrigation*, vol. 1, xx.

acres of cultivated land, with average landholdings of 3.9 acres. In summer they grew cotton, millets, maize, sugar cane, and rice. In winter, the main crops were clover, wheat, beans, and barley. Principle exports were cotton, cereals, and until 1890 when its cultivation was banned, tobacco. (After the ban, cigarettes made from imported Chinese and Japanese tobacco were a key export.)

The most important export crop was long-stapled cotton (*Gossypium barbadense*)—a species with longer threads than those grown in India and elsewhere, which commanded higher prices because it could be spun into stronger, finer, silkier thread. Average annual production rose steadily between 1860–4 (nearly one million cantars) and 1885–9 (nearly three million cantars), but spurted in the 1890s to reach six million cantars by the end of the decade (1 cantar = 44.928 kg). Owen attributes this in part to 'near-continuous' improvements in perennial irrigation, which meant the young plants could be watered throughout the summer when the Nile was at its lowest level. Also, cotton growers gained more access to seeds, credit, ginning, transport, and marketing, and could get higher returns than for any other crop. The area under cotton more than doubled between the early 1880s and 1912, covering just over 20 per cent of the country's fields by the end of the nineteenth century.[42] Since 1820, British companies had played a role in the mechanization of ginning Egyptian cotton production, and dominated this industry.[43]

Agriculture was a hostage to floods and drought, which in bad years led to a massive loss of revenue; after the flood of 1877 nearly one million acres remained uncultivated, causing a loss of more than £1m.[44] In years of low flood, water levels had to be raised artificially. Before mechanization, water was raised and brought to the fields from canals using waterwheels and *shadoofs*, a simple bucket-and-pole system. Settlement followed irrigation, but population numbers had risen more rapidly than cultivation and the peasants had only been saved from calamity, said Willcocks, by the great rise in the prices of exported goods, mainly raw cotton. At this time, Egypt first started importing foodstuffs—her people could no longer feed themselves.

---

[42] Roger Owen, 'A Long Look at Nearly Two Centuries of Long Staple Cotton', in Bowman and Rogan, *Agriculture in Egypt*, 348–51.

[43] Ghislaine Alleaume, 'An Industrial Revolution in Agriculture? Some Observations on the Evolution of Rural Egypt in the Nineteenth Century', in Bowman and Rogan, *Agriculture in Egypt*, 341.

[44] Willcocks and Craig, *Egyptian Irrigation*, vol. 1, 312.

The Egyptian system of basin irrigation involved building dykes to enclose basins that were seasonally flooded. The British aim was to bring perennial irrigation (initiated in Egypt by Muhammed Ali in the first half of the nineteenth century) to the whole of the Nile Valley. This meant irrigation from canals that flowed all year round, instead of relying on floods. Basin irrigation only allowed one crop per year, while canals permitted multiple cropping. By 1913, just over four million acres had been brought under perennial irrigation. Since the building of the Aswan reservoir alone, more than 400,000 acres of 'basin land' had been converted in this way. Lessons learned in India were applied in Egypt.[45]

All this required juggling acts, and sometimes the sacrifice of one crop to another. There was a constant battle with cotton boll worm, which thrived in damp and humid conditions and 'wreaked havoc' in the cotton fields. The trick was to keep the fields dry and the plants hard and fibrous during June and July, a critical time in the worm's life cycle, and to irrigate clover upon which worms fed until the young cotton plants were ready. Following Willcocks's advice, the Khedive issued two decrees in 1911 to ensure that this happened.[46]

The cost was enormous. The Delta Barrages and canal heads (completed in 1861) cost £4m, and had to be expensively repaired in the late 1880s.[47] The first Aswan Dam cost £2.4m. However, overall production increased because cultivable land had been greatly extended; in this sense Egypt as a whole was an economic beneficiary, and the state's investment—partly recouped in tax revenue—could be seen as worthwhile. There were winners and losers, and some sections of the population benefited more than others.

The British initially took over the corvée system of forced labour by fellahin or peasants. Willcocks believed the abuses which had always accompanied the system worsened once perennial irrigation was introduced. These included forcing all agricultural labourers to do canal clearance, and moving them from province to province. Corvée took farmers away from their own fields at times of year when they most needed to tend them. Willocks considered this hard labour analogous with the building of pyramids. He condemned corvée as torture, and graphically described watching 'thousands of naked

---

[45] *Ibid.*, vol. 2, 662.

[46] *Ibid.*, vol. 1, 413–14.

[47] The Delta Barrages were the first of their kind in the world. Their function was to stop the flow of the river, raise the water surface, and enable the river to feed the canal at a much higher level so that canals, in summer, were not dependent for their discharge on the level of river water. Willcocks and Craig, *Egyptian Irrigation*, vol. 2, 630 ff.

labourers struggling through slush and mud to clear canals'.[48] He vowed to end the system by the time his five-year contract was up, and did so by 1889. It was replaced by contract labour.

As in India, Willcocks was quick to criticize European as well as Egyptian malpractice and what he saw as the negative impacts of imperial intervention. Such non-conformism was regarded as dangerous, and consul-general Lord Cromer forced him to sign a statement promising not to write anything critical while he was still an employee of the Egyptian government. He later wrote: 'When I left the Egyptian service in 1897 I took my revenge on my long abstinence and wrote on every subject under heaven.'[49] He forfeited promotion by standing up to Cromer, and sometimes disobeying him.

However, he continued to work in the colonial service, went on to report on irrigation in South Africa, and spent 1908–11 in Mesopotamia as adviser to the Turkish government, designing projects to control the Euphrates and Tigris and irrigate three million acres. Willcocks's *Plans of the Irrigation of Mesopotamia* map in fantastic detail dozens of canals, drains, and banks ringed by desert, through which these mighty rivers snake.[50]

Some Effects of Irrigation

The extreme effects of high and low floods were mitigated by various hydraulic improvements. But the British engineers have been accused of being far less successful at providing drainage than 'new water', a failure that led to increased waterlogging and salinity.[51] In the twentieth century, more money had to be spent on drainage than on building the Aswan High Dam.[52] Scholars argue that the spread of perennial irrigation incurred major environmental and social costs that included a growing dependency on export cash crops, particularly cotton, at the expense of subsistence food crops; the breakdown of village communalism and cooperation in the local management of water; the gradual replacement of communally held land with private landholdings; a move towards large estates owned by wealthy individuals and companies, many of them foreign; and higher taxes which had to be paid in money, not kind. The pink boll worm began to cause great damage to the cotton crop after 1900, and together with waterlogging and

---

[48] Willcocks, *Sixty Years*, 89–90.   [49] *Ibid.*, 116–18.

[50] Willcocks, *Plans of the Irrigation of Mesopotamia* (London: E. & F. N. Spon; New York: Spon & Chamberlain, 1911).

[51] Owen, 'A Long Look', 350.   [52] Bowman and Rogan, *Agriculture in Egypt*, 4.

increased salinity, this led to a 'significant decline in yields just before the First World War and continued to provide a brake on development for the rest of the twentieth century'.[53] By the end of the nineteenth century, these were among the factors that had led to deepening poverty, landlessness, and ill health among peasants, who had become chronically indebted to moneylenders.[54]

This picture, particularly the emphasis on an earlier communal management of water, does not entirely square with the evidence about pre-British coercive irrigation systems. Also, some scholars claim that domestic food supplies were not in fact jeopardized by export cash crops; Egypt could consistently produce 'enormous surplus'.[55] In this view, the decline in wheat and beans was linked to foreign competition 'and not from a devilish design on the part of the British to starve the Egyptians by misdirecting all their energies to cotton production'.[56] Agricultural production increased as a result of land reclamation, and was largely sustained into the twentieth century—apart, for example, from the fall-off in wheat and sugar production in 1943 following a malaria epidemic.[57]

However there is little doubt that the expansion of irrigation encouraged the spread of environmentally related and waterborne diseases into previously uninfected areas. A 1913 survey by the Rockefeller Foundation found that about 60 per cent of the population of Egypt was infected with bilharzia, hookworm, the relatively mild non-falciparum malaria, and other parasitic diseases. The high prevalence of malaria in Lower Egypt was confirmed by another survey in 1939. The following year, leading Oxford-trained physician and professor of hygiene Abd al-Wahid al-Wakil (see Chapter 10 for his work on plague) claimed that 15 per cent of the whole population suffered from malaria, and 75 per cent from bilharzia.[58] When mosquitoes carrying falciparum (malignant) malaria invaded the country in 1942, they 'flourished in the new irrigation regime' and killed some 130,000 Egyptians.

[53] Owen, 'A Long Look', 350.

[54] R. O. Collins and R. L. Tignor, *Egypt & The Sudan* (New Jersey: Prentice-Hall, 1967), chs. 1 and 4; Gabriel Bahr, *A History of Land Ownership in Modern Egypt, 1800–1950* (London: Oxford University Press, 1962).

[55] Bowman and Rogan, *Agriculture in Egypt*, 4–5.

[56] C. Issawi, *Egypt: An Economic and Social Analysis* (London: Oxford University Press), 26–7.

[57] Nancy E. Gallagher, *Egypt's Other Wars: Epidemics and the Politics of Public Health* (New York: Syracuse University Press, 1990), 6–15.

[58] *Ibid.*, 33–4; McNeill, *Something New*, 205.

In the long term, the twentieth-century irrigation works that built upon what the British imperial engineers had begun have had devastating environmental consequences for Egypt and the entire region. These include salinization, a heavy reliance on chemical fertilizers to replace silt (now stopped in its tracks by the Aswan Dam), the shrinking of the Nile Delta, the destruction of sardine and shrimp fisheries, the upset of Mediterranean waters and biotic species, the corrosion of ancient monuments, the flooding of Nubian villages in the Sudan, and an explosion of water hyacinth which clogs up waterways and harbours the snails that carry schistosomiasis (bilharzia). Infection rates shot up in rural communities.[59]

To Conclude

Water was increasingly regulated and commodified by British colonial administrations. Some supplies had been dominated by pre-colonial powers, but not transformed into a commodity in quite the same way, nor articulated to transnational systems of production and consumption (of cotton, rice, indigo, opium, and other export crops) that in turn transformed, and left deep marks upon, environments and societies. A major aim of irrigation in India was both to feed the people, and in Arthur Cotton's words, to free up labour which could be put to work 'in raising whatever their country is best suited to produce for foreign countries'.[60] In spatial terms, irrigation works formed networks that profoundly altered physical space. Cultivation expanded, 'wastelands' were reclaimed, but roaming pastoralists lost out to settled cultivators, while new canals rode roughshod over local property rights. Local elites did well out of irrigation and coalesced around it, forming human networks empowered by the British to extract revenue and police the peasants on their behalf; individuals were often rewarded with land titles.[61]

Irrigation ultimately helped to change the political landscape, too; for example, 'profitable irrigation in the Punjab, both in Pakistan and India' led to 'water [becoming] valuable enough to add to the friction between the two countries'.[62] On the Nile, regional water wars intensified through the twentieth century and into the twenty-first, as Willcocks forewarned. The battle for control of the river has been spurred by urbanization and

---

[59] McNeill, *Something New*, 170–3.   [60] Singh, *Taming the Waters*, 37.

[61] David Ludden, *An Agrarian History of South Asia*, *The New Cambridge History of India* IV: 4 (Cambridge: Cambridge University Press, 1999).

[62] McNeill, *Something New*, 160.

population growth—today an estimated 160m people in ten countries depend on the Nile and its tributaries. Some states in the region, such as Tanzania, have increasingly challenged Egypt's hegemonic share of the waters, safeguarded in the Nile Water Agreement of 1929, drafted by Britain on behalf of its colonies and hotly resented by their successors.

As was the case with scientific forestry, and the physicians and bacteriologists involved in tackling plague (Chapter 10), the water engineers 'increasingly drew on an international discourse' generated by fellow professionals and the institutions established in this era.[63] Important networks of knowledge were created, whose legacy was long lasting. As in other parts of the Empire, forced attempts at land reclamation and agrarian 'betterment'—in this case using irrigation—sometimes backfired, triggering resistance. Engineers were handmaidens of capitalist enterprise, charged with turning a profit from water; their conservationist concerns were bound up with efficient and effective long-term use of this key resource. As with forestry, and other fledgling sciences, this demand sometimes led to profound tensions between individual officials and the state—evident in many of the exchanges between Willcocks (avowedly more concerned with peasant welfare than government wealth) and his superiors.

[63] Gilmartin, 'Models', 211.

9

Colonial Cities: Environment, Space, and Race

Colonial Cities in the Imperial Environment

Colonial cities have dotted our narrative as points on the emerging map of imperial commodity extraction or as centres of transport and administration. In this chapter, the first to adopt a synthetic overview approach, our attention turns specifically to urban zones, their changing role in the emerging spatial and environmental history of empire, and the character of their built environments. Cities will also be a specific focus in discussing the environmentally linked disease of bubonic plague (Chapter 10).

Cities transform, sometimes obliterate, nature in their immediate environments. Such urban concentrations have also acted as hinges for the broader process of environmental and social change across large swathes of land described in the first half of this book. Cities, as human creations, sometimes seem to have 'broken from nature'.[1] Yet the rise of many colonial cities was intimately connected with the changing relationships between people and nature in the regions they touched. We will argue that their environmental boot-prints were varied and hybrid in character, but in part moulded by specifically British planning and styles.

British trade, shipping, and planning helped to plant the kernel of new cities across the globe. Of the fifty largest cities in the world by the early twenty-first century, fifteen had at least partial roots in the British Empire, and if US cities founded in the colonial period are included (New York, Boston, Philadelphia, and Washington), the total is nineteen.[2] British imperialism may not, alone, have been 'the greatest creator of towns' but urbanism was surely one of 'the most lasting of the British imperial

---

[1] Cronon, *Nature's Metropolis*, 14.

[2] <http://www.citypopulation.de> uses 'urban agglomerations' as the basis; <http://www.citymayors.com> has a different order, and includes both greater urban areas (with some gaps) and delimited municipalities, based on UN figures.

legacies'.[3] Nine of those fifteen are in areas of South Asia which fell under British control; three—Cairo, Lagos, and Johannesburg—are in Africa.

Imperialism also contributed to the rise of British ports and manufacturing towns, and the growth of London. London was the largest city in the world at the height of the British Empire between the 1820s, when it overtook Beijing, and 1925, when it was overtaken by New York. Its population expanded from about 1.3 million in 1825 to a height of nearly 9 million around 1950.[4] It dwarfed the other European, metropolitan, imperial cities of its era, notably Paris, Vienna, and Berlin, as well as those which had grown in earlier phases of European expansion, such as Madrid and Lisbon.[5]

The term 'colonial city' should not disguise the diversity of urban concentrations in the British Empire. Some, such as Delhi, Cairo, or Zanzibar, pre-dated British trade and conquest; in these places, colonial growth was spliced onto pre-colonial roots. In Australia, New Zealand, and Canada, most cities were long dominated by descendants of English-speaking Europeans, but elsewhere urbanizing indigenous communities or non-British immigrants, such as the Chinese in Singapore and Penang, rapidly became demographically predominant. Even those cities dominated by British people were forging their own demographic and social identities. We should also be cautious about seeing colonial cities as young, fresh upstarts of the urban world. Some trading entrepôts of the Americas and Asia, such as Boston, Mumbai, and Kolkata, were established when the manufacturing centres of Birmingham and Manchester, which became England's second and third largest conurbations, were but villages. These colonial ports grew together with the industrial cities of Britain.

The location of many early colonial cities was initially shaped by the maritime character of the British Empire. Water-borne transport remained the cheapest form of moving commodities up to the late nineteenth century: it created the opportunities for expansion, and knitted the Empire together. It is striking how little emphasis is placed on these points in key overviews of the city in history.[6] Robert Home, who floats the idea of imperial cities

    [3] James Morris, *Stones of Empire*, quoted by Robert Home, *Of Planting and Planning: The Making of British Colonial Cities* (London: E. and F. N. Spon, Chapman & Hall, 1997), 1.

    [4] <http://www.geography.about.com/library>.

    [5] Felix Driver and David Gilbert (eds.), *Imperial Cities: Landscape, Display and Identity* (Manchester: Manchester University Press, 1999).

    [6] These tend to be focused on the ancient world and Europe: Lewis Mumford, *The City in History: Its Origins, its Transformations, and its Prospects* (London: Secker & Warburg, 1961);

as thalassocracies, is an exception.[7] Ports were funnels for the commodities extracted from colonial hinterlands, for manufactured goods pouring out of industrial Britain, and for cross-Empire trade. They serviced imperial shipping itself, on its long, fragile routes across the globe. Their urban economies and communities were thus interconnected, sometimes more closely than with their respective hinterlands. Some were sited largely for their naval or military advantages and were at the centre of an exchange of military personnel. Because movement to and from Britain, and through the Empire, was largely dependent upon shipping, the ports were conduits for mobile people: imperial armies, settlers, slaves, indentured workers, traders, and bureaucrats. As the key nodes of supply and communication back to Britain, they also often became administrative centres, and they were the routes to far-flung, inland official and military posts.

No part of the coastal world was beyond the reach of shipping by the eighteenth century, but the scale of growth of each particular port depended on its locus in this global map of finance and exchange, as well as the societies and commodities it was servicing. Ports mapped expanding British trade and naval power. Boston, New York (1664, originally Dutch), Montreal (1760, originally French), Bridgetown, Barbados and Kingston, Jamaica (1692) were seventeenth-century products of the early Atlantic economy trading fish, furs, sugar, and slaves. Although the value of Caribbean sugar exports was comparatively high in the seventeenth and eighteenth centuries, no major city emerged on an island under British control. This applies even to Jamaica around 1810, when it was the world's largest sugar exporter, and produced 30 per cent of traded coffee.[8] Island hinterlands were spatially restricted and each needed to develop its own harbour. None rivalled Cuba's Havana, which became a major administrative and religious centre for the Spanish Empire.

In South Asia, Madras/Chennai (originally Indian, 1639), Mumbai (Portuguese, 1665), and Kolkata (1690), were at the heart of East India Company operations prior to conquest. West Africa had indigenous urban concentrations in the interior, but for the reasons suggested in Chapter 2, acquired forts

Peter Hall, *Cities in Civilization* (London: Weidenfeld & Nicolson, 1998); and John Reader, *Cities* (London: William Heinemann, 2004). The comment applies also to books with a wider focus such as Anthony D. King, *Colonial Urban Development: Culture, Social Power and Environment* (London: Routledge & Kegan Paul, 1976) and Aidan Southall, *The City in Time and Space* (Cambridge: Cambridge University Press, 1998).

[7] Home, *Of Planting and Planning.*

[8] Porter (ed.), *Atlas of British Overseas Expansion*, 63.

rather than colonial ports in the era of the slave trade.[9] Freetown, Accra, and Lagos became nodes of imperial influence in the nineteenth century, after abolition, in the era of legitimate trade and formal colonialism. Gibraltar was taken in 1704, and Malta in 1800, to secure routes through the Mediterranean. Cape Town (1806, originally Dutch), Port Louis (1810, Dutch and French), and Durban (1824) marked British determination to command sea-routes to the East during and after the Napoleonic wars, as well as growing South African trade. Penang, Singapore, Hong Kong, and Rangoon were founded or expanded by British trading companies as they penetrated South-East and East Asian markets from the late eighteenth century. Sydney, Melbourne, Adelaide, and Christchurch were established to service antipodean settlers, including wool exporters.

Imperial (metropolitan) cities are sometimes distinguished from colonial, yet as noted they were interconnected. Glasgow in Scotland developed particularly strong imperial links. Although it had monastic and medieval origins, including an ancient university, it rose to prominence on the back of the American tobacco trade in the eighteenth century.[10] The city housed about 24,000 people in the 1760s, when James Watt began his experiments with steam engines there.[11] Matthew Boulton manufactured the engines and by 1825, Glasgow boasted 310, in textile mills, pits, and steamboats. Coal and iron ore deposits nearby cemented its advantages and it became the centre for building metal, steam-driven, and screw-propelled ships: the 'art of boiler making', Peter Hall notes, 'led to the art of iron shipbuilding'.[12] As the Suez Canal (1869) confirmed the advantages of steam for eastern routes, and steel replaced iron, so the Clyde and Glasgow dominated shipbuilding, and quickly displaced wood and sail, at the peak of British naval domination in the second half of the nineteenth century.

Steam-engine technology was expanded to railway locomotives, and engines from Glasgow carried the freight of many colonial countries. Iron-works were exported throughout the Empire. For example, as Malaysian museum guides now proudly point out, MacFarlane's in Glasgow supplied the unlikely ornate, iron pillars for the Chinese-style mansion of Cheong Fatt Tze, the leading shipowner in Penang in the early twentieth century.[13]

[9] David M. Anderson and Richard Rathbone (eds.), *Africa's Urban Past* (Oxford: James Currey, 2000).

[10] John MacKenzie, ' "The Second City of the Empire": Glasgow—Imperial Muncipality', in Driver and Gilbert (eds.), *Imperial Cities*, 216.

[11] Hall, *Cities in Civilization*, 350.   [12] *Ibid.*, 353.   [13] Visit by Beinart, January 2004.

Glasgow was the home of Lipton's tea company, which also owned plantations in Sri Lanka. The city grew tenfold between 1801 and 1911 (800,000 people) into the largest in Scotland, and the third largest in the United Kingdom, as the kingpin of the revolutionary new maritime fleet.[14] It was the second port in Britain, after London. Glasgow, MacKenzie argues, like other imperial ports, evinced a combination of grandiosity and poverty.

Within the Empire as a whole, Hong Kong catered for the largest tonnage of shipping at the time, but had a relatively small population. By 1911, Kolkata (1.7 million) and Mumbai (1 million) had overtaken the population of all British cities except London. Mumbai's imperial rulers and Indian middle class aspired to rival British cities and, with increasing trade, manufacture, and monumental Victorian architecture, it was compared both to Liverpool and Manchester. The city's planners also had great ambitions for the sewerage system, although it never won the 'sanitary race'.[15]

Cities, Natural Resources, and Commodification

In his urban environmental history of Chicago, William Cronon evolved a model of the city at the centre of a web of commodification.[16] The city sucked in natural resources and raw materials, consumed or processed them, and spewed them out, along newly developed transport routes. Chicago was also a hub of machinery, which helped to transform the surrounding countryside, socially and environmentally, from buffalo plains to rangeland, and then to grain-producing homestead farms. Some of its wealth came from the natural bounty of the indigenous forests to the north, easily floated down the rivers and southwards across Lake Michigan: 'axes and saws bit the bark of century-old trees, stimulated by this city's energy'.[17] Timber was treated in giant sawmills to become railway sleepers and building materials for North America's most rapidly growing city. By the 1850s, Chicago was the single largest timber market in the world and its vast yards were imbued with 'an aroma of pine mingled with the smell of sewage from the river'.[18] Meat from cattle that converted the rangeland grasses to human food was processed in industrial pack-houses and, when refrigeration became available, transported along railway routes to cities across America.

Colonial cities do not always fit comfortably into this model. Certainly many ports, whatever their other functions, handled commodities and

[14] MacKenzie, 'Second City', 218.   [15] Home, *Of Planting and Planning*, 73.
[16] Cronon, *Nature's Metropolis*.   [17] *Ibid.*, 4, 150.
[18] *Ibid.*, illustration between 168 and 169.

6. Warehouses and boats, Weld Quay, Penang.

Credit: Khoo Salma Nasution and Malcolm Wade, *Penang Postcard Collection, 1899–1930s* (Penang: Janus, 2003).

provided markets; in that sense they transformed their hinterlands. But the degree of processing and manufacturing, along the lines described by Cronon, was uneven. As sugar had to be crushed immediately after the cane was harvested, the mills it spawned tended to be near plantations rather than in the ports. Settler-farmed wool was increasingly exported in the 'grease', hardly treated; the washing and scouring of this product on farms and in local factories had largely ceased by the end of the nineteenth century. Most textile production was located in Britain and Europe rather than the colonial ports. Similarly the imperial economy sucked in unprocessed peasant-grown staples, such as cotton from Indian, palm oil and cocoa from West Africa.

This colonial relationship affected the spatial structure of colonial cities, their environments, their workforces, and their housing. In the nineteenth century, at least, most colonial ports were cities of warehouses rather than factories. By the early twentieth century, this pattern was changing quickly. Indian cities developed their own industrial capacity, despite the competition with Britain. Kolkata jute mills employed close on 200,000 people and Mumbai's cotton mills also grew rapidly over the next few decades. In the longer term, many ports developed significant manufacturing capacity, sometimes, but by no means always, in areas related to their commodity exports.

The extraction of minerals also spawned urban development. The Witwatersrand was probably the single most significant conurbation built around mines, reflecting the value of this gold deposit as the largest mineral treasure trove in the British Empire. In many other contexts, however, the short-lived character of mineral booms, the relative dispersal of mining activities, or the existence of an expanding port or administrative centre nearby, militated against the growth of large mining cities. Ballarat, the Australian gold-mining centre in Victoria, is a case in point; its gold exports were briefly more valuable than wool in the 1850s but output could not be sustained. The population of Victoria grew from about 80,000 to 540,000 between 1851 and 1861, far faster than the Witwatersrand half a century later.[19] But the majority of these people did not establish themselves on the goldfields. Similarly, the late nineteenth- and early twentieth-century tin-mining boom in Malaysia, which helped to can so much Empire food, took place in widely dispersed locations, away from the coast. The towns it produced, such as Taiping and Ipoh, did not rival Singapore, Kuala Lumpur, and Penang—which also became rubber ports. The gold-mining industry in Zimbabwe was scattered, and the works developed separately from the cities of Harare and Bulawayo. Surprisingly few major colonial cities were specifically located around mines.

Founded in 1886, following the discovery of gold in the Transvaal, Johannesburg's population climbed to a quarter of a million by 1914.[20] Along with oil and rubber, gold became one of the Empire's three most valuable traded commodities in the twentieth century. The geology of this deposit fundamentally shaped patterns of exploitation. Outcrops found on the surface were just the tip of the iceberg. Gold-bearing rock occurred in seams dipping diagonally, underground to the south. The mineshafts had to be sunk deep below the surface. Vast quantities of rock had to be extracted, then pulverized in giant batteries, and treated with a cyanide-based solution to extract the gold.

W. C. Scully, long-serving rural Cape magistrate, saw the dominance of machine over man on the Rand as responsible for the human and

---

[19] Geoffrey Searle, *The Golden Age: A History of the Colony of Victoria, 1851–1861* (Melbourne: Melbourne University Press, 1963).

[20] Charles van Onselen, *Studies in the Social and Economic History of the Witwatersrand, 1886–1914*, vol. 1, *New Babylon* (Harlow: Longman, 1982), 2.

environmental damage wrought by the mines. For him, in 1913, the cost of twenty-five years of underground mining barely justified the wealth that was generated. 'This roaring vortex of passion and greed', he wrote, devoured all before it, working 'without intermission' night and day. The product of mining was unnatural. When gold had been extracted, trolleys tipped the 'crushed earth ... over the summit of the dump in the form of sterile white powder'.[21] Scully thought that the mines would soon be exhausted, and rejoiced in the thought that 'fragile fingers of vegetation may ... veil the nakedness of these livid, monstrous dumps' and the land might revert to a time 'when the wild game moved over its crest in the early morning to greet the rising sun; when those streams of white water from which it took its name flashed down the shallow valleys'.[22] But Scully underestimated the Rand's longevity and wealth. The dumps, strung out along the Witwatersrand, became a distinctive signature in the landscape, almost an object of pride. The urban landscape was by then densely covered by Victorian and Edwardian buildings, distinctively secular, around the market square, finance houses, and stock exchange.[23]

The mines produced acute environmental health problems: 'almost every aspect of the industrial process that evolved in the mining industry prior to World War I ... contributed to the production of tuberculosis.'[24] Fine dust from drills and explosions filled the lungs of both white and black mineworkers. Before the introduction of water-fed drills around 1910, many contracted silicosis, and this diminished their resistance to tuberculosis. Scully saw disease as the penalty for 'machines that tried to conquer their creator, man' so that human life was 'often as much a waste product as is the material forming the dumps'.[25] White miners initially suffered even more than black in that they tended to work continuously for longer periods, while most Africans came as migrant workers for contracts of nine to eighteen months. For 1900–2, the average age of death of Cornish miners who worked on rock drills in Transvaal gold mines was 36 and, of those who died, the average working life on the Witwatersrand was

---

[21] William Charles Scully, *The Ridge of the White Waters* (London: Stanley Paul, 1913), 125–6.

[22] Scully, *Ridge of the White Waters*, 131–2.

[23] Clive M. Chipkin, *Johannesburg Style: Architecture and Society, 1880s–1960s* (Cape Town: David Philip, 1993).

[24] Randall M. Packard, *White Plague, Black Labor: Tuberculosis and the Political Economy of Health and Disease in South Africa* (Pietermaritzburg: University of Natal Press, 1989), 67.

[25] Scully, *Ridge of the White Waters*, 125, 133.

less than five years.[26] By 1912–13, tuberculosis rates of black mineworkers were about double those in the African population as a whole.[27] Aside from the dust, crowded compounds and barracks facilitated the spread of disease. However, after intervention by the state and mining companies, with respect to diet, housing, and underground conditions, rates of tuberculosis were reduced from eighteen per thousand in 1912 to three per thousand in the 1930s.[28] Improved medical screening kept infected African men back in the rural areas, where rates continued to be much higher.

Johannesburg required large quantities of food, more than could be provided initially by local agricultural production. The gold mines were developed in the railway era and provided an immediate target for the Cape Colonial and Natal systems. Very soon the city had access to foodstuffs from a global market, including grains from Argentina and Canada. Like Chicago, Johannesburg also provided a spur to agricultural modernization in its immediate hinterland. Lord Milner's post-South African War reconstruction government (from 1902), and the Union Department of Agriculture (from 1910), helped to transform settler farming so that by the interwar era, the city relied very largely on South African produce. Unlike many other colonial mining towns, Johannesburg's economy diversified, underpinning an increasingly sophisticated industrial base.

Mining and rapid urban development created specific environmental pressures, not least a huge demand for water. An early visitor to Johannesburg noted the 'absence of a convenient river; indeed paucity of the water supply (one and sixpence a small barrel being the price paid)'.[29] South African schoolchildren later learnt, perhaps incorrectly, that Johannesburg was the largest city in the world without a river. Water initially had to be collected from the streams and springs located mostly to the north of the mines and there were many competing interests. Concessions were granted to commercial companies which drove up the price. Commercial washeries, manned by Zulu migrants, members of the Amawasha guild, jostled for space at the relatively few streams running near the city until they were displaced

---

[26] Gillian Burke and Peter Richardson, 'The Profits of Death: a Comparative Study of Miners' Phthisis in Cornwall and the Transvaal, 1876–1918', *Journal of Southern African Studies*, 4/2 (1978), 147–71.

[27] Packard, *White Plague, Black Labor*, 74.   [28] *Ibid.*, 159.

[29] Maryna Fraser (ed.), *Johannesburg Pioneer Journals, 1888–1909* (Cape Town: van Riebeeck Society, 1986), 9, quoting C. Du-Val, 'All the Worlds Around!!! With Pencil, Pen, and Camera' (1888).

by licensing laws and steam laundries.[30] The mines were particularly thirsty, consuming about half the water supply by the 1910s.[31] A Rand Water Board, established in 1903, centralized activities, rapidly reduced the price, and determined that the Vaal river, 70 km to the south, was the only long-term solution to the water shortage. The attention of imperial engineers was increasingly absorbed by urban water supplies, as much as irrigation. William Ingham, chief engineer, visited Egypt to inspect the Nile works and a Vaal barrage was completed in 1923; it was opened by Prince Arthur.[32] The city's water-supply problems were only solved by the construction of the Vaal Dam in 1938, the largest in the country. It also took many years to develop an underground sewage system. Up to the 1930s, nightsoil was collected by teams of 'bucket boys'—most of them African migrant workers and numbering up to 6,000 at their height.

Johannesburg mushroomed in a regional colonial context where a degree of racial segregation was already entrenched. Initially, as thousands of people from all backgrounds poured into the new town, spatial segregation was blurred. But the prevalence of African migrant labour was one factor in redefining sharper boundaries. The bulk of mineworkers were migrant African men, housed in compounds next to the gold mines along the southern edge of the city and in an arc along the Witwatersrand. The city centre was situated directly north of this industrial zone. Slum-yards occupied by black people close to the centre were cleared in the interwar years. Apartheid Group Area policies in the 1950s finally destroyed black inner-city settlements; people were decanted to Soweto (South Western Townships). The wealthier, white suburbs spread further out, mainly to the north and east.

Colonial cities were not only formed around ports and mines. Administrative and political priorities came into play. Ottawa grew first as a timber-yard. Logging was a winter activity, using sledges on ice paths for transport, till the timber could be tumbled into the thawing rivers. It was chosen as the Canadian capital in the 1860s because it offered a neutral site between Ontario and Quebec, and was further away from American influences than existing colonial cities. Railways and inland transport routes became equally important to the siting of cities and administrative

---

[30] van Onselen, *Studies in the Social and Economic History of the Witwatersrand, 1886–1914*, vol. 2, *New Nineveh* (Harlow: Longman, 1982), 74–110.

[31] Phil Bonner and Peter Lekgoathi, *Rand Water: A Century of Excellence* (Johannesburg: Rand Water Publications, 2004).

[32] Bonner and Lekgoathi, *Rand Water*, 51.

centres. Nairobi, for example, grew into the largest East African urban centre for these reasons, on the back of the railway line, military priorities, settler influx, and Government House.[33] The advent of mass air transport at the end of the colonial era in the 1960s tended to cement the growth of existing urban zones, though it also allowed the ports to be bypassed.

The Urban Environment in Colonial Cities

The urban built environment was shaped by the variety of physical locations, of commercial functions, and of populations. There were no blueprints for planning and it was always a contested area. Some townscapes were influenced by their previous histories of settlement. Yet a significant number of colonial cities, especially in the settler states of the Americas, southern Africa, and Australia were new creations, in which British administrators and settlers had a large hand. Some commonalities can be found in colonial cities amidst the diversity.

Spanish colonial cities, which were among the first, were generally laid out on a rectilinear grid with a central plaza for the market as well as ceremonial and religious events.[34] British colonial cities, boasting wide thoroughfares, emulated them from the eighteenth century.[35] It was a style difficult to impose on older European towns, which had grown from close-knit medieval hearts, with winding narrow streets, and arterial roads probing out, like the strands of a spider's web, to the surrounding countryside. Grids were also sometimes the result of more concentrated political authority, in the hands of a few colonial officials. They required prior control of vacant or public land. Oglethorpe, for example, laid the foundations for a handsome combination of rectilinear treed squares and boulevards in the (then British) mid-eighteenth-century Savannah, Georgia. Kolkata was foremost in imperial grandeur when Lord Wellesley, Governor-General in the 1790s, had a massive new Government House constructed, modelled on a British country manor. A grid was laid around it. This was sharply different to the architecture and environment of the bazaar. Lord Curzon later commented of the project that India was to be ruled 'from a palace, not

---

[33] L. Thornton White, L. Silberman, and P. R. Anderson, *Nairobi: Master Plan for a Colonial Capital* (London: HMSO, 1948).

[34] Southall, *The City*, 255; Reader, *Cities*, 250.   [35] Home, *Of Planting and Planning*, 11–12.

from a counting-house; with the ideas of a Prince, not with those of a retail dealer in muslins and indigo'.[36]

Commerce could in fact be married happily to ordered urban settlement, and the warehouses flanking dockside quays, or retailers in Victorian main streets, were a feature of many colonial cities and often essential to municipal finances. Similarly, the squares at the heart of colonial cities, while they may have symbolically put 'human order on the wilderness', were also functional. They were military centres, transport hubs, showcases for parades as well as venues for sport, equestrian activities, and public pleasure. They were decorated with trees and monuments, largely to monarchs, founders, and military heroes. In the nineteenth century, statues of Queen Victoria were ubiquitous (see Chapter 18).

Raffles in Singapore, William Light in Adelaide (son of Francis, the colonial founder of Penang), and Montgomerie in Rangoon all tried to impose strict planning on the spatial structure of these ports, with areas reserved for the military, commerce, different communities, and compounds for workers.[37] Raffles required a covered five-foot walkway in front of houses to ensure a sheltered public thoroughfare for pedestrians; the style spread to other British cities in South-East Asia. Christchurch, promoted by Edwin Gibbon Wakefield, the advocate of planned settlement in New Zealand, and established in 1850, was modelled on a grid; so were Grahamstown, the first British colonial centre in the Eastern Cape (1812), Pietermaritzburg, capital of Natal, and Ottawa.[38]

Public buildings, even when they were not planned as an ensemble, reflected a British institutional approach.[39] The urban aesthetic of Victorian colonial cities was often dominated by a form of British neo-classicism, including the 'wasted space of useless peristyles and costly detached columns'.[40] Proud, symmetrical, rather squat buildings with columns, porticos, and sash windows spoke of power and government authority, at the physical heart of the

[36] Thomas R. Metcalf, 'Architecture in the British Empire', in Robin W. Winks (ed.), *Oxford History of the British Empire: Historiography*, vol. V (Oxford: Oxford University Press, 1999), 590, quoting Lord George Curzon of Kedleston, *British Government in India*, 2 vols. (London and New York: Cassell, 1925), I, 71.

[37] Home, *Of Planting and Planning*, 70.

[38] Porter (ed.), *Atlas of British Overseas Expansion* for city maps.

[39] James Morris, *Farewell the Trumpets: An Imperial Retreat* (Harmondsworth: Penguin, 1982).

[40] Thomas A. Markus, *Buildings and Power: Freedom and Control in the Origins of Modern Building Types* (London: Routledge, 1993), 292.

colonial city. Churches, sometimes of a different, neo-Gothic, style, provided a focal point for the administrative or settler community. Spired cathedral designs by Gilbert Scott, the prominent Victorian architect, spanned the Empire—from Glasgow to Grahamstown and Christchurch. Alongside or near them lay cemeteries; Anglicans, unlike Catholics, buried next to the church. In Penang and Kolkata there are imposing colonial tombs 'moulded together by age and dilapidation', often with biographical detail, recording anything from arrival to marriage, careers, battles fought, and not least early and painful death from fever. Penang's old city-centre cemetery was, by the early twenty-first century, flanked by busy roads and decaying mansions. A forest of old frangipani trees carpeted the ground with creamy flowers—in this case redolent of tropical rather than English vegetation.[41]

Many of the streets close to the ports in the Asian colonial cities of Singapore, Hong Kong, Penang, and elsewhere were planned as shop-houses where families, largely Chinese, lived and worked or ran small businesses. This allowed for dense settlement, and intense economic activity around the ports without requiring daily, long-distance travel. In Singapore, these shop-houses were largely cleared in post-colonial modernization. But they survive in Georgetown, Penang, some serving their old functions, and, flanked by an exhilarating variety of street-food vendors, catering for a new tourist market. They may be a model for those city planners, like Richard Rogers, who again advocate diversified inner-city economies and dense, mixed, integrated neighbourhoods.[42]

A number of British colonial cities, however, became sharply segregated: spatially, functionally, and racially.[43] Even around docklands, which often housed mixed populations of transient sailors and racially diverse workers in the nineteenth century, patterns changed. As steamships displaced sail, tonnages increased and the demand for dockside coal, water, and cranes developed, so the larger ports were transformed and new massive, concrete facilities were built. As a corollary, inner-city settlement was cleared. City planners were increasingly prioritizing sanitation and disease control. Especially after late nineteenth-century outbreaks of bubonic plague (see next chapter), the 'sanitation syndrome' encouraged physicians and administrators to remove racially defined groups of people, particularly in South

---

[41] Morris, *Farewell the Trumpets*, and Beinart visit.

[42] Richard Rogers and Philip Gumuchdjian, *Cities for a Small Planet* (London: Faber & Faber, 1997).

[43] King, *Colonial Urban Development*; Home, *Of Planting and Planning*.

African cities, who were seen to carry infection. Responses to sanitation and plague were not uniform, however, and did not always result in segregation. Moreover, in colonial cities where domestic labour was cheap, and social expectations high, houses were large enough to accommodate live-in servants. They created their own networks and social geography, complicating the racial and spatial exclusivity of wealthier suburbs. Public spaces could also subvert strict segregation. Racetracks were established in many colonial cities, venues not only for officials and settlers, but also a surprising number of local people. Horses and betting brought diverse races and classes to a shared, if still hierarchical, space.

Robert Home's study of British colonial cities, while strong on ports, suggests that their planners disregarded the traditions of the colonized at least until the early twentieth century. But, as noted above, British architectural imports were already hybrid in style. And Anthony King argues explicitly for the significance of local influences on colonial architecture. For example, the bungalow housing of East India Company military cantonments (large camps) drew partly on indigenous sources and left an enduring legacy.[44] From the late eighteenth century, some of these cantonments covered extensive areas on the peripheries of town settlements, such as Kolkata, with single-storey bungalow housing for officers. The word was derived from bangolo, the peasant hut in rural Bengal. In colonial India, their construction initially depended on local workers, and the earlier versions were sometimes temporary structures using local materials such as mud-brick and thatch. The style was developed in the nineteenth century into open, outward-facing buildings, and wide verandahs on large plots. As they were located on protected military sites, there was no concern for security. Their architecture was in sharp contrast to established Indian urban houses, walled around the outside, with inner courtyards providing light and protected outdoor space.

Bungalows were seen as conducive to health in the tropics.[45] Nineteenth-century medical thinking attributed disease partly to bad air and miasmas, so that space and ventilation were highly valued. Sited away from Indian settlements, military cantonments, and later European civil lines or suburbs, expressed both social and spatial distance.[46] Servants' quarters stood separately on the edge of plots, some way from the main building. Roads,

---

[44] Anthony King, *The Bungalow: The Production of a Global Culture* (New York: Oxford University Press, 1995).
[45] King, *Colonial Urban Development*, 108–54.   [46] King, *The Bungalow*, 35.

carefully maintained, were 'watered, morning and afternoon, to keep the dust at bay' and 'hedges trimmed, so as to set off the bungalows to effect'.[47] Bungalows were adopted by the Public Works Department in the mid-nineteenth century and standardized with flat, fire-resistant roofs. They became the colonial vernacular as an element in Indian urban planning after the 1857 rebellion, when the British government took direct control, and the white population expanded to 120,000 by 1913 (excluding troops). The bungalow became the norm on rural plantations and in hill stations. Similar Victorian houses were being built in the smaller towns and farmlands of Australia and South Africa. In Nigeria also, spacious bungalows were seen as providing the necessary light, drainage, and separation from local people. The 1917 Township Ordinance specified one-and-a-half- to two-acre sites for Europeans with servant quarters along a 'back line'.[48]

Bungalows, culturally hybrid in origin, were vigorous global spreaders in anglophone settler cities, partly by route of Britain and North America. They became ubiquitous as suburban houses, prized by upwardly (and outwardly) mobile communities desiring to escape crowded inner-city squalor. The Indian middle classes also came to favour bungalows. Suburbs consumed urban space and in turn were made possible by comparatively cheap land, and better, more individualized forms of transport, especially cars. Americans, Canadians, Australians, and white South Africans led the world in per capita car ownership by the mid-twentieth century. Bungalows were also associated with the 'modern, informal, individual and artistic houses, suggesting simplicity and style'.[49] They were adopted into new garden cities: the major urban development at Canberra in the 1920s, for example, reproduced 'low-density suburban extensions', with large areas of green space around the urban centre.[50]

Local professionals and skills helped to create other distinctive hybrid styles.[51] In South Africa, Cape Dutch architecture was borrowed and developed by some British settlers; many key examples are from the period after Dutch rule and 'nowhere else in the world did historical accident bring together the Dutch and British colonial traditions so abruptly or

---

[47] King, *Colonial Urban Development*, 120, quoting Mulk Raj Anand, *Morning Face: An Autobiographical Novel* (Bombay: Kutub, 1968).

[48] The term 'townships' was later used in southern Africa for segregated sub-economic developments on city peripheries for blacks.

[49] King, *The Bungalow*, 154.   [50] Powell, *An Historical Geography*, 177.

[51] Markus, *Buildings and Power*, 23.

so completely'.[52] Herbert Baker absorbed the style in some of his late nineteenth-century projects, notably Rhodes's urban Prime Ministerial residence, Groote Schuur (the big barn). For large buildings in India, architects tried to develop a Saracenic style that again drew local motifs into modernist building. The Cheong Fatt Tzee mansion in Penang, with its ornate art deco stained-glass windows and imported Glasgow ironwork, nevertheless incorporated elements of Chinese layout, guided by the principles of feng shui, including a large hallway with ornate screen.

The public streetscapes of colonial cities included not only churches but also richly varied places of worship. The Empire provided an umbrella for Chinese, Jewish, and Muslim migration so that mosques, synagogues, and Buddhist temples proliferated in unlikely contexts. Indigenous people came into colonial cities from their foundation. They, and non-British immigrants, brought with them their own ideas of public and private space. City fathers also faced spatial resistance. However the streets had been laid out, however building was regulated, their use depended to some degree on the cultural practices and economic priorities of their inhabitants. Street-vending, street calls, and markets, licensed or not, leant many cities character. Penang's reputation as the street-food capital of the world had small beginnings with Chinese noodle stalls and Tamil immigrants hawking Nasi Kandar (rice and meat or fish) in the late nineteenth century.

Many cities, even those dominated by settlers, were characterized by an eclectic mix of vegetation. Except in North America, most British colonial cities were outside the frost belt and it was possible to grow a subtropical and Mediterranean bricolage of exotics: sweet-scented oleander, hedges of bougainvillea and lantana, and the ubiquitous geraniums, many developed from South African rootstock. Suburban streets were often lined with trees, such as lilac-flowered Latin American jacaranda, and parks echoed nineteenth-century British concerns about the need to create public spaces for environmental health and recreation. Some of these were the outgrowths of botanical gardens, established since the seventeenth century in the Dutch, French, and British Empires. While gardens had a commercial and scientific purpose, as botanists tested the commercial potential of plants, this was combined with varying degrees of public access. Cape Town's old Dutch Company Garden was revived by the British in the nineteenth century. Penang's Waterfall Gardens (1884) was a favourite public space for visitors

---

[52] Ronald Lewcock, *Early Nineteenth Century Architecture in South Africa: A Study in the Interaction of Two Cultures, 1795–1837* (Cape Town: A. A. Balkema, 1963).

and featured on many postcards.[53] Typically they mixed both indigenous and exotic species—another manifestation of hybridity in colonial cities. The Kalizoic Society in Melbourne, established in 1879 as one of Australia's first environmental movements, aimed at beautifying the new suburbs with a similar diversity of vegetation.[54]

Urban Planning and Urban Environments

Professional urban planning increasingly shaped city environments from the late nineteenth century and brought monumental buildings to new capitals such as Ottawa, Pretoria, Delhi, and Canberra. All of these were compromise administrative sites, chosen to balance the geopolitical interests of rival colonies or regions that had come together in larger states. New Delhi and Canberra were probably the largest projects in the early twentieth-century Empire. Delhi had been a royal centre for pre-colonial Mughal rulers. From 1873, it was the site of the Durbars—great ritual processions that displayed imperial power and Indian princely wealth. But compared with the major ports, it was still a provincial city in the late nineteenth century, separated into an Indian town, military cantonment, and civil station. The urban design of New Delhi is particularly interesting, King argues, because 'its post-1911 development gave the colonial power the opportunity to utilise half a century and more of experience, and to provide what was perceived as the optimum planning solution for the administrative capital of the largest territory of the colonial empire'.[55] As it transpired, Delhi played this role for only a few decades before independence (1947).

Delhi was chosen as the capital over Kolkata in 1911 because of its deep historical associations with Mughal power, its centrality in northern India, and its location at the junction of major railway lines. Construction was entrusted to the British architect Edwin Lutyens who was 'keenly sensitive to the newest developments in the art and science of town planning'.[56] The planning committee chose ground free of major settlement on the peripheries of the city. Lutyens, assisted by Herbert Baker, drew on classical layouts from Rome and Washington, monumental in scale, with avenues radiating outwards to provide vistas for buildings of imperial grandeur.

---

[53] Khoo Salma Nasution and Malcolm Wade, *Penang Postcard Collection, 1899–1930s* (Penang: Janus, 2003), 159–69.

[54] Bonyhady, *The Colonial Earth*, 220.   [55] King, *Colonial Urban Development*, 183.

[56] Robert Grant Irving, *Indian Summer: Lutyens, Baker, and Imperial Delhi* (New Haven: Yale University Press, 1981), 87.

They incorporated new ideas about garden cities, embowered by trees, which emphasized 'air and light and greenery'—bringing the countryside within the city. Wide streets were also seen as hygienic. This element ran parallel with the planning of Canberra by an American architect. Raisina Hill in Delhi, on which key buildings were sited, and the Jumna River, provided effective natural features. Lutyens and Baker self-consciously used high ground to elevate buildings and underline their prominence. Housing and commercial sites were separated from government: 'the enlightened planning and homogenous clarity of the new Delhi formed, to British eyes, a symbolic contrast with the heterogeneous confusion and narrow, twisted byways of the existing city ... A monument to their belief in ordered governance and that elusive but keenly sought goal, progress.'[57]

The effect was somewhat spoiled because Lutyens fought bitterly with Baker over the positioning of buildings, and eventually lost the argument about the centrality of his majestically domed Government House. Its dominance was diminished by the fact that a hill in the major approach road, routed through Baker's Secretariat buildings, obscured the vista.[58] Baker repeated many features of his earlier Union Buildings in Pretoria: the scale, the brown stone, and the neoclassical columns. Lutyens and his colleagues designed over 1,000 bungalows around the government complex to house officials in the comfort expected by the Indian Civil Service. While the public buildings survived, these, and the associated greenery, were rapidly disappearing by the early twenty-first century as denser housing developments took their place.

Alternatives to monumental planning and rectilinear grids were also being canvassed in India. Public housing, in low-rise blocks of flats, was constructed in Mumbai from the late nineteenth century to improve the conditions and health of the urban poor. These chawls became a model for subeconomic public housing in many other cities. Patrick Geddes, influenced by William Morris's socialism, argued from the 1910s that communities, as much as planners, should make their city in order to avoid a dehumanizing, industrial megalopolis. Rapidly growing cities should be developed as 'a succession of village groups, each with its own centre'.[59] 'Town planning', he suggested, must be 'folk planning' as well as 'place planning'; planners should 'keep in view the whole city, old and new alike'.[60] In particular he was critical of the segregationist post-plague interventions: 'the policy of

[57] Ibid., 89.   [58] Ibid., 154.   [59] Hall, Cities of Tomorrow, 246.
[60] Jacqueline Tyrwhitt (ed.), Patrick Geddes in India (London: Lund Humphries, 1947), 9.

sweeping clearances should be recognised for what I believe it is; one of the most disastrous and pernicious blunders in the chequered history of sanitation'.[61] The rats, Geddes argued, would simply move on. Geddes consulted widely in India, and established a base in the industrializing and modernizing princely state of Indore. This was soon also to become home to Albert Howard's agricultural experiments (Chapter 12). Geddes felt Indore could be turned by 'small removals' and 'replannings' into a clean and pleasant town, while preserving the 'old life of the Mohallas and Bazars'.

Geddes's view was not popular with the Indian Civil Service, and he made little direct impact. A friend of his on New Delhi's planning committee did, however, win support from Viceroy Hardinge to modify Lutyens's original plan for 'numerous long straight roads': these were seen to lack visual interest and provide channels for wind and dust.[62] By the interwar years, colonial India was a surprising experimental ground for urban design. Le Corbusier, the arch-priest of modernism, was given the freedom to plan Chandigarh as a new capital for the Punjab.[63] It was his only major project, and perhaps building on this scale required a patron with the authoritarian traditions and financial capacities of the British Raj. He produced a spread-out grid, dependent on motor transport, unsuited to community neighbourhoods, and with housing densities strictly segregated for different social groups. While the quality of housing was high, this was planned segregation by class rather than race, and the irony of Chandigarh's layout, as in the case of other new towns in poor countries, was that it produced a parallel city of informal settlements and traders. As rural people flocked to cities, the environmental problems of slums and peri-urban informal settlements vexed city managers who struggled to maintain a colonial, or modernist spatial order. But elements of that order, in varying and hybrid forms, were a long-lasting legacy of imperial urban environments.

[61] *Ibid.*, quotes from 22, 32, 45.   [62] Irving, *Indian Summer*, 57.
[63] Hall, *Cities of Tomorrow*.

10

Plague and Urban Environments

Our themes have so far been commodity frontiers, the transformation of nature, the beginnings of imperial environmental regulation, and the spatial dimensions of colonial cities. In this chapter we open an interrelated enquiry—into disease, specifically the third pandemic of plague. The link between environments and disease has long been made. By the late nineteenth century, as parasitology and tropical medicine made rapid strides, the precise causes of life-threatening maladies could be identified with increasing accuracy. Ross pinpointed mosquitoes as bearers of malaria and yellow fever; Bruce and others discovered the trypanosome borne by tsetse flies (see Chapter 11). Such discoveries gave environmental investigation and understanding a new urgency. They also provided arguments and scientific rationales for environmental regulation that seemed to offer the possibility of controlling disease. State intervention in controlling disease had a profound impact on some colonial environments, both urban, in this case, and rural (Chapter 11). While environmental controls were conceived as beneficial, both for British and indigenous people, they were also one way in which imperial subjects experienced political and social domination. Medical management of environmentally related diseases was sometimes strongly contested by the colonized. The same dilemma is explored in relation to conservation (Chapter 16).

In a seaborne empire, as we have noted, ports were often critical sites for urban development, and formed the fundamental web of early empire. Cities, especially ports, were also centres of disease. Infections were brought into them, both by ships and from their hinterlands. They provided large concentrations of people in which disease could easily take hold, especially in the absence of efficient sanitation and healthcare. More people were becoming urbanized, living on top of one another in unsanitary and overcrowded conditions that were ideal spawning grounds for new and old infections. By the 1890s, Mumbai, a major centre of infection in India, had about 800,000 people—along with Kolkata this was a new scale of city in the subcontinent. Colonial medical services usually prioritized the protection of governing classes, elites, and soldiers, and managing the urban environment was a critical tool in disease control. In the imperial context, environmental management of diseases—especially epidemics—helped to shape the character and internal boundaries of the city.

Plague is described as an acute febrile, infectious, highly fatal disease whose more common bubonic form is characterized by inflamed and painful swellings of the lymph nodes, or buboes, in the groin, armpits, or neck. It strikes suddenly with chills and fever, and is accompanied by vomiting, thirst, general pain, headache, mental dullness, and sometimes delirium. After three days, black spots (which gave it the name Black Death) may appear on the skin.[1] There are two other forms of plague—pneumonic (transmitted via droplets produced by coughing and sneezing) and septicæmic. All three are fatal without antibiotic treatment.[2] Bubonic plague is a disease of wild rodents that only accidentally leaps to humans via the bites of rat fleas (*Xenopsylla cheopis*), although other fleas can also transmit it. In the etiology of plague, a population of rats sufficiently close to humans must be infected by wild rodents so that, when the former die, their fleas—and the plague bacillus—migrate to people and a new blood meal.[3]

The plague pandemic that began in China in 1894 and encircled the world in the next ten years was the third in recorded history. But it differed in fundamental respects from the other two. The first major outbreak of plague, in the sixth century AD, lasted for more than fifty years, and the second, known as the Black Death, killed more than twenty-five million people—a quarter of the population of Europe—in the fourteenth century.[4] The 1665 Great Plague of London was comparatively minor. What was new about this late nineteenth-century 'plague trail' was how it leapt from one continent to another, on steamships that speedily carrying infected fleas and rats from port to port. Imperial trade was burgeoning, urban centres growing, and imperial railroads snaked across the land. Above all it was seaborne, because rats find

---

[1] *Miller-Keane Encyclopaedia and Dictionary of Medicine, Nursing, and Allied Health*, 6th edn. (Pennsylvania: W. B. Saunders, 1972), 1257.

[2] William H. McNeill, *Plagues and Peoples* (New York: Anchor Press/Doubleday, 1976), 124; *Miller-Keane*, 1257.

[3] Myron Echenberg, 'Pestis Redux: The Initial Years of the Third Bubonic Plague Pandemic, 1894–1901', *Journal of World History*, 13/2 (2002), 434.

[4] A recent study puts the figure much higher, at around 50 million deaths from 1347 to 1353; Ole Benedictow, *The Black Death, 1346–1353: The Complete History* (Woodbridge: Boydell Press, 2004).

ships 'the most convenient way to travel', and can easily scramble on board via mooring ropes.[5] Other factors in its spread included the bigger size of ships (hence larger colonies of rats), the large shipments of grain (which provided food and nests), and the passing of infection from ships' rats to susceptible populations of wild rodents in California, Argentina, and South Africa. Moreover, the medical and official response was uniquely imperial, and involved segregationist controls and other strongly interventionist measures which had less to do with epidemiological requirements than socio-political ones. Everywhere it went, plague triggered a crisis in both state medicine and relations between rulers and subjects. This chapter will follow the trajectory of the infection, and explore the nature and significance of the response.

In 1871 the traveller Émile Rocher described seeing bubonic plague in Yunnan, a western province of China, where it had probably been endemic for at least 100 years.[6] The outbreak followed warfare and famine, and it spread across southern China over the next twenty years via trading routes and troop movements. In 1894 the disease struck Canton, the main port and largest city in southern China, and at least 100,000 people were said to have died by the end of the year.[7] Hong Kong, British-held since 1841, was just eighty miles away, linked to Canton by river traffic. Plague inevitably spread there, but petered out a few months later with the loss of some 3,000 lives. International teams of bacteriologists descended on the port, where a Japanese (Shibasaburo Kitasato) and a Franco-Swiss bacteriologist (Alexandre Yersin) independently discovered the plague bacillus, *Pasteurella pestis* (later renamed *Yersinia pestis*).[8] The two were respectively students of Robert Koch and Louis Pasteur. The following year, Yersin was among the first bacteriologists to successfully inoculate animals with anti-plague vaccine. Yersin spotted the connection with rats in 1894, but few people believed him until a series of confirmatory investigations in India (published 1898), Australia (1900), and South Africa (1902). These challenged and overturned prevalent theories that plague was transmitted

[5] McNeill, *Plagues and Peoples* (repr. London: Penguin, 1994), 120.

[6] W. J. Simpson, *A Treatise on Plague, Dealing with the Historical, Epidemiological, Clinical, Therapeutic and Preventive Aspects of the Disease* (Cambridge: Cambridge University Press, 1905), 48–54; Carol Benedict, *Bubonic Plague in Nineteenth-Century China* (Stanford, CA: Stanford University Press, 1996).

[7] No official count was made and figures are unreliable, according to Echenberg, *Plague Ports* (New York: New York University Press, 2007). For a summary, see Echenberg, 'Pestis Redux'.

[8] L. Fabian Hirst, *The Conquest of Plague* (Oxford: Clarendon Press, 1953), 107.

by air, water, and food. The mechanism of transmission was only fully established in 1908.[9]

The next major stop on the plague trajectory was Mumbai in August 1896. It spread from there to the Bombay Presidency, and then to other provinces. Indian workers were blamed for importing plague to East Africa in the late 1890s—the disease became 'the first passenger on the yet unfinished Uganda Railroad', which its unfortunate victims were building.[10] Between 1894 and 1904 it would also afflict populations along the sea routes of empire in South Africa, South America, California, the Middle East, and Australia. Plague turned up in London's docks as early as September 1896, in a ship that left India before the epidemic had taken hold. It entered Senegal by ship in 1914, killing almost 9,000 people. Fresh outbreaks struck Manchuria in 1911 and 1921.[11] French-controlled Madagascar was infected in 1898 and again in 1921.

By the end of the nineteenth century, the medical profession was in a much better position to develop new knowledge and win 'the race between skills and ills'.[12] Public administrators operated in a context where states were expanding their powers, and new technologies facilitated improvements in municipal sanitation. The plague pandemic came in the wake of cholera and smallpox outbreaks, travelling similar routes. And as with other branches of imperial science, the careers of certain medical practitioners followed the plague trajectory across the Empire. Among them was Scottish-born William Simpson (1855–1931), whose posts included first Medical Officer of Health (MOH), Calcutta (1886–98); Professor of Hygiene at King's College, London, from 1898 to 1923; Medical Adviser to the Government of Cape Colony during the 1901 plague outbreak; commissioner in charge of investigating plague in Hong Kong (1902) and the Gold Coast (1908); and Director of Tropical Hygiene at the Ross Institute and Hospital for Tropical Diseases, London, which he co-founded (1926–31).[13] He wrote a major report, published in 1915, on sanitation and disease in East Africa. Simpson was knighted in 1923 for his services to tropical medicine, particularly his researches into

[9] James R. Busvine, *Disease Transmission by Insects: Its Discovery and 90 Years of Effort to Prevent It* (Berlin and London: Springer-Verlag, 1993), 64.

[10] Davis, *Late Victorian Holocausts*, 201.

[11] McNeill, *Plagues and Peoples*, 156. This also draws on Simpson's global map 'Distribution of Plague from 1894 to end of 1904', in *A Treatise on Plague*, before 75, and R. Pollitzer, *Plague* (Geneva: World Health Organization, 1954).

[12] McNeill, *Plagues and Peoples*, 260.

[13] Simpson, *A Treatise on Plague*, title-page; *Dictionary of National Biography, 1931–1940* (Oxford: Oxford University Press), 812–13.

plague on several continents. His presciptions for plague in some cases led to enforced urban racial segregation.

Plague in Colonial Cities

Hong Kong, the first infected colonial city, boasted giant warehouses that stored merchandise from the provinces, waiting for the ships that would take it overseas. Though the port was only sixty years old, it already had strong trading links with islands in the Pacific and China Seas, India, Australia, Japan, and North America. It was one of the largest in the Empire. More than half China's imports and over one-third of its exports passed through here. Rats thrive in warehouses as much as they do in ships. Hong Kong lacked an MOH and sufficient hospitals, and was totally unprepared in public health terms. The demands of imperial trade had rapidly swollen its population with 100,000 Chinese labourers. Plague dispersed quickly in the unsanitary, overcrowded slums, which had a population density five times higher than the most crowded areas of London.[14] The poorest Chinese workers bore the brunt of this disease; out of 2,552 plague deaths in 1894, 2,514 were Chinese.[15] As elsewhere, these figures only included the hospitalized or those whose bodies were counted; plague was under-reported and actual numbers were probably much higher.

The measures taken to combat it included disinfection and sometimes the razing of houses, isolation of patients and suspects on a hospital ship, house-to-house searches by teams including soldiers and convicts to find and remove the sick; and undignified burial in mass graves under a layer of cement. Many Chinese resisted, or fled. They objected not only to state intrusiveness but also to what they saw as absurd and alien approaches to medicine. There was no effort to catch rats, or to vaccinate, before the early twentieth century. Unlike some other cities, there was no attempt to introduce racially segregationist controls here, and Chinese elites—including hospital directors—blocked isolationist measures in general. However, Europeans saw plague as a 'filth disease' peculiar to the Chinese, and dreaded that it would spread to their enclave.[16] Plague burned itself out after four months, but returned again in 1896.

India suffered worst in this pandemic. Mumbai had been free of the disease for nearly 200 years: 'by many it was considered an extinct disease so

[14] Echenberg, *Plague Ports*, citing J. Dyer Ball, *Things Chinese, or Notes Connected with China* (Hong Kong: Kelly and Walsh, 1903), 537.
[15] Benedict, *Bubonic Plague*, 177.   [16] *Ibid.*, ch. 5.

far as modern times were concerned, and at the most could only prevail to a limited extent among filthy and uncivilised people.'[17] It remained free even during outbreaks in other areas of India earlier in the nineteenth century and when plague was epidemic in Mesopotamia (Iraq) in 1891–2. But there was a link with famine and the social unrest that also surrounded it. In 1896 famine had driven many villagers to Mumbai from the countryside; railways facilitated movement. The city's slums swelled and became 'a particularly receptive environment for disease'.[18] These half-starved people were highly susceptible to plague, and their gaunt faces haunt the pages of doctors' photo albums.[19] Equally, once the city's plague mortality rose, trains, carts and every other kind of transport filled with a reverse exodus of frightened people, accompanied by rats and fleas. Also, the movement of grain aid to famine-affected rural areas in turn ferried rats and fleas from city to village, thereby completing the circle of epidemic. Gandhi later described the railway as a 'distributing agent for the evil one'.[20]

The first cases, mistaken for diphtheria and fever, appeared near the Mumbai docks in August 1896. Large numbers of rats were also seen to be dying, but no one made the connection at this point. Grain merchants began to sicken, too. Indian physician Dr A. G. Viegas officially reported the disease as plague, but was only believed when Russian-born government bacteriologist Waldemar Haffkine reconfirmed the diagnosis in a laboratory. Haffkine, the only full-time bacteriologist in the country, helped to develop a cholera vaccine in Paris in 1892 and went on to develop an anti-plague vaccine in India in 1897. Wherever rats started dying, human plague cases followed. Health officials began disinfecting houses, and forcibly segregating the sick and those suspected of 'harbouring' plague. Indians reacted with hostility, as many Chinese had done in Hong Kong. Simpson wrote: 'People did not and would not understand that the disease was infectious ... Every sanitary measure was opposed. Denunciations and protests were soon followed by active demonstrations of ill-feeling by stoning of the officers engaged in plague work, attacking of the ambulances, and even storming

---

[17] Simpson, *A Treatise on Plague*, 66.

[18] Home, *Of Planting and Planning*, 74.

[19] Sunita Puri, " 'Catching" the Plague: Visual Narratives of the Indian Body, Colonial Power, and Infectious Disease in Bombay, 1896–1897', unpublished M.St. thesis, Modern History (University of Oxford, 2003).

[20] I. J. Catanach, 'Plague and the Indian Village, 1896–1914', in Peter Robb (ed.), *Rural India: Land, Power and Society under British Rule* (London and Dublin: Curzon Press, 1983), 218–20.

of the plague hospital'.[21] After three weeks, compulsory hospitalization had to be suspended. Contemporary writers singled out Muslims as the main objectors to plague controls, one street orator insisting that segregation was contrary to the principles of Islam.[22] But this is challenged by some modern scholars who claim opposition to plague measures came from every class, caste, and ethnic group.[23]

By December the mortality had doubled, and carried on rising until plague reached its zenith in February 1897. Panic set in, shops were closed, and homes abandoned as thousands fled. Stringent new laws were introduced, including the Epidemic Diseases Act 1897, which applied to the whole of India. This marked a major turnabout in British policy towards epidemic disease in India. The change of approach was forced in part by international diplomatic and economic pressure, but the new science of bacteriology and the confidence that accompanied it also came into play. Relatively cautious responses to smallpox and cholera gave way to measures that were now aggressively interventionist.[24] Ships were quarantined, plague committees created in every large centre where the disease appeared, and temporary hospitals and segregation camps built. The sick were forcibly taken from their homes by search parties hunting down plague cases. Private hospitals were set up, catering for different religions and castes; by early 1898 there were more than thirty of them in Mumbai.

Burning down houses, and flooding dwellings and sewers with disinfectant in the mistaken belief that germs produced plague, actually helped to spread it, since rats merely ran elsewhere. Also, with fewer rats around, infected fleas deprived of a blood meal were forced to seek out other mammals.[25] However, environmental plague controls did not lead to residential segregation on racial lines. Europeans—who were relatively unaffected by plague—had lived in separate urban quarters since the eighteenth century; for example, in Chennai (Madras) they congregated around the fort, and there was a separate 'Black Town' for Indians. In the hot season, they fled to the hill

[21] Simpson, *A Treatise on Plague*, 68.

[22] W. F. Gatacre, *Report on the Bubonic Plague in Bombay, 1896–97* (Bombay: Times of India, 1897), 14. He was chairman of the Bombay Plague Committee.

[23] Rajnarayan Chandavarkar, 'Plague Panic and Epidemic Politics in India 1896–1914', in T. Ranger and R. Slack (eds.), *Epidemics and Ideas: Essays on the Historical Perception of Pestilence* (Cambridge: Cambridge University Press, 1999), 203–40.

[24] David Arnold, *Colonizing the Body: State Medicine and Epidemic Disease in Nineteenth Century India* (Stanford, CA: University of California Press, 1993), from 203.

[25] Hirst, *Conquest*, 117.

stations, which were believed to be more hygienic. Mark Harrison points out that urban separation had more to do with cultural preferences. It did not have a sanitary rationale until the 1860s, and there was no attempt to move whole Indian populations within or from cities, even after plague. Once the epidemic had passed, Improvement Trusts were established in the larger cities with the aim—for both sanitary and commercial reasons—of clearing slums, building new dwellings, and making roads (Chapter 9). Boundaries were permeable. European homes housed Indian servants and even military cantonments, often established some miles from major cities, contained significant Indian populations.[26]

The epidemic spread, by sea and land, to Ahmedabad, Pune (Poona), and Karachi, following railway lines, roads, shipping routes and pilgrimages, with rats and fleas travelling alongside humans and merchandise. Between late 1897 and June 1898 there was a second wave of epidemic in the Bombay Presidency, twice as severe as the first. A third epidemic followed, the worst of all, reaching many parts of India. In 1902 plans for mass inoculation were announced, prompting great alarm about doctors being poisoners. The strength of Indian opposition eventually forced the government to change tack and replace coercion with more cooperative measures. By 1903–4 over 1.3 million had died. This was probably underestimated by 20 to 25 per cent, because many people hid their dead and dying or ran away from urban centres.[27] Between 1896 and 1933 more than 12 million people died of plague, and these were only the recorded deaths.[28]

Military Links and Segregation

Plague in South Africa coincided with one of Britain's major imperial conflicts—the South African War, which necessitated moving in half a million troops. The disease struck the ports of Cape Town, Port Elizabeth, East London, and Durban in 1899–1901.[29] Grain and fodder for British

[26] Personal communication with Mark Harrison; Home, *Of Planting and Planning*, 80–1.

[27] Simpson, *A Treatise on Plague*, 71–4. His figures are contradictory. For more reliable statistics see Echenberg, *Plague Ports*; Ira Klein, 'Urban Development and Death: Bombay City, 1870–1914', *Modern Asian Studies*, 20 (1986), 725–54; Arnold, *Colonizing the Body*.

[28] *Miller-Keane*, 1257. Arnold gives 12m by 1930, in *Colonizing the Body*, 202, and in 'Touching the Body: Perspectives on the Indian Plague, 1896–1900', in Ranajit Guha (ed.), *Subaltern Studies V: Writings on South Asian History and Society* (Delhi: Oxford University Press, 1987), 55.

[29] Elizabeth van Heyningen, 'Cape Town and the Plague of 1901', ch 3 in C. Saunders, H. Phillips, and E. van Heyningen (eds.), *Studies in the History of Cape Town*, vol. 4 (Cape Town: University of Cape Town, 1984), 66–107; Maynard W. Swanson, 'The Sanitation Syndrome:

army horses was being imported from Argentina, India, and Australia, and it harboured rats and fleas that carried the bacillus. In March 1900 the SS Kilburn arrived from Rosario in Argentina with a cargo of fodder for the British cavalry. Her captain had died a day before docking in Cape Town and five crew members were ill. The cases were confirmed as plague and a quarantine camp quickly opened at Saldanha Bay, to which all the crew were sent under guard.

The colony had been taking plague precautions since 1899 and the outbreak seemed to be contained. But by September 1900 people were noticing large numbers of rats dying in the Cape Town docks; the affected zone was the South Arm, an area taken over by the military when war began. According to Simpson, who happened to be in the country investigating typhoid among troops and was then loaned to the Cape government by the War Office as plague adviser, new cases were reported among black dockworkers in early 1901.[30] The city, like the other affected ports, was then bursting with troops and refugees fleeing conflict, as well as struggling to cope with a growing population of migrant African workers. Its poverty and overcrowding led Simpson to declare: 'Next to Bombay, Cape Town is one of the most suitable towns I know for a plague epidemic'.[31] He went on:

Cape Town for its size has a very large proportion of filthy slums and insanitary houses ... overcrowded with a heterogeneous population, consisting of natives, coloured people, Indians, Arabs, and whites of almost every nationality. The natives coming direct from their kraals in the native territories to work in Cape Town, being unused to town life, are unable to adapt themselves to their new conditions and crowd together when permitted to an extraordinary degree.[32]

Nearly 100 people were found to be living in one plague-affected house of moderate size. The subtext to his explanations was highly racialized. Similar links had been made by British officials in India.[33] Simpson concluded that clean-living people in clean houses (in other words, wealthier white people) were not at risk, or so the town's citizens were told.[34]

Bubonic Plague and Urban Native Policy in the Cape Colony, 1900–09', *Journal of African History*, 18 (1977); F. K. Mitchell, 'The Plague in Cape Town in 1901 and its Subsequent Establishment as an Epidemic disease in South Africa', *South African Medical Journal*, Special Issue (29 June 1983), 17–19.

[30] Van Heyningen, 'Cape Town', 75.
[31] Simpson, 'Lecture on Plague' (Cape Town, 1901), 8.
[32] Simpson, *A Treatise on Plague*, 191.   [33] *Ibid.*, 180–3.
[34] Van Heyningen, 'Cape Town', 79; Home, *Of Planting and Planning*, 78.

Official concerns about the environmental and sanitary conditions in South Africa's urban areas focused on black people in general as a threat to public health and social order, though anti-semitism also featured. Imported Indian labour was seen as a further potential threat. In 1897, Gandhi—who arrived from India with some 600 passengers on two ships (his first visit had been in 1893)—was blamed by white demonstrators for bringing the plague from Mumbai, as well as swamping Natal with Indians. He was assaulted on disembarking in Durban.[35] Two years later, whites in Port Elizabeth protested at the clearance of ships from plague-infected countries. The *Cape Times* condemned the racial nature of these riots, urging people to de-link the 'anti-Coolie movement' from plague concerns.[36] Nevertheless the authorities swiftly decided that Africans were the main source of the disease, although the number of African cases was lower than among whites or coloured people.[37]

When plague arrived, Cape Town's ruling class, and its Medical Officer of Health, Barnard Fuller, were extremely concerned about the perceived threat to its 30,500 whites. The plague authorities set about removing the city's African population, with some exceptions made for black freeholders and lease-holders, domestic servants, and dockworkers. The first cases and contacts were isolated in a tented camp on the beach, and soon afterwards a 'native location' was created near a sewage farm at Uitvlugt, a few miles away on the Cape Flats. Plague intensified racial segregation in some South African cities. Swanson called it the 'sanitation syndrome', and urban race relations were, he argues, widely influenced by the imagery of infection and epidemic disease. The forced removal was made possible under a Public Health Act, first intro-duced in 1883 after a smallpox epidemic. Between 6,000 and 7,000 Africans were moved to Uitvlugt and settled in lean-tos, huts, and barracks alongside a twenty-bed hospital. Port Elizabeth city fathers pursued a similar policy.

Once plague had waned, hostility grew among Africans, and there were riots at Uitvlugt and unrest in Cape Town itself, where African dock labourers struck in protest at the new controls. In March 1901 mounted police broke up a public meeting called to protest against removals. On several occasions crowds of slum dwellers also tried to prevent plague victims and contacts being removed from houses. Muslims in particular opposed the isolation of patients, and the handling of their dead by non-Muslims. The government

---

[35] Victor Lal, *A Fateful Encounter: H. S. L. Polak (A Jewish Idealist) and M. K. Gandhi (An Indian Nationalist) in South Africa, 1893 to 1914* (forthcoming); Swanson, 'The Sanitation Syndrome', 28.

[36] Van Heyningen, 'Cape Town', 72–3.   [37] Swanson, 'The Sanitation Syndrome', 31.

made some concessions to this community, but threatened to move them to a location if protests continued. People of all races and classes joined together to oppose mass vaccination.[38]

Plague exacerbated and focused racial prejudice. The issue thrown into greatest relief by the epidemic was the position of urban Africans. But although plague contributed towards the emerging segregationist pattern in South African cities, Swanson places too much emphasis on its role in prompting early segregation policies—residential patterns were already partly segregated when plague arrived. And once plague departed, Africans moved back into several city centres, including Cape Town, Johannesburg, and East London. A range of other social forces lay behind the subsequent imposition of urban apartheid.

In Nairobi similar attempts were made, at Simpson's suggestion, to see racial segregation as a partial answer to urban disease and sanitation problems. These had previously been dealt with by burning down the entire, plague-hit Indian Bazaar in 1902, and sections of it in later years.[39] The central plank of his blueprint, the Simpson Plan, was residential racial segregation—an idea previously mooted but not implemented. Public defecation near European housing, and 'the proximity of...natives with their flocks and herds', were seen as 'a constant source of annoyance to the Europeans', according to a Sanitary Commission that reported in 1913. Asian witnesses were no less unhappy about the conditions they lived in, particularly in the bazaar, but they blamed bad drainage and lack of sanitation, not other races.

The commissioners overwhelmingly accepted the need for segregation after Principal Medical Officer A. D. Milne spoke sternly, in relation to malaria transmission, of the 'danger of proximity of races'—and flatly blamed Asians for plague: 'where there were Indians there was plague'.[40] The subtext was official unease at the numbers of Indian migrant labourers who had chosen to stay on in East Africa after building the Uganda Railway between 1896 and 1902 (6,500 of 32,000 remained).[41] At the same time, white settlers were agitating to keep the highlands free of Indian and Jewish people.

---

[38] Van Heyningen, 'Cape Town', 98–101.

[39] Thornton White, Silberman, and Anderson, *Nairobi: Master Plan for a Colonial Capital*, 14.

[40] *East Africa Protectorate: Nairobi Sanitary Commission Report and Evidence* (Nairobi: 1913), 11, 3, 5–6.

[41] Anthony Clayton and Donald C. Savage, *Government and Labour in Kenya, 1895–1963* (London: Frank Cass, 1974), 13.

(They succeeded on both counts, at least in the short term.) Though the 1902 plague outbreak had been blamed on 'importation from India'—there were cases on board ship among migrants—by now it was recognized that the disease had already been present in Kisumu, the railway's northern terminus in Uganda.[42] Milne had gathered oral histories there that indicated it was endemic; in fact, Africans had abandoned the site chosen for the railway headquarters because of plague.[43] Since it was a rural phenomenon in Uganda, and this country was never a settler colony, urban racial segregation was not suggested. Simpson's plan to provide separate quarters for Europeans, Asians, and Africans in every Kenyan town and trade centre was not extensively implemented and was aborted in the 1920s.[44]

Alternative Models

Myron Echenberg demonstrates that Egypt's experience of the third pandemic was different to other parts of the Empire in length, intensity, and both public and official responses.[45] The disease struck Alexandria, one of the busiest ports in the Mediterranean, in May 1899, seventeen years after the start of the British occupation. Members of the 18,000-strong Greek community were the first to succumb, followed by Jews, Syrians, and Egyptians. (Around 15 per cent of the city population of 340,000 was non-Egyptian.) It was over in seven months, with a death toll of forty-five out of ninety-three cases. The reasons for this mildness have been put down to sanitary reforms, started by a French doctor, that transformed the disease environment, and the fact that modern medicine had made the city's residents relatively healthy and resistant to infection. It was believed Alexandria had become a modern city and modern cities did not get plague, but this wasn't entirely true: plague returned annually for the next thirty years, killing nearly 100 people in the worst years. Perhaps more important was that plague measures were quickly implemented with the support of the majority of residents. Apart from a couple of incidents, there was no popular resistance to plague controls. The official response

[42] Nairobi Sanitary Commission Report, 5.

[43] E. N. Thornton, A Report on an Investigation into Plague in the Protectorate of Uganda (Entebbe: Government Printer, 1930), 5.

[44] W. J. Simpson, Report on Sanitary Matters in the East Africa Protectorate, Uganda, and Zanzibar (published by the Colonial Office as African No. 1025, 1915), 53; Milcah Amolo Achola, 'Colonial policy and urban health: The case of colonial Nairobi', Azania, 36–7 (2001–2), 119–37; Andrew Hake, African Metropolis: Nairobi's Self-Help City (London: Chatto & Windus for Sussex University Press, 1977), 129, 176; Thornton White, Silberman, and Anderson, Nairobi, 15.

[45] Echenberg, Plague Ports, chapter on Alexandria.

here was markedly different from some of the other cities we have described because its plague controls did not involve racial segregation, and the authorities were relatively sensitive to local cultural concerns, including gender issues. They gained the cooperation of important Muslim leaders and healers.

The Greek victims were mostly people working in and living above groceries, bakeries, and wine shops, in tenements called *okelles*. But rather than blame this community and its cultural habits, medical experts like epidemiologist Abd al-Wahid al-Wakil surmised that Greeks caught the disease simply because they lived in rat-infested areas and worked in 'trades attractive to rats'. Wakil wrote: 'In Egypt plague does not differentiate between nationalities'.[46] Residential patterns followed class divisions more than racial ones. The Quarantine Commission concluded that plague had arrived via used sacks exported from Mumbai via Suez, but the health authorities preferred to think it had come in Greek merchants' baggage from Jeddah. Either way, once it had arrived, the railway network and Nile boats appear to have played a role in transmission.

The Anglo-Egyptian government had been relatively prepared for plague, sending a public health team to Mumbai in 1897 to study ways of keeping Egypt free. They were mindful of French criticism that the British had 'carelessly imported cholera from India'; there were severe epidemics of cholera in 1883 and 1896. The medico-political tensions kept resurfacing, eminent physician André Proust (father of author Marcel) condemning 'Britain's appropriation of the Persian Gulf and the Suez Canal as its private waterways, and its persistent refusal to cooperate with international sanitary bodies to keep bubonic plague out of Europe'.[47] Moreover, Alexandria had the only modern sewage and water-treatment system in the country, and a public health system established at the behest of Khedive Muhammad Ali (who ruled 1805–48). This pre-dated British occupation, though all the reforms had not been implemented by 1882, and did not apply to all districts.

A long-established Islamic medical tradition existed in Egypt that remained separate from the European biomedical system. Although European doctors looked down upon indigenous healers, and some of their activities were curbed under British rule, their assistance—and that of mosque officials whose duties included keeping health records—was sought when epidemics struck. Local hygiene committees run by women *hakimas*

---

[46] A. W. Wakil, *The Third Pandemic of Plague in Egypt* (Cairo: The Egyptian University, 1932), 161–2.

[47] Echenberg, *Plague Ports*, 79.

(traditional doctors) and religious leaders were closely involved in managing plague, as they had been in earlier campaigns against cholera. In marked contrast to India, Muslim leaders and healers had supported—and oversaw—compulsory vaccination for smallpox from 1890. Such was the reliance of ordinary Egyptians on *hakimas* and *shaykhs*, and their avoidance of western-style hospitals, that the British realized they could not afford to ignore them when combating plague. By bringing these people and other Muslim elites (including Egyptian doctors trained in western medicine, such as Wakil) on board, and allowing them to play key roles, they won the population over. Indeed, Wakil was ahead of many contemporary European plague experts in his thinking. One religious leader and university teacher, Sheikh Muhammad Abdu (1849–1905), was particularly influential. He believed 'science and modernity were compatible with Islam', and said so.[48] Significantly, Egypt was run jointly by the British and an Egyptian elite who could partly shape the outcome of the encounter.

Sydney provides another example of plague responses that did not lead to racial residential segregation as such, though the Chinese community was already living in a virtual ghetto, and was treated separately by public health officials. The epidemic that shook the city in the spring and summer of 1900 was the first of its kind in Australia; Sydney would go on to face nine more by 1922. The number of casualties in these ten outbreaks was low compared with other parts of the Empire—196 deaths in total, and 535 for the whole country in the same period.[49] The disease arrived by ship, and the first case involved a carter who handled goods on the wharves. The outbreak prompted mass hysteria, and the official response included closing off large parts of central Sydney to traffic and pedestrians, house-to-house cleansing and fumigation, the forced removal of nearly 2,000 people into a quarantine station, the demolition of homes and outbuildings, and the mobilization of teams of rat catchers. Citizens were encouraged to burn barrels of tar in the streets to purify the air. Businesses were closed and many traders ruined. Other Australian colonies boycotted goods from New South Wales and quarantined its ships, adding to the financial hardship. And in a repeat of what had happened during the smallpox epidemic of 1881–2, the Chinese community became the victims of 'a virulent campaign of personal abuse and vilification', much of it media-led. Many people believed they

[48] Echenberg, *Plague Ports*, 104.
[49] P. H. Curson, *Times of Crisis: Epidemics in Sydney, 1788–1900* (Sydney: Sydney University Press, 1985), 137.

could catch plague from an infected person, who was very likely to be Chinese.[50]

An Infectious Diseases Act had been passed in 1882, and the rat-flea theory was accepted almost from the start by the Chief MOH, J. Ashburton Thompson, who reported on the outbreaks in 1900 and 1902.[51] Rodent control rather than cleansing became his top priority, though it was difficult to convince politicians and public of the need for this. His published work helped to establish that a rat epizootic always preceded an epidemic, and fleas were the intermediaries. Ashburton Thompson was ahead of his time in his grasp of the environmental dimensions of epidemiology. Similar observations were made about tsetse (see Chapter 11), by those who grasped that trypanosomiasis could best be understood holistically.

Plague primarily targeted working-class males, especially those handling hay, chaff, maize, potatoes, and other warehoused goods, and a few self-employed people in central Sydney—such as butchers, bakers, and carters—whose work brought them into contact with these other labourers. It also affected people working in suburban factories, mills, and stores whose supplies and raw materials came from the wharves and warehouses. They sometimes carried the disease home to infect family and friends. Apart from certain places of work, the disease was most prevalent in poor, high-density residential areas such as tenements in Lang Ward, facing the harbour. While plague shone a light onto Sydney's appalling housing and sanitary conditions, it barely touched the middle and upper classes in outlying suburbs.[52]

The fact that its victims were largely working class allowed the authorities to impose 'more draconian measures than might otherwise have been possible'.[53] Like non-whites in other parts of the Empire, the poor white working class was in no position to object. Isolation and segregation were key. Vaccination was also carried out, and special hospitals created. Not only were plague-infected people forcibly removed from their homes, but also all those who had come into contact with them. Chinese people were forced to live in tents on the beach near the quarantine station, while whites lived in cottages. Though there were violent scenes when people refused to be taken away by police, there were no formal protests apart from a riot by people demanding vaccination. By March the authorities also decided to quarantine large parts of the city's wharves. More than 108,000 rats were killed with a 2d

[50] *Ibid.*, 138–9.   [51] *Ibid.*, 140. The reports were published in 1901 and 1903.
[52] *Ibid.*, 143–6.   [53] *Ibid.*, 150.

reward per rat brought in for cremation, later increased to 6*d*. The clean-up became a spectator sport.

In racial terms, it was the 4,000-strong Chinese community who suffered most (both in proportionately higher morbidity and mortality and discriminatory treatment), and they were the only group to be compulsorily vaccinated. Many of the city's carpenters and joiners were Chinese, and their businesses were boycotted. As with smallpox and leprosy, they were accused of introducing the disease to Australia and hiding cases. Plague reinforced pre-existing prejudice against the Chinese, provoked in part by smallpox in 1881–2. But plague controls did not lead to residential segregation; this was pre-existing. In the long run, the state was convinced of the need to improve public health systems and government administration, and plague forced the pace of health and social reforms.

Disease, Environmental Regulation and Segregation

At the time of the third pandemic, the role of the rat, gerbil, and other flea-carrying rodents was not fully understood. It also took time for public health officials to understand the vehicular role of trade goods such as rice and other grains, and make the connection with cotton, which rats found very attractive for food, nesting, and breeding.[54] Particularly in the first decade of the twentieth century, recently discovered germ theory held sway. Only a few individuals such as Wakil in Alexandria and Ashburton Thompson in Sydney held radically different views, and these did not catch on immediately. Hence early controls largely focused on quarantine, segregation, and disinfection, aimed at cleansing buildings and conveyances of the so-called 'filth' disease. These were ineffectual against *Y. pestis* without also targeting rodents, their food supplies, and their modes of transport. Controls often targeted mobile people, including Indian immigrants to South and East Africa, Chinese to Australia, African labour migrants within South Africa, travellers and 'criminal tribes' in India, vagrants and 'vagabonds' everywhere. Racial scapegoating was the order of the day as officials sought to curb this mobility, seen to pose a threat to decent, settled society. In India in particular, plague inspectors detained travellers by ship, rail, and road and publicly examined them; people suspected of being sick were pulled off

---

[54] Thornton, *A Report*; Hirst, *Conquest*, 316; H. H. King and C. G. Pandit, 'A summary of the Rat-Flea Survey of the Madras Presidency with a Discussion on the Association of Flea Species with Climate and with Plague', *Indian Journal of Medical Research*, 19/2 (1931), 357–92.

trains. The state kept a photographic record of these controls, which shows just how invasive they were.[55]

Yet administrators faced a conundrum: at this time the Empire required greater global mobility of labourers, soldiers, animals, and merchandise, not less. Plague led to a crisis of globalization, long before the word was invented. Should the door to economic and other types of migrant remain open, and risk one kind of disaster, or be closed and risk labour shortages? For the colonized, plague controls temporarily curtailed freedoms and in some countries intensified forms of urban segregation. In this sense, disease regulation helped to change the social and built environment of colonial cities. But Swanson's argument about the specific influence of the sanitation syndrome on segregation in South Africa, which must be qualified over the longer term there, is not easily generalized to the Empire as a whole. Echenberg in particular highlights alternative official and medical responses to plague. The controls over migration were temporary, and within the next decade large numbers of Indians were indentured to imperial sugar fields, and Chinese to the Rand goldmines.

As for Simpson, although he drew attention to environmental issues and poverty, appalling housing and lack of sanitation, he never entirely took on board the flea vector theory, insisting to the end that infected food was largely to blame. While many health workers paid lip service to the new discourse and insect vectors, they did not abandon their old ideas. With the notable exception of Ashburton Thompson, they treated plague as if it were cholera, typhus, or smallpox, applied outdated assumptions, and generally failed to grasp the implications for human health of a crossover disease. They did not see plague primarily in terms of environmental causes, apart from erroneously linking it to soil and foul air. Nevertheless, what is remarkable is that with the exception of India, many parts of the Empire did largely manage to contain the third pandemic, suggesting that isolation of people and disinfection did have some effect.

---

[55] Puri, ' "Catching" the Plague'.

11

Tsetse and Trypanosomiasis in East and Central Africa

Colonialism and the Spread of Tsetse

Disease, we have argued, influenced patterns of colonization, especially in West Africa, the Americas, and Australia (Chapter 2). In turn, imperial transport routes facilitated the spread of certain diseases, such as bubonic plague. This chapter expands our discussion of environmentally related diseases by focusing on trypanosomiasis, carried by tsetse fly, in East and Central Africa. Unlike plague, this disease of humans and livestock was endemic and restricted to particular ecological zones in Africa. But as in the case of plague, the changing incidence of trypanosomiasis was at least in part related to imperialism and colonial intrusion in Africa.

Coastal East Africa presented some of the same barriers to colonization as West Africa. Portugal maintained a foothold in South-East Africa for centuries, and its agents expanded briefly onto the Zimbabwean plateau in the seventeenth century, but could not command the interior. Had these early incursions been more successful, southern Africa may have been colonized from the north, rather than by the Dutch and British from the south. Parts of East Africa were a source of slaves and ivory in the eighteenth and early nineteenth centuries. The trading routes, commanded by Arab and Swahili African networks, as well as Afro-Portuguese further south, were linked with the Middle East and the Indian Ocean.[1] In the early decades of the nineteenth century, slave-holding expanded within enclaves of East Africa, such as the clove plantations of Zanzibar. When Britain attempted to abolish the slave trade in the early nineteenth century, and policed the West African coast, East and Central African sources briefly became more

---

[1] Lovejoy, *Transformations in Slavery*; Edward A. Alpers, *The East African Slave Trade* (Nairobi: East African Publishing House, 1967) and *Ivory and Slaves in East Central Africa: Changing Patterns of International Trade to the Later Nineteenth Century* (London: Heinemann, 1975).

important for the Atlantic slave trade. African slaves from these areas were taken to Latin America and the Spanish Caribbean.

Britain did not have the same intensity of contact with East Africa as with West and southern Africa until the late nineteenth century. There was no major natural resource that commanded a market in Europe and British traders had limited involvement in these slave markets. But between the 1880s and 1910s, most of East and Central Africa was taken under colonial rule, sometimes initially as protectorates: by Britain in Kenya and Uganda; Germany in Tanzania; Rhodes's British South Africa Company in Zimbabwe, Zambia, and Malawi; and by King Leopold of Belgium in the Congo. The opening of the Suez Canal (1867), European military dominance, and the growing technological gap facilitated conquest by limited numbers of colonial troops and their African allies.

East African conquest coincided with rapidly advancing medical understanding of tropical diseases. Malaria remained a major scourge, although the Native American remedy of quinine, derived from the bark of the cinchona tree, greatly reduced mortality for Europeans in the British Empire in last few decades of the nineteenth century. For example, the British expedition that sacked Kumasi, capital of the Asante kingdom in Ghana, in 1874, lost only 2 per cent of its European troops to disease.[2] Malaria was definitively linked to mosquitoes by Ronald Ross, working in India, in 1897–8. His research prepared the way for new modes of attack on the disease, not least environmental management of mosquito breeding grounds. The late nineteenth century proved to be a critical period for advances in parasitology when insect vectors such as mosquitoes, ticks, fleas, and flies were confirmed as carriers of a number of diseases, particularly tropical diseases, of humans and animals. In this period, also, scientists identified the trypanosome, the protozoa or parasite that caused sleeping sickness in humans, as well as its tsetse fly vector, and linked it to an animal disease.

Tsetse is the name given to a genus of flies found over a wide range of the African continent. It is a word taken from the southern African language Setswana, adopted into English in the nineteenth century, and then generalized. There are twenty-two species and some additional subspecies of fly, as well as many different trypanosomes.[3] The two most dangerous

[2] Curtin, Feierman, Thompson, and Vansina, *African History*, 446.

[3] David Bourn, Robin Reid, David Rogers, Bill Snow, and William Wint, *Environmental Change and the Autonomous Control of Tsetse and Trypanosomosis in Sub-Saharan Africa* (Oxford: Oxford Environment Research Group, 2001), 3.

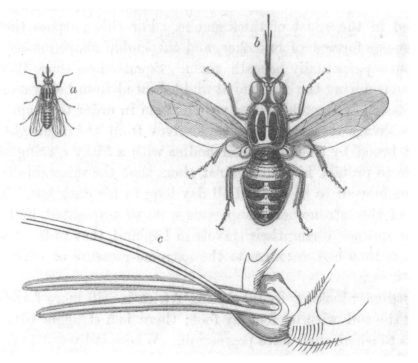

7. A late nineteenth-century image of the tsetse fly, *Glossina morsitans*.
Credit: Mary Evans Picture Library.

groups are the riverine tsetse or *Glossina palpalis* and the savannah tsetse or *Glossina morsitans*. The latter predominates in East and Central Africa, and causes trypanosomiasis in humans and cattle. Sleeping sickness, the common name for the human form, is a wasting disease affecting the central nervous system. It has many manifestations, partly dependent on the variety of the trypanosome. In southern Africa, the animal disease associated with tsetse was called *nagana*, derived from a Zulu word.

Tsetse flies are in turn dependent upon hosts, largely wild animals, sometimes human or livestock, for their diet of blood and for their reproduction. Trypanosomes survive in the bloodstreams of mammals. The fly—one of the few insects that is born alive rather than from a deposited egg—does not carry the parasite from birth, but once it matures, it must have a blood meal every few days. It thus picks up the trypanosome from a host, becomes a vector, and remains so throughout its lifespan of up to six months. Trypanosomes also multiply in the body of the tsetse. Wildlife, which have harboured them over a very long period, appear immune to their effects. However, trypanosomes can in certain cases counter the immune system of livestock and humans. It is interesting that humans, whose genetic ancestors have survived in Africa for millions of years, have not become more immune. It is less surprising that cattle succumb as their introduction to Africa is more recent, perhaps 5,000 years ago, and less in the case of southern Africa.

Except for occasional epidemics, the foci of human infection have been relatively concentrated. But the zones of continuous animal infection were far larger, and the percentage of domestic animals that are carriers and victims usually far higher. Some trypanosomes infect livestock but not people and some have a differential impact on animals. For example, the *brucei* (named after David Bruce, a scientist who made early breakthroughs in identifying the parasite) is particularly lethal for horses. John Ford argued that this trypanosome made it especially difficult to colonize parts of Africa—because it precluded the use of cavalry (Chapter 2).[4] Livestock can also experience the disease as acute, leading to death within in couple of weeks, or chronic. Infected cattle become emaciated and if they are subjected to exertion, such as trekking or ploughing, they can succumb to this or another disease. Poor nutrition also greatly affects death rates.

A history of trypanosomiasis requires some understanding of the relationship between humans, domestic animals, wild animals, flies, the trypanosome, and their habitat—in other words it must in part be an environmental history. Tsetse flies need warm, even temperatures and a degree of humidity. Their range is therefore limited by the dry heat of the Sahara to the north, and the desert and cold in the west and south of southern Africa. Highland areas with sharp temperature variations are also largely free from tsetse. But given the range of species, each adapted to specific habitats, they managed to survive in many areas. Aside from keeping horses out of large swathes of the continent, the prevalence of tsetse limited the expansion of pastoralism and the use of animal draught in cultivation and transport. Even where cattle could be kept in tsetse zones, they tended not to be used for the demanding requirements of draught. This may have diminished the value of wheeled transport in sub-Saharan Africa, an absence often noted in the earlier comparative literature on what was considered Africa's backwardness. While limited numbers of livestock could be kept in, or on the margins of, tsetse belts, the fly tended to push livestock farming into more arid

---

[4] John Ford, *The Role of the Trypanosomiases in African Ecology: A Study of the Tsetse Fly Problem* (London: Oxford University Press, 1971), 64–5.

zones, which were often also more environmentally vulnerable, and in some parts of Africa, the intensive mixed agriculture of Europe and Asia was less feasible.

We should, however, be careful about exaggerating the impact of tsetse on African economic and social development. Perhaps the greatest kingdom in eighteenth- and nineteenth-century sub-Saharan Africa was Asante, which sat squarely in the West African tsetse belt. Its armies, which commanded areas hundreds of kilometres from the capital Kumasi, were made up of footsoldiers only, armed with muskets.[5] Agriculture was by hoe and transport by porterage and canoe. By contrast cattle were an economic cornerstone of the Zulu state in southern Africa, which at its peak in the 1820s and 1830s was probably a fifth the size of Asante and its production systems less intensive. In Central Africa, major states such as the Bemba (northern Zambia) were also largely without cattle.[6] It is difficult to generalize, in that there were centralized and decentralized political systems with, and without, cattle in Africa. In some contexts livestock gave local communities mobility, and local political units freedom to accumulate. Where space was available for pastures, livestock may have inhibited as much as facilitated agricultural intensification.

Some types of African cattle, such as the West African N'dama breeds, and humped East African Zebu, are to varying degrees trypanotolerant.[7] This seems largely to be genetic but they may also acquire immunity through surviving early exposure to infection. And while Africans did not know about trypanosomes, some did believe that the fly was an infecting agent, and that it was related to wildlife. They could thus take precautionary action. Although African explanations of disease were often couched in the language of witchcraft, this did not preclude more instrumental forms of understanding, avoidance, and treatment. As noted in Chapter 4, Zulu kings, whose land was on the southern margins of the tsetse belt, organized

[5] Ivor Wilks, *Asante in the Nineteenth Century: The Structure and Evolution of a Political Order* (Cambridge: Cambridge University Press, 1975); Jack Goody, *Technology, Tradition, and the State in Africa* (London: Oxford University Press, 1971).

[6] Audrey I. Richards, *Land, Labour and Diet in Northern Rhodesia: An Economic Study of the Bemba Tribe* (1939; Oxford University Press: International African Institute, London, 1995).

[7] Ford, *The Role of the Trypanosomiases*, 86–90; Bourn, Reid, Rogers, Snow, and Wint, *Environmental Change*; James Giblin, 'Trypanosomiasis Control in African History: An Evaded Issue?', *Journal of African History*, 31 (1990), 59–80; A. M. Jordan, *Trypanosomiasis Control and African Rural Development* (Harlow: Longman, 1986), 56–60.

bush clearance campaigns and large hunting parties to drive back the habitat for tsetse. Tsetse was an issue for many pre-colonial and early colonial travellers, hunters, and potential colonizers, from Livingstone in southern Africa to Burton in East Africa, because it affected their movements. Early colonial governments in East Africa found that they had to address it. In Uganda, a British protectorate from 1890, perhaps 250,000 people died from sleeping sickness between 1900 and 1908. An even larger number probably succumbed in the Congo.[8] Trypanosomiasis infection also spread through Tanzania, Mozambique, Zambia, and Malawi, though not on the same scale. The no-go areas for livestock expanded steadily, and over a longer period of time. British colonial authorities had a major stake in dealing with the problem because it was prevalent in so many of their colonies.

John Ford, who worked in the British colonial service, published a path-setting book on trypanosomiasis in 1971 that associated its spread with colonialism.[9] He also suggested that Africans had in some contexts reached a modus vivendi with the fly and achieved partial immunities through regular low-level contact. Total eradication was unlikely to succeed and opened the way to future infection. Similar arguments were made by some malaria experts. Helge Kjekshus developed his argument in *Ecology Control and Economic Development in East African History*, which also helped to set the framework for much subsequent writing on African environmental history by highlighting colonial responsibility for environmental degradation.[10] The core of his thesis is that in pre-colonial times, Africans established some degree of balance with the fly. This was achieved in part by dense settlement and intensive cultivation—an 'agro-horticultural prophylaxis'—and in part by keeping areas round settlements relatively free from bush and wildlife—for example by fire.[11] Avoidance strategies involved moving livestock seasonally to areas where the fly was less dangerous, or through fly zones at night, which was less risky. For example, Zulu livestock owners

[8] Kirk Hoppe, *Lords of the Fly: Sleeping Sickness Control in British East Africa, 1900–1960* (Westport, CT: Praeger, 2003), 1; Maryinez Lyons, *The Colonial Disease: A Social History of Sleeping Sickness in Northern Zaire, 1900–1940* (Cambridge: Cambridge University Press, 1992).

[9] Ford, *The Role of the Trypanosomiases.*

[10] Helge Kjekshus, *Ecology Control and Economic Development in East African History* (London: Heinemann, 1977).

[11] Kjekshus, *Ecology Control*, 25.

avoided the fly-prone lowlands in hot, wet summer months.[12] Various temporary repellents were also employed, such as smoke, human and animal excrement, and lion's fat.

Kjekshus drew on late pre-colonial travellers such as Speke and Burton to describe a basic mastery by East Africans in Tanzania over their environment. Burton found wildlife rare in the densely settled areas of the East African coast and suggested that the people were often 'superior in comforts, better dressed, fed and lodged and less worked than the unhappy Ryot of British India'.[13] Similar pictures were drawn of abundance, fertility, and environmental control in the Ganda kingdom.[14] The 'dangerous combination of trypanosomes, their hosts (wildlife) and their vectors (tsetse flies)' could be kept at bay because they tended to be concentrated in woodlands, or wilderness zones between the major chiefdoms, where they did not contest for space with humans. But ecological control, Kjekshus argues, proved to be vulnerable.

The 1890s has been seen as a decade of unmitigated disaster for many imperial subjects.[15] Environmental conditions, in part triggered by an El Nino event in 1896, coincided with conquest and disease to cause widespread famine. (See Chapters 8 and 10.) In East Africa, conflict was compounded by the indirect consequences of imperialism such as the cattle disease rinderpest, probably imported from India in 1891—which destroyed up to 80 per cent of herds—as well as human ailments such as smallpox, plague, and sand flea or jiggers from Latin America. Malaria remained a major killer and it was possibly spreading, along with maize cultivation, because mosquitoes seem to thrive on maize pollen.[16] German colonial conquest of Tanzania was followed by brutal suppression of the Maji Maji Rebellion in 1906; over 75,000 people were killed. The Germans used scorched earth methods of warfare and control. East Africa was one of the theatres of the First World War. Both Germans and Allied troops, including South African forces invading on behalf of the Empire, required porters on a large scale and used disruptive and sometimes coercive labour recruitment methods. In 1918, the global influenza epidemic killed perhaps 3 per cent of the Tanzanian

---

[12] Ford, *The Role of the Trypanosomiases*, 481; Karen Brown, 'uNakane: The Ecological and Chemical Campaign against Livestock Trypanosomiasis in KwaZulu Natal, 1894–2004', unpublished paper, Wellcome Unit for the History of Medicine, Oxford (2004).

[13] Kjekshus, *Ecology Control*, 4, 72, quoting Burton, 1860.

[14] Hoppe, *Lords of the Fly*, 33.   [15] Davis, *Late Victorian Holocausts*.

[16] McCann, *Maize and Grace*.

population. 'The people of southern Tanganyika had not lost only a hope of regaining freedom', Iliffe affirmed, 'they had lost a battle in their long war with nature'.[17]

Kjekshus believed that taken together, these processes reduced cattle numbers, halted population growth, and allowed bush and tsetse to spread. Early colonial conservation controls, such as wildlife reserves and hunting laws, further inhibited Africans' capacity to restore environmental controls. British rulers, taking over Tanzania as a mandate after the Treaty of Versailles (1918), carved out the Selous Game Reserve, named after the hunter and leader of the pioneer column into Zimbabwe (Chapter 5). Tsetse continued to spread, at least till the 1930s, by which time it had engulfed very large new areas. In a number of African colonies, fly belts seemed to reach their peak extents around this time, with sporadic epidemic outbreaks of sleeping sickness up to the 1940s. In sum, the breakdown of the pre-colonial balance allowed wildlife, bush, and fly to expand at the cost of settled areas and it proved very difficult to regain such territory. Kjekshus's analysis is similar to that of West Africanists who have laid emphasis on the demographic impact of the slave trade in retarding economic development.[18] Both use Boserup's model suggesting that population increase tends to lead to agricultural intensification, specialization, and development.[19] Depopulation had the opposite impact, and in Africa its effects were compounded by the undermining of local manufactures such as iron-working and cloth production.

Giblin, analysing coastal northern Tanzania, reaffirms this general picture, although he has a slightly different understanding of disease control.[20] Also drawing on Ford, he suggested that frequent low-level contact with the disease stimulated partial immunity. Rinderpest also killed trypanotolerant stock in the 1890s and the replacement animals were almost certainly less immune. Famine, out-migration, and probable demographic decline, set in train a downward spiral, a 'narrative of ecological decline', which persisted through to the 1930s at least.[21] The experience of Maasai communities

---

[17] John Iliffe, *A Modern History of Tanganyika* (Cambridge: Cambridge University Press, 1979), 202.

[18] Inikori (ed.), *Forced Migration*; Walter Rodney, *How Europe Underdeveloped Africa* (London: Bogle L'Ouverture Publications, 1972).

[19] Esther Boserup, *The Conditions of Agricultural Growth* (London: Faber, 1965).

[20] Giblin, 'Trypanosomiasis control'.   [21] *Ibid.*, 79.

in British-ruled Kenya adds a further dimension to the arguments about colonialism and tsetse. Many Maasai were forcibly removed from their northern reserve on Laikipia in 1911–13 to Western Narok in the south of the protectorate, where trypanosomiasis was far more prevalent.[22] They thus experienced greater losses from the disease. There was still room for evasion of tsetse but this strategy was more difficult for the Purko Maasai section than it had been in Laikipia, because environmental resources were more scarce. There were fewer uplands and less water—and they had to share these with other sections. They saw this southern reserve as 'bitter' by comparison with the sweet (*sidai*) north.

Attempts to deal with the epidemic in early twentieth-century Uganda and Congo exacerbated epidemics.[23] Colonial states corralled people in dense settlements in order to separate them from tsetse. On the one hand, this intensified control, and created what some African people saw as 'death camps', where rates of infection were higher. In epidemics at least, humans could act as a reservoir. On the other hand, the concentration of people in these camps may have had the counterproductive result of increasing the range of the fly. Whereas the Belgians largely abandoned this policy of concentrated settlements, the British authorities in Tanzania pursued it, unevenly, for much of the colonial period.

Modifications to Arguments about Colonial Intrusion and Disease

While the association between colonialism and the spread of tsetse is well established in historical literature on Africa, a number of qualifications have been made. Viewed over a longer time-span, including the period both before and after the early colonial era, disease incidence and colonial responsibility may have a more complex history. The first problem concerns the relation between people and nature in the pre-colonial period. John Iliffe sees African society as more vulnerable to disease, famine, and environmental constraints in the nineteenth century. On the one hand, he recognizes that Africans' control of the land and 'struggle with their enemies in nature' in this 'immensely difficult continent' was a major contribution to human

---

[22] Lotte Hughes, 'Moving the Maasai: A Colonial Misadventure', D.Phil., University of Oxford (2002), published under the same title (Basingstoke: Palgrave Macmillan, 2006).

[23] Lyons, *The Colonial Disease*; Maryinez Lyons, 'Sleeping Sickness Epidemics and Public Health in the Belgian Congo', in David Arnold (ed.), *Imperial Medicine and Indigenous Societies* (Manchester: Manchester University Press, 1988), 105–24.

history.[24] On the other hand, these achievements did not represent a far-reaching mastery of the environment, and in many African societies 'men measured out their lives in famines'.[25]

Iliffe notes that tsetse may have been spreading in parts of Tanzania in the second half of the nineteenth century, prior to direct colonial intrusions. With the importation of firearms from the 1860s, African villagers along the ivory and slave-trading routes to the interior sought security by concentrating their settlements in fortified villages. Bush, and tsetse fly, 're-conquered' areas from which people had moved.[26] This process continued, probably at a more rapid pace, in the early twentieth century but it did not start then. He emphasizes labour migration and the removal of male labour from agriculture as key factors. Similarly, bush and tsetse spread in some Maasai areas of Kenya in the early colonial period, but not primarily because of colonialism or capitalism.[27] Firm conclusions are elusive because of the inadequacy of sources on the pre-colonial period. It is very difficult to establish a historical baseline and chart definitively the zones of infection at various periods of the nineteenth century.[28] The controls over tsetse cited by Kjekshus were likely to have been very uneven.

Secondly, scientific discoveries in the early colonial period resulted in a much fuller understanding of the disease and hence a better ability to trace and record it. Africa attracted some ambitious and high-profile scientists as tropical medicine became defined as a field and the colonies provided a laboratory for testing the possibilities of the new bacteriology and parasitology; 'scientific reputations could be made'.[29] The trypanosome was first seen in the blood of mammals by microscope in 1880, and it was associated with a wasting disease of horses in India. A key breakthrough was made in 1894 when David Bruce, of the British Army Medical Service, was sent to recently conquered Zululand to investigate cattle disease there.[30] He confirmed that

---

[24] Iliffe, *Modern History of Tanganyika*, 4.

[25] *Ibid.*, 13; David Johnson and David Anderson (eds.), *The Ecology of Survival: Case Studies from Northeast African History* (London: Croom Helm, 1988).

[26] Iliffe, *Modern History of Tanganyika*, 76, 163.

[27] Richard Waller, 'Tsetse Fly in Western Narok, Kenya', *Journal of African History*, 31/1 (1990), 81–101.

[28] Juhani Koponen, *People and Production in Late Precolonial Tanzania: History and Structures* (Helsinki: Monographs of the Finnish Society for Development Studies, 2, 1988), 248.

[29] M. Vaughan, *Curing Their Ills: Colonial Power and African Illness* (Cambridge: Polity Press, 1991), 37.

[30] Brown, 'uNakane'.

the trypanosome was the cause, that the same parasite was infecting horses, and that it was carried by healthy wildlife. The trypanosome was identified in the blood of a human sufferer of the so-called Gambia fever in that colony in 1901; further connections were made by Alberto Castellani in Uganda in 1902, during the epidemic there (1900–5). He identified trypanosomes in the cerebro-spinal fluid of a patient with sleeping sickness. Bruce headed a delegation to Uganda and identified a specific species of tsetse fly as the key carrier.[31] Deaths which might have been attributed to a range of other factors, by both Africans and whites, could now be pinpointed more effectively, although it is possible that trypanosomiasis was still confused with tickborne diseases in cattle. In sum, tsetse became more visible in the early colonial period.

Thirdly, while there is little doubt that trypanosomiasis was initially spread by colonial intrusions, Malawian material suggests important qualifications not only as to the causes but also the longer-term trajectory of tsetse incidence.[32] Despite the fact that Malawi had a denser population than most of Zambia or Tanzania in the nineteenth and early twentieth century, tsetse belts also spread there from about 1890 to 1920. This was not colonially induced—or not directly so. Rather, the process was initiated by the disruption of dispersed settlement patterns from the mid-nineteenth century. Southern Malawi was invaded by slavers, mostly Yao-speakers from the east coast, and northern Malawi partly conquered by the Ngoni (an offshoot from the Zulu kingdom). Many communities took refuge in stockaded villages, on islands in the lakes and rivers, or on plateau areas. In the Tchiri highlands, formerly one of the most densely populated areas, much land was reclaimed by bush and game. In the north, the Ngoni cleared land around them of people and thus allowed tsetse to encroach; according to one source they 'made a wilderness' of this land so that it became 'the favourite resort of game and beasts of prey'.[33]

[31] Ford, *The Role of the Trypanosomiases*, 240. K. A. Hoppe, 'Lords of the Fly: Colonial Visions and Revisions of African Sleeping Sickness Environments on Ugandan Lake Victoria, 1906–1961', *Africa*, 67 (1997), 86–105.

[32] John McCracken, 'Colonialism, Capitalism and Ecological Crisis in Malawi: A Reassessment' in David M. Anderson and Richard Grove (eds.), *Conservation in Africa: People, Policies and Practice* (Cambridge: Cambridge University Press); John McCracken, 'Planters, Peasants and the Colonial State: the Impact of the Native Tobacco Board in the Central Province of Malawi', *Journal of Southern African Studies*, 9/2 (1983); John McCracken, 'Conservation and Resistance in Colonial Malawi: The "Dead North" Revisited', in William Beinart and JoAnn McGregor (eds.), *Social History and African Environments* (Oxford: James Currey, 2003).

[33] McCracken, 'Colonialism, Capitalism', 67; Leroy Vail, 'Ecology and History: The Example of Eastern Zambia', *Journal of Southern African Studies*, 3 (1977), 129–55.

In this scenario the spread of tsetse and bush began before the colonial invasion. However, there was not a major sleeping-sickness epidemic till the colonial period. In the 1890s, the British South Africa Company established its authority over this part of Central Africa and, as the intensity of slave raiding diminished, the population began to disperse again. People abandoned stockaded settlements, and reinvaded old land around Ngoni territory, to find space for cultivation. They and their livestock moved into tsetse terrain and became highly susceptible to infection. Thus greater freedom of movement in the early colonial period set the scene for trypanosomiasis deaths. Moreover, new settlements disturbed the wildlife that hosted the fly and as a result probably enlarged the areas that were subject to infection. The gradual decline of internal slavery in Tanzania in the early twentieth century, which enabled more people to establish independent homesteads, may have had the same effect.

'Once sleeping sickness erupted', McCracken argues, 'it spread with terrifying speed.'[34] In the first decade of the twentieth century, a missionary commented that tsetse had swept across the Kasungu district in the central province, almost to the lakeshore. Cattle and horses could no longer be moved freely. By the early 1920s, whole villages had to be evacuated. Cattle keepers in the north were cut off from markets in the south, and they found the disease intruding on their territory.

In Malawi, the early colonial state found it difficult to establish areas for European plantations. Nor was there initially much scope for cash crops grown by Africans in this landlocked colony, far from the coast and markets. The state encouraged migrant labour, and provided facilities for labour recruiters to the South African and Zimbabwean mines. As in Tanzania, there was a large demand for porters, so that male labour was siphoned off and unavailable for agriculture and land clearance.

David Bruce was commissioned in 1911 to study trypanosomiasis in Malawi. Convinced of the link between wildlife and tsetse, he supported culling. The evidence of the Transvaal, where tsetse had apparently been eradicated, seemed proof that this was indeed a potentially effective measure. Hunters had decimated the wildlife, and many larger antelope which survived had been killed off by rinderpest in 1896–7. In northern KwaZulu/Natal and in Zimbabwe, policies of wildlife eradication were also pursued as a strategy

---

[34] McCracken, 'Colonialism, Capitalism'.

of tsetse control.[35] In certain areas, this priority outweighed the colonial concern to control hunting and protect wildlife. However, when applied in Malawi in the 1910s, in a less systematic way, culling probably scattered animals and accelerated the advance of the fly. Smaller animals, which were difficult to shoot, like warthogs, bush pigs, and bush buck were major carriers, although this was not known at the time. (Kudu, the second largest African antelope, was also a major host.) It was only from the 1930s that sufficiently careful research was done to discover which animals were the key hosts. Malawi was an impoverished colonial state and never made sufficient expenditure for systematic game clearance. Thus even attempts to shoot out wildlife were at best hit and miss, and probably exacerbated trypanosomiasis.

The driving back of fly belts happened in a quite unexpected way, which was unrelated to the colonial campaigns. However, it could be argued that this was also a result of colonialism. Various cash crops had been tried in Malawi with limited success. In the 1920s, African peasants started to farm tobacco with the encouragement of the colonial state and a few large-scale European landowners, especially in the central province. Male labour was absorbed back into agriculture, both on estates, where Africans lived as tenants, and on smallholdings. Tobacco required large areas of land to be cleared and timber to be felled as fuel for the drying process. This had a decisive impact in diminishing the fly's habitat. The expansion of markets for dried and smoked fish from the lakes also impacted on Malawi's woodlands.[36]

This analysis complicates the links between British colonialism and the spread of trypanosomiasis and alerts us to regional specificity—different stories can be told about various parts of East and Central Africa. After the Second World War, and the rapid expansion both of population and cultivation in most African countries, the disease gradually diminished in severity. More intensive and diverse strategies of control were deployed. Culling was used over a long period in some countries—notably Zimbabwe. For example, in four years between 1948 and 1951, more than 100,000 head of wildlife were destroyed, largely on the white-owned farmlands, for tsetse

[35] MacKenzie, *Empire of Nature*; Shirley Brooks, 'Playing the Game: The Struggle for Wildlife Protection in Zululand, 1910–1930', unpublished MA thesis, Queen's University, Kingston (1990).

[36] Wiseman Chijere Chriwa, 'Fishing Rights, Ecology and Conservation along Southern Lake Malawi, 1920–1960', *African Affairs*, 95/380 (1996), 351–77.

control.[37] Re-infection could then be prevented by fencing. But culling was not always effective. In Ngamiland, northern Botswana, British officials hoped to expand the cattle economy by eradicating wildlife and tsetse from ranching areas. The Okavango delta—a reservoir for wildlife with limited human settlement and livestock—impeded this process. When tsetse control by culling failed, the local chieftaincy supported the development of the Moremi Game Reserve, which became the country's major and most profitable national park.[38] In general, trypanosomiasis control hastened the urgency of separating wildlife from people. Game reserves and national parks seemed the best solution in tsetse territory; they served as a compromise between those wanting elimination of wild animals and those that prioritized conservation.

British policy in Tanzania included resettlement in concentrated villages up to the 1950s. Although there was no major epidemic, the colonial state tried to prevent infection by moving tens of thousands of people, largely in districts around Lake Victoria.[39] In 1938 an estimated 160,000–200,000 people lived in these villages. As the post-war government increasingly espoused a policy and rhetoric of development, new settlements were conceived as a means of regulating rural society, modernizing agriculture, facilitating education, and introducing services such as roads and water. The battle against sleeping sickness became tied up with a battle for improved land use; elsewhere villagization strategies were closely linked with other kinds of environmental management, notably soil conservation. Resettlement was not very widely implemented at the time, because most states in Africa lacked the capacity for major social engineering and these measures faced deepening resistance from rural communities (Chapter 16).

British colonial officials were split over the policy of moving people as a means of trypanosomiasis control. Aside from causing social upheaval, some scientists felt that relocation opened the way to reinfestation. Swynnerton in Tanzania, Nash in Nigeria, as well as South African scientists tried instead to control the vector, tsetse.[40] Sustained experiments were devoted to fly traps. While these started with unlikely attempts to use human and animal

---

[37] Roben Mutwira, 'A Question of Condoning Game Slaughter: Southern Rhodesian Wildlife Policy (1890–1953)', *Journal of Southern African Studies*, 15/2 (1989), 250–62.

[38] Maitseo Bolaane, 'Wildlife Conservation and Local Management: The Establishment of Moremi Park, Okavango, Botswana in the 1950s–1960s', unpublished D.Phil. thesis, University of Oxford (2004).

[39] Hoppe, *Lords of the Fly*, 3, 110–14.   [40] Jordan, *Trypanosomiasis Control*.

baits, they evolved into complex entomological research, deploying various colour and odour traps, together with poisons. After the Second World War, the newly available DDT provided a temporary solution to remaining fly belts in South Africa.[41] Drug treatments became available from the 1920s, and medicines were far more effective—if expensive—by the late colonial period.

Trypanosomiasis infection declined in the mid-twentieth century, so that by the end of the colonial period human sleeping sickness was no longer a serious killer. As in the case of plague, imperialism may initially have facilitated the spread of this disease, but over the longer term, mechanisms of control and social processes combined to diminish its impact. In the early years of African independence, the range of the tsetse fly narrowed further. In Nigeria, for example, reported sleeping sickness cases soared to over 80,000 a year in a widespread epidemic in the 1930s.[42] By 1960 fewer than 5,000 were registered and by 1975 human cases were comparatively rare. Land clearance and farming in Nigeria has in recent decades pushed tsetse southwards so that animal trypanosomiasis also declined; hunting for bushmeat helped to diminish wildlife carriers. As a result, cattle could be used in an expanding zone of mixed farming and pastoralists, initially assisted by trypanocidal drugs, could also extend their ranges.

In some countries, however, there has been a noted resurgence of trypano-somiasis since the 1970s. The World Health Organization (WHO) reported about 10,000 new cases a year between 1969 and 1975, mostly in Congo and West Africa; of countries in Central and eastern Africa, only Tanzania was still seriously affected.[43] By 1990 45,000 deaths were reported annually and WHO believed the figure to be far higher, possibly between 300,000 and 500,000.[44] The collapse of the state in the Democratic Republic of Congo, political conflicts, as well as the devastation of primary health-care facilities, all contributed to re-infection. Even in South Africa, where eradication was successful, *nagana* re-emerged in the 1990s as a significant cattle disease in a few districts of KwaZulu/Natal.[45] Control programmes broke down and exotic eucalyptus plantations may have provided a haven for one species of

---

[41] Brown, 'uNakane'.

[42] Bourn, Reid, Rogers, Snow, and Wint, *Environmental Change*, 94–107.

[43] Jordan, *Trypanosomiasis Control*, 34–5.

[44] See <http://www.who.int/mediacentre/factsheets/Fs259>, 'African Trypanosomiasis (sleeping sickness)'.

[45] Brown, 'uNakane'.

fly. This scenario has given strength to those who, following Ford's hypothesis, suggest that complete eradication is impossible and it is better to seek local balances and partial immunities. Malaria eradication presents similar problems. However, WHO argues that systematic campaigns and medical controls still hold considerable promise and cites past successes up to the 1970s. Ambitious programmes have been launched to introduce sterilized flies, and reduce tsetse reproduction rates.

The history of trypanosomiasis presents challenges for imperial environmental history. Some have condemned colonial destruction of natural resources such as wildlife, woodland, and forests. But human habitation requires a degree of environmental control and, in the case of tsetse, lack of control had disastrous results. In the eyes of Kjekshus and others, socio-environmental dislocation resulted from a thickening of indigenous vegetation and increase in wildlife that would, in other contexts, be welcomed by environmentalists. There is a profound irony here. Conversely, prophylaxis against trypanosomiasis benefited from the eradication of tsetse flies, but, as some colonial officials noted, fly belts could contribute to the protection of wildlife habitat. This example suggests that environmental degradation or improvement must be judged in social as well as simply ecological terms.

Kjekshus's argument that tsetse inhibited economic development is also questionable. Some of Africa's most powerful pre-colonial states, with varied export economies, grew up in tsetse belts. Even in the colonial period, economic development was not significantly impeded by trypanosomiasis. Peasant cash cropping of palm oil, cocoa, and coffee in West Africa are cases in point. Uganda, the British colony which suffered worst from sleeping sickness in the early twentieth century, also became one of the most successful centres of African agricultural production, especially of cotton, in East Africa. In colonial Kenya, by contrast, where tsetse was less prevalent, African economic development was more generally constrained by the demands of the settlers for a monopoly of valuable cash crops, such as coffee, and their concerns about protecting their labour supply. Imperialism could help trigger loss of environmental control. But capitalist markets and colonial administrations could also provide the technology or motor for new controls over ecologically related diseases. And although the overall picture is mixed, agricultural production generally expanded in the colonial period.

12

Imperial Scientists, Ecology, and Conservation

Scientists in the Empire

Imperial scientists have appeared in a number of our chapters: Cleghorn, protagonist of forest conservation in India; Willcocks, the self-critical dam-builder extraordinary in Egypt and India; Simpson, the plague doctor, and Bruce, who researched trypanosomiasis in southern Africa. The early centuries of empire preceded professionalization, but scientific interests were even then at its heart. Species transfers were, as we have suggested, a long-term preoccupation and closely related to scientific enterprise.[1] The maritime empires that characterized the last half-millennium depended upon nautical technology and navigation science, and this distinguished them from preceding, more geographically restricted, land empires. Naval power and the expansion of shipping permitted a different social geography of empire, linking Europe to the Americas, the tropics, and the southern temperate zones, and partly bypassing the torrid task of conquest in Europe and the Muslim world. Shipping carried the freight of trading empires, literally and metaphorically.

Especially from the mid-nineteenth century, scientists were central actors in imperial development.[2] They helped to pioneer new technologies that facilitated discovery, and vastly more effective exploitation, of hidden natural resources, such as gold, oil, and rubber. A growing arms gap underpinned the European power bloc and conquest was so rapid and so widespread in the later decades of the nineteenth century not least because it was relatively easy and inexpensive. Constraints imposed by environment and disease were gradually driven back, by dams, boreholes, and the partial prophylaxis against malaria. Communications, based around steam and iron, telegraphs, railways, and roads were the 'tentacles of progress' in the new empire,

---

[1] Brockway, *Science and Colonial Expansion*; Drayton, *Nature's Government*; Schiebinger, *Plants and Empire*.

[2] Daniel R. Headrick, *The Tools of Empire: Technology and European Imperialism in the Nineteenth Century* (New York: Oxford University Press, 1981).

opening up new routes for exploitation.[3] They bound together increasingly modern, planned cities, zones of hydraulic imperialism, mining, and similar enterprises.

Scientists and science in empire have received intense critical attention over the last couple of decades. This is especially so in African history and social sciences which, from their inception as self-conscious areas of academic enquiry, in the dying days of colonialism, tried to write from the vantage point of Africans and to decolonize European minds. From the late 1970s, when it was clear that African nationalist narratives and ambitions had been corrupted, Africanists tended to evince an unease with modernization and development, so closely linked to both the late colonial and nationalist projects. Drawing on a long lineage of anthropological writing, research burgeoned on indigenous or local knowledge—and as a corollary, its counterpoint, a critique of colonial science. This ran parallel to similar discussions in South Asian subaltern studies, so evident in academic writing on Indian forestry (see Chapter 7).

Colonial science was seen as a particularly problematic enterprise, moulded by authoritarian colonial states. Some of the most interesting writing developed in the rapidly growing field of medical history, where, David Arnold noted, authors saw 'medicine and disease as describing a relationship of power and authority between rulers and ruled'.[4] Literature on India and Africa emphasized the exploitative and regulatory aspects of science in imperial settings. More intensive use of colonial natural resources often restricted access by indigenous people, or actually displaced them. Scientific advances quickened the pace of raw material extraction. The movement of colonial resources to the industrial hub of Europe intensified asymmetrical economic relationships. Scientific prescriptions could cut across local patterns of resource use, disrupt social relations, or demand resettlement of communities.

Scientists, as we have illustrated, also became increasingly concerned about the long-term viability of natural resources in the face of intensive use. Their work fed into the establishment of exclusive, protected zones for forests, wildlife, or watersheds. Historians of colonial Africa have argued that technical officers grew in influence from the 1920s, and increasingly prescribed to peasants how they should farm and which areas they should

[3] Headrick, *The Tentacles of Progress: Technology Transfer in the Age of Imperialism, 1850–1940* (New York: Oxford University Press, 1988).

[4] David Arnold (ed.), *Imperial Medicine and Indigenous Societies* (Manchester: Manchester University Press, 1988), 2.

protect. Critical analyses have sometimes included an appeal to the common-sense idea that peasants best knew how to farm, and how to manage local environments. As John McCracken typically reminded us, 'the best experts are those who recognise that rural people are the best experts'.[5]

While it is clearly mistaken to exaggerate the impact of academic work and of history in particular, such discussion was part of a far-reaching rein-terpretation of science, knowledge, power, and environmental management. It helped to change the terms of debate, and even policy, by questioning the value of big, intrusive, authoritarian development projects. It legitimated ideas of community management of natural resources that have attracted a great deal of NGO energy and donor funding. This perspective was power-fully developed in overviews such as Michael Adas's *Machines as the Measure of Men* (1989) and Fairhead and Leach on *Misreading the African Land-scape* (1996).[6] James Scott's *Seeing like a State* epitomized, on a far broader front, the anti-statist critique of 'high-modernism' and scientific planning, reducing many of its forms—Stalinism, forestry, urban planning, colonial agricultural projects—to symptoms of the same simplified, standardized vision born in the Enlightenment.[7] He echoes ecofeminist views, except that they also saw science as intimately connected with male power, of which imperialism was an extreme version.[8] Quoting Isaiah Berlin, Scott compares 'the scientific forester and the cadastral officer', the administrative man, to the hedgehog, who knows only one big thing, while farmers, peasants, and naturalists were like the fox who knows a great many things.[9] Hedgehogism narrows knowledge, and provides a 'rather static and myopic view'. Admin-istrative man, the utilizer of science, 'perceives a drastically simplified model of the buzzing, blooming confusion that constitutes the real world'.

But scientists in the Empire should be analysed in a more complex frame-work. There was another side to scientific endeavour, also touched upon in earlier chapters, in that they became important agents in conservationist

[5] John McCracken, 'Experts and Expertise in Colonial Malawi', *African Affairs*, 81/322 (1982), 101–16.

[6] Michael Adas, *Machines as the Measure of Men: Science, Technology, and Ideologies of Western Dominance* (Ithaca: Cornell University Press, 1989). James Fairhead and Melissa Leach, *Misreading the African Landscape: Society and Ecology in a Forest-Savanna Mosaic* (Cambridge: Cambridge University Press, 1996).

[7] James Scott, *Seeing Like a State: How Certain Schemes to Improve the Human Condition Have Failed* (New Haven: Yale University Press, 1998).

[8] Shiva, *Staying Alive*; Merchant, *The Death of Nature*.

[9] Scott, *Seeing Like a State*, 45.

initiatives and ecological thinking. In this chapter, we will examine their role largely in the latter contexts. The reference points will be African, Australian, and Indian in the period from about 1900 to 1960. First, it is important to understand the developing disciplines and institutions within which scientific officers worked. For many historians of science, this is an unproblematic statement—although they in turn sometimes neglect power relations and social context. Scientific disciplines were not divorced from power, but they retained a relative autonomy. The term 'colonial science' is itself problematic in that scientists were trained in generalizing and to some degree universalist modes of thinking. Many worked in multiple centres of calculation, drawing on wide comparative circuits of knowledge, with reference points outside of particular colonies and their economic priorities. Their disciplines were advancing rapidly and subject to intense internal debate and division. Some were capable of developing their own original research trajectories.

Secondly, some scientists and technical officers drew on local knowledge systems; Willcocks is an interesting case. There was interpenetration of ideas in practice, even if it was not always acknowledged; experts could act as generalizers and developers of local knowledge. Anthropologists, at least, also tried to explain it. Thirdly, some colonized countries, such as India, produced their own scientifically trained experts who could contribute to a critique of imperialism, and the development of a national approach. Fourth, scientists could sometimes try to rectify the environmental ills caused by imperial exploitation. This was evident in wildlife conservation and forestry, even when they excluded local people from land and resources, as well as in the emerging discipline of ecology.

Ecology, Empire, and the Interpenetration of Knowledge

Ecology was from its inception, Libby Robin argues, conceived in pursuit of a global understanding of the natural world. It grew out of the sciences of exploration such as geology, botany, and zoology, but came of age as one of the 'sciences of settling'. Ecology, she continues, 'in its guise as a self-conscious, twentieth-century science, was partly an artefact of empire'.[10] But it could also be, as Helen Tilley suggests, potentially subversive because it crossed disciplinary boundaries, and encouraged totalizing and holistic

---

[10] Griffiths and Robin (eds.), *Ecology and Empire*, 63.

thinking.[11] Ecologists were critical of anthropocentric approaches, and their ideas were a major stream feeding into radical modern environmentalism. We can see both of these strands in ecological work in the Empire.

Robin is not suggesting that ecology was simply a science for imperialism. As a British discipline it was initially more theoretical: concerned to map vegetation types and, in the hands of Tansley, who spearheaded its institutional development, to understand the competition between plants and their relations to animals. Ecologists did not focus only on undisturbed habitats. In the 1920s Elton studied plant and animal invasions for which ecological thinking was well suited.[12] Echoes of his approach can be found in Crosby's work. Population ecology was an adjunct enterprise, exploring the dynamic interaction between species, their reproductive strategies, food supplies, and habitats.

Ecology was largely a field science and it soon became tied to conservation: both the concern to protect species and to exploit natural resources more effectively and sensitively. Aldo Leopold, sometimes invoked as a founding father of twentieth-century American environmentalism, made his name in the 1920s explaining the 'value of varmints'—or what happened to a forest ecology when the predators were exterminated, and the deer population exploded. For Americans and Australians, ecology was strongly related to the development of agriculture in difficult new environments. In the Mid-West, for example, locust plagues threatened agriculture, and the growth of applied entomology, as a means of analysis and control, fed into ecology.[13] Clements studied plant succession as part of an attempt to understand and improve the exploitation of pastures for ranching. From this grew his highly influential arguments about the existence of a climax vegetation—a vegetation at its most diverse and productive equilibrium. This was desirable both for the benefit of nature and for livestock production. Clements's

[11] Libby Robin, 'Ecology: a Science of Empire' in Tom Griffiths and Libby Robin (eds.), *Ecology and Empire: Environmental History of Settler Societies* (Edinburgh: Keele University Press), 63–75; Anker, *Imperial Ecology*; Helen Tilley, 'Africa as a "Living Laboratory": The African Research Survey and British Colonial Empire: Consolidating Environmental, Medical, and Anthropological Debates, 1920–1940', unpublished D.Phil. thesis, University of Oxford (2001), 128, quoting Paul B. Sears; Helen Tilley, 'African Environments and Environmental Sciences', in Beinart and McGregor (eds.), *Social History and African Environments*, 109–30.

[12] Charles Elton, *Animal Ecology* (first pub. 1927: Chicago: University of Chicago Press, 2002); Elton, *The Ecology of Invasions by Animals and Plants* (London: Methuen, 1958).

[13] Paulo Palladino, *Entomology, Ecology and Agriculture: The Making of Scientific Careers in North America, 1885–1985* (Amsterdam: Harwood Academic, 1996).

ecological understanding helped to guide range-management practices in the British Empire and Commonwealth for over half a century.

While metropolitan training often remained important, the locus of environmental sciences changed during the first half of the twentieth century. Britain tended to neglect its agricultural sciences in the late nineteenth and early twentieth centuries, because agriculture was in the doldrums, and settler states were more attuned to the value of public science in this sphere. Scientific work was increasingly associated with national rather than imperial priorities and formed an important part of intellectual life and new national identities; government departments and universities provided a career structure for scientists.[14] India also began to produce natural scientists in significant quantities. In Africa, there was increasing interaction between scientists based in the settler states of South Africa and Zimbabwe, many in government service, and those in British colonies, around such intractable local concerns as trypanosomiasis control and soil conservation—although racial barriers and exclusion from higher education delayed African participation.

Historians of science in India have a greater sense of the long history of interactive knowledge, and of an earlier localization of institutions and national science.[15] In the eighteenth century, some British officials, as 'orientalists', were deeply absorbed in recording Indian achievements. Bayly suggests that 'colonial knowledge was derived to a considerable extent from indigenous knowledge, albeit torn out of context and distorted by fear and prejudice'.[16] In the nineteenth century, the gap grew and Europeans felt they had little to learn.[17] By the late nineteenth century, India was being seen not so much for its technological legacy as for its spirituality, which could be an antidote for the 'disease of invention'.[18] 'Technical men' were less interested in local knowledge and practices. Their discourse was universal and their 'real concern was to ensure the most efficient use of nature in the service of the state'.[19] Indian professionals in the early decades of the twentieth century drew on this legacy, even if they were part of a nationalist rather

[14] Dunlap, *Nature and the English Diaspora.*

[15] Adas, *Machines as the Measure of Men*, 99.

[16] C. A. Bayly, *Empire and Information: Intelligence Gathering and Social Communication in India, 1780–1870* (Cambridge: Cambridge University Press, 1996), 7.

[17] Satpal Sangwan, *Science, Technology and Colonisation: An Indian Experience, 1757–1857* (New Delhi: Anamika Prakashan, 1991).

[18] Adas, *Machines as the Measure of Men*, 351.

[19] Roy MacLeod and Deepak Kumar (eds.), *Technology and the Raj: Western Technology and Technical Transfers to India, 1700–1947* (New Delhi: Sage Publications, 1995), 13.

than imperial project. A group of Indian scientists around the journal *Science and Culture* opposed both British rule and the Gandhian influence in the Indian National Congress. While they accepted that Gandhi was genuinely sympathetic to those marginalized by modernity, they believed that science alone was 'capable of improving conditions of life when fully applied in a planned economy.'[20] They rejected the 'dubious Gospel of the Spinning Wheel and the Bullock Cart'.

Even at the height of modernist confidence, however, there were contested approaches to progress in the colonial world. The imbrication of scientific and local knowledge, and the subversive potential of science, is evident in the career of Cambridge-trained Albert Howard, who cut his teeth as an agricultural officer in the West Indies before going to India in 1905. He began as an economic botanist at Pusa, the newly established all-India government agricultural station. His wife, Gabrielle Matthaei, was a Cambridge-trained botanist who worked with him. In 1910 he was able to start a station in a far more arid zone at Quetta, Baluchistan. His work involved systematic observation of the practices of Indian peasants: 'We have before us an old civilization, with a corresponding volume of traditional experience in the growth of crops. This has helped to crystallize and define the agriculture of the country'.[21] His first focus was on methods of contouring and field drainage, which developed into the study of soil aeration. He also had major successes with breeding new strains of wheat, which were widely adopted. As Pusa's departments became more specialized, he felt that his increasingly practical and cross-disciplinary approach was being stifled and by 1924 he had established a new station in the princely state of Indore.

Howard became fundamentally concerned with soil fertility—'the first condition of any permanent system of agriculture'. He accepted that 'the agricultural systems of the Orient have passed the supreme test—they are almost as permanent as those of the primeval forest'.[22] They achieved this often through leaving plant residues in the soil as well as transferring animal and human wastes. Indian agriculture, he observed, was less successful on

[20] Dinesh Abrol, ' "Colonised Minds" or Progressive Nationalist Scientists: The Science and Culture Group' in MacLeod and Kumar, *Technology and the Raj*, 266; Arnold, *Science, Technology and Medicine in Colonial India*, ch. 6.

[21] Louise E. Howard, *Sir Albert Howard in India* (London: Faber & Faber, 1953), 36 quoting Albert Howard, 'The Improvement of Crop Production in India', 1920; Arnold, *Science, Technology and Medicine in Colonial India*, 152–3.

[22] Albert Howard, *An Agricultural Testament* (London and New York: Oxford University Press, 1940), 10.

this front than Chinese and Japanese, except that there were often particularly fertile patches around villages where excrement was deposited. His aim was to examine the scientific basis of fertility and, in part, he sought a fuller incorporation of Chinese systems in India.

Howard became deeply critical of Western agriculture, which seemed everywhere to cause a rapid decline in soil fertility. At this time, Liebig's ideas about soil chemistry dominated scientific soil research. Inorganic agricultural chemistry, with its focus on nitrogen, phosphorous, and potassium proposed that the solution to fertility was fertilizer. In the early decades of the twentieth century, as areas of cultivated land increased and mechanization displaced animals and their manure, so fertilizer became more essential and chemical companies more powerful. Howard sought alternatives that could be pursued by Indian peasants. One, he believed, was the widely practised, ancient system of mixed and rotational cropping with pulses or legumes and cereals, from which both benefited. Leaving plant residues could produce very uneven results, unless part of a careful cycle, because of the competition between decomposing vegetation and new plants for nitrogen. He experimented extensively with green manuring as a way of solving this problem. He was attracted to green manures not only as a means of restoring soil fertility but also because nature, he believed, clothed most bare soil with forest or pasture, and abhorred a vacuum of plants.

His war cry was increasingly 'humus' and the restoration of this organic matter, prepared away from fields, to the soil was perfected in what he called the Indore process between 1924 and 1931. The physical properties of humus were to some degree recognized, especially its capacity to hold water, and to aerate soils, but not its nutritional qualities *per se*. Howard argued that humus, correctly prepared, contained nutritional material, including chemicals, essential for plant growth. The ideal mixture required vegetable and animal wastes and the management of micro-organisms in its preparation. Compost made in this way was 'soft to the feel with the smell of rich woodland earth'; that made with chemical activators was 'harsh to the touch with a sour odour ... The soil must have its manurial rights'.[23]

Plant health, Howard argued, was closely related to organic matter, soil aeration, and porosity, and these were the key to control of pests such as greenfly in fruit. Correct composting could greatly enhance the nutritional status of animals and people, as well as disease resistance. So confident was Howard of

---

[23] Howard, *An Agricultural Testament*, 42.

his methods that he tried to have boll worm imported from the United States in order to show that Indore cotton would be immune. A composting system that used human wastes also promised to solve the problem of night-soil treatment in Indian villages, and related diseases: 'cleaner and healthier villages will go hand in hand with heavier crops'.[24] Howard 'believed fundamentally in peasant shrewdness', or 'peasant wisdom', and 'that any worthwhile suggestion would earn an immediate and lasting success'.[25] He was equally committed to scientific methods and schedules—'nearly thirty years of the most exacting investigation, conducted on strict scientific lines'.[26] But he believed that science had to be broadly conceived and he criticized some British scientists for their narrowness of focus.

Howard employed Indian scientists, with one of whom he co-authored a book. It seems that he did secure Indian acceptance of some of his wheat seeds, his systems of field contouring, as well as composting. Cotton growers found the Indore process useful and elements of it were quickly taken up on some coffee and tea estates in East Africa. But labour was always a problem, for larger as well as smaller farmers. As he recognized, 'Artificials are easy of application, easily purchased in good times … whereas humus means more labour, more attention, transport and trouble.'[27]

On his return to England in 1931, Howard energetically promoted his ideas and was one of the key influences in the foundation of the organic agriculture movement. The Soil Association, leading advocate of organic methods in Britain, has taken up his legacy with an annual Sir Albert Howard Memorial Lecture. In 2002, this was given by Vandana Shiva, doyenne of Indian radical environmentalists. In the colonial era and now, Howard's life and legacy are an instructive example of the dynamic interpenetration of knowledge. As mechanized chemical farming spread, his was a subversive voice—yet its roots were in colonial science, or better named, we suggest, science in the Empire.

Science, Agriculture, and Conservation

In both Australia and South Africa, disease and pestilence were an important initial focus for environmental sciences: understanding and coping with plague and trypanosomosis, phylloxera in grapes, with livestock diseases, and with invasive plants and animals such as prickly pear and

---

[24] Howard, *Sir Albert Howard*, 215.   [25] *Ibid.*, 15.   [26] *Ibid.*, 12.
[27] Howard, *An Agricultural Testament*, 71.

rabbits (Chapter 6).[28] Australia, followed by South Africa, introduced Latin American insects, cactoblastis and cochineal, to destroy the rampant prickly pear, which threatened agriculture, in one of the most ambitious biological control campaigns undertaken in the Empire. Eradication of prickly pear was closely tied up with experimentation in natural sciences such as entomology. It was seen in both countries as a conservationist initiative, because the campaign promised both to remove a threat to agriculture and to protect indigenous vegetation.

Conservationist concerns were equally important in rabbit control. Francis Ratcliffe went to Australia from Britain in the early 1930s, trained in the new methods of population ecology. He worked on giant fruit-eating bats, the flying foxes, which had become a pest to Queensland farmers and then—after a spell lecturing in Aberdeen—on soil erosion in Australia. His book, *Flying Fox and Drifting Sand*, became a classic, which influenced environmental consciousness in Australia 'about the ecological limits of agricultural enterprise'.[29] He was also centrally involved in rabbit-control work, which linked population ecology and conservation because rabbits not only destroyed the pastures for sheep, but also consumed indigenous plant species. As in the case of prickly pear, biological control provided a solution—this time in the shape of the disease myxomatosis, which killed 90 per cent of Australia's rabbits in the 1950s. The wool clip grew quickly, stimulated also by a period of high prices. Even if the primary purpose of such interventions was connected with economic production, the potential for restoration of biodiversity was a significant side product. Dunlap exaggerates when he argues that 'the great story of the settlers and their lands in the last forty years [to 1998] has been the impact of ecology's knowledge'.[30] But ecological thinking did penetrate into agriculture and popular discourse, as well as the social sciences; it influenced broader environmental consciousness by introducing new concepts, and knowledge of complex interactions. Science for development was increasingly including science for conservation.

There are similar strands in the career of Edgar Barton Worthington, who was an advocate of ecology, and to some degree transcended his role as a colonial scientist. He graduated as a zoologist in 1927 from Cambridge, and, aware of the potential for research in 'untrodden territory'—after the

[28] Beinart, *Rise of Conservation*; Tyrrell, *True Gardens of the Gods*.

[29] Robin, 'Ecology', 70; Frances Ratcliffe, *Flying Fox and Drifting Sand: The Adventures of a Biologist in Australia* (London: Chatto & Windus, 1938).

[30] Dunlap, *Nature and the English Diaspora*, 245.

mode of Darwin and Wallace—took a post with the Fishing Survey of Lake Victoria.[31] This was established in response to a crisis of over-fishing in the lake, following the introduction of improved nets, which affected the supply both to settlers and Africans. Fish were of great importance in local food supplies, and fishing provided many lakeside villagers with an income. Worthington also looked into the possible effects of a dam proposed by the Sudanese government that might raise the lake level, and expand the shallow areas of the lake, to the benefit of the fishing industry. His analysis was based on understanding complex food chains, and how they might alter.[32] Ecology in his hands was, at one level, a route to 'farm the waters' and he suggested the introduction of Nile perch to expand the fisheries.[33] Although this was not then pursued, the perch was later to have a major impact both by increasing yields and destroying small, indigenous cichlid fish species.[34] But Tilley notes that he spent two years researching the lakes of East Africa and worked extensively with local African sailors and fishermen, accepting that they 'probably taught us more about the fish and fisheries of Lake Victoria that we were able to teach them'.[35]

Worthington was asked to coordinate the scientific research and publication for Lord Hailey's ambitious *African Survey*.[36] He consulted widely with scientists working on and in Africa; his task was not only to summarize the position, but explore how science could be better coordinated, turned to administrative use, and improve social welfare. About 275 scientists and administrative officers were consulted and the extensive survey, *Science in Africa*, gave considerable prominence to rising environmental knowledge and conservationist concerns in the Empire.[37] From 1937 to 1946 he worked at Lake Windermere in England, researching for the Freshwater Association, exploring how certain fish favoured by anglers could be increased in number and others diminished. In the late colonial period, he

---

[31] Tilley, 'Africa as a "Living Laboratory"', 88; E. B. Worthington, *The Ecological Century: A Personal Appraisal* (Oxford: Oxford University Press, 1983).

[32] Peder Alter, 'The Ecology of Nations: British Imperial Sciences of Nature, 1895–1945', unpublished Ph.D., Harvard University (1999), 234.

[33] Anker, 'The Ecology of Nations', 235.

[34] Tijs Goldschmidt, *Darwin's Dreampond: Drama in Lake Victoria* (Cambridge, MA: MIT Press, 1996).

[35] Tilley, 'Africa as a "Living Laboratory"', 89.

[36] Worthington, *Science in Africa* (London: Oxford University Press, 1938); Lord Hailey, *An African Survey: A Study of the Problems Arising in Africa South of the Sahara* (London: Oxford University Press, 1938).

[37] Tilley, 'Africa as a "Living Laboratory"', 100 and ch. 4.

moved into an international coordinating role, seeking to apply scientific research to the solution of emerging global environmental and agricultural problems.

Worthington's influence can be traced in scientific bureaucracies and in spreading ecological and conservationist initiatives. One idea that attracted him was the potential of farming wildlife in Africa. Here he worked with Fraser Darling, a Scottish ecologist, who made his name with a study of *A Herd of Red Deer* in the 1930s.[38] This was a pioneering work on animal ethology, based on observing deer over the long term and in their natural habitat. Drawing on Elton, and influenced by earlier work on termites, Fraser Darling saw the herd as an organism.[39] He looked beyond individual animals to explore how the herd functioned as a unit in pursuit of reproduction, food resources, and maintenance—even if it implied sacrificing some animals. He also emphasized adjustment and flexibility in interaction with the natural environment.

Darling developed interests in Africa, and became the Director of Research at the Conservation Foundation of New York.[40] Neither he nor Worthington invented the idea of wildlife farming or utilization in Africa—this had been suggested at least since the late eighteenth century when Anders Sparrman, the Swedish traveller at the Cape, argued that domesticated antelope species would be less damaging than livestock to the veld.[41] A number of attempts were made in South Africa and the Middle East to domesticate the eland, largest of the antelopes and known for its meat. South African sheep farmers kept springbok in their fenced, enclosed camps and British estate owners, as Darling was well aware, farmed deer for venison. Anthropologists noted that indigenous peoples in many parts of the world used fire to facilitate hunting of wildlife, and regulated the periods when this could take place. National parks were increasingly interventionist in environmental management, providing borehole water, culling, burning, and fencing—what one sceptical commentator later called 'elephant farming'.[42] The idea of wildlife farming had many antecedents.

[38] F. Fraser Darling, *A Herd of Red Deer* (London: Oxford University Press, 1937).

[39] Sandra Swart, 'The Ant of the White Soul: Popular Natural History, the Politics of Afrikaner Identity, and the Entomological Writings of Eugene Marais', in Beinart and MacGregor, (eds.) *Social History and African Environments*, 219–39.

[40] John Morton Boyd (ed.), *Fraser Darling in Africa: A Rhino in the Whistling Thorn* (Edinburgh: Edinburgh University Press, 1992).

[41] Beinart, *Rise of Conservation*.

[42] Patrick Marnham, *Fantastic Invasion: Dispatches from Africa* (London: Abacus, 1981).

After the Second World War, the Canadian, Australian, and New Zealand governments all formed agencies to apply science to wildlife problems and management.[43] Together with some officials in British colonies, leading scientists such as Elton, Darling, and Worthington encouraged research on wildlife ecology in Africa.[44] South African wildlife societies and zoologists were turning their attention to the same issues from the early 1950s. An American scientific conservationist, Raymond Dasmann, author of *The Destruction of California*—which set the tone for many later critiques of irrigation—conducted influential research in Zimbabwe showing the advantages of farming wildlife as opposed to livestock.[45]

The arguments were both ecological and economic.[46] Wild animals were best adapted to the African vegetation. The variety of wildlife species allowed for less damaging utilization of a very broad range of plants. Wildlife moved more regularly than livestock and were less likely to overgraze. By using the vegetation more efficiently, farming would become less damaging but also potentially give higher yields. Wildlife farming was never restricted to venison in that from the start it was also linked to commercial hunting and tourism. Wealthy landowners in South Africa had begun to buy wildlife and trout estates on the borders of the Kruger National Park and it was an easy transition to see the commercial tourist potential. In Kenya, attempts were made to encourage community management of wildlife in Maasai districts in the 1960s. It took some time before economic gains could be realized, and here the large settler farm proved to be a more adaptable base than African areas. But ecological thinking and imperial scientists played some role in evolving such new agricultural strategies that promised to increase biodiversity and could include an element of local community management. This came to a difficult fruition in the CAMPFIRE project, initiated in the 1980s in independent Zimbabwe (see Chapter 17).

Mainstream interpretations of new environmental movements, post-Rachel Carson and CND, have assumed a largely metropolitan momentum, yet there are important strands of thinking which fed in from the formerly colonized world. Scientists who worked in the Empire, and who often travelled and researched across national boundaries, slid easily into the International Union for the Conservation of Nature, the World Wildlife

---

[43] Dunlap, *Nature and the English Diaspora*, 245.

[44] Dawn Nell, 'Ecology, Agriculture and Wildlife Utilization in South Africa and Kenya, c.1950–1970', unpublished D.Phil dissertation, University of Oxford (2003).

[45] Raymond Dasmann, *African Game Ranching* (Oxford: Pergamon Press, 1964).

[46] Nell, 'Ecology, Agriculture and Wildlife Utilization'.

Fund, and UN agencies such as the Food and Agriculture Organization. Science became more multi-sited, and influenced by a greater range of political forces, in the post-colonial era. But we should be cautious about dismissing the varieties of science in the imperial period.

Exact science was necessary to make and operate the many machines that drove the Empire. Scientific ideas, languages, and practices increasingly suffused multiple spheres of activity that included categorizing the natural world, identifying and treating disease, extracting usable natural resources, and conserving environments. They became inescapable elements of modernity, intruding with varying degrees of acceptance into the lives of most imperial subjects. But exactness did not preclude scientific attempts to see the whole. Scientific modes of thought have been central in exploring the unity of complex, extraordinarily varied, natural systems. Colonial technical imaginations were brought to bear on enhancing production but also, for example, in seeing river valleys and watersheds as a whole, incorporating forestry, soil science, hydraulics, climatology, ecology, and sometimes forms of social development. Increasingly sophisticated and varied scientific approaches brought a new overview within the grasp of colonial governments. Even if officials worked within authoritarian states and were often insensitive to the social context, their approach was not, in Scott's terms, hedgehogism, but came closer to foxism—viewing the landscape as a whole and making a multitude of calculations about its potential.

Scientists and administrative people could also adopt complex models through which to understand and represent the world. They may have written on restricted topics, because the norms of discipline and publication demanded that they did so, but their contributions were often perceived as part of a greater research effort. Scientific models may not have been complex enough, but ecology, in particular, was a means of expanding the boundaries of interdisciplinary scientific enquiry. Scientists also increasingly shaped the concepts through which all disciplines understood the natural environment. These concepts are impossible to escape, and are widely, if unselfconsciously, used by historians and social scientists. In exploring a modified view of science in the Empire, however, we are not suggesting that technologically influenced development projects were generally welcomed by colonized people. Conservationist interventions that threatened access to natural resources or challenged patterns of local usage were often contentious. This was a major irony of colonial environmental policy: that interventions perceived by their authors as well-intentioned could prove most contested (Chapter 16).

13

Empire and the Visual Representation of Nature

Science and technology helped to shape resource frontiers in the Empire and conquer environments. They also framed new understandings of environmental change and conservationist policies. In a different way, visual representations conjured the Empire for British people and permeated their view of it. They were an inescapable element in the imagining of imperial nature. The growing range of images, we will argue, similarly had potential for encouraging possession, exploitation, and conservation of natural resources.

In 1926, an Empire Marketing Board was established in Britain to promote the consumption of food and products from the colonies and dominions. In its short life till 1933, it produced some of the most striking pictorial representations of empire in the shape of over 700 posters.[1] These were carefully commissioned with explicit instructions to some of the leading designers and poster artists in the country. Many captured the central themes that we have tried to illustrate: they depicted commodities, such as South African fruit, Australian wool, Ghanaian cocoa, or Malaysian pineapples, against a background of vivid landscapes, and sometimes the people who worked to turn nature into commodities. They promoted a positive image of an interdependent empire, in which exotic and beautiful environments, partly tamed, gave forth their riches for the British consumer.

In this chapter, we try to describe some of the images transmitted about the landscape and environment of empire, especially in the century from about 1850. While our major focus is on British-based representations, some reference is made to artistic work elsewhere that fed into the imperial visual store. Visual material such as Marketing Board posters familiarized British audiences with far-flung conquered zones, and naturalized their exploitation. However, these images were only one style of representation; there were many others and it is important to capture some of the complexity and variety of

---

[1] Stephen Constantine, *Buy and Build: the Advertising Posters of the Empire Marketing Board* (London: HMSO, 1986).

visual imaginations, developed in many different media. Images could transcend their intended purpose, and, as in the case of approaches to nature itself, there were conflicting and contending voices. Jostling alongside images that celebrated exploitation were others that championed nature or portrayed it sympathetically. Because of the power of visual media, it is arguable that these had a particular influence on environmental thinking. More recently, visual images have been a significant feature in the reassertion of indigenous rights and local knowledge about the environment. This chapter explores briefly advertising, photography, settler art, exhibitions, posters, and wildlife film.

Images, Commodification, and Advertising

In *Propaganda and Empire*, John MacKenzie innovatively analysed visual images as part of imperial propaganda.[2] His frontispiece—and clearly a personal favourite—is a postcard of imperial troops, with elephants and mountains in the background, entitled 'Defenders of the Empire' and used for selling Scotch whisky. It nicely sums up some of the core constituents of empire: conquest and military might, men in elaborate uniform, some on horseback, exotic animals and locations, royalty, and commodities. The troops are marching forward, a metaphorical statement about progress. His book was part of an argument against the view that the British were indifferent to imperialism. He wanted to survey the impact of empire on Britain and the creation of a British imperial world-view. While empire may have been fragmented, images such as this postcard attempted to put it all together, by 1924, with the king at the centre, juxtaposed by symbols of Africa, India, Canada, and Australia. Whatever the political reality, as settler states asserted their dominion status, and as rumblings of Indian nationalism grew louder, visually it was still possible to contain the Empire in a single, eclectic picture.

The development of a rich and multifaceted imperial iconography was gradual and incremental, but picked up pace in the late nineteenth and early twentieth centuries. Technical advances in photography, lithography, and mechanized printing facilitated the reproduction of multiple copies, and from the early twentieth century colour could be added. The driving force for dissemination of these images was not least commercial. On the one hand, they helped to sell books and popular magazines. By the late nineteenth

---

[2] John M. MacKenzie, *Propaganda and Empire: The Manipulation of British Public Opinion, 1880–1960* (Manchester: Manchester University Press, 1984).

century, British people were largely print literate. They were simultaneously becoming visually literate in new ways as such 'material became available at prices so low as to place them in almost every home'.[3] On the other hand, images became saleable commodities in themselves. The postcard industry flourished, as did lantern slide shows before the beginnings of cinema. In the second half of the nineteenth century, stereoscopic slides of two pictures seen through a viewfinder became a widespread craze in the Western world.[4] By the turn of the century, one American company produced seven million a year.

The very act of reproducing and selling a picture of landscape was a form of commodification.[5] Imperial visual images, drawing on design as well as photography, also became significant motifs in advertising. Alongside the ubiquitous Britannia, Victoria, John Bull, and Union Jack, were Stanley selling bootlaces, Baden-Powell whisky, and Kitchener selling stove polish. (He was known for this before his stern and uncompromising image fingered First World War recruits.)[6] More specifically relating to nature, balmy palms sold the purity of soap (and recognized its source), West Indian landscapes sold lime cordial, Camp coffee portrayed many evocative scenes of bivouacked imperial armies, and, less connectedly, Huntley and Palmer biscuits used an Indian scene with elephants.[7] Cocoa and tea advertisements often invoked the geographical context from which the products came. Selling cigarettes by camel and desert (R. J. Reynolds from the 1910s) must have been intended to stimulate thoughts both of fine tobacco and crisp, clean air rather than dry throats. Arid climates had been thought suitable for the curing of tuberculosis and chest diseases. Settler societies echoed these developments. Just as the springbok was emblazoned on everything from cigarettes to oranges (in Britain as well as South Africa), so the evocation of wilderness by canoe and water was deployed to advertise milk, lager, and cigarettes in Canada.[8]

[3] MacKenzie, *Propaganda and Empire*, 16.

[4] Neal Sobania, 'Stereoscopic Imagery in Support of a Colonial Project, South West Africa, 1905', paper for a conference on 'Encounters with Photography', South African Museum, Cape Town (1999); and 'But Where Are the Cattle? Popular Images of Maasai and Zulu across the Twentieth Century', *Visual Anthropology*, 15 (2002), 313–46.

[5] James R. Ryan, *Picturing Empire: Photography and the Visualization of the British Empire* (London: Reaktion Books, 1997), 57.

[6] Robert Opie, *Rule Britannia: Trading on the British Image* (Harmondsworth: Viking, Penguin, 1985), 7.

[7] Opie, *Rule Britannia*, 102–9.

[8] Benidickson, *Idleness, Water, and a Canoe*, between 16 and 17.

The advertising industry was stimulated by greater competition, more rapid transport facilities, and the globalization of markets as other industrialized countries caught up with Britain in the late nineteenth century. Manufacturers felt that they could trade on specifically British and imperial illustrations. Foreign manufacturers also used such images to penetrate the British market; 'African Traders' matchboxes, resplendent with an exchange encounter in the tropics, were made in Sweden.[9] If imperial patriotism was profitable, so it seems was the depiction of imperial nature.[10] These brands in turn became a comfortable and recognizable element in consumer visual culture—sometimes a tangible reminder of the provenance of commodities. Advertising helped to naturalize imperial environments as places from which products came. The absorption of such products as sugar and tea into British consumer taste at an earlier stage had been a more gradual process of osmosis, sometimes swept along by a wave of fashion. By the late nineteenth century, aggressive, sometimes visually inspired, marketing characterized the attempts to create new tastes for colonial products.

The View through the Camera Lens

Photography provided opportunities for image-making beyond this print and advertising culture. James Ryan argues that photography enabled British people 'symbolically to travel through, explore and even possess [colonial] spaces'.[11] Photographs were not a transparent reflection of the world they represented, but shaped by conventions of what was photogenic, what photographers saw as interesting, and which patterns of pictorial composition they followed. He argues that they 'reveal as much about the imaginative landscape of imperial culture as they do about physical spaces of people pictured within their frame'.[12] Others go further in suggesting that, like the scientific travelogue before it, 'the camera became a coloniser, a preparer of the route to European expansion in the late nineteenth century'[13] (Chapter 5).

From the start, photography was linked with travel and landscape and it certainly hugely expanded the range of representation that had begun

---

[9] Opie, *Rule Britannia*, 103.   [10] MacKenzie, *Propaganda and Empire*, 3.

[11] Ryan, *Picturing Empire*, 13.   [12] *Ibid.*, 19.

[13] Paul S. Landau, 'With Camera and Gun in Southern Africa: Inventing the Image of the Bushmen c.1880 to 1935', in Pippa Skotnes (ed.), *Miscast: Negotiating the Presence of the Bushmen* (Cape Town: University of Cape Town Press, 1996), 132; Paul S. Landau and Deborah D. Kaspin (eds.), *Images and Empires: Visuality in Colonial and Postcolonial Africa* (Berkeley, CA: University of California Press, 2002); MacKenzie, *Propaganda and Empire*, 19.

with art, maps, and illustration in travelogues. Photography was directly and quickly incorporated into the professional recording of imperial space. The Royal Geographic Society encouraged travellers to build photographic records, which it collected and stored. Topography and natural history featured strongly in early photography and, in turn, scientific enterprise encouraged the recording and mapping of terrain and resources.

Photography, however, was a difficult medium to control—more so as access to the technology spread. Some caution is required before we requisition it as a handmaiden of imperialism. First, there can be a problem in interpreting specific photographs. Ryan suggests that nineteenth-century photographs of Africa tended to emphasize disease, death, and barbarism. He illustrates this point with an 1860s photograph of vegetation taken by John Kirk, exploring with Livingstone in Central Africa. Ryan sees this photograph as a 'wall of impenetrable, twisted vegetation' symbolic of savagery and redolent of darkest Africa.[14] Kirk had a specific interest in tropical diseases and Ryan suggests he is illustrating a 'medical topography' of miasma. Certainly this language was pervasive at the time and Livingstone pictured himself as bringing light to Africa. Nevertheless this image could be interpreted in other ways, as a fascinating, tangled, romantic treescape in the manner of Marianne North (Chapter 5). Sympathetic images of dense fern vegetation in Australia were being painted at the same time. Ryan himself provides a very different photograph by Kirk, of a couple of statuesque baobab trees. The composition captures their gigantic scale and otherness, but it is redolent of an open English parkscape, with lime or oak, rather than darkest Africa. Of course a series of photographs can give a strong sense of a photographer's aims and style. But unless we know what was intended, many images can be read in different ways. While compositions were often suborned to established conventions of what was considered photogenic, they were sometimes taken with no very clear intent. Moreover, once photographic or artistic images are captured, they become documents that to some degree have a life beyond the intentions of their creators.

Secondly, photographs, even those taken by one person, can be very diverse. Elsewhere, Ryan discusses Samuel Bourne, who worked as a commercial landscape photographer based in Mumbai in the 1860s and 1870s. The quality of his nature photographs is extraordinary and he was important in developing an Anglo-Indian aesthetic. Ryan emphasizes that Bourne was

---

[14] Ryan, *Picturing Empire*, 38.

attracted by picturesque scenes, often with water, reminiscent of British land-scapes. One carefully and symmetrically composed photograph of Srinigar, Kashmir, recalled Constable.[15] Yet his mountainscapes were rugged and solemn—too arid to be simply part of a copycat imagery of Europe. They may have been containable within conventions of European alpine painting but they were not recreations of 'the softness of the English countryside'.[16]

Thirdly, photography was adopted by colonized people themselves. Judith Gutman argues that photography by Indians, especially in the nineteenth century, was significantly different from that by Europeans.[17] Much Indian photography recorded formal scenes, their content influenced by domestic social hierarchies. Physical representation and landscape were less important. Indian photographers did not try to produce symmetrical, choreographed, and romanticized landscapes. They expressed Indian life views—a different aesthetic and a different view of history in which individual lives were less significant. In particular she suggests that photographs, like some Indian art, presented the scene to the viewer flat on. The eye was not led to a focal point, or a single subject, as in much Western photography; there are seldom horizons. Gutman's revelation came when she was considering a picture of a group of women at a market. No woman stood out. The eye is not led through the peripheries or background to the foreground; it has to traverse the photograph and settle on each sub-scene separately. Family groups, in a single line, required similar viewing. Gutman uses a photograph of Indian public works (1903) to suggest that landscapes are peopled and the earth often raw and used, rather than choreographed.

These are exciting ideas, but caution is also needed here. Christopher Pinney feels that Gutman essentializes the otherness of Indian photography.[18] Indian photography in the late nineteenth and early twentieth century was shaped by the importance of studio work and by subjects who could pay for it. How different are these formal scenes to similar European studio material? Moreover, European photography at the time could also present scenes with little focal point. Two striking 1870s photographs of South Africa, published somewhat at random in a photo book on Africa, are a case in

---

[15] Ibid., 49; Judith Mara Gutman, Through Indian Eyes (New York: Oxford University Press, 1982), 17.

[16] Anne Newlands, The Group of Seven and Tom Thomson: An Introduction (Willowdale, Ontario: Firefly Books, 1995), 8.

[17] Gutman, Through Indian Eyes.

[18] Christopher Pinney, Camera Indica: The Social Life of Indian Photographs (London: Reaktion Books, 1997), 93–6.

point.[19] One taken at the Port Elizabeth Club in 1870 presents club members scattered around the garden. The eye has to explore each cluster separately and the subjects do not all face the camera, or a focal point. Many crowd scenes, and many formal photographs of large groups of people standing in lines, require this form of detailed reading. Technology also influenced pictorial possibilities. And earthy photographs are not unique to Indian styles. Famous images of the Big Hole diamond mine in Kimberley, in the 1870s, around the time that Bourne was creating his landscapes, evoke the grit, work, and chaos of a barely regulated industrial scene. By 1903 Western photographs showing workers in mines, railway construction, and quarries were commonplace. Gutman's argument requires qualification but she does remind us of the huge variety of photographers at work in the Empire and the possibility of images, taken by colonized people, that did not involve colonial 'possession' or simple replication of European styles.

Fourthly, as Ryan notes, photographs could be used directly in anti-imperial advocacy. Images sent by British missionaries to the Aborigines Protection Society of atrocities in Leopold's Congo were an attack on a certain form of imperialism. And by the early twentieth century, if not before, the careful and sympathetic images being taken of African animals were potentially subversive of imperial modes of natural resource exploitation, in particular hunting.[20] They differed from the woodcuts of hunting in nineteenth-century sagas and some were specifically conservationist in intent.

Landscape Art and Conservation

Painting and drawing were popular pastimes for English-speaking amateurs at home and abroad, but probably a technique less available than photographic technology and with less diverse picture makers. Art has a clearer professional body, a more controlled process of selection and display. Artists have more licence to shape their subjects and tend to organize themselves into self-conscious movements and styles which advertise their meaning. While the literature on photography tends to emphasize imperial possession and domination, Dunlap suggests that landscape art in Anglophone settler societies departed from such perspectives, and became both conservationist and nationalist during the early decades of the twentieth century.[21]

---

19 John Fabb, *Africa: The British Empire from Photography* (London: B.T. Batsford, 1987), 9.
20 C. A. W. Guggisberg, *Early Wildlife Photographers* (Newton Abbot: David & Charles, 1977).
21 Dunlap, *Nature and the English Diaspora*.

Most nineteenth-century art by settlers and travellers is seen, like photography, to reproduce European styles in new environments. 'Art in Canada', a critic later grumbled, 'meant a cow or a windmill'.[22] Artistic vision focused on the cabin in the wilderness, or the farmyard, signifying the early phases of encroachment upon nature. Yet in Australia Eugene von Guerard, working in the 1850s and 1860s, transcended this genre. He did paint scenes of 'wilderness converted'—the 'hut with smoking chimney' surrounded by trees with a family, dog, and chickens in a clearing.[23] But often, he specifically tried to capture the wild grandeur of nature. His most famous painting of 'Ferntree Gulley in the Dandenong Ranges' seemed a 'quasi-religious' recording of one of nature's 'loveliest cloisters'.[24]

While von Guerard's work can be seen in the context of lush, romantic European nature painting, he tried to illustrate what was specific about Australia—the fern trees, the density of vegetation, and lyre birds.[25] The painting became celebrated as typically Australian, although this particular site was soon to be destroyed by tourists and loggers. Another of von Guerard's paintings, Tower Hill, was commissioned by a landowner in the 1850s. Later in the century it was used by this emerging conservationist as a record of what the area had looked like in its pristine condition. Tower Hill did become part of a national park in the early twentieth century. After a sorry saga of mismanagement and exploitation, the original painting was used to reconstruct the vegetation during 1960s restoration work.[26]

Marianne North's paintings, hung in a special building at Kew from 1882, and 'bursting with colour and light', show a similar artistic transition.[27] (See Chapter 5.) Her depiction of the colonized and tropical world as vivid and exciting, rather than dark and dangerous, represented a different version of tropicality and captured something of her own personal conflicting desires.

In Australia, Arthur Streeten's 'Cremorne Pastoral', painted in 1895, was explicitly intended as a shot across the bows of business interests that wished to develop mining near Sydney Harbour.[28] He was part of the Heidelberg school of artists, who painted the Australian landscape in the open air,

[22] Newlands, *The Group of Seven*, 8, quoting A. Y. Jackson.

[23] Tim Bonyhady, *Australian Colonial Paintings in the Australian National Gallery* (Melbourne: Australian National Gallery, 1986), 186.

[24] Bonyhady, *Australian Colonial Paintings*, 176.

[25] Schama, *Landscape and Memory*.   [26] Bonyhady, *The Colonial Earth*.

[27] Michelle Adler, 'Skirting the Edges of Civilization: British Women Travellers and Travel Writers in South Africa, 1797–1899', unpublished Ph.D. thesis, University of London (1995), ch. 7.

[28] Bonyhady, *The Colonial Earth*.

borrowing from European impressionists but celebrating the 'light, heat, and space' of the country.[29] Dunlap sees their vision as different from von Guerard's; they were Australians rather than visiting Europeans, totally immersed in the landscape, rather than representing the exotic. But the art of both was absorbed into conservationist politics. In the settler dominions in the early twentieth century, commercial artists and politicians placed local animals and plants in coats of arms, stamps, and tourist brochures as well as advertisements; they became officially part of national iconography. Landscape and climate 'became central to national myths' in art as well as literature.[30] National art was still strongly influenced by styles of painting emerging from metropolitan schools and fashions and it is possible to detect similarities in landscape art in the different settler colonies. But each developed its own distinctive variant and colonial artists increasingly reflected a rootedness in local environments and identities.

An often-cited example of landscape art as nationalism is the work of the Canadian Group of Seven, formed in 1920.[31] They were inspired by Tom Thomson's colourful, modernist landscapes painted in the 1910s. Thomson died in a canoeing accident in 1917 at Canoe Lake in the Algonquin park north of Toronto.[32] The Group of Seven drew on his attempt to reflect the mood of wilderness, focusing on the treescape, the contours of hills, and the multicoloured water. Nature was conceived at the historical heart of nation, and psychologically embedded in settler society. They were searching for a deeper, more elemental identity at a time when Canadian society was industrializing rapidly and many Canadians, including new immigrants, were absorbed into cities. The Group of Seven explored the wilderness, and 'the grandeur and beauty of their country'. They wanted to do 'native' art, 'native as the rocks, or the snow, or the pine trees' and to find 'oneness with the spirit of the whole land'.[33] Their landscapes were of power, rather than tranquillity; they represented the forces of nature, rather than the homesteads and farmyards that tamed it. This is nowhere more apparent than in Lawren Harris's stark green, white and dark views of 'Mountains and Lake', or 'North Shore Lake Superior'.

The Group of Seven's modernism and their emphasis on symbol, line, and colour offended some local critics. Ironically, their status was enhanced

[29] Dunlap, *Nature and the English Diaspora*, 101.

[30] *Ibid.*, 99.   [31] *Ibid.*, 104–5; viewed at the Royal Ontario Museum, Toronto.

[32] Benidickson, *Idleness Water, and a Canoe*, 5.

[33] Harry Hunkin, *The Group of Seven: Canada's Great Landscape Painters* (Edinburgh: Paul Harris Publishing, 1979), 35; Newlands, *The Group of Seven*.

at the Wembley Empire Exhibition in London in 1924. British critics, formerly disdainful of derivative colonial art, now saw 'real triumphs'; 'Canada has arrived', one wrote, 'she has a real national style', giving 'the very feel of Canada'.[34] Landscape and environment, rather than culture, underpinned Canadian uniqueness. There are echoes of this modernist, nationalist art in the South African landscapes by Pierneef at this time. He employed cubist perspectives and a striking incorporation of blue, purple, and grey, as well as natural colours, to evoke heat and isolation. His work became very public, adorning Johannesburg Station and South Africa House in London, amongst other sites. Pierneef was claimed by Afrikaner nationalists as 'teaching us to see, understand and to appreciate the rolling miles of veld with the blue mountains in the distance'.[35] These artists were learning to view the landscape in a new way, claiming a special status in interpreting it, rather like white South Africans were learning how to sight animals in the Kruger National Park. They saw themselves as particularly perspicacious, and well-suited to this pursuit, because of their background.[36] (See Chapter 17.)

Depictions of indigenous people were less central to, but not entirely absent from, such re-imaginings. In the nineteenth century, Native Americans featured in settler art and photography; everywhere in the British Empire they came under the scrutiny of the ethnographic camera.[37] Even then, some photographers gave their subjects dignity. By the interwar era of the twentieth century, anthropological sensitivities, and new ideas about cultural relativism, began to intrude into art. In the Canadian case, some painters focused on indigenous symbols in their natural landscapes. Emily Carr's ambitious recording of standing totem poles began before the Group of Seven was formed, between 1908 and 1912, and she continued to paint them through the next few decades.[38] (Harris tried to persuade her, unsuccessfully, to concentrate on landscapes.) Her paintings of indigenous motifs may have started as a mode of anthropological recording but they reflected the stern and powerful images of another representation of nature. Through her

[34] Hunkin, *The Group of Seven*, 115–16.

[35] Alrika Hefers (ed.), *J. H. Pierneef, The Station Panels* (Perskor, no place or date).

[36] Bunn, 'An Unnatural State'.

[37] Elizabeth Edwards (ed.), *Anthropology and Photography, 1860–1920* (New Haven: Yale University Press, 1992).

[38] See website: <http://www.emilycarr.org>, Stuart Macnair Inc. cultural consultants, 'To the Totem Forests: Emily Carr and Contemporaries Interpret Coastal Villages' (1999) and notes from museum visit.

work, indigenous carved symbols in the totem poles were absorbed into a naturalistic settler art, which helped to give them an authority and a visibility.

Carr painted on different scales, depicting whole First Nations settlements in their natural settings, as well as clusters of poles, and specific motifs such as birds. Her images are powerful and appreciative of First Nations art. By comparison, Herbert Baker's incorporation of the Great Zimbabwe birds into his design for Rhodes House, in Oxford, acknowledged an indigenous art form, but submerged the symbol in his own amalgam of classical, colonial, and Arts and Craft architecture. Totem poles had become a symbol of survival and regrouping for the devastated West Coast First Nation communities in the nineteenth century. They were resuscitated in twentieth-century British Columbia, becoming ubiquitous in the public and commercial sphere. Some totem pole carving is traditional, some explores new artistic routes, and some is part of a highly commercialized industry, produced as decorative pieces or as souvenirs for tourists. Canadian First Nation and Inuit artists, as also Australian Aboriginal, have reasserted themselves since the 1960s, winning international recognition in a post-colonial era. Much of their work represents the spirit of nature and landscape, but, intriguingly, it revives older forms of abstraction. There is less direct representation of nature than in settler nationalist work, except in carvings of animals.

Propagandist Visions and Empire Produce

Photography and art expressed a plethora of visions, and evolved in a number of sites. Exhibitions were more centralized and organized ventures juxtaposing industry, machines, decorative arts, commodities, and new consumer goods. Exhibitions were not invented for the Empire but they became a resplendent vehicle of imperial display, helping to fix and link images, rather like MacKenzie's whisky postcard. They ran in tandem with imperial pageantry and served as a visual encyclopaedia of knowledge about empire, a 'museum of global explanation'.[39] Organized by eminent committees, exhibitions nevertheless gave some scope for individual entrepreneurs. Imre Kiralfy, an immigrant Central European, was 'more responsible perhaps than anyone for the vivid and vulgar understanding the British population had of its foreign territories'.[40] He liked to have indigenous people, as well as their material culture, on display.

[39] Paul Greenhalgh, *Ephemeral Vistas: The Expositions Universelles, Great Exhibitions and World's Fairs, 1851–1939* (Manchester: Manchester University Press, 1988), 20.
[40] *Ibid.,* 93.

Trade, technology, and progress were the central motifs of Victorian exhibitions, mixing the exotic with the practical and material, simultaneously glorifying and domesticating. In the twentieth century there were stronger political goals: plenty, peace, imperial achievement, and unity. Imperial exhibitions increasingly gave independent space to India and the dominions. At least twenty-four Indian palaces were built for exhibitions between 1886 and 1939. The two key early twentieth-century events were the 1911 London White City Exhibition, Kiralfy's apogee, and the 1924 British Empire Exhibition at Wembley. With a £2.2 million fund and a site of 216 acres, the scale of Wembley was often called 'vast' in contemporary literature: the Great Exhibition of 1851, in the Crystal Palace, 'was a village fair if compared', according to one exuberant author.[41] Wembley was all the more ambitious because an Empire Stadium, initially holding over 100,000 people, was completed in less than a year.[42] Opened by King George V, it was among the first major projects built with ferroconcrete, not only for the structure, but also for every detail from lamp posts and bridges to finishes: a 'city of concrete ... fresh, vigorous, beautiful and essentially of the present day'.[43]

Central buildings were devoted to Industry, Engineering and Government, mainly with displays from the 'Great Mother of all this wonderful family'.[44] A 'giant relief map of the world', in the Government building, captured the vastness of empire 'which could be seen at a glance, and where moving ships show the great trade routes of the world'. Exhibitions celebrated 'resources yet untapped', such as 'virgin forests' in Canada. Buildings were provided for each of the dominions and colonies to house its exhibits, 'transforming what had been a drab London suburb into an imperialist's dreamland'. The red walls of 'West Africa in Middlesex' faced the Canadian Pacific building and the India pavilion, glinting in an artificial London pond. A Cape Dutch house, modelled on Groot Constantia, nestled alongside 'A Moonlight Fantasy of East Africa', with stone castle, dhow, palms, and Zanzibar courtyard.[45] Scenes from a disparate Empire were literally and metaphorically brought together—like an enlarged Commonwealth stamp

[41] Donald Maxwell, *Wembley in Colour: The British Empire Exhibition of 1924* (London: Longmans, 1924), 112.

[42] Donald R. Knight, *The Lion Roars at Wembley: British Empire Exhibition, 60th Anniversary 1924–5* (New Barnet: Private Publication, 1984), 5–9.

[43] Knight, *The Lion Roars at Wembley*, 8.   [44] Maxwell, *Wembley in Colour*, 95.

[45] *Ibid.*, 23.

collection—within a single space, where the mountains of Canada tumbled onto the palm beaches of Africa.

These juxtapositions, however, could compress real as well as imaginary sequences. Imperial travellers did go by ship via Gibraltar and Malta, through the Suez Canal, down the East African Coast, or to India, Malaysia, and Australia, glimpsing each along their way. Many en route to Australia caught a snippet of Cape scenery. Wembley made sense partly because it also drew on a growing visual experience, and literacy. It is difficult to imagine this now, when all bow before the god of football, but Wembley was known in the interwar years for its imperial lions, not those on the England shirt. Over seventeen million people visited during the first seven-month opening, at an average of 104,000 a day, and nearly ten million in 1925 when it was re-opened for six months. It is true that an amusement park, with a mile-long rollercoaster, was part of the attraction, but the exhibition was also a version of empire to which the British were drawn. The visitor figures would make the sponsors of London's Millennium Dome weep.

The panoramic dioramas at Wembley depicted work, play, and nature. 'Modern commerce and machinery', one recorder noted, 'often enrich the pictorial possibilities of landscape'.[46] So a Canadian grain port, or elevator, dubbed one of 'the castles of Canada' was pictured against a soaring mountain landscape, and was accompanied by 'interesting travel films of Canadian scenery'. Group of Seven influence is evident in the pictures of landscape, though their paintings were exhibited separately in the Arts building. Two enormous sculptures of bison flanked the entrance to the Canadian Pacific railway building.

The dioramas were emulated in natural history museums. In London, the British Museum concentrated less on colonial objects than on classical culture and archaeological riches. The lineage of culture that was seen to have reached its apogee in early twentieth-century Britain was the sequence of civilization through Egypt, Greece, Rome, and the Renaissance. But British natural history and hunting museums presented stuffed colonial animals in increasingly imaginative ways, recreating the exhibition style. Colonial museums, burgeoning during the late nineteenth century, emphasized nature as much as culture, specializing in local animals and resources.[47] They became a means by which the middle classes of settler societies, or the intellectual elite

---

[46] Maxwell, *Wembley in Colour*, 38.
[47] Lewis Pyenson and Susan Sheets-Pyenson, *Servants of Nature: A History of Scientific Institutions, Enterprises and Sensibilities* (London: HarperCollins, 1999).

of the Indian Civil Service, could participate in popular scientific education, learn about resources in their territory, and view it as a whole.

In some senses Wembley laid the groundwork for the Empire Marketing Board's posters. Established in 1926 to promote the consumption of imperial, including British, food and products, the Board arose out of debates on imperial preference and trade.[48] Champions of empire wished to combine tariff protection at home with imperial preference to increase the flow of intra-empire trade. In 1926, only 30 per cent of British trade was with the empire. But free trade sentiment was strong and after the Conservatives lost the 1923 election, Baldwin abandoned a protectionist platform. On coming back to power in 1925, his government compromised by reserving £1 million a year for research and publicity to promote Empire trade and products, especially agricultural commodities. A key figure in the campaign was Frank Pick, formerly managing director of London Underground, where posters were a major feature of publicity. The Empire Marketing Board spent £427,000 on posters over eight years. Many were part of themed sequences of five, on their own hoardings, located separately from commercial adverts.[49] Interestingly, the Board did not use photography.

A number of posters represented nature as background for the commodity. Cattle-raising in Australia took place in big sky country with fields, eucalypts, and distant hills. South African orange orchards were pictured against the backdrop of mountain scenery, as were deciduous fruits. Malaysian pineapples were grown amidst intensely green, pristine, tropical vegetation. A blue, clean sea often featured in posters on shipping and transport routes. In some posters, animals were used to sell products. An attractive springbok appeared, somewhat incongruously, in a poster urging consumers to 'Buy South African Oranges', as did a bison, slightly less so, in 'Buy Canadian Hams and Bacon'. Some posters included local people who worked to turn nature into commodities. McKnight Kauffer's distinctive modernist design to promote cocoa, for example, showed an abstract, lush, yellow and green background, with black female shapes wearing pink cloths. His banana poster was similar. Others depicted cocoa in an exotic, colourful soup of African women, baskets, and trees. Ceylon tea featured women in sarongs picking in a sea of green plants, set against hills and sky.

---

[48] Mark Havinden and David Meredith, *Colonialism and Development: Britain and its Tropical Colonies, 1850–1960* (London: Routledge, 1993), 150–2; Constantine, *Buy and Build*.
[49] *Ibid.*, 5.

8. Gathering Cocoa Pods. An Empire Marketing Board poster from 1928.

Credit: G. Spencer Pryse, artist, British National Archives ref. CO956/5.

Such designs vividly linked nature, work, and trade. The commodity
gained freshness and interest from nature, and perhaps the women were
intended to add wholesomeness. They were barely sexually suggestive. Toil
was hard but it was not pictured as exploitative. Only in a few images,
such as tobacco-growing in Rhodesia and Nyasaland, were white planters
also included amidst the indigenous workers and landscape. These are
strong images that both fed off and influenced the popular art of this era.
Constantine argues that they were explicit propaganda, and attempted to
draw the Empire together and purvey the idea of mutual dependence.[50] Even
more striking is the embodiment of nature and wilderness in commodity.
The commodity chain was pictorially represented by the collective work of
the poster artists and their commissioners.

   Some posters were reproduced in other forms: 2–3,000 of a map entitled
'Highways of Empire', mimicking Wembley's imperial cartography, for
schools; 250,000 images of the springbok and buffalo for cigarette cards.[51]
They appeared in the press, and at Empire Shopping Weeks. One million

---

[50] Mark Havinden and David Meredith, *Colonialism and Development: Britain and its Tropical
Colonies, 1850–1960* (London: Routledge, 1993), 5; Constantine, *Buy and Build*.

[51] *Ibid.*, 10.

people, many of them schoolchildren, visited the Empire Marketing Board Cinema at the Imperial Institute in South Kensington. The posters were designed to sell an idea as much as specific products; some criticized them as ineffective because they were insufficiently aggressive and too subtle.[52] By the early 1930s, after the depression, the Board became redundant—replaced by imperial preference and protection. Poster production was abandoned. Though the images have not been revived, in the manner of London Underground adverts of the time, as part of a retro visual culture, they remain as evidence of a creative period of public design. They would have been seen as part of a broader poster culture advertising everything from films to seaside resorts. In that sense, they almost certainly integrated images and knowledge of imperial commodities in a wider set of expanding consumer possibilities for British people.

The Colonial Origins of Natural History Film

By the interwar years, film was shouldering other media aside in the Western world as the most powerful maker of visual images; the rise of television after the Second World War further accelerated that process. Dominated by the US, feature film shown in British and dominion cinemas did not always present an explicitly imperial view of the world. Nevertheless, Hollywood's version seldom challenged the basic tenets of Western dominance—whether in Westerns affirming the morality of conquest or in its hierarchical depiction of race relations. Some British-made feature films addressed imperial themes. *The Four Feathers* (1939)—by Alexander Korda, a Hungarian expatriate—dealt with heroism and cowardice in the conquest of Sudan. Documentaries made by the Colonial Film Unit were used for propaganda and education in fields such as health and rural development.

Film, especially expensive feature film, was more restricted in authorship than either photography or art. Yet it could also be ambiguous in respect of the imperial ethos. The gradual shift from predatory hunting to conservationism in the British Empire, exemplified by the rise of the imperial wildlife reserves, was reflected in and reinforced by visual images (Chapters 4 and 17). Photographic safaris began in the early twentieth century, as did published books of photographs, promoting the beauty and fascination of wild animals.[53] Photographs were certainly used to record hunting. Rather

---

[52] Havinden and Meredith, *Colonialism and Development*, 151.
[53] Ryan, *Picturing Empire*; Guggisberg, *Early Wildlife Photographers*.

like the stuffed trophy before them, they became a certificate of human prowess and animal death. Yet such public evidence of slaughter was an increasingly uneasy display.

By the 1930s, wildlife films that concentrated very largely on animals rather than hunters had become an established genre in Britain and the US. Kenya in particular was a favourite site for filming, because of the imperial connection and the accessibility of large African mammals. Park Rainey, Cherry Kearton, and Douglas and Osa Johnson, among others, won large audiences for feature-length wildlife films.[54] While their intention was to highlight the animals, and their film-making practices already involved long patient waits at waterholes, the Johnsons in particular found it necessary to ramp up the excitement for audiences by provoking animal charges and fights. But after the Second World War, styles changed. Natural history films flourished and were able to command prime slots, with audiences of millions, on British television. Some of the most important film-makers in the 1950s and 1960s, when TV became a mass medium in Britain, were part of a network of ardent animal lovers and conservationists.[55]

Armand and Michaela Denis, filming largely in Kenya, had a weekly slot on the BBC. David Attenborough began his *Zoo Quests*—the first to Sierra Leone.[56] Joy and George Adamson brought up the motherless lion cub Elsa, and then released it into the wild. She wrote a best-selling book *Born Free* (1960), with sequels, published by Collins who specialized in this material. They set the scene for the eponymous, widely screened, film (1965), made on location in Kenya, for which George relived their experiences with another lioness.[57] Vets Sue Hart and Toni Harthoorn, who became the model for the American series *Daktari*, were based in Nairobi and also key figures in filming and writing about African wildlife in the 1960s.[58] They all depicted wild animals sympathetically. As privileged interlocutors, they were experimenting with what they felt to be a new set of relationships between

---

[54] Pascal James Imperato and Eleanor M. Imperato, *They Married Adventure: The Wandering Lives of Martin and Osa Johnson* (New Brunswick, NJ: Rutgers University Press, 1992).

[55] William Beinart, 'The Renaturing of African Animals: Film and Literature in the 1950s and 1960s', *Kronos: Journal of Cape History*, 29 (2003), 201–26.

[56] David Attenborough, *Life on Air: Memoirs of a Broadcaster* (London: BBC, 2002).

[57] Joy Adamson, *Born Free: A Lioness of Two Worlds* (London: Collins, 1960); George Adamson, *Bwana Game: The Life Story of George Adamson* (London: Collins and Harvill, 1968); Adrian House, *The Great Safari: the Lives of George and Joy Adamson* (London: HarperCollins, 1995).

[58] Sue Hart, *Life with Daktari: Two Vets in East Africa* (London: Companion Book Club, 1969).

people and wild animals. They were not necessarily the first to do so, but they had access to the combined force of mass publishing, photography, film, and television. They were determined to change the image of wild animals in human minds. Though they have not perhaps been claimed by modern environmental movements, they did influence some strands of popular environmentalism, especially its animal-centric anglophone forms.

Film, and especially television, was a medium that lent itself to the project of connecting Western audiences to African wildlife. It could capture movement and dramatic encounter; it could compress time to transmit action, energy, and excitement. Improved telephoto lenses, slow motion, and synchronized sound helped enlarge the scope for filming animal activities—to include mating, birth, and predator kills. On television wild animals were brought into people's front rooms to produce the 'absurdly intimate filmic reality we now take for granted'.[59]

The images of African animals projected at this time were essentially for Western people. They coincided with major and heavily publicized Commonwealth achievements, such as the conquest of Everest by Edmund Hillary and Tensing Norgay. Most of the film-makers and publicists still saw the primary responsibility for protecting African wildlife to lie with themselves and Western society. Thus although elements of their conservationist projects were subversive of an earlier imperial hunting ethos, they were not directly challenging the pre-eminence of Western ideas. It is striking that natural history film in this period tended to write out or diminish the presence of African people who had lived so long with wild animals. Some were, however, shown as auxiliaries in the enterprise and especially after independence in the early 1960s, there is greater recognition of African involvement. The film of *Born Free* included both African and Indian actors and attempts were made to win the support of the new Kenyan government.

We began with John MacKenzie's argument about visual media forming an element in the propaganda of empire. His thesis was part of a book about propaganda, rather than about images. Undoubtedly, some images were used in this way—notably the posters of the Empire Marketing Board. But industrial society produced a multiplicity of visual technologies, which could not easily be controlled. Images themselves could mean different things to diverse audiences. Photography, art, and film were all on occasion deployed

---

[59] Donna Haraway, *Primate Visions: Gender, Race, and Nature in the World of Modern Science* (New York: Routledge, 1989), 42.

by critics of empire or targeted at practices that had been associated with imperialism. Some new technology, particularly photography, was available to colonized peoples. Indigenous artists developed their own genres and were, in the longer term, able to reach wider audiences.

The natural environments of conquered territories were recorded and presented for a range of purposes. While these representations sometimes reflected 'possession' by dominant groups and hugely increased the familiarity of British people with colonized places, they also facilitated links between those places. Cinema-goers in South Africa in the 1950s and 1960s were fed on a diet not only of American Westerns, but also Canadian forestry films and the Kenyan-made *Born Free*. Such interactions helped to create a visual commonwealth. And in certain respects, the multiplicity of images about nature and animals in the colonial era were important in stimulating conservationist impulses.

14

Rubber and the Environment in Malaysia

The rise of the motor car created two very different commodity frontiers in the British Empire, one producing oil and the other rubber. The demand for rubber followed an often-repeated pattern in that it was shaped by scientific invention, technological change, and new patterns of consumption in the industrialized world. It was related directly to the development of new fossil fuels. Coal transformed shipping and overland transport by rail. Oil (Chapter 15) opened new realms for mobility. The invention in 1867 of the internal combustion engine by a German, Nikolaus Otto, and in 1885 of automobiles powered by gasoline-driven engines revolutionized transport, culture, and the South-East Asian environment.[1]

During the late nineteenth century, wild natural rubber booms swept through the tropical world, from Brazil to the Congo, leaving in their wake hardship and scandal. In Malaysia, there was a very different outcome—the development of plantations on a new capitalist agrarian frontier. Rubber became one of the single most important commodities produced in the Empire, and was enormously valuable to Britain not only for its own motor industry but also to sell to the United States. Whereas demand for some earlier imperial commodities was largely British, there was also significant consumption of rubber and oil in other parts of the Empire, especially the settler dominions. In the early decades of the twentieth century, rubber plantations, in parallel with expanding sugar production in Queensland, Natal, Trinidad, and Fiji, extended and intensified Britain's engagement with the tropical zones of the world. Indentured workers replaced slaves as the major plantation workforce. South India was the major labour source for Malaysia, where the ports and tin-mining centres already had substantial Chinese communities. British colonialism in Malaysia left as its legacy a multi-ethnic society. By the 1930s about 55 per cent were indigenous Malays and Orang Asli, 35 per cent of Chinese origin, and close to 10 per cent Indian.

---

[1] N. Georgano *et al.*, *Britain's Motor Industry: The First Hundred Years* (Sparkford: G. T. Foulis, 1995).

Although capital was increasingly mobile by the late nineteenth century, extraction and production of the three major commodities of the twentieth-century Empire proved to be highly location specific. Gold and oil were trapped in particular geological formations. The sites of exploitation result-ed partly from the serendipity of pre-colonial discovery, and partly from colonial sensitivity to potential mineral wealth. In the case of rubber, other environmental factors were more significant—notably those which shaped where the trees could be grown and tapped successfully. While foreign capital was essential in moulding the growth of the industry and, until independence in 1957 the majority of production remained in foreign hands, capital had to go to the lowland forests of South-East Asia. There, plantations tore into the peninsula's timber resources. But rubber did not require such massive alienation of land and displacement of indigenous populations that was characteristic of Caribbean plantations. Malays were not decimated by dis-ease, nor did the rubber industry spawn a significant settler population. Our arguments in this chapter are that rubber production was shaped by environ-mental opportunities and constraints, that it transformed parts of Malaysia and underpinned rapid economic growth, but that in comparative terms, the social and environmental impact of this plantation complex was constrained.

The Origins of Malaysian Rubber

Rubber-producing plants are restricted to the tropics; their latex is an adaptation to heat and assists resistance to insects that bore into the bark. Rubber-producing vines were found in many tropical forests, including South-East Asia, where *Ficus elastica* or rambong was used locally. The Amazon forests housed vines and trees such as manihot and seringa, which Native Americans tapped. Brazil was an important source of natural rubber, and in the 1850s Portuguese settlers rushed into the forested interior, using their own and indigenous labour to collect the sap.[2] A complex trade network evolved, bringing rubber down the river system to Belem where seringa rubber was used for shoe-making. By the 1860s, Brazilian experiments suggested that hevea species, and especially the tree *Hevea braziliensis* was the best natural source for manufacture. The largest trees, up to fifty metres high, tended to be on elevated, well-drained ground, on the lower slopes of river valleys.

[2] Warren Dean, *Brazil and the Struggle for Rubber: A Study in Environmental History* (Cambridge: Cambridge University Press, 1987).

Manufacturers in North America and Europe saw the potential of natural rubber in the early decades of the nineteenth century, but its use was restricted by its propensity to become tacky when warm, and more rigid when cold; it also had a pungent smell. In 1839 the bankrupt and formerly imprisoned American storekeeper, Charles Goodyear, stumbled across a solution.[3] He linked up with an unsuccessful rubber entrepreneur, Nathaniel Hayward, who had found that the addition of sulphur improved rubber's quality. To this Goodyear added, by accident, heat. The compound, so treated, could better withstand changes in temperature and lost its smell. In Britain Thomas Hancock, hearing of this American discovery, and working with a company called Mackintosh, developed his own process of vulcanization—so named after the Roman god of fire.

Experiments quickened with other solutions, chemical additives, and colours. These opened the way to a wider range of uses including machinery components, bottle stoppers, bouncing balls, and rainproof garments or Mackintoshes. When rubber aged, it became brittle, and this remained a major problem, eventually solved by chemical antioxidants. But rubber had attractive properties of flexibility and elasticity, as well as imperviousness to water and many chemicals, and it was easily cleaned. British imports increased from £300,000 in 1854 to £1,300,000 (nearly 60,000 kg) in 1874, putting a premium on a reliable colonial source of supply.[4]

Plant collectors were assigned to find seeds of the *H. braziliensis*. Some brought to London in 1873 were purchased by the Pharmaceutical Society for Kew, the spider in the web of the botanical Empire. Twelve of them germinated. Henry Wickham, an Englishman then living in Brazil, employed Native Americans to harvest thousands of seeds from wild trees in what was later found to be the northern part of the tree's range, along an Amazon tributary, in 1876. He believed that the natural rubber in this area was particularly sought after. Wickham brought the seeds back himself by ship. He exaggerated the dangers of his export by stealth—in fact such seed transfers were not illegal—and this helped to assure him recognition in Britain and notoriety in Brazil.[5] (Brazilian pique at this transfer should be tempered, Warren Dean argues, by the recognition that they acquired coffee in the eighteenth century through a similar stealthy import from the French colony of Cayenne.) Most of Wickham's seeds went to Kew, where nearly

---

[3] Austin Coates, *The Commerce in Rubber: The First 250 Years* (Singapore: Oxford University Press, 1987).

[4] Drayton, *Nature's Government*, 249.   [5] Dean, *Brazil*, 22.

3,000 were planted. In 1876–7 about 2,000 seedlings were sent to Sri Lanka, and a few to the British trading settlement at Singapore. It was from these two consignments that the main Malaysian stock was derived.

Following earlier Dutch incursions at Molucca, British trading settlements, in which Chinese immigrants predominated, were established in Malaysia in the late eighteenth century. Penang and Singapore emerged as the main centres, two of the ports collectively known as the Straits Settlements (Chapter 5). Colonial intrusions were limited during the nineteenth century and proceeded in part by agreements negotiated with Malay sultans. Tin mining, largely in the hands of Chinese owners and workers, took off in Perak in the 1870s to supply the growing global canning industry. By the late nineteenth century, perhaps 200,000 hectares of land nearer to the trading centres had been cleared for plantations to grow spices, gambier for dyestuffs, sugar, tapioca, coconut palms, and coffee.[6] None of these was very successful; both Chinese and British landowners were hungry for a profitable crop.

Rubber was one of many they tried. South-East Asian planters, experimenting with various Asian as well as Latin American rubber plants, were attracted to the quicker-growing vine species, but the yields of hevea appeared to be heavier. Henry Ridley, appointed curator at the Botanical Gardens at Singapore in 1888, became an ardent protagonist of the tree as a solution both to the problems of British rubber supply, and to those in the Malaysian plantations. More than anyone, he evolved methods of cultivating and tapping the trees. Most of the wild rubber gathering in Latin America and Africa involved cutting or slashing—and often killing—the plants. Even the more careful attempts to pierce or bore holes in the bark tended to destroy the source. Ridley perfected the herringbone form of excision, peeling away a limited area of the outer bark, but leaving the inner cambium intact; carefully done, this permitted maximum flow of sap from the tree while allowing the bark to recover. Sap would flow diagonally downwards and drip into containers. In Malaysia, at least, indigenous Orang Asli people in Perak used a similar technique on wild vines.[7] The area cut away would gradually be widened, downwards. Frequent tapping did not seem to damage the plants nor result in disease; morning tapping seemed to yield better than evening.[8]

---

[6] Colin Barlow, *The Natural Rubber Industry: Its Development, Technology, and Economy in Malaysia* (Kuala Lumpur: Oxford University Press, 1978), 23.

[7] D. J. M. Tate, *The RGA History of the Plantation Industry in the Malay Peninsula* (Kuala Lumpur: Oxford University Press, 1996), 203.

[8] Barlow, *The Natural Rubber Industry*, 21.

Prompted by Ridley, a Chinese landowner, Tan Chay Yan, put 17 ha. under rubber trees in 1896. This was generally recognized as the first successful commercial planting. Rubber's future in Malaysia was then shaped by an extraordinary conjuncture of climate, disease, and events. *H. braziliensis* requires a tropical climate with high rainfall—preferably over 1800 mm annually. The tree was quite adaptable and was tried amongst other places in Cambodia, Congo, India, Indonesia, Liberia, Mozambique, Sri Lanka, and Uganda. But it did best in locations where there was little variation in temperature, relatively little wind, and good drainage. Highly seasonal rainfall did not produce optimum growth. Yields were low in the dry season, and heavy monsoon rains—such as those experienced in South India and Burma—restricted tapping for long periods.[9] Thus while rubber would grow in many wet tropical zones, the best conditions were quite restricted. Malaysia and Sri Lanka, as well as parts of Dutch-controlled Indonesia and French-controlled Vietnam, soon emerged as the most favoured sites.[10]

The Singapore and Sri Lankan seeds, mostly from Wickham, and further selected by Ridley, proved to be the best available. Some of the African plantations used inferior seed collected at a later date in Brazil and this was one factor that inhibited their growth. Collecting forays were subsequently made, notably by the Dutch for their Indonesian plantations; they were unable to find a better stock, and it took at least seven years from planting to test the result. Seeds purchased from established plantations proved cheaper and more reliable. Rubber growers largely drew their stock from the selected survivors of about 2,000 seedlings: 'within thirty years, a few basketsful of seeds had been transformed into an agricultural resource of immense consequences in world trade and industry'.[11]

Dean argues that disease as well as climate shaped the location of successful rubber growing. Frequent attempts were made to establish plantations in Brazil itself, which had by definition a suitable climate. Many domesticated species do thrive in regions where their wilder forebears were located: maize, potatoes, tomatoes, and prickly pear or spineless cactus are all American cases in point. But rubber provides an example of a species that could not easily be exploited in its local context. While there were many technical and agricultural problems that constrained production on individual estates, it is worth pointing out that coffee plantations were spreading rapidly in Brazil

---

[9] Voon Phin Keong, *Western Rubber Planting Enterprise in Southeast Asia, 1876–1921* (Kuala Lumpur: Penerbit University, 1976), 129.

[10] Dean, *Brazil*, 32.   [11] *Ibid.*, 34.

at the time. Ironically, the success of Brazilian coffee in the late nineteenth century, which drove down world prices, undermined attempts by Malaysian planters to compete with this crop, which briefly looked most promising, and pushed them towards alternatives such as rubber.

Natural rubber in its domestic environment was subject to parasitic fungi and leaf blight that greatly diminished its productivity, and this problem was not resolved, despite a major research effort in Brazil in the first half of the twentieth century.[12] In the other cases mentioned, such as maize, domestication and intensification were a slow process, allowing experimentation and selection, which seemed to circumvent the problem of disease. The demand for rubber was both huge and sudden. Brazilians tried to import *Ficus elastica*, the main Asian rubber-yielding species, in an attempt at reverse plant transfer, but this lacked the attributes of hevea. South-East Asia, by contrast, proved to be relatively free of hevea pests and some of these were left behind. Many species travel with their pests but perhaps the limited number of plants initially transferred, and their long route via London, destroyed accompanying microbes. This gave Malaysia an enormous advantage. Diseases that did occur in the plantations were also systematically countered.

Ridley's enthusiasm and the early experiments coincided with the beginnings of motor-vehicle and bicycle manufacture, which vastly increased the market for rubber. Solid rubber tyres were used first but vibration damaged both vehicles and people. Pneumatic tyres were rediscovered by an Edinburgh vet, John Dunlop, for bicycles in 1888. His rubber and sailcloth technique rapidly became more sophisticated in the hands of the Michelin brothers who produced trimmer versions. In 1895 they fitted a car for the Paris-Bordeaux race and though it required twenty-four spares, they finished the journey.[13] The Goodrich company in Akron, Ohio, constructed a pneumatic tyre with layers of rubber and fabric in 1896; others joined them so that Akron became Rubber City. Car tyres soon created the major demand for natural rubber and Ford's innovations in mass manufacture after 1908 cemented the relationship between South-East Asian producers and the motor industry. Tyre technology improved by the use of cord, later wire, in the casing and, from the First World War, the addition of carbon black, made from oil residues, which boosted strength and durability.[14]

---

[12] Dean, *Brazil*, 22.   [13] Coates, *The Commerce in Rubber*, 88.
[14] Colin Barlow, Sisira Jayasuriya, and C. Suan Tan, *The World Rubber Industry* (London: Routledge, 1994), 196.

Prices for primary commodities were comparatively high during the first decade of the twentieth century; those for rubber remained particularly so until the First World War. Malaysian growers responded quickly. By 1905, 20,000 ha. was under rubber, by 1910, over 200,000 ha., by 1914 over 400,000 ha., and by 1922 over one million.[15] By the latter date, nearly 40 per cent was grown on smallholdings, some by Chinese but mostly by Malay people.[16] Malaysia outstripped Sri Lanka, and gained a headstart on Indonesia as a centre of rubber production. British planters in Uganda, the most successful in growing *H. braziliensis* in Africa, made little progress after the First World War and there was no other competition within the Empire.[17] Ridley proved correct that cultivated rubber would soon exceed the quantity, and undercut the price, of wild gathered rubber, where extraction often destroyed the supply. African exports of natural rubber peaked in 1910. The Brazilian boom faded soon after and by 1914 overall cultivated production, nearly two-thirds of it in Malaysia, overtook wild exports.[18] Manaus in the Amazon, and Belem on the coast, which had flourished as European submetropoles, the former boasting a gilded opera house, gave way to the Anglo-Chinese cities of Singapore, Penang, and Kuala Lumpur.

This combination of innovation and industrialization, ecology and economy, underpinned the fastest-growing plantation complex in the Empire at the time, outstripping sugar which was also expanding rapidly in more diverse sites. Malaysia became by far Britain's most valuable tropical colony. It is true, however, that other agrarian frontiers ploughed their way across even greater areas of unexploited land. Wheat spread like wildfire across the Canadian prairies, covering over ten million hectares by the mid-1930s—a fivefold increase since 1900. The successful breeding of hard, quick-growing Marquis wheat, by crossing Red Fife seeds with an Indian variety called Red Calcutta, enabled farmers to cope with short growing seasons and difficult environmental conditions. New roller mills, required to grind the hard

---

[15] J. H. Drabble, *Rubber in Malaya, 1876–1922: The Genesis of an Industry* (Kuala Lumpur: Oxford University Press, 1973), 117, 205, 215; Barlow, *The Natural Rubber Industry*, 26. Figures in these and other sources differ: K. S. Jomo, Y. T. Chang, and K. J. Khoo, *Deforesting Malaysia: The Political Economy and Social Ecology of Agricultural Expansion and Commercial Logging* (London: Zed, 2004), 27, mentions 549,000 ha. by 1911.

[16] Drabble, *Rubber in Malaya*, 216; Barlow, *The Natural Rubber Industry*, 69; Jomo, Chang, and Khoo, *Deforesting Malaysia*, 28–9.

[17] H. N. Whitford and A. Anthony, *Rubber Production in Africa* (Washington, DC: Government Printing Office, 1926).

[18] Havinden and Meredith, *Colonialism and Development*, 109.

grain, played an 'essential part in the conquest of the prairies under the Union Jack'.[19]

Rubber production was concentrated in British and Dutch colonial possessions, with London dominating the market, despite the fact that the US was the major consumer. This global pattern persisted until after the Second World War and provided an economic boost for the Empire and the sterling area. At the outbreak of the war, when production was disrupted by the Japanese invasion of Malaysia, about 75 per cent of natural rubber was used for tyres, 9 per cent for machinery such as shock absorbers, seals, hoses, and engine mountings, and 7 per cent for footwear.[20] Sponge rubber production grew quickly and techniques were being developed to process liquid latex into foam rubber.

The Environmental Impact of Rubber

Henri Fauconnier described how land was opened up for plantations in his novel, *Malaisie* (*The Soul of Malaya*), which won the Prix Goncourt in 1930.[21] A French planter, who arrived in 1906, he became one of the pioneers in cultivating the West African palm oil tree in Malaysia. Palm oil was eventually, in the 1980s, to overtake rubber as the country's major agricultural export. Fauconnier was no stranger to the havoc that such new commodities could wreak in the tropics. His sponsor, the Belgian entrepreneur Adrian Hallett, had major interests in the Congo at the time of 'red rubber'—as E. D. Morel called Leopold's bloody pursuit of the product.[22] But he did not write primarily about the social disruption caused by rubber booms. *Malaisie* was in part a romanticization of the tropics, in part a story of personal quest, and in part an attempt to evoke interrelationships and racial characteristics in a multi-ethnic plantation society. Trapped in the mores of his time, while also standing outside them, he was equally revealing of the psyche of the male colonist.

Malaysians in contract teams cleared the forests. First they chopped out the undergrowth.

---

[19] Hancock, *Problems of Economic Policy*, 159.

[20] K. E. Knorr, *World Rubber and its Regulation* (Stanford: Stanford University Press, 1945), 47.

[21] Henri Fauconnier, *The Soul of Malaya* (1931; Singapore: Archipelago Press, 2003), translated by Eric Sutton.

[22] E. D. Morel, *Red Rubber: The Story of the Rubber Slave Trade Flourishing on the Congo in the Year of Grace 1906* (London: T. F. Unwin, 1906).

Then they attack the forest trees. On all sides I hear the axe-blows biting steadily into the trunks. The night moisture falls from the higher branches in great drops. The jungle smells of fresh shavings and crushed leaves ... The fellers begin by observing the line and angle of the tree ... [T]hey cut one deep gash in one side only so that the tree is left standing. But the colossus that towers above the throng of giants, is the last to be felled, and its collapse will bring down all the rest. Sometimes the structure of it is so vast, it grips the earth with such an array of buttresses, that it has to be surrounded with scaffolding like a cathedral before the cylindrical part of the trunk can be reached. Then, balanced on a frail-swaying framework, little brown men nibble at the enormous column. ... And then, suddenly ... I would hear the rending shriek of a tornado; then a moaning sound, a sort of long drawn out neigh that ended in a roar. The earth shook beneath my feet. On a slope of the hill, in a cloud of flying wreckage, a whole stretch of jungle had crashed.[23]

The felled timber was burnt, totally devastating the indigenous vegetation. Malaysia did export timber but in that period clearing, rather than logging, was the priority. It is an irony that this intriguing novel, with its heartfelt plea for the difference and validity of Malay society, and its celebration of a tropical environment, should have been written by a successful planter as his industry ran amok in the rich Malaysian forests.

Although clearing and tapping were labour intensive, this did not preclude smallholder production. A significant number of Malay, as well as Indonesian, peasants planted rubber on their land. Some maintained trees as part of mixed farming, but smallholders also developed plots with predominantly rubber and later sold them to plantation owners. While this was not a *kumri* system as discussed in relation to Indian forests (Chapter 7), it had the effect of preparing land for rubber at relatively low cost. In 1913 the Federated Malay States government passed legislation preventing further sales of Malay land and effectively establishing reserves.[24] This coincided with the passing of the Natives Land Act, partly for the same purposes, in South Africa. However, a far larger proportion of land was reserved in Malaysia than in South Africa, and Malays were still able to purchase land outside of their reserves. Nor did the colonial state prioritize the mobilization of Malay labour for rubber. While this Act was partly aimed at protecting Malay landholdings, it was also intended to, and did, inhibit rubber production by smallholders.

---

[23] Fauconnier, *The Soul of Malaya*, 128–9.
[24] Collin Abraham, *The Naked Social Order: The Roots of Racial Polarisation in Malaysia* (Subang Jaya, Selangor: Pelanduk, 2004); Barlow, *The Natural Rubber Industry*, 37.

Much of the Malay population was settled in kampongs, traditional village groups, near the coast, and along rivers, dependent upon fishing and seafood as much as cereals, mixed farming, and forest produce. The clearing of forested land for rubber on slopes in the interior did not initially displace large numbers. Orang Asli people, the original inhabitants, whose ancestors predated the Malay migration, could find some protection in the highland forests. Compared with much of the rest of Asia, the Malaysian peninsula was not heavily populated in the pre-colonial period. At the turn of the twentieth century, even with Chinese immigration, the total population was around two million, in a country with high rainfall that was larger than the United Kingdom. There were few intensively developed agrarian systems, or major irrigation works; the exception was the north-western Sultanate of Kedah where rice was produced on a significant scale. Rubber did not usually compete with rice for the same land, because the tree thrived best on well-drained sites, and waterlogging was inimical to its growth. So even though it was usually a higher-value crop it did not generally threaten the major riverine and delta rice-production areas in Malaysia specifically, or in South-East Asia more generally.

Much of Malaysia remained under a form of indirect rule, and it was to some degree necessary for the colonial state to negotiate with the sultans. The government encouraged the planting of food crops in the reserves, particularly rice, or padi, where this was possible.[25] Rice was less profitable, because of competition from Burmese imports, and Malaysian smallholders were not always willing growers. State policy was explained by the need to secure food supplies. The sultans by and large supported it because they had greater control over traditional modes of agriculture, and saw these as less threatening to their authority than smallholder rubber production. Reserves and food crops were seen to diminish the pace of social change.

As a result, most Malays were not forced by displacement, or rapid social differentiation, to become plantation workers. Their domestic subsistence economy, together with limited production of cash crops, was initially sufficiently strong for many to sidestep the labour market or to engage more selectively, on their own terms, as seasonal workers in forest clearance. The great bulk of the rubber workers on European-owned estates were Tamil-speaking Hindus recruited as indentured workers from the south of India. They were part of a growing imperial diaspora of impoverished South

[25] Abraham, *Naked Social Order*; John H. Drabble, *Malaysian Rubber: The Interwar Years* (Basingstoke: Macmillan, 1991).

Asians seeking a living wage on the sugar estates of Natal, Fiji, and Trinidad as well as in Malaysia. They lived a rather segregated existence, isolated in the plantation 'lines' or barracks.

The colonial government and estate owners were also concerned that smallholder production would undercut the consolidation of a large-scale, plantation-based industry and dilute the quality of rubber. Rubber was increasingly processed in small factories on the estates—most commonly to produce ribbed smoked sheets, which involved heating and solidifying the raw latex into large sheets for transport. Plantations were seen as the most suitable vehicle for improving quality. Because of the increasing expense of initiating and financing rubber production, and the long time gap between clearing forest, and tapping the planted trees, ownership of plantations became increasingly concentrated. Sudden downturns in rubber prices, in 1912–13, 1920–2, and 1930–2 contributed to the failure of smaller planters and further concentration. Individual, resident owner-occupier planters were largely displaced by corporate agencies, mostly based in London. This was a gradual process but by the 1950s, about 70 per cent of the total plantation acreage was controlled by agencies. Harrison and Crosfield, the biggest, owned 63 estates, totalling over 90,000 ha. One result was that the growth of a stable, permanent planter class was greatly inhibited. British men managed the estates, but they were largely recruited in Britain, and where families came, the children were usually educated at home. Most of these managers returned to Britain.

The rapidity of expansion and the unevenness of market demand caused sudden crashes in rubber prices. For most of the interwar years, rubber made up over 80 per cent of Malaysia's agricultural exports. When prices fell, so did government revenues, as well as planter and company incomes. In 1917, and again in the 1920s, the Federated Malay States government imposed restrictions on the expansion of plantations, and also on export sales. It hoped to stabilize the price by limiting production. There was a further reason for these measures: US purchasers encouraged expanded production in the hope of lowering raw material prices and US rubber firms began to acquire land in Malaysia. The colonial government's attempt to restrict clearing of new land was also a reaction to the influx of American capital. While the measures had some temporary impact on prices, they were in some ways counterproductive. Restrictions in Malaysia opened up opportunities in Indonesia, where smallholder production thrived and threatened to undercut British plantations. Malaysian smallholders were further constrained, even though some planted illegally.[26] Artificially maintained prices also discouraged efficiency and innovation. The colonial government was not out of step with global trends in this interwar period when agricultural support and protection, not least of settlers, was becoming widespread. But by 1927, restrictions were abandoned and after the Depression they were replaced by an international producer agreement including Dutch Indonesia and Thailand.

Malaysian and Indonesian producers were, however, lucky in the failure of American companies to open up plantations elsewhere. Ford purchased a huge Amazonian concession in 1927, which was locally dubbed Fordlandia. It was not the best land for rubber and production was hampered especially by *Dothidella ulei*, the leaf blight. This had not been a major threat to the highly dispersed wild trees but struck the concentrated plantations with a vengeance.[27] Managers failed to destroy wild rubber trees, and hence carriers of the blight, in the neighbourhood of plantations. After an investment of over $10 million, the estate first produced rubber in 1943. Firestone, the tyre company, bought a derelict estate in Liberia in 1924. They were hampered by the lack of infrastructure and a port, which they had to build, as well as by human diseases. By the 1940s, 15,000 ha. was under cultivation and the company began to produce rubber more effectively.

Despite the rapid growth in the rubber market, demand was not limitless, and for a period, state intervention constrained an expansion of the area cleared. The agencies were also aware that overproduction would drive down prices and they themselves tried to limit expansion, as well as the expense of preparing new land. From the 1920s, increasing attention was devoted to maximizing yields in the established plantations and a Rubber Research Institute was founded in 1925. Planting distances were debated and improved; densities in general diminished. Extension services were launched and soil conservation strategies researched. New types of spiral cuts increased yields. The most important technical innovation, however, with major environmental implications, was the replacement of planting by seed with the use of clones or bud grafting.

Most of the seeds used in establishing the Malaysian plantations came from the limited number of trees that Ridley nurtured in Singapore and their descendents. During the period of rapid expansion, rubber seeds were at a premium. Planters used what was available and they did not always have the information, or the opportunity, to select carefully. The result was that

---

[26] Barlow, *The Natural Rubber Industry*, 68.   [27] Dean, *Brazil*; Tate, *The RGA History*, 361.

9. Gathering rubber on a Malaysian plantation, *c.*1960.
Credit: Getty Images.

trees yielded very unevenly. Seed selection could improve yields by up to 40 per cent, but not always reliably.[28] Moreover, reproduction by seed could not be fully controlled. Rubber produced male and female flowers that were fertilized by insects. Local insects adapted to this introduced plant, and even

[28] Barlow, *The Natural Rubber Industry*, 115.

the best selected female trees could thus be pollinated from poor male trees. This further increased the unpredictability of yield, even when seeds were taken from selected trees.

Cloning or bud grafting was developed by Dutch scientists in Indonesia in the 1910s and commercially pioneered in Malaysia from the 1920s by E. T. N. Gough of the Sungai Recko estate. After collaborative observation of yields from a huge range of trees on a variety of plantations, he selected 391. Buds from the selected mother trees were bound into flaps of bark from seedlings, and when they had taken, the upper growth of the seedling was cut back. The resulting grafted trees were in turn carefully observed as they came to bear. These were long-term trials because full information about the quality of new trees required recording until they were mature. Even if higher yields were apparent within a decade, there was uncertainty about their resistance to disease and wind, and their longevity. It was only by the 1970s, after sustained experimentation, that the properties of different cloned cultivars could be fully and reliably assessed. Planters had to take risks with clones that were not fully proven. But the biggest agency houses, such as Harrisons and Crosfield, soon recognized that bud grafting could transform their yields. The major estates were gradually replanted with the best cultivars. Average yields roughly doubled between 1920 and 1940, and doubled again, to 2,000 lb per acre annually, by 1965. Rubber production grew far more quickly than the area of the estates. These did, however, nearly double in size over that period, despite the Japanese occupation in the Second World War and the Emergency of the 1950s, so that by 1965 they occupied about 900,000 ha.[29] Smallholder production expanded even more quickly to about 1.3 million ha. or 60 per cent of the total area and was strongly encouraged by the independent Malaysian government. Even then, rubber occupied only about 6 per cent of the country's land area and about 15 per cent of the cultivable area.

While rubber displaced botanically diverse forest and its wildlife with a monocrop, the trees themselves did to some degree cover and hold the soil on slopes. Compared to other crops, rubber made limited demands on soil nutrients.[30] In the early years of production, the environmental impact was greater because planters pursued heavy weeding regimes in order to keep the

---

[29] Donald W. Fryer, *Emerging Southeast Asia: A Study in Growth and Stagnation* (London: George Philip, 1970), 67. Figures differ: for example Tate, *The RGA History*, 502, has lower areas.
[30] Fryer, *Emerging Southeast Asia*, 67.

earth clear between the rows. This was the system developed in Sri Lanka and adopted in Malaysia because it was believed that the trees would grow more quickly, produce more, and be less susceptible to disease. Some estates also used sodium arsenite to control weeds and undergrowth, which probably affected the roots of the rubber trees. Ridley was not an advocate of this practice, and was alarmed by the soil erosion that resulted on sloping land. As another official commented, 'our rugged pioneers were no respecters of the soil'.[31] Chinese plantation owners, by contrast, tended to intercrop rubber with bananas, peppers, and agave, which covered the soil better. Smallholdings were generally more densely planted, with more frequent tapping, and less clean weeding: 'many looked overgrown and neglected, especially in comparison with the overseas estates, and their thick stands led inevitably to spindly trees of small girth.'[32]

By the 1920s estate owners began to change their views and some, like Howard in India, saw recycled plant matter as contributing to soil fertility (see Chapter 12). An American, H. N. Whitford, who reported for US interests on African and Malaysian rubber, proposed a 'forestry system' of rubber production.[33] Noting that rubber trees came from a forest environment, he argued that they would thrive best amidst a range of other species.[34] He also suggested denser planting with 'near-Asiatic methods'.[35] Whitford visited during the early 1930s, spoke at public gatherings, published, and generated interest in these ideas. Although denser planting was rejected and the forest system was not proven experimentally, cultivation was gradually modified. During the early 1930s Depression, when prices plummeted and costs had to be cut, some of the first casualties were Indian workers, and with them went the most energetic clean-weeding regimes. Yields nevertheless increased. When the Japanese occupied Malaysia in the Second World War, and many managers and workers fled, plantations became overgrown, without affecting the trees. As cultivation systems changed, environmental damage was more limited than it might have been. While only a restricted range of species could grow under the dense foliage of rubber trees, the dangers of soil erosion diminished. British estates did not, however, intercrop, and the Indian workers had little opportunity, or land, to grow food.

---

[31] Tate, *The RGA History,* 405–6.   [32] Barlow, *The Natural Rubber Industry,* 71.
[33] Whitford and Anthony, *Rubber Production in Africa*; H. N. Whitford, *Estate and Native Plantation Rubber in the Middle East, 1930* (New York: Rubber Manufacturers Association, c. 1931).
[34] Tate, *The RGA History,* 405–6.   [35] Drabble, *Malayan Rubber,* 54–6.

Post-Colonial Deforestation

The rate of clearing forests for rubber planting continued to increase rapidly after independence in 1957. In some respects this was surprising because of the development of synthetic rubber.[36] During the Second World War, both the Germans and Russians, who were cut off from natural rubber supplies, developed synthetics—from oil and alcohol respectively. The German product, Buna rubber, was more resistant to heat, oil, and abrasion. After the War, it was adopted by the major American tyre companies, such as Goodyear, as well as the shoemakers Bata in Czechoslovakia. US manufacturers enthusiastically pursued a breakthrough that would disrupt the European monopoly of natural rubber and drive down prices. They had considerable success, and from the 1950s, the proportion of synthetic rubber sold on the world market gradually increased. But overall demand grew more quickly and synthetic rubber remained expensive to produce. Malaysian rubber production actually doubled from 409,000 tonnes in 1946 to 915,000 in 1966 and only reached its peak in 1986. Economic growth was still largely based on export commodities such as rubber and tin.[37] There was thus plenty of scope for smallholders to produce rubber on newly cleared land after independence.

The most important causes of further deforestation, however, were land reform and logging after independence, especially in Sarawak and Sabah, which were fully absorbed in the Federation of Malaysia in 1963. By the 1950s, many Malays were becoming more integrated into wage labour as land shortage, ecological disturbance, and population growth impacted on their heartlands.[38] Population increased on an African scale, tenfold in the twentieth century. The independent government was committed to giving special entitlements to *bumiputera*, Malaysian 'sons of the soil', and in catering for the growing number of landless poor. Malay cultivators were already diversifying their activities, and pushing into forested areas. The state satisfied the demand for land not so much by redistribution of estates, but by opening new forest land through its Federal Land Development Agency.[39]

---

[36] Barlow, Jayasuriya, and Tan *World Rubber Industry*.

[37] Edmund Terence Gomez and K. S. Jomo, *Malaysian Political Economy: Politics, Patronage and Profit* (Cambridge: Cambridge University Press, 1997), 16.

[38] Tim Harper, *The End of Empire and the Making of Malaya* (Cambridge: Cambridge University Press, 1994).

[39] Jomo, Chang, and Khoo, *Deforesting Malaysia*, 28–9.

At independence, the proportion of rubber planted in smallholdings was already close to 50 per cent of the total and this increased again to roughly 80 per cent when rubber output reached its peak in the 1980s. Careful selection of planting stock enabled smallholders to gain high yields, although these remained, on average, about 20 per cent lower than plantations. The Land Development Agency alone cleared a further one million hectares by 1990, most of which went under plantation crops such as rubber and palm oil. This was government planning on a large scale, involving the establishment of villages and services as well as export crops. Thus the period after independence, and especially the 1970s, when half a million hectares were cleared, heralded a new phase in destructive exploitation of forest land, similar to that in the first decade of the century.[40] Government schemes and plantations were extended on a large scale to Sarawak and Sabah.

By the 1980s, rubber ceased to be the major export crop. Production of synthetics, coupled with new rivals such as Vietnam, finally knocked the bottom out of the market for Malaysian producers. Many of the rubber trees were cut for timber before their useful life was over. While rubber and tin had been the twin pillars of the colonial economy, they were replaced with other higher-value agricultural products and a rapidly expanding manufacturing sector. Palm oil became Malaysia's major agricultural export and, like rubber, the trees in plantations in Malaysia proved to be more successful and productive than those in their home territory of West Africa. Palm oil production expanded most quickly in the forested lands of Sabah, where rubber had not taken a major hold. Again, while this monocrop reduced biodiversity, palm trees held the soil well. By the late twentieth century, long rows of thickset palm trees, rather than rubber, dominated the plantation landscape.

Logging of tropical hardwoods became equally important in the export economy. This involved a different form of forest exploitation in that it did not usually imply total clearance. Between 1970 and 1990, roughly half of peninsular Malaysia's remaining forest area was logged and partially destroyed.[41] Sarawak's forests were reduced by about a third over the same period.[42] Deforestation for logging was barely controlled. Private enterprise

---

[40] David Lee, *The Sinking Ark: Environmental Problems in Malaysia and Southeast Asia* (Kuala Lumpur: Heinemann, 1980); Consumers' Association of Penang, *The Malaysian Environment in Crisis: Selections from Press Cuttings* (Penang: Consumers' Association of Penang, 1978).

[41] Jomo, Chang, and Khoo, *Deforesting Malaysia*, 50.

[42] Drabble, *An Economic History of Malaysia, 1800–1990* (Basingstoke: Macmillan, 2000), 226.

timber companies won concessions from the state, sometimes through political connections. Local state governments, which had responsibility for licences and conservation, colluded with contractors or justified their approach on the grounds of economic growth and creating employment.[43] By the 1990s, the peninsula was close to being logged out of the best commercial species, largely for export to Japan.

In conclusion it is instructive to compare the environmental influences on the rubber plantations with those shaping the history of sugar. Both required warm, frost-free environments, and both were very largely colonial export crops. But sugar could be adapted to a wider range of climates and terrain. Sugar also seems to have been freer from devastating diseases. It proved very difficult to control the natural diseases and predators of rubber in their Latin American habitat and this provided South-East Asia with great advantages. The quick expansion of rubber plantations in Malaysia in the early twentieth century necessitated widespread deforestation. Despite this, the limits of international demand, and rapid increases in yield, restricted the areas of growth. Malaysia was not environmentally transformed on the scale of the Caribbean sugar islands. Some of the most devastating environmental change, and especially deforestation, took place after independence, as land reform gave smallholders access to new zones for cultivation, and logging expanded to supply the global market for hardwoods.

Malaysia's indigenous society was only partly displaced, and was to some degree able to participate in the expansion of commodity production. Chinese migration over a long period, and Indian indentured workers, profoundly changed the demographic make-up of the peninsula so that the Malay population was barely a majority at the time of independence. But since independence, Malays have been able to assert themselves, demographically and politically, in a way that the remnant indigenous societies of the British American plantation economies, or of Australia, have not.

---

[43] Consumers' Association of Penang, *State of the Environment in Malaysia* (Penang: Consumers' Association of Penang, 1997).

15

Oil Extraction in the Middle East: The Kuwait Experience

Oil has been the lubricant of international relations and industry since the turn of the twentieth century. The fabulous wealth it has generated for a clutch of individuals, states, and corporations has skewed global politics, fed human greed, fuelled conflict, and brought as much destruction as delight in its wake. The struggle for access to and control over oil was central to the final stages of imperial expansion, and the Middle East saw a regional equivalent of the 'scramble for Africa'. European powers sought to carve up the area as the twentieth century turned, their eyes fixed on oil as the main prize.

Central to our argument is that empire followed natural resources, in unpredictable ways. It created commodity frontiers that had enormous implications for routes of expansion and relations with local societies. The future of the Middle East, then under the sway of the crumbling Ottoman Empire, was already of great concern to Britain at the beginning of the twentieth century. But oil provided a new urgency, and shaped patterns of intervention; the history of the Middle East over the next century would have been profoundly different without it. Although capital became more mobile from the late nineteenth century, some of the most valuable natural resources in the twentieth-century Empire proved to be rooted to specific regions. In this sense, oil as a natural resource shaped the geography of empire, as had fur and forests before it. But the specific character of oil and of imperialism in the region (our focus is on Kuwait), resulted in rather different outcomes for local societies than those experienced on some other earlier commodity frontiers. Although the oil companies were largely foreign-owned, Middle Eastern people were, to a much greater degree, beneficiaries of resource extraction. In this respect, there are parallels with Malaysia. An important concern in this chapter is to chart the impact of oil on Bedouin pastoralists in Kuwait, their use of the desert, and its environmental implications. We also explore briefly other environmental impacts of oil exploitation.

These are issues less frequently rehearsed than the political and economic consequences.

The energy needs of the metropolitan world led to increasing demands for oil as the twentieth century advanced. In the early days of the industry, petroleum products were largely used for lubricants, construction, and lighting fuel. The scientific and technological advances that facilitated the development of motor vehicles blew the field of possibility wide open and made it possible to manufacture various new oil-based products on an industrial scale. In addition to the use of oil as fuel, PVC (polyvinyl chloride), now one of the world's most widely used plastics, was invented by a French physicist in 1835 and industrially produced from 1912. The development of the petrochemical industry, particularly from the 1940s, spawned paints, plastics, fertilizers, synthetic fibres, synthetic rubber, resins, and other products made from petroleum-based raw materials (including natural gas) that had myriad domestic, agricultural, military, and industrial uses. While these discoveries were not primarily British, imperial power gave Britain an early advantage in the exploitation of oil.

Oil and the Middle East

The word petroleum comes from the Latin *petra* (rock) and *oleum* (oil). It is a form of bitumen made up largely of hydrocarbons, and existing in a gaseous or liquid state in natural underground reservoirs in sedimentary rocks—generally sandstone or limestone. There must be a natural barrier or trap so that petroleum can accumulate and be prevented from escaping to the surface, though oil does naturally seep and migrate underground from the source rock. Because oil is lighter than water, it can often be found in the highest part of an underground structural fold or anticline.[1]

As is the case with other resources, some of its properties were already well known. Crude oil was produced in such quantities in the ancient Arab world that discussion of the legal aspects of oil concessions formed a central part of Arab law by the tenth and eleventh centuries; lawyers decided that the sultans owned all exposed minerals—such as petroleum and bitumen—which could be garnered at the earth's surface or not far below it.[2] Early uses of oil in the region included light distillates (naft in Arabic)

---

[1] John M. Hunt, *Petroleum Geochemistry and Geology*, 2nd edn. (New York: W. H. Freeman, 1996), 3, 23–4.

[2] R. J. Forbes, *Studies in Early Petroleum History* (Leiden: E. J. Brill, 1958), vii.

for military grenades, flame-throwers, and other weapons, as well as torches, medicines, lubricants, and boat tar. (The indigenous peoples of Canada also sealed birch bark canoes with tar bitumen.) The ancient Egyptians used bitumen to embalm the dead. As part of a building mortar, bitumen glued the walls of Jericho and Babylon. Some seepages and petroleum gases burned continuously, and became objects of fire worship. Medieval medical handbooks in Europe reiterated classical and Arab writings on the virtues of petroleum and bitumen. Marco Polo returned from his travels in northern Persia in 1271–3 with stories of rich oil reserves at Baku on the Caspian Sea, in what is now Azerbaijan. He noted: 'People come from vast distances to fetch it, for in all the countries round about they have no other oil.'[3] In 1600, the English missionary John Cartwright visited Baku and described its thriving oil trade.

Although oil was long known about and used, both in this region and other parts of the world, the oil industry awaited the development of new uses, scientific methods of detection and extraction, and the invention of the long-distance pipeline. In the 1850s new drilling techniques were developed, using either churn or rotary methods, or a combination of the two. In 1859 the first successful drilling in the US triggered an oil rush, but the first big US strike was not made until 1901 in Texas. By the 1870s, under Russian control, Baku's petroleum industry had expanded to twenty-three refineries. Russian oil production led the field and for a time surpassed its US rivals, competing with American kerosene in Europe. Kerosene was extracted from petroleum, and had replaced whale oil in street and other lamps by the late nineteenth century. It also fuelled small cooking stoves and later small motors. After the perfection of the electric light bulb in 1879, demand for kerosene began to fall off—at least in the industrialized world. Gasoline was simply an industrial waste left over when kerosene was distilled; before the automobile was invented, it was regarded as worthless. Asphalt was used for roads from around 1880. Faster, motorized transport required relatively dust-free roads, so these two discoveries went together.

The Middle East became the major multinational hunting ground for oil, partly because of geological factors: its oil reserves were rich and relatively close to the surface, and therefore easier and cheaper to tap. Prospecting was extended around known seepages in Persia, Iraq, Bahrain, and elsewhere in the Gulf. Anticlines—places where the rock arched upward, and could

[3] Forbes, *Studies*, 155, quoting *Marco Polo's Travels* (London: Dent, 1908).

hold trapped oil—were relatively easy to identify in a desert environment. Oil fields were often not far from the coast and favourably located on sea routes both to Europe and the East. Later, scientists confirmed that Middle Eastern deposits were contained in very thick sequences of porous rock that held huge quantities of oil in anticlines and other traps. The accessibility and size of these reserves made the region a lasting focus for the world's superpowers.[4]

As the demand for oil increased, coal went into gradual decline as a source of fuel and petrochemicals. The fuel that had fired Britain's industrial revolution and shored up her imperial domination in the late nineteenth century was heavy and less flexible. The beauty of this 'new' fossil fuel was its flexibility and mobility—'oil is essentially a fuel on the move', easier and cheaper to shift than coal.[5] Other advantages over coal included its relative cleanliness, lightness, and much higher power-to-weight ratio, which was particularly useful to shipping. Following a decade of gradual switching, the Royal Navy adopted oil in 1912 and welcomed the fact that ships could now refuel at sea.

All this was advantageous to commerce, and vital to warships. But the major use of oil was in motor vehicles. By 1913, there were 1.25 million automobiles registered in the US, while Britain, France, and Germany between them had more than 400,000.[6] Britain's motor-car industry was founded in 1896 and grew out of iron-working, engineering, bicycle-making, and other established industries. Total British vehicle production reached 34,000 by 1913, the year the first moving-track assembly lines arrived at Ford factories in Detroit and Trafford Park, Manchester. Ford, Wolseley, and Humber were the three leading manufacturers. The Sunbeam (not cheap at £390 and £670, compared to £125 for a Model T Ford) proved one of the biggest pre-war commercial successes. The more expensive Lanchesters or Napiers (favoured by Indian princes) came in four-cylinder 'Colonial' and 'Extra-Strong Colonial' models with higher ground clearance. Imports of fuel oil rocketed, between 1902 and 1918, from just below 300 million

---

[4] For geological explanations of why the Middle East has such large oil reserves, see S. T. Longrigg, *Oil in the Middle East: Its Discovery and Development*, 3rd edn. (London: Oxford University Press, 1968), 2–5.

[5] J. E. Hartshorn, *Oil Companies and Governments: An Account of the International Oil Industry and its Political Environment* (London: Faber & Faber, 1962), 36.

[6] Fiona Venn, *Oil Diplomacy in the Twentieth Century* (Basingstoke: Macmillan, 1986), 5, table 1.1; Daniel Yergin, *The Prize: The Epic Quest for Oil, Money and Power* (London and New York: Simon & Schuster, 1991), 208.

gallons to about 1,350 million gallons, reflecting wartime demands as well as the beginnings of mass production.[7] In 1918 a committee was formed to investigate the oil needs of the Empire; retaining control of Middle Eastern oil fields was seen to be crucial, partly in order to reduce 80 per cent dependency on US supplies.[8]

By 1939 there were two million cars on British roads, and after the Second World War great efforts were made to improve British models for 'colonial conditions' because exports were vital to the industry.[9] Cars became a major consumption item in Britain, especially for men. The language of cars and driving appealed to the new freedoms of post-war Britain, which found an outlet on the open road. This was the realization of the 'century of travel and restlessness', foreseen in 1916 by oil tycoon Henri Deterding of Royal Dutch-Shell.[10] Oil exploitation was also a field for male swagger, a world of gushing derricks and 'Hydrocarbon Man'.[11] Freedom of thought, action, and movement came to be considered basic rights in democratic societies, and affordable, private transport played a central role.

Early Concessions

Following a number of earlier agreements, the first major oil concession in the Middle East was granted in 1901 to British engineer William Knox D'Arcy.[12] He was given a sixty-year 'exclusive privilege' to find and develop oil, gas, and asphalt across almost the entire Persian empire—a concession covering 500,000 square miles. The British government backed D'Arcy's efforts, which eventually paid off handsomely. In 1905 D'Arcy joined forces with the British-owned Burmah Oil Company and three years later discovered one of the world's largest oilfields, on the site of an ancient fire temple. Britain was indirectly responsible for what had by 1909 been renamed the Anglo-Persian Oil Company, and also helped to guard its operations, sending Indian soldiers from the 18th Bengal Lancers to protect the drilling area from local people who were trying to defend their grazing grounds. The troops were led by Arnold Wilson, who was to become general manager of Anglo-Persian, and Acting Civil Commissioner for Mesopotamia (1918–20). As elsewhere

---

[7] Marian Kent, *Oil and Empire: British Policy and Mesopotamian Oil, 1900–1920* (London: Macmillan, 1976), 206, fig. 2, UK Petroleum Imports 1900–19.

[8] *Ibid.*, 6–7, 125, 133–4.   [9] Georgano *et al., Britain's Motor Industry.*

[10] Quoted in Yergin, *The Prize*, 208.   [11] *Ibid.*, 14 *passim.*

[12] George W. Stocking, *Middle East Oil: A Study in Political and Economic Controversy* (London: Allen Lane, Penguin Press, 1971); Longrigg, *Oil in the Middle East.*

in the Empire, military, extractive, and government roles could be closely linked. The Navy, increasingly dependent on oil, signed a twenty-year supply deal with the new company. Under Winston Churchill, First Lord of the Admiralty, the British Government took a 51 per cent controlling interest in Anglo-Persian at a cost of £2.2 million. It was in the strong position of being both the largest shareholder and the main customer.[13]

Iraq (then Mesopotamia) was the site of the second major concession in this period. Again, the prize went to a British-dominated company, the Turkish (later Iraq) Petroleum Company and its subsidiaries. Initially German banking interests held a 25 per cent share in the company, forfeited to France after the First World War; Dutch and Americans also held shares. These interests came together to exploit the deposits at Mosul from 1914.[14] After the Ottoman Empire crashed in the First World War, its former Arab territories were shared out between Britain (which took Iraq and Palestine) and France (Syria and Lebanon). Petroleum resources became an increasing focus of Western rivalry. Iraq became a British mandated territory in May 1920 and a rebellion by Iraqis, including demobilized soldiers and disaffected Shiites, was brutally suppressed with the aid of oil-powered aircraft.[15]

Kuwait, Before and After Oil

Kuwait provides a fascinating case study of how natural resources and their extraction shaped empire. This small territory provided a winning conjuncture: the distance between the oil reserves and the coast was short, and the deep natural harbour at what became Kuwait City was said to be the best in the Gulf. Kuwait's strategic position at the mouth of the Gulf, near shipping lanes, made it an important conduit to India. The discovery of oil was to transform this corner of the Gulf into a vital hinge of the Empire.

The country was founded in the early eighteenth century—in an area under nominal Ottoman control—by nomadic Bani Utub people, a branch of the Anizah, driven out of the Arabian interior by civil conflict and drought. The ruling Al-Sabah family dominated Kuwaiti political life from

---

[13] Stocking, *Middle East Oil*, 22–39.

[14] Henry Longhurst, *Adventure in Oil: The Story of British Petroleum* (London: Sidgwick & Jackson, 1959); Jill Crystal, *Oil and Politics in the Gulf: Rulers and Merchants in Kuwait and Qatar* (Cambridge: Cambridge University Press, 1990), ch. 2.

[15] Peter Sluglett, *Britain in Iraq 1914–1932* (London: Ithaca Press, 1976), 41. Elie Kedourie, *England and the Middle East: The Destruction of the Ottoman Empire 1914–1921* (London: Bowes & Bowes, 1956), ch. 7.

the beginning. For two centuries before oil was discovered, the nation's wealth did not lie underground but below the waves—in the form of pearls, lifted from the seabed by divers who were often bonded labourers. A ruling coalition centred on the sheikh and merchants who relied on the oyster-pearling economy. Fishing, dhow-building, and seafaring were also important, and horses, wood, spices, wool, hides, coffee, and Iraqi dates passed through Kuwait on their way to India, East Africa, and elsewhere.[16] Nomads used the deserts for livestock herding, and traded products such as ghee, sheepskins, wool, and goats' hair.

The British came to monopolize Gulf trade, despite having only a few trading posts, by acting as brokers between rival sheikhs along the Arabian side of the Gulf. Britain and Kuwait maintained friendly relations, both fearing Ottoman encroachment on their interests. British anxiety over German penetration, in the shape of a proposed Berlin–Baghdad railway with a terminus in Kuwait, combined with Kuwait's desire to stay independent of the Turks, brought the two nations together in an important alliance under Mubarak the Great (who ruled from 1896 to 1915).[17] In 1899 he signed a treaty setting out Britain's relationship with Kuwait, which was to pave the way for her effective absorption into the British Empire. The political resident who signed it went 'under cover of a game-shooting expedition to the salt marshes of southern Iraq' so as not to alert the Turks.[18] In 1914 Britain formally recognized Kuwait as an independent state under British naval and military protection, though it was not formally made a protectorate. By the 1920s Kuwait was a 'veiled protectorate', an arrangement that seemed to suit both parties.[19]

In this period, foreign oil prospectors began to threaten British hegemony. An eccentric New Zealander, Major Frank Holmes, visited the ruling sheikh in the 1920s to discuss a concession. Holmes had secured prospecting rights in Saudi Arabia's Al-Hasa province and in Bahrain; the latter were bought by Standard Oil of California in 1928. People like Holmes were charming and skilled negotiators, tough 'men of the desert' seeking the pot of black gold by every means necessary. British political agent Harold Dickson said

---

[16] Alan Villiers, 'Some Aspects of the Arab Dhow Trade', in L. E. Sweet (ed.), *Peoples and Cultures of the Middle East: An Anthropological Reader*, vol. 1 (New York: Natural History Press, 1979), 155–72.

[17] Crystal, *Oil and Politics*, 22; David H. Finnie, *Shifting Lines in the Sand: Kuwait's Elusive Frontier with Iraq* (London: I.B. Tauris, 1992), ch. 2.

[18] Finnie, *Shifting Lines*, 15–16.

[19] Andrew B. Loewenstein, 'The Veiled Protectorate of Kowait' [*sic*], *Middle Eastern Studies*, 36/2 (April 2000), 104–5.

of him: 'He carried a large white umbrella lined green, wore a white helmet as issued to French troops in Africa, and over his face and helmet a green gauze veil—quite like pictures one has seen of the tourist about to visit the Pyramids'.[20]

Holmes appealed to greed, and his client's money was all the more attractive because it 'had an American tang about it'.[21] Anglo-Persian and Gulf Oil, controlled by the powerful Mellon family, began wooing Sheikh Ahmad Al-Sabah, who was desperate to find a new source of income since Japanese cultivated pearls had (from 1905) knocked the bottom out of the natural pearl market. Kuwait faced ruin—export earnings had fallen, merchants were bankrupted, boats grounded, and divers sent back to their desert homes. The sheikh was tempted by Gulf Oil's offer—sweetened by its bribe of a Sunbeam car—but dared not alienate his old friends the British.

In 1933, Gulf and Anglo-Persian agreed to merge in a joint venture called the Kuwait Oil Company. London insisted that Britain must control ground operations, and the sheikh signed a seventy-five-year concession for a down payment of £35,700—all this before any oil had been found. Exploration began in 1935 and oil was struck three years later in the Burgan field in south-eastern Kuwait. To gauge how large the find was, crude oil was allowed to flow into a sand reservoir and set on fire: 'the heat from the flaming oil was so intense that the sand walls of the banked reservoir were transformed into sheets of glass.'[22] A few weeks later, new finds in neighbouring Saudi Arabia sparked a scramble for concessions. Oil exploitation was then interrupted by the Second World War. All Kuwait's oil wells were plugged with cement in case they fell into enemy hands. Production did not resume until 1946, and had reached 1.83 million barrels per day by 1962.

The Kuwait Oil Company concession covered almost the entire country and its islands, apart from the island of Kubbar. This gave it great manoeuvrability; drilling could be shifted from one well to another whenever production costs started rising. It was not subject to any environmental protection laws, and was therefore free to move its drilling sites.[23] Also, because the terrain was so flat and barren, entire rigs could be 'skidded'

---

[20] H. R. P. Dickson, *Kuwait and her Neighbours* (London: George Allen & Unwin, 1956), 269. Quoted in Stocking, *Middle East Oil*, 111. Dickson was Political Agent in Bahrain and Kuwait before becoming Chief Local Representative for the Kuwait Oil Company in 1936, and its acting General Manager during the Second World War.

[21] Stocking, *Middle East Oil*, 111.   [22] Yergin, *The Prize*, 300.

[23] Y. S. F. Al-Sabah, *The Oil Economy of Kuwait* (London: Kegan Paul, 1980), 39–40.

across country on tractor-drawn trucks by the 1950s.[24] The main problems facing the oil company were lack of fresh water and locally grown food, both of which had to be imported in the days before a condenser plant was built to produce drinking water, and agriculture developed. Drilled boreholes supplied brackish water suitable only for industrial use and livestock. The oil flowed from wells into nine 'gathering centres' before being pumped up to the tank farm at Ahmadi, five miles from the coast. From there, the oil ran down to the port and refinery at Mina al Ahmadi. Pipes under the seabed linked the refinery to five sea loading berths. By the end of 1949 the world's largest tanker-loading pier had been built offshore.[25]

Outside Kuwait proper lay a buffer Neutral Zone to the south, fifty miles long and forty wide, shared with Saudi Arabia. The first concession to drill here went in 1948 to the American Independent Oil Company, and a year later to the American Pacific Western Corporation. The Neutral Zone was to make John Paul Getty 'not only the richest American, but also the richest private citizen in the world'.[26] Kuwait won full independence from Britain in June 1961, a year after becoming a founding member of OPEC. By the early twenty-first century it was ranked fourth among world oil producers. After the government, the oil industry is the second largest employer in the country. Almost all of it is government owned—Kuwait was the first Arab oil-producer to gain total control of its own output, and the Kuwait Oil Company was fully nationalized in 1974–5.

Oil and the Bedouin

Oil made the desert bloom in one sense, but also partially depopulated it. The numbers of nomadic Bedouin in Kuwait were estimated at 13,000 in 1916, out of around one million for the central Arabian desert as a whole.[27] Even at that time, Bedouin groups regularly moved between desert and port. Some members of the Beni Khalid tribe, renowned breeders of horses and cattle who also owned large date groves, had partly settled in Kuwait and other towns and become pearl divers.[28] They followed the example of the Bani Utub founding tribe, moving seasonally between sea, city, and desert.

---

[24] Longhurst, *Adventure in Oil*, 235.
[25] Dickson, *Kuwait and her Neighbours*, 581–3.   [26] Yergin, *The Prize*, 444.
[27] Admiralty Naval Intelligence Division, *A Handbook of Arabia*, vol. 1 (London: HMSO, 1916), 286, 18. Population was estimated according to tent numbers.
[28] *Ibid.*, 84–5.

The Hawāzin were also no longer full-time pastoralists, but engaged in diving, fishing, and served in the sheikh's army.[29]

New frontiers impinged on regional nomadic migration long before oil was commercially exploited, though nomads from Kuwait and Saudi Arabia were allowed free access to the water wells of the Neutral Zone when its borders were drawn in 1922.[30] Urban populations gradually swelled with former desert dwellers, some attracted by opportunities in the city, others forced to seek alternative livelihoods where traditional pastoralism alone could no longer sustain the family group. Severe droughts in 1940–1, and a tuberculosis outbreak that killed many Bedouin, also prompted emigration to Kuwait City and surrounding villages. More Bedouin took up wage labour and many found jobs in the police, army, and oil industry, where they tended to fill relatively unskilled posts such as those of guards and drivers. With the appreciation of land values, oil triggered a burst of land speculation in the 1940s and 1950s. The ruling sheikh gave out land around Kuwait City as a way of rewarding friends and consolidating his family. Some plots were given to the sheikh's Bedouin followers as a reward for loyalty. The desert, however, was still accessible to Bedouin tribal confederations, each with extensive pastures at their disposal. Some continued to move between urban and rural areas, maintaining flocks and selling wild fruits and other consumables in the city bazaar.

If oil displaced anything, it was the camel—the most highly specialized desert animal. It had been prized as a source of food, as well as for wool, leather, and the sheer wealth and prestige it represented. It provided the main means of transport, and was an article of exchange for grain, hardware, and textiles including tent cloth. The camel had modest forage needs, could survive on very little water, and it converted brackish water and sparse pastures to a nutritious milk for humans. Female camels lactate for 11 to 18 months— much longer than most animals. This allowed camel pastoralists to use areas of desert well beyond the limits of sheep and goats. It gave them power over the territory itself, enabling the Bedouin to travel and raid far and wide.[31]

Up until the First World War, camels had provided the only means of regional transport to Bedouin, traders' caravans, and pilgrims. Bedouin

---

[29] Admiralty Naval Intelligence Division, A Handbook of Arabia, vol. 1 (London: HMSO, 1916), 93.

[30] Douglas L. Johnson, The Nature of Nomadism; A Comparative Study of Pastoral Migrations in Southwestern Asia and Northern Africa (Chicago: University of Chicago, 1969), 46–7.

[31] Louise Sweet, 'Camel Raiding of North Arabian Bedouin: A Mechanism of Ecological Adaptation', in Sweet (ed.), Peoples and Cultures, 1, 272–4.

sold and rented animals to travellers, worked as guides, and supplied Hajj pilgrims with fodder.[32] Motorized transport and highways began replacing camel caravans, and by the mid-1950s, the minimum forty-day pilgrimage to Mecca by camel took six days by car.[33] This further undermined Bedouin economic independence. The Anizah people still owned about one million camels in the 1950s, but there were only 9,000 left in the whole of Kuwait by 1998.[34] Camels were increasingly bred for racing, which became a major televised spectator sport in which Bedouin breeders and trainers predominated.

In villages with good wells vegetables could be grown for market; the gardeners were mostly from the Nejd Awazim community. But by the 1950s oil was beginning to make inroads here: 'Owing to the new growing port of Mina al Ahmadi a mile south of the [fishing] village of Fahaheel

10. Camels resting near Khurais Well, Saudi Arabia, mid-twentieth century.
Credit: Getty Images.

[32] R. H. Sanger, *The Arabian Peninsula* (Ithaca, NY: Cornell University Press, 1954), 164.
[33] Dickson, *Kuwait and her Neighbours*, 571.   [34] *Ibid.*, first figure 87.

most of the male population are in the Oil Company and not doing any gardening.'[35] Mina al Ahmadi was to grow into a major township, built for oil workers. Anthropologist Peter Lienhardt, who was particularly interested in the sedendarization of Kuwaiti nomads and the effects of economic change on their lives, described the refinery town in the 1950s as 'a well-appointed foreign enclave, the home of a little, *ad hoc*, oil company society' from which 'the desert had been expelled'.[36] His observations of oil-fuelled urban environmental and social change are also telling:

The modernisation of the city [of Kuwait] was beginning, whether people wished it or not, to produce a corresponding change in the pattern of residence ... Whereas traditional neighbourhoods had housed richer and poorer people together, residential preference and the means and availability of transport were beginning to produce suburbs between which there was some noticeable economic differentiation. This is not to suggest that the Kuwaitis were ceasing to be a community, but their wealth was changing them into a community of a less constricted and less integrated sort.[37]

By 1953, there was hardly any pearl fishing and little left of the dhow trade. Lienhardt noted:

The gap of time between the collapse of pearl fishing and the start of oil revenues, though a time of great hardship, had only been about twenty years. The established families had survived and been able to take up again where they had left off. In the modern situation, their capital was freer than it had ever been before because they now had no clients ... Men who had been pearl fishers talked about the old days without any hint of nostalgia. Wage labour had replaced a profit-sharing system, debts had been forgiven, and no one seemed sorry to see the end of an era.[38]

But the impact on urban environment and society was complex. While houses were being pulled down to make new streets and modern shops, and mud dwellings replaced by concrete and steel, the old bazaars—the centre of public life for men—still flourished. While the commercial value of urban land was shooting up, profits stayed entirely in Kuwaiti hands

[35] Viola Dickson, *The Wildflowers of Kuwait and Bahrein* (London: George & Allen Unwin, 1955), 112.

[36] Peter Lienhardt, *Disorientations: A Society in Flux: Kuwait in the 1950s*, ed. A. Al-Shahi (Reading: Ithaca Press, 1993), 31.

[37] Unpublished observations. Our thanks to Dr Ahmed Al-Shahi, his literary executor, for permission to quote.

[38] Lienhardt, observations; Nels Johnson, 'Ahmad: A Kuwaiti Pearl Diver', in Edmund Burke III (ed.), *Struggle and Survival in the Modern Middle East* (London: I.B. Tauris, 1993), 91–9.

because foreigners were not allowed to buy or own land. Kuwaitis were to some degree able to control the impact of oil extraction.

Changing Landscapes

The interior, heavily used by pastoralists and criss-crossed by caravans, was not pristine before oil, but oil had an important impact on wildlife. The writings of European travellers and imperial officials evoke powerful images of a desert environment. Of the Arabian desert in general, political agent Colonel Samuel Miles declared: 'Probably no other part of the world's surface can compare in its desolation with this wilderness, where save camels, goats, wild animals and a few wandering Bedouins, no life exists, and where its immutable aspect is characterized by dreariness, lethargy, and monotony.'[39] Bedouin called it Al-Jafoor, or the 'unfrequented space'.

Yet it is striking how many also record the diversity of the vegetation. 'The general character of the country is that of an horizon-bounded prairie, undulating like long low waves,' wrote political resident Lewis Pelly, as he journeyed south-east of Kuwait City in 1865. He saw plains 'sprinkled with low brushwood ... which the camels browsed as we went along', and three or four parallel 'roads' along which people migrated annually to the Arabian interior.[40] 'Grass and flowers newly sprung above the soil impart a greenish and blue tinge to the land,' wrote Danish adventurer Barclay Raunkiaer in 1912, as he left Kuwait City for Al Safah (to the south) by camel caravan. He saw many different annual grasses, and other plants including irises, plantain, and yellow-flowering artemesia. His big find was white truffles, for a while his party's main subsistence food: 'During the march we collect great sacks of them ... Ali daily prepares for me an excellent dish of truffle curry.'[41] The caravan moved from well to well, arguing en route with tribesmen who demanded tolls for passing through their territory. Viola Dickson wrote on the vegetation of Kuwait in the 1950s and gave a more exact picture of the rich variety of perennial and annual plants, many of them valuable to grazers. She makes clear there was no lack of desert life a few years after the establishment of an oil industry.[42]

---

[39] S. B. Miles, *The Countries and Tribes of the Persian Gulf* 2nd edn. (1919; London: Frank Cass, 1966), 385–7.

[40] Louis Pelly, *Report on a Journey to Riyadh* (Bombay: 1866; Cambridge and New York: Oleander Press, 1978), 15, 24, 18.

[41] Barclay Raunkiaer, *Through Wahhabiland on Camelback* (London: Routledge & Kegan Paul, 1969), 59, 62–3, 69.

[42] Dickson, *Wildflowers*.

Early twentieth-century observers listed a rich variety of wildlife—oryx, wild ass, gazelle, wolf, hyena, hedgehog, hare, jerboa, field rat, and ostrich in the north and western desert.[43] Birdlife (besides ostrich) included partridge, bustard, sandgrouse, hawks, and hoopoe. It was the use to which cars were put, rather than oil *per se*, that was ruining the desert by the 1940s. Companies built roads into the interior. Hunters with firearms began shooting from cars instead of camels, a new practice condemned as 'revolting' by Stanley Mylrea, a doctor practising in Bahrain and Kuwait. 'Up to a few years ago', he wrote, 'gazelle hunting took skill, perseverance, endurance, and the hunter got his game one by one. Now the Ford goes out and simply runs the game down. What chance has a gazelle against a 25 horsepower engine in the open desert? And so the Fords come back, reeking with blood and bulging with gazelles. One car is said to have brought in forty in one day.'[44] Dickson lamented that vehicles had done most to change the desert and the 'thinking of the desert Arab'. He abhorred the fact that falconry, 'once the chief Arab sport, has developed into the systematic slaughter of thousands of *hubára* [lesser bustards] annually, for it is done by motor-car today'. And he concurred on the danger to gazelles 'hunted to such an extent in fast-moving automobiles that this beautiful animal is now nearly extinct'.[45] In 1964, the Sultan of Oman—facing the same problem of motorized hunting—banned the use of vehicles for hunting gazelles and oryx, and established a 'gazelle patrol' to protect them.[46] More recently, the new Gulf fad of 'crest driving', a sport that involves surfing the crests of sand dunes at speed in four-wheel-drive vehicles, has added another dimension to the car's erosion of the desert.

However, the advent of motor vehicles also brought benefits for Bedouin who could fetch water, firewood, and fuel, and transport their small stock and entire households by lorry or truck. Chatty has documented this major shift from camel to truck, describing how it aided the commercialization of sheep rearing.[47] Feed supplement could be carried to the flocks, and fattened sheep

---

[43] Miles, *Persian Gulf*.

[44] 'Before Oil Came to Kuwait: Memoirs of C. Stanley G. Mylrea, Pioneer Physician in Bahrein and Kuwait, 1907–1947', 92, 26–7. Unpublished papers, Middle East Centre Archives, St Antony's College, University of Oxford.

[45] Dickson, *Kuwait and her Neighbours*, 571.

[46] Dawn Chatty, 'Animal Reintroduction Projects in the Middle East: Conservation without a human face', in Chatty and M. Colchester (eds.), *Conservation and Mobile Indigenous Peoples* (Oxford: Berghahn, 2002), 228.

[47] Dawn Chatty, *From Camel to Truck: The Bedouin in the Modern World* (New York: Vantage Press, 1986).

taken to market without losing weight en route. The use of trucks boosted sales of goat and sheep milk, and enabled some pastoralists to integrate more effectively into the regional economy without becoming sedentary cultivators. It also enabled them to cut out exploitative middlemen when marketing pastoral products, and to extend seasonal migration into previously unusable areas along new road networks. By the 1960s, trucks had replaced camels.

The Al-Dhafir of Northern Arabia (some of whom lived in Kuwait and crossed the border at weekends by car to visit their relatives) also switched from camels to sheep as their principal livestock, grazing them over a wider area than was possible before. By the 1980s, sheep had become more economically useful and the Al-Dhafir only kept small numbers of camels 'for milk and for nostalgic reasons'.[48] Sheep, however, had some negative environmental impacts. Overgrazing and desiccation of rangelands resulted from larger flocks, which were being raised to meet rising urban demand for meat and dairy products. Tribal leaders could no longer regulate and safeguard land use because of state moves to open up their territory. Concerns about environmental degradation encouraged the Syrian Government to try and revive traditional range-management systems from the late 1960s, and the Saudis did likewise from 1977.

Oil and urbanization therefore created limited opportunities for a modified pastoralism in this world of fluid frontiers, and in certain respects it resulted in more intensive use of the desert. Governments have used modern drilling technology to dig deep water wells for Bedouin—free for use by all. Settlements have sprung up around these, and young men working in the oil fields, urban areas, or the military have helped to develop these townships through remittances. The new-style oases fit well into the changed pastoral economy, which concentrates on sheep and goats produced primarily for urban markets instead of subsistence. Settlements boasting diesel and petrol pumps are particularly important—'feeding' the trucks so crucial to modern herding, where once Bedouin fed passing pilgrims and camels.

As we have noted, nomadic communities in the Middle East did not historically exist in isolation from settled societies; the very instability of marginal environments forced them to engage with sedentary communities, including settling from time to time.[49] Pastoralists held land, grew

---

[48] Bruce Ingram, *Bedouin of Northern Arabia: Traditions of the Al-Dhafir* (London and New York: KPI, 1986), 48.

[49] Cynthia Nelson (ed.), *The Desert and the Sown: Nomads in Wider Society* (Berkeley: University of California, 1973); Chatty, *From Camel to Truck*, introduction.

dates and other crops for human and stock consumption, and sent men away periodically for military service.[50] They have long had multi-resource livelihoods, not purely pastoral ones, and using the proceeds of work in the oil industry to fund other economic activities could be seen as another diversification though this strategy tended to put more of a burden on women. For example, woman are now involved in cheese-making, to meet the rising urban demand for dairy products.[51] Across the region as a whole, however, Bedouin men drifted away from the livestock economy and grasped new opportunities to earn cash by working in the oil industry and government.[52] Livelihoods were increasingly generated through wages or the urban economy. Most workers have not reinvested this income in livestock but in land, automobiles, increased cross-border trade, diesel-powered water pumps for their date gardens, or, for wealthier individuals, petrol-station franchises.[53] By the 1980s, young Saudi Bedouin reportedly spent their income on bridewealth and cars.[54] Some families that did invest in livestock could afford to pay hired labour (often foreign) to herd and do other manual work.

The connection with livestock, however, is manifest in reinvented traditions. The development of camel racing since the 1980s, from small-scale social celebration to a major heritage revival sport and European tourist attraction (particularly in the United Arab Emirates), illustrates cultural adaptation by Bedouin as well as the central role of automobiles. Camel owners compete for prizes of luxury cars such as Mercedes and BMWs. Trucks carrying camels to racetracks near most major cities became a familiar sight on the highways. But in a nod to the past, the stadium at Nad Al Shiba near Abu Dhabi, for example, is built in the shape of a large white tent. Bedouin are said to have 'shift[ed] their traditional knowledge and skills to the breeding of racing camels in the context of the new oil economy ... Camel

    [50] Donald P. Cole, 'The Enmeshment of Nomads in Sa'udi Arabian Society: The Case of Al Murrah', in Nelson, (ed.), *The Desert and the Sown*, 113–28.

    [51] Chatty, *From Camel to Truck*, 143–8.

    [52] D. Chatty, 'Petroleum Exploitation and the Displacement of Pastoral Nomadic Households in Oman', in Seteney Shami (ed.), *Population Displacement and Resettlement: Development and Conflict in the Middle East* (New York: Center for Migration Studies, 1994), 89.

    [53] D. Chatty, 'The Bedouin of Central Oman: Adaptation or Fossilization?' in P. Salzman (ed.), *Contemporary Nomadic and Pastoral Peoples: Asia and the North* (Virginia, US: College of William and Mary, 1981), 22, 28–30.

    [54] Donald P. Cole, 'Bedouin and Social Change in Saudi Arabia' in J. G. Galaty and P. C. Salzman (eds.), *Change and Development in Nomadic and Pastoral Societies* (Leiden: Brill, 1981), 139.

races as cultural performances provide a cultural link between the modern changing society and the old cultural lifeways.'[55]

Oil, Colonialism, and War

As was the case with resource extraction right across the Empire, the triumphalist conversion of 'wastelands' to valuable national resource was a major end result of oil exploitation in the Middle East. The winning ethos was summed up by J. W. Williamson, writing of Anglo-Persian's exploitation of Persian oil fields, in the 1920s.

Before the Company came to Persia the area around Masjid-i-Sulaiman was little else than a wilderness of crumpled hills, the loneliness of which was disturbed only by the wandering nomads or by the prowling hyaenas and jackals ... [To] reflect that but a few short years ago there was nothing at Fields but a hilly wilderness and at Abadan only a bare desert, is to realise what a great thing has been done for Persia, for Britain and for civilisation in this area of the Middle East. It is inspiring to remember that all these results have come from British enterprise, industrial organisation and, not least of all, from the steady, persistent application, continuously directed from the head, of scientific knowledge and methods to the whole business of getting and refining a black liquid from the bowels of the earth.[56]

Compared to some of the earlier imperial resource frontiers we have examined, the impact of oil could be accommodated by indigenous communities, and local elites became the major beneficiaries. Britain's role as a colonial power was constrained. Pastoral life that had long evolved in this difficult environment to some degree survived, in modified form. A combination of power relations, the disease environment, the late development of the oil frontier, and the fact that oil exploitation did not require the conquest and alienation of large areas of land, assisted local societies in negotiating the terms of colonial intrusion. Initially at least, oil did not require large amounts of cheap labour, and local communities were able to supply some of the company's requirements.

The uses of the desert changed during the period of oil exploitation. Despite the decline of camel keeping, other intrusions such as motorized hunting and small stock farming brought new environmental pressures. As

[55] Sulayman Khalaf, 'Continuity and Change in Camel Racing in the UAE', *Anthropos* (1999), 85–106, viewable online at <http://www.enhg.org/articles/camelrac>.

[56] J. W. Williamson, *In a Persian Oil Field: A Study in Scientific and Industrial Development* 2nd edn. (1927; London: Ernest Benn, 1930), 190–1.

for the longer-term effects on Kuwait, these are impossible to gauge separately from the consequences of the 1990–1 Iraqi invasion of the country, and the first Gulf War. In brief, Iraqi forces reportedly destroyed more than 700 oil wells, spilling 60 million barrels of oil that formed 246 oil lakes in the desert. Soil was poisoned and a major groundwater aquifer, two-fifths of Kuwait's entire freshwater reserve, was contaminated. Ten million barrels of oil were emptied into the Gulf, devastating 1500 km of coastline. The costs of the environmental clean-up have been estimated at more than US$40 billion. It took nine months to put out the oil fires, and some assessors claim that 'the desert will be contaminated forever'.[57] The resource base for Bedouin was, and remained, badly damaged.[58] The use of the Kuwaiti desert by US-led forces in this war, and in the 2003–5 invasion of Iraq, added to the environmental loss.

[57] Green Cross International, 'An Environmental Assessment of Kuwait Seven Years After the Gulf War' (August 1998); Duncan McClaren and Ian Wilmore, 'The Environmental Damage of War in Iraq', *The Observer*, 19 January 2003.

[58] Andrew Gardner, 'The New Calculus of Bedouin Pastoralism in the Kingdom of Saudi Arabia', *Human Organization*, 62/3 (2003), 267–76.

16

Resistance to Colonial Conservation and Resource Management

In the remaining chapters we will focus increasingly on the response by colonized people to competition for, and commodification of, conquered environments. Political conflict over natural resources had deep historical roots in the Empire, and these issues were not resolved by dominion status for the British settler states nor decolonization after the Second World War. They fed into the politics of decolonization and into environmental debates within and beyond the post-colonial Commonwealth. Subsequent chapters traverse the moment of decolonization and explore elements of late twentieth-century political ecology.

In South Asia and Africa state attempts to control and regulate natural resources changed power relations in the countryside and triggered popular resistance. Through conquest or annexation, some colonial and protectorate governments not only alienated large swathes of territory, but also assumed responsibility for and asserted rights over the natural environment. The governments of settler states moved to protect environments from careless settlers who ransacked it for wildlife or timber, and from indigenous peoples whose land-management systems were regarded as destructive. In some cases conservators recognized that European settlers wreaked more havoc than indigenes; Sim said of the Cape forests that the 'Hottentot and Bushman inhabitants … were not intentionally destructive … But the advent of European civilization boded greater ill to the forests, and rapidly enough that ill has been accomplished.'[1] And some, such as Howard, saw value in local agrarian systems. But although regulation could affect all colonial subjects, it tended to bear most heavily on indigenous people. Colonial governments introduced policies of excluding humans from protected areas, as well as a wide range of other measures aimed at curbing customary

---

[1] T. R. Sim, *The Forests and Forest Flora of the Colony of Cape of Good Hope* (Cape Town: Government of the Cape of Good Hope, 1907), 43.

user rights and maximizing state revenue. Stiff penalties were introduced to punish those who broke the new regulations, and thus the rise of bureaucratic conservationism often led to the criminalization of local resource extractors.

In settler colonies the privatization of land transformed socio-environmental relationships, barring local communities from accessing resources they had long regarded as communally held and managed. In some early colonial settlements, this process echoed the enclosures of common land in eighteenth-century England. At a fundamental level it changed the value people placed upon land, setting in train a process towards individualized tenure, commercialization, and subdivision of territory. In non-settler states such as British India, where the Crown acquired a fifth of the total land area for state forests, imperial interventions altered relationships in the countryside between different social strata and castes, landlords and tenants, peasants and graziers, tribals and non-tribals. Struggles for control of land and resources are ancient everywhere, and private land title was not a new concept in India. What was new was (in part) the 'impact of western legal forms and principles on the distribution of rights to the land'.[2] Following decolonization from 1947 in India, through the 1950s and 1960s elsewhere, there were both changes and continuities in intrusive conservationism and environmental policies. Independent Malaysia, for example, loosened forest protection (Chapter 14), but African countries such as Tanzania and Botswana extended the areas devoted to exclusive wildlife management (Chapter 17).

Colonial governments wanted to see natural resources used as efficiently as possible, for what they perceived as the public good (see Chapter 7). Conservation in this context meant protecting resources in order to optimize the economic capacity of land in the long term. There was often a tension between conservationist measures and the commercial development of natural resources—the contradictions embedded in scientific forestry being a prime example. But driving both was often the belief that the state and its scientists perceived natural resource use more rationally than the local inhabitants. In their eyes, this legitimized their role as ultimate stewards of the land. Colonial states also tended to reject the idea that nomadic and transhumant communities should have the right to roam over more land than they were peceived to need or use; pressure was put upon them to settle down, cultivate, take up wage labour, and pay taxes.

---

[2] C. A. Bayly (ed.), Eric Stokes, *The Peasant Armed: The Indian Revolt of 1857* (Oxford: Clarendon Press, 1986), 9.

Popular protest over land alienation and conservationist regimes manifested itself in grass-roots resistance over access to resources such as land, forests, pasture, water, flora, and game. This chapter will look at some aspects of conservation and resource management and describe the different forms of resistance that erupted in response to new policies. These included passive resistance such as peaceful demonstrations, refusal to pay tax or work, through to poaching, deliberate killing of wildlife, burning of forests and symbols of white rule (such as bungalows and offices), land invasion, riots, and murder. Some of our examples show how quiet evasion and encroachment were transformed over time, in a new political climate, into open, loud, and violent defiance—frequently prompted by state action. In the twentieth century, some anti-colonial rural and nationalist movements placed land and other resource rights at the centre of their demands; there was often an environmental angle to conflicts attending the political transition to independence.

Resistance was evident from the earliest phases of British colonial occupation. Grove has shown how the introduction of forest reserves and environmental legislation in the islands of St Vincent and Tobago from the late eighteenth century sparked confrontation with the remaining Caribs.[3] In mapping the land and creating forest reserves, little provision was made for Caribs, and there was no official recognition of common landholding. Caribs on St Vincent harassed survey teams, and razed a new military barracks. In a symbolic gesture, they burned the government cartographer's survey maps, which he had hidden in a field. Grove calls the resistance successful, since the British were forced to accept the legitimacy of Carib claims to common rights in land, but the Caribs were ultimately decimated. They used the forests as military bases and retreats. White settlers, by contrast, successfully demanded the right to clear more of them for sugar and cotton. Caribbean precedents were echoed elsewhere in the British Empire. The connection in the official mind between lawlessness and forests became a much-repeated refrain across the Empire. In West Africa, for example, forests were not only a focus for conflict between traditional authorities and the colonial state, but seen as 'a potential source of African resistance and self-empowerment'.[4] Since many local people regarded forests as sacred spaces, there was often a spiritual dimension to the relationship.

---

[3] Grove, *Green Imperialism*, ch. 6.
[4] McEwan, 'Representing West African Forests', 31–2.

Carib use of forests as resistance refuges was echoed in Maasai warrior rebellion and the Mau Mau emergency in Kenya in the 1900s and 1950s respectively.

Resistance to ecological and related controls did not simply come from indigenous communities, or peasants, but from a wide cross-section of society including European settlers. For example, the beef baron Gilbert Colvile delighted in breaking the law of British East Africa by deliberately setting large bush fires, stealing vaccine from government vets, evading taxation, and allegedly making freelance cattle raids with Maasai warriors into neighbouring German territory during the First World War.[5] Ewart Grogan flouted Forest Department rules in the same protectorate in the 1920s, in his exploitation of the Lembus Forest—later a site of political struggle by Tugen residents, who successfully resisted state attempts to erode their rights to use it.[6] Many early settlers were irked by the official development conditions that came with land grants, and blatantly defied them.

Rural Resistance in India

Especially for some peasant and *adivasi* (tribal or indigenous) communities, one of the most profound socio-ecological changes under British colonial rule followed the reservation of forests by the state (see Chapter 7). Their resistance to forest laws was also linked to other issues including increased rents, taxation, indebtedness to moneylenders, opposition to incomers, displacement, forced labour, and drives for autonomy. Of the many rural insurrections in British India, we shall mention only some of those arising at least in part from forest controls, while recognizing how difficult it can be to disaggregate this from other factors—at both the symbolic and material level. Also, it is important to note that attacks were not simply directed at European and government targets but more generally against a range of oppressors including landlords and moneylenders.[7] There are in some cases continuities in patterns of resistance over long periods; for example, in the

[5] Hughes, 'Moving the Maasai', ch. 6. Chapter 7 of published version, same title.

[6] David Anderson, *Eroding the Commons: The Politics of Ecology in Baringo, Kenya, 1890–1963* (Oxford: James Currey, 2002), ch. 8; David Anderson, 'Managing the Forest: The Conservation History of Lembus' in Anderson and Grove, (eds.), *Conservation in Africa*, 249–68.

[7] Ranajit Guha, *Elementary Aspects of Peasant Insurgency in Colonial India* (Delhi: Oxford University Press, 1992), 3, 26.

Gudem-Rampa uprisings in the hill tracts of what is now Andhra Pradesh between 1839 and 1924.[8] Though British claims to forests long preceded this legislation, restrictions enforced under the Indian Forest Act of 1878 affected all forest-dependent people, both tribal and caste Hindu. Fluid, once porous boundaries became fixed. Village 'wastelands' (unoccupied and uncultivated commons) were in many places incorporated into state forests, which meant villagers lost free grazing and wood supplies. Some were demarcated and handed to (Indian) revenue collectors who allowed villagers to continue using them, but under strict conditions.

Just as *kumri* was never fully controlled, administrators were forced in many cases to give pastoralists forest grazing rights; for example, by the 1890s grazing was still allowed in about 80 per cent of forests in the Punjab Hills. In the Kangra Forests villagers were given a share of timber revenue in order to keep them sweet, and in the Kumaun Division there was a dramatic policy change in 1916 when officials decided to allow villagers to burn the forest floor. These small gains indicated the scope for resistance although they could hardly make up for the losses; the system remained in place, with some modifications.[9]

Even in highly localized movements, rural leaders often linked demands concerning forest use to broader anxieties about dispossession. For example, the people of the Garo Hills in Meghalaya state, North-East India, opposed forced labour and protested to the government in the 1900s about rights to disputed lands in nearby plains. Garo leader Sonaram R. Sangma, challenged in court about his role in mobilizing resistance to the British, explained: 'They [the Garos] expect the reserved forests to be thrown open and impressed labour to be abolished. They want to cut trees and bamboos wherever they like ... and also to *jhum* [practise shifting cultivation] where they please, inside the reserves. They think their own lands have been taken from them by Government and turned into forest reserves.' Sangma was unusual for his time in seeking legal redress for Garo grievances, and was labelled a 'professional agitator'. But his actions forced the British to set up an investigative commission in 1906.[10]

[8] David Arnold, 'Rebellious Hillmen: The Gudem-Rampa Risings 1839–1924' in Ranajit Guha (ed.), *Subaltern Studies I*, 88–142.

[9] D. Hardiman (ed.), *Peasant Resistance in India, 1858–1914* (Delhi: Oxford University Press, 1992), 49.

[10] Bengt G. Karlsson, 'A Matter of Rights: Forest Reservations, Legal Activism and the Sangma Movement in 20th Century Garo Hills', paper presented at the International Conference on the

Frustration with a range of controls similarly triggered rebellion in Bastar state, Central India, in 1910—a place of 'interminable forest'.[11] People saw a series of droughts and disease outbreaks as a sign that 'the earth had turned bitter against them', and vowed to fight the British, believing they could turn guns and cannons into water. Sundar asserts that 'forest reservation was perhaps the most drastic of colonial interventions', but Bastar did not experience systematic forest management until the British took over direct control of the state in 1891, and there were no reserves before the century turned. Fury over hiked land revenue, bans on shifting cultivation, and the burden of forced labour (not banned until 1929 by administrator W. V. Grigson, also Bastar's first major anthropologist) were among other factors behind the rebellion. It is popularly called the Bhumkal, meaning a political council but also anger displayed by the earth: a clear indication of its roots in the soil. The revolt began with the looting of bazaars and killing of a trader, beaten to death by a 500-strong mob. Burning of property, schools, and police stations followed. Grain was redistributed, mail stolen, and telegraph lines cut. Just as colonial states recognized the centrality of communications in control, so rural rebels attempted to counter the asymmetries of technology. Traders, police, foresters, officials, and immigrants were singled out for attack, as hated representatives of the state or other types of alien exploiter.[12]

Gadgil and Guha describe a sequence of protests in the eight hill districts of Uttar Pradesh state (known collectively as Uttarakhand) as 'perhaps the most sustained opposition to state forest management' in these Himalayan tracts.[13] They took place between 1904 and the late 1940s, and included organized attacks on forest officials, mass violation of regulations, and appeals to the Crown to lift various bans. In 1904, villagers in the Khujni area attacked the conservator's staff. Two years later, villagers in Khas branded the conservator's face with a cattle iron, forcing him to run for his life. The rebels declared they objected to any state interference with forests, asserting they had full and exclusive rights to them. In Kumaun Division in 1921, people entered state forests en masse, burning commercially grown pine

Forest and Environmental History of the British Empire and Commonwealth (University of Sussex, March 2003), 1.

[11] Nandini Sundar, *Subalterns and Sovereigns: An Anthropological History of Bastar, 1854–1996* (Delhi: Oxford University Press, 1997), xi.

[12] Sundar, *Subalterns and Sovereigns*, 104–6, 132.

[13] Gadgil and Guha, *This Fissured Land*, 163; Gadgil and Guha, 'State Forestry and Social Conflict', 279–80.

trees as well as government buildings. This campaign 'virtually paralyzed the administration', which had to abolish forced labour (*begar*) and relinquish control over some woodland. In 1930, the peasants of Rawain rebelled against cuts in the amount of forest produce villagers were allowed to gather. They refused to obey the rules, drove state officials out, and declared their own government. Soldiers sent to put down the revolt killed many protesters when they fired on an unarmed crowd.[14]

Peasant rebels tended to make two claims: they asserted their rights of use and control over forests and other resources, and they accused the government of privileging state or commercial gain over their subsistence needs. Here was a clash between different concepts of property and ownership, as well as opposing concepts of forest management and use. Both forest and game laws treated local people as predators, assumed to be 'involved in an unrestrained, senseless and indiscriminate destruction of forest resources' whose counterpoint was the supposed restraint, logic, and planned preservationist goals of state conservators.[15] Resisters were often united by religious convictions, and the belief that ecological controls threatened their spiritual well-being as much as their livelihoods. They frequently sought divine approval for their actions, and made sacrifices to the gods beforehand. Religious appeals could instil a broader sense of common identity, courage, and solidarity. Arnold writes of the Gudem-Rampa rebellions—in which forest grievances and curbs on shifting cultivation featured—that religion 'expressed the hillmen's dissatisfaction with their subjugation and offered a means by which they hoped for deliverance from oppression'.[16] The final uprising in this series (1922–4) was led by a Hindu holy man, Rama Raju, regarded by *adivasi* as having magical powers. The British wrote him off as insane, and ultimately shot him. (Unlike most other rebel leaders, he was unusually 'an outsider from the plains'.)[17]

Simultaneously, Gandhi's philosophy of *satyagraha* or peaceful non-cooperation (he spurned the term passive resistance), and his call for a rejection of modern industrialized capitalist society in favour of a return to simple, communal, and cooperative village life, struck a chord with

---

[14] Ramachandra Guha, 'The Malign Encounter: The Chipko Movement and Compelling Visions of Nature', in T. Banuri and F. Apfell Marglin (eds.), *Who Will Save the Forests?* (London: Zed Books, 1993), 86–9; Ramachandra Guha, 'Forestry and Social Protest in British Kumaun, c. 1893–1921' in Ranajit Guha (ed.), *Subaltern Studies IV*, 54–100.

[15] Saberwal, Rangarajan, and Kothari, *People, Parks and Wildlife*, ix.

[16] Arnold, 'Rebellious Hillmen', 121.   [17] *Ibid.*, 134–40.

millions of people and influenced both the style of revolt and the content
of anti-colonial critiques.[18] By the 1920s and 1930s peasant struggles had
acquired a more nationalist fervour, and were directed more overtly against
government. Rama Raju was a case in point; inspired by Gandhi, he sought
to liberate India from the British, and hoped localized rebellion could act as a
springboard for this larger battle—but unlike Gandhi, he believed liberation
could only be achieved by force.[19]

Forest *satyagraha*, a new form of peasant mobilization, began in 1930 in the
Central Provinces and soon spread to other areas. Though spearheaded by
the Congress Party as part of its civil disobedience campaign (1930–4), 'these
movements actually enjoyed a considerable degree of autonomy' and some
violent protests were carried out 'in defiance of nationalist leaders' who
favoured peaceful means.[20] Notable grass-roots leaders included Ganjam
Korku, a Gond from Banjaridhal, Central Provinces. Resistance mainly
took the form of grass and wood cutting, teak felling, non-cooperation,
forest invasions, and boycotting of fuel and timber auctions, but there
was some arson and clashes with police; women played a key role in
throwing large cordons around their men to prevent arrest. As one British
administrator described it, 'large bands' of protesters were 'raging [*sic*]
the forests, emotionally cutting grass and wood'.[21] In 1930 there was a
wave of killings of elephant and rhino by Kachari tribals in Assam, actions
echoed three decades later in East African parks.[22] Though the movement
was quashed, its importance was longer lasting, since the nationalists had
extended their support base to the rural areas and would build on this in
the years leading up to independence. In 1945–7, the Warlis tribal people of
Maharashtra launched partly successful strikes against landlords and forest
contractors, whom they accused of gross exploitation.[23]

India's post-independence governments, committed to rapid industrialization, allowed increasingly aggressive commercial forest exploitation. This
was accompanied by more restrictive regulations, and a reiteration, in the

---

[18] Sunil Sen, *Peasant Movements in India: Mid-Nineteenth and Twentieth Centuries* (Calcutta
and Delhi: K. P. Bagchi, 1982).

[19] Arnold, 'Rebellious Hillmen', 135, 141.

[20] Gadgil and Guha, 'State Forestry and Social Conflict', 279; also Sumit Sarkar, 'Primitive
Rebellion and Modern Nationalism: A Note on Forest Satyagraha in the Non-Cooperation and
Civil Disobedience Movements', in K. N. Panikkar (ed.), *National and Left Movements in India*
(Delhi: Vikas, 1980), 19, 23.

[21] Sir Montagu Butler to Irwin, 30 July 1930, quoted in Sarkar, 'Primitive Rebellion', 66.

[22] Sarkar, 'Primitive Rebellion', 23.   [23] Sen, *Peasant Movements*, 66–7, 126–7.

National Forest Policy of 1952, that the state would remain in control of forests. Newly built roads penetrated more woodlands, and down the roads poured outside contractors who took forest produce to industrial process-ing plants and cities. Some forms of intensified exploitation, such as resin tapping, drew on older skills, while others, such as paper making, using chir left over from the manufacture of railway sleepers, were industrial activities. Together with the creation of protected areas, they drove a new dynamic of displacement both in relation to settlements and in local processing of forest produce. Opposition to these policies grew from the early 1970s, culminating in possibly the world's most famous environmental movement: Chipko, meaning 'embrace' or 'hug the tree'. Launched spontaneously in Uttarak-hand in 1973, but rooted in much earlier protest, it mobilized grass-roots resistance to deforestation in the Himalaya. Protesters hugged trees in order to prevent contractors from felling them. The early protests in Uttar Pradesh resulted in a major victory in 1980 with a fifteen-year ban, ordered by Indira Gandhi, on green felling in the Himalayan forests of that state. Later the movement spread to other areas, multiplying into hundreds of autonomous initiatives, and achieved other felling prohibitions in the Western Ghats and Vindhyas in Central India.

Chipko has been remarkably enduring and provided a bridge between localized protest and globalized action, evolving into a social movement that claims to challenge the full range of development policies. Notably, it has not only involved peasants but also all social groups and ages, including children. Prominent activists have included Chandi Prasad Bhatt, whose organization coordinated early protests against commercial forestry, and Sunderlal Bahuguna, a philosopher and disciple of Gandhi, who successfully appealed to Mrs Gandhi, and who coined the Chipko slogan 'ecology is permanent economy'. The prominent role of women in Chipko has led some to call it a feminist movement. Guha regards this as a simplistic analysis. 'In the act of embracing the trees … women are acting not in opposition to men (as feminist interpretation would have it), but as bearers of continuity and tradition in a culture threatened with fragmentation'.[24] His assumption that feminists necessarily oppose men is wrongheaded, while his description of hill women as 'bearers of tradition' itself belongs to eco-feminist analysis, albeit a problematic one. Chipko is an instructive example of mobilization by women that was specifically, although not exclusively, around natural resources.

---

[24] Guha, 'Malign Encounter', 100–1.

Other later twentieth-century resistance linked to forest and wildlife controls, or loss of tribal lands, has included the Jharkhand (meaning forest land) movement which included resistance to commercial teak planting in 1978–9, and the killing of tigers with poisoned bait in Dudhwa National Park in the mid-1980s. This and subsequent poisonings by Naxalite anarchists in various parts of Andhra Pradesh have also been interpreted as evidence of unabated animosity towards forest and conservation controls.[25] The Jharkhand movement is the oldest indigenous peoples' struggle for autonomy in post-colonial India, and culminated in the creation of a separate state of the same name in 2000. For Jharkhandis, many of whom earned their living from forests, plans to replace their beloved sal trees with teak were the last straw in a century of dispossession and oppression—including frustration over forest rules, bonded labour, indebtedness, and displacement by giant power and irrigation projects.[26]

Wilderness Myths and Wildlife Parks

The conservation of wildlife in Africa produced similar tensions to those around forest reservation in India. Early African wildlife reserves did not generally exclude all indigenous people. In the Kenyan case, game reserves were deliberately created in the 1900s to overlap partially with areas set aside for the Maasai.[27] In South Africa, the Kruger National Park had African inhabitants until the interwar years and there was initially a similar tolerance—up to the 1940s—of the indigenous residents of the Matopos Hills in Zimbabwe (see Chapter 17).[28] But as national parks were gradually established, policy changed and a cordon was thrown around scenery, wildlife, and habitats that were believed to be endangered. African hunters were labelled 'poachers'. Barriers led to deepening alienation, and growing hostility to conservation. This set governments, conservationists, and indigenous peoples on a collision course that became increasingly acrimonious in parts of Africa as the twentieth century advanced.

---

[25] V. Saberwal and M. Rangarajan (eds.), *Battles Over Nature: Science and the Politics of Conservation* (Delhi: Permanent Black, 2003), introduction, 16.

[26] Amit Roy, 'Second Phase of Jharkhand Movement', in R. D. Munda and S. Bosu Mullick, (eds.), *The Jharkhand Movement* (Copenhagen: IWGIA, 2003), 74.

[27] David Collett, 'Pastoralists and Wildlife: Image and Reality in Kenya Maasailand', in Anderson and Grove (eds.), *Conservation in Africa*, 140.

[28] Carruthers, *Kruger National Park*; Terence Ranger, *Voices from the Rocks: Nature, Culture and History in the Matopos Hills of Zimbabwe* (Oxford: James Currey, 1999).

Outside of the reserves, where hunting was usually permitted, white trophy hunters were able to plunder game, at a price. Licensed guns were acceptable, while traps, snares, bows, spears, nets, and poison were widely outlawed. Both in Africa and India, indigenous hunters were accused of cruelty, while the law explicitly recognized gun users as humane.[29] The new regulations did not stop African hunting, least of all in remote and hard-to-police areas, but merely drove it underground. In Kenya, however, African hunters had a surprising defender in leading settler Lord Delamere. He publicly admitted poisoning lions to prevent them from killing livestock; this was legal, on private land, under the game laws. In a speech to the local parliament, Delamere urged the government to take firmer action against predators for the sake of all farmers and stock keepers, black and white, for 'lions were useless vermin and it was impossible to deal with them as the Game Reserves were breeding places for them'. Furthermore, he declared, 'if government took away natives' grazing land and gave it to Europeans it had not the right to tell the natives that they must not kill the game which was eating up their crops'.[30]

For other influential individuals, African wildlife came to be seen as part of a paradise that had to be defended. In 1903, the Society for the Preservation of the Fauna of the Empire (SPFE) was created by a group of aristocratic hunters, naturalists, and colonial officials. One of its aims was to ban hunting by Africans, in the belief that this endangered the big game animals, particularly elephant and rhino. Former US president Theodore Roosevelt, who made a celebrated East African safari in 1909, was a self-proclaimed conservationist as well as a hunter. In his best-selling account of this journey, published the following year, Roosevelt propagated the 'wilderness myth', but it took a long time before reserves or national parks had a secure legal footing in Africa.

African hunters were not the only group singled out for blame. Pastoralists were believed to compete with wildlife for pasture, water, and space, and damned for doing so. This ignored the fact that many communities had coexisted with wild animals for centuries, and jointly helped to shape the landscape. For example, the Maasai did not eat game unless facing severe famine, and customarily only killed predators if they threatened their livestock—though there was an element of trophy sport involved here, too,

---

[29] MacKenzie, *The Empire of Nature*, 209.
[30] *Legislative Council Debates*, Kenya Colony (Nairobi: Government Printer, 1930), 102–3.

in so far as lions' manes and ostrich feathers were prized as headdresses, and Maasai traded in ivory and other wildlife products in the nineteenth century.[31] Their domestic grazing regimes interacted with those of wildlife, and by working in tandem both made the best use of available grasses, bushes, and their nutrients. Within limits, grazing stimulates new plant growth. Studies of grazing succession in the Serengeti show that different species of game and domestic stock modify the pasture in sequence, improving its condition for the next herd that comes along.[32] Similar arguments that grazing by livestock was beneficial to wildlife have been used in an Indian national park.[33] This is not to say that Maasai and other communities can still coexist with wildlife without negative impact. Population growth, sedentarization, and changing land use have altered the dynamics, while a static cultural model should not be held of Maasai (or any other) society.

The coexistence of Maasai and game was understood by the administration of British East Africa (later Kenya) when it gazetted a game reserve within the Southern Maasai Reserve in 1906, and allowed the Maasai to continue living there on the grounds that 'native and game alike have wandered happily and freely since the Flood'.[34] A Northern Game Reserve also overlapped with the Northern Maasai Reserve, until the latter was closed in 1913 and its residents forcibly moved south to western Narok. It was only later that pastoralists were barred from areas reserved exclusively for wildlife, and efforts to sedentarize them intensified. Game regulations led to an increase in predators such as lion, which posed a growing threat to Maasai livelihoods by the 1920s. Game warden Captain Ritchie noted in 1926 that lions 'grown overbold as a result of immunity from molestation … attack cattle and their drovers impartially, and that with the sun at high noon'.[35] Furthermore, wildlife in Kenya was not (and is not to this day) confined to parks or

---

[31] Noel Simon, *Between the Sunlight and the Thunder: The Wild Life of Kenya* (London: Collins, 1962), 87; Thomas Hakansson, 'The Human Ecology of World Systems in East Africa: The Impact of the Ivory Trade', *Human Ecology*, 32/5 (2004), 574, 576–80.

[32] K. M. Homewood and W. A. Rodgers, *Maasailand Ecology: Pastoralist Development and Wildlife Conservation in Ngorongoro, Tanzania* (Cambridge: Cambridge University Press, 1991), 98, 125.

[33] Ramachandra Guha, 'The Authoritarian Biologist and the Arrogance of Anti-humanism: Wildlife Conservation in the Third World', in Saberwal and Rangarajan (eds.), *Battles Over Nature*, 152.

[34] B. F. G. Cranworth, *A Colony in the Making* (London: Macmillan, 1912), 310. Cited in W. K. Lindsay, 'Integrating Parks and Pastoralists: Some Lessons from Amboseli', in Anderson and Grove (eds.), *Conservation in Africa*, 152.

[35] Game Department Annual Report 1926, in *SPFE Journal*, New Series, VIII (June 1928), 79.

reserves but moved seasonally in and out, competing for grazing and water with domestic stock in surrounding dispersal areas.

This was the case with Amboseli, a small reserve (600 square km) with a huge wildlife dispersal area. It was declared a national reserve in 1947, but pastoralists were initially permitted to use it. The Southern Game Reserve was abolished in 1952 and replaced by three smaller national reserves; a fourth, Maasai Mara, lay further west. Hunting was banned in the reserves but licensed shooting allowed in adjoining areas. Concerns were raised after a 1955 drought forced African herders to concentrate in Amboseli's central basin, where there are large perennial springs, and administrators tried to draw them away by sinking bore holes and controlling grazing patterns. Administration of Amboseli was handed over to the local African county council in 1961, in an attempt to encourage it to take responsibility for conservation by offering financial and managerial inducements. David Western links this move to the imminent end of British rule (1963): 'With independence approaching, the colonial government did not wish to alienate the Maasai by establishing a national park.'[36] Now conservation of the reserve was in African hands, but this did not satisfy those Maasai who received no direct benefit from it. Increasing numbers of tourists were visiting Amboseli by the 1960s; the council got some of this revenue, as well as hunting fees from shooting in a Controlled Area outside the park. A livestock-free area was created in central Amboseli, after negotiations with the council and pastoralists. Maasai feared that more restrictions would follow if they did not occupy more areas, and so they increased their use of the park's central basin.

The warriors then decided to take direct action. In the mid-1960s they began killing wildlife in protest at the threatened loss of their dry season grazing. This was widely interpreted as a political act; warriors were deliberately targeting the 'big five' that tourists had come so far to see. Western is explicit: 'Rhino, which numbered over 150 in the 1950s were virtually exterminated by 1977, with only 8 remaining—largely the result of spearing by the Maasai to show their political dissatisfaction with their prospects in Amboseli'.[37] These acts were an extension of the warriors' customary defensive role; the well-being of the community was threatened and the warriors can be seen as taking responsibility for pre-emptive action. They

[36] David Western, 'Amboseli National Park: Enlisting Landowners to Conserve Migratory Wildlife', *Ambio*, 11/5 (1982), 304.

[37] *Ibid.*, 308.

were also acting defensively against predators that attacked their livestock, and protesting against an apparent lack of predator control by the Kenya Wildlife Service (KWS). Former game warden Ian Parker claims Maasai deliberately poisoned predators in this period, using acaricide supplied by vets to kill disease-carrying ticks.[38] Lion killing by Maasai in protest at cattle losses and KWS inaction against predators continued in the 1990s, and more recently around Nairobi National Park.

After 1977, when a new project was launched which aimed to give the Maasai direct development benefits from Amboseli, the incidence of deliberate spearings fell sharply and the numbers of wildlife in the ecosystem increased. But other forms of protest were evident after the reserve became a park in 1974 'when events occurred that made conservation costly or supported their suspicions of a predatory government'.[39] When promised water supplies were not maintained, and tourism revenues failed to end up in group ranch coffers, 'Maasai moved their cattle herds back into the park ... And they continued to kill wildlife that threatened their cattle.'[40] In late 2005, however, the story came full circle. In a surprise move, the Kenyan government capitulated to Maasai political pressure and 'handed' Amboseli back to the local county council, illegally changing its status back again from national park to reserve. This act was widely seen as a bribe aimed at encouraging Maasai to vote 'yes' in the November referendum on the country's new constitution (they took the bribe but voted no), and was condemned by conservationists and others who launched a 'save Amboseli' campaign and challenged the move in court.

Kenyan Maasai were at least consulted over the creation of protected areas in Amboseli and Maasai Mara, and have had a stake in their management, which may or may not continue in the case of Amboseli. Across the border in Tanzania, from the late 1950s, plans were laid for people-free parks without fully consulting the people concerned. The man behind them was instrumental in influencing East African governments, in partnership with Western conservation bodies, to implement such policies. Bernard Grzimek, former veterinary officer turned Director of the Frankfurt Zoo, caught the imagination of the Western public and raised thousands of

---

[38] Ian Parker, *What I Tell You Three Times Is True: Conservation, Ivory, History and Politics* (Librario Publishing , 2004), 45; Gibson, *Politicians and Poachers*, 212n.; David Western, personal communication.

[39] Western, 'Amboseli', 307–8.

[40] Gibson, *Politicians and Poachers*, 145. His source is Western.

pounds for African conservation through his writings, films, and television programmes. 'Pure, unperverted nature, a bit of "paradise", still exists today in the great national parks, for which I have fought all my life', he wrote. 'It is a piece of countryside in which only indigenous animals and plants live, the animals naturally without being hunted, the woodland quite without forest management, hence a piece of genuine wild land.'[41]

When Serengeti was declared a National Park in 1940, the rights of some 9,000 Maasai living within the area were to some extent safeguarded. Grzimek, observing park occupation from a light aircraft in 1958, argued for the Maasai to be expelled because 'no men, not even native ones, should live inside [its] borders'. He claimed that the ecosystem could not support wild animals and domestic stock simultaneously, and that this community had 'no right' to be in Serengeti's western portion.[42] He also sought to prevent the British rulers of Tanzania privileging Maasai over wildlife by reducing the size of the park. In the introduction to *Serengeti Shall Not Die*, Grzimek and his son's highly influential hymn to people-free parks, the travel writer Alan Moorehead erroneously wrote of Serengeti: 'But year by year the numbers of the herds grow less as poachers and tribesmen attack them and make inroads upon their waterholes and grazing grounds.'[43] Maasai were driven from the western Serengeti plains in 1959, which prompted a backlash. Warriors speared thirty-one rhinos in the 8,000-square-km Ngorongoro Conservation Area in 1959–60, and another twelve in 1961—compared to seventeen rhino killings in the previous seven years, and only three per year between 1962 and 1967. Evidence suggests that in earlier years the vast majority of commercial poaching was not carried out by Maasai, who tended to deter poachers and helped the park authorities pursue them; these acts were qualitatively different. As tensions grew in Ngorongoro between pastoralists and officials, cooperation broke down, and some Maasai are said to have become guides and hunters for poaching gangs.[44]

Resistance in both Amboseli and Ngorongoro was parochial, though its impact had international dimensions. Elsewhere in Africa, as earlier in India, resistance to conservation measures became increasingly connected with nationalist and anti-colonial movements around the mid-twentieth century.

---

[41] B. Grzimek, R. Messner, L. Riefenstahl, and H. Tichy, *Visions of Paradise* (London: Hodder & Stoughton, 1981), 100.

[42] Bernhard and Michael Grzimek, *Serengeti Shall Not Die* (London: Collins, 1965), 177, 178.

[43] Alan Moorehead, introduction to Grzimek and Grzimek, *Serengeti Shall Not Die*, 13.

[44] Homewood and Rodgers, *Maasailand Ecology*, 138–9.

Opposing Soil Conservation

Official efforts to combat soil erosion played a major role in colonial rural reconstruction in Africa, which also met with widespread resistance. After the 1930s Depression, settler and colonial states, armed with new ideologies of development, expanding technical departments, and increasing state revenues, felt empowered to expand their role. Conservation schemes, as part of their drive to progress, struck at the most basic resources of all: earth and water, and how people used them. In this case, rural people were not generally excluded from land but the aim was to change their systems of agriculture, under the banner of 'betterment'. The finger was pointed at African farming practices, pasture management, and increasing 'population pressure'. By the 1930s this had become a constant refrain in southern and eastern Africa, and the subtext was in part racial.

In South Africa, the 1932 report of the Native Economic Commission identified overstocking by subsistence farmers in the reserves as a particularly urgent concern and warned of impending desertification.[45] Commissioners feared that growing rural poverty and environmental degradation would drive larger numbers of Africans to the cities, where they would swamp white communities. Agricultural officials had long promoted soil conservation on white-owned farms; now images of the American Dust Bowl, with swirling sandstorms and impoverished farmers trudging westwards to California, helped to catapult erosion up the agenda of state concern in many parts of the Empire in the 1930s.[46] Subsequent policy documents, recommended the total reorganization of African rural society, including cutting stock numbers, concentrating settlements into villages, and fencing pastures so that rotational grazing could be introduced. There were echoes of earlier imperial initiatives, such as mission villages or those developed to combat tsetse. Betterment areas were envisaged both in existing African settlements and in land newly acquired under the 1936 Native Trust and Land Act. This promised more land for exclusive African occupation, in order to make real the national policy of racial segregation. Africans in turn would increasingly lose their remaining political rights in the broader society. The Native Affairs

---

[45] Peter Delius, *A Lion Amongst the Cattle: Reconstruction and Resistance in the Northern Transvaal* (Oxford: James Currey, 1996); P. Delius and S. Schirmer, 'Soil Conservation in a Racially Ordered Society: South Africa, 1930–1970', *Journal of Southern African Studies*, 26/4 (December 2000), 719–41.

[46] Beinart, *Rise of Conservation*.

Department was determined not to let any of this additional land 'be ruined by malpractice'.[47]

Betterment and the 1936 Act soon triggered opposition in rural Transvaal, where much of the newly purchased Trust land lay. This began not in reserves but among African labour tenants on white-owned farms, whose position was also threatened by the Act. In 1940, resentment grew in the Pietersburg area after people were prosecuted for cutting down trees without permission. Culling of livestock (usually by enforced sale following an assessment of local carrying capacity) was particularly unpopular and some rural communities refused to register with the Native Trust or move to designated sites. They cut fences, wrecked beacons, and ploughed on land set aside for grazing. By 1943 the conflict had become violent. A man arrested for illegal ploughing was forcibly freed from police custody; the crowd then threatened the native commissioner and threw assegais at agricultural officers. Some 500 armed people took to the bush. The authorities reacted by deporting some of the alleged leaders, and rewarding cooperative headmen. But the seeds of unrest had been planted, and grew into organized grass-roots movements such as the migrant worker-led Zoutpansberg Balemi Association and Sebataladi Motor Cottage Association. Though these did not last long, those behind them had 'tested the political and economic constraints which held them fast'.[48]

After the Second World War, which saw a lull in conservationist intervention, officials launched another major push to transform the African areas, which included plans to build 'healthy rural villages' for families who did not earn their living from the land. In 1945 a 'new era of reclamation' was announced. Whereas the old betterment process had in theory been voluntary—'the change must come largely from the people themselves'—policies were increasingly compulsory.[49] South African rural rehabilitation in the 1950s had much in common with land-use plans evolved in Zimbabwe and some British colonies but its aims were more far reaching, and the use of fencing distinctive. People were forced to sell cattle, and to keep fewer donkeys and goats.[50] At the same time, chiefs were being asked to play an increasingly central role in implementing these reforms. Their involvement was required under the Bantu Authorities Act of 1951, passed by the new National Party government, which cemented an administrative system based

---

[47] Delius and Schirmer, 'Soil Conservation', 722.   [48] Delius, *A Lion*, 71.
[49] Delius and Schirmer, 'Soil Conservation', 727–8.
[50] Nancy Jacobs, *Environment, Power and Injustice: A South African History* (Cambridge: Cambridge University Press, 2003).

on tribal authorities. Rural communities felt that the state was attempting to 'penetrate and dominate every nook and cranny of their world'.[51]

This was the last straw. Resistance in the Transvaal culminated in the Sekhukhuneland Revolt of 1958, which arose from fears that chiefs were becoming an instrument of the central government and the Trust. It was linked to wider campaigns organized principally by the African National Congress. As in the case of Indian forest resistance, rural opposition to conservationist controls was a significant plank in popular mobilization against the apartheid state, and catapulted several individuals into national politics. In Zimbabwe, resistance to the removals from the Matopos and surrounding areas in the 1950s fed into popular mobilizations by African nationalist politicians: 'people thought that "nationalism would bring them freedom" and a return to the Matopos'.[52] The park became a site of armed struggle and an attempt was made to desecrate Rhodes's grave, sited on a prominent rock with scenic views over the reserved land.

Across the British colonial areas of the continent, rural opposition to state intervention in African husbandry was a significant element in anti-colonial struggles. Opposition to compulsory terracing, designed to control soil erosion, in Central Kenya has been identified as one of the roots of Mau Mau. Kikuyu peasants saw communal hard labour on terracing come to nothing as heavy rains destroyed much of their work. Anger followed disillusion.[53] The use of women to dig terraces was a particular focus of discontent, and an issue raised with the colonial government by Jomo Kenyatta. In 1948, 2,500 women marched on district headquarters in Central Province where they 'danced and sang and informed everyone that they would not take part in soil conservation measures because they had quite enough to do at home'.[54] A month later they also refused to plant grass, and launched an all-out revolt. When leaders were arrested, 'they were quickly released by a large crowd of their own sex brandishing sticks and shouting Amazonian war-cries'. The resistance was not just anti-government, but as in South Africa was also directed at acquiescent chiefs and headmen.

Women played a significant role in resistance movements in colonial Africa even though it was sometimes difficult for them to become public actors. In 1947 and 1950, together with men, Kenyan women started cultivating

---

51 Delius, *A Lion*, 72.   52 Ranger, *Voices*, 175.

53 D. W. Throup, 'The Origins of Mau Mau', *African Affairs*, 84/336 (July 1985), 399–433.

54 A. Fiona D. Mackenzie, *Land, Ecology and Resistance in Kenya, 1880–1952* (Edinburgh: Edinburgh University Press, 1998), 1.

swampland—an activity banned under a Land and Water Preservation Ordinance.[55] Their continued growing of drought-resistant millet can also be seen as resistance to official orders to plant maize, though it was simultaneously a hedge against hardship and a way of preventing men from controlling what they produced.[56] There were cases in Africa where officials, chiefs, and people cooperated successfully on soil-conservation measures.[57] But for many the ubiquitous colonial presence—asking questions, making rules about land use, and convicting those who transgressed—seemed to constitute a 'conservation imperialism'.[58] Unwittingly, the state helped set in motion the irresistible rock that would roll towards decolonization.

Some of the most effective resistance involved 'massive withdrawal of compliance', to use Scott's phrase, rather than outright revolt. Overtly violent actions which avoided shedding human blood, such as the killing of valuable wildlife by warriors in and around East African parks, do not easily fit his categorizations. They do, however, bear out his claim that resistance is often both instrumental and symbolic. Indian examples include the branding of the conservator's face in Uttarakhand and 'messenger boughs'—traditionally used to summon villagers to a communal hunt—which featured in the Kol insurrections of 1831–2 and the 1910 Bastar rebellion. In the 1930s in what is now Karnataka state, women garlanded and painted men with ritual paste before they entered the forests to cut sandal trees, and symbolically broke the regulations themselves when invoking the god Krishna and his wanderings in the woods.[59]

There is a direct line to be drawn between the alienation of people from forests and other communally held land, and the development of political struggle and consciousness in the colonized world. As Karl Marx noted in his 'Debates on the Law of the Thefts of Wood' (1842), reservation sowed the seeds of revolution.[60] Popular resistance to colonial forest controls often preceded other types of protest and helped to shape it; for example, the roots of the Indian Naxalite movement which emerged in the late 1960s arguably lay in much earlier opposition to forest controls and curbs on shifting

[55] Mackenzie, *Land, Ecology, and Resistance*, 3, 165, 167.

[56] A. Fiona D. Mackenzie, 'Contested Ground: Colonial Narratives and the Kenyan Environment, 1920–1945', *Journal of Southern African Studies* 26/4 (2000), 704–5.

[57] Grace Carswell, 'Soil Conservation Policies in Colonial Kigezi, Uganda', in Beinart and McGregor, *Social History and African Environments*.

[58] Guha, 'Authoritarian Biologist', 154.

[59] Gadgil and Guha, *This Fissured Land*, 162; 'State Forestry and Social Conflict', 279.

[60] *Rheinische Zeitung*, 298 (October 1842).

cultivation.[61] Joint action to stop dam building, inundation of homes and wildlife habitats, and mining in watershed areas echoed the earlier alliances.[62] In South African reserves, soil-conservation controls helped trigger broader political movements, while opposition to terracing schemes in 1940s Kenya played a role in the development of Mau Mau. However, it is a mistake to see all peasant or indigenous resistance in terms of either nationalist or class struggle. It may be more helpful to view it as a response to the destruction of community and collective practices and identities, or more broadly the colonial 'rupture of continuities'.[63]

The legacy of colonial conservationism can be seen more recently in certain official, developmentalist, and environmentalist discourses and policies. Similarly, isolated rural protest movements have more recently been able to find support in the international context from human rights NGOs and UN bodies dedicated to indigenous rights. For example, the voices of peasants, pastoralists, activists, politicians, social scientists, international sympathizers, and a few environmentalists have all been heard in debates about the relevance of national parks to rural people. Exclusionist policies have increasingly come under intense scrutiny. (See Chapter 17.)

[61] Grove, 'Colonial Conservation', 34; Hardiman, *Peasant Resistance*, 5–6.

[62] M. Rangarajan, 'Battles for Nature: Contesting Wildlife Conservation in 20th Century India', paper presented to a conference at the University of Florida, December 2000, 16.

[63] Guha, 'Malign Encounter', 88, Hardiman, *Peasant Resistance*, 8–10.

17

National Parks and the Growth of Tourism

Conservation and Tourism: National Parks in Africa

Imperial expansion transformed and destroyed nature in many areas; yet, as we argue, it also contained conservationist impulses. On the one hand these involved attempts to modify practices on land that was used for agriculture both by settlers and indigenous people. On the other, land was reserved more directly by creating zones where human settlement was disallowed. In the case of forests, this often implied scientific management and controlled commercial logging—although some forests were more tightly protected. With regard to wildlife and protected habitats, settler and colonial governments placed greater emphasis on exclusion in their conservation strategies. This chapter will chart changes in attitude and policy towards protected areas, as tourists replaced elite travellers and white hunters in answering the call of the wild.

As in the last chapter, our discussion moves beyond the colonial period. While we focus on countries that became part of the Commonwealth, independent states were operating in a changing international context of which the imperial heritage was only one element. We recognize the shift towards community management of natural resources, and the potential for tourism to generate income for poor people. But we argue that the legacy of exclusive conservation, informed partly by new concerns and interests, remained powerful. It is an ambivalent legacy, still the subject of intense debate and contestation, and heavily criticized in recent literature on Africa.[1] While conservation has helped to preserve some habitats and threatened species, a point not often recognized in critiques, it has not often won local legitimacy.

In discussions of wildlife protection, policies of preservation are some-times distinguished from conservation. The boundaries between these ideas

---

[1] Beinart, 'African History and Environmental History'.

are not easily drawn. In general, preservation is seen as an earlier phase and 'is posited on ... the prevention of any active interference whatsoever'.[2] More recently, such strategies have been adopted in highly protected wilderness zones. Conservation is seen as a later, more interventionist phase. It implies wise usage or management to ensure the long-term viability of a natural resource—much in the way that 'sustainable' is used now. In fact, preservation often also requires some degree of management. With respect to wildlife, conservationist approaches became associated with viewing by tourists. Wildlife, once the object of hunting, was both being conserved and commodified in another way. In some protected areas, culling and sale of animal products was also pursued.

In the early years of wildlife protection, colonial officials and others attempted to set aside areas when they began to realize the failure of hunting laws and the enormity of the destruction. Colonial states established reserves by proclamation and decree that could easily be revoked. From the 1920s, and especially after the Second World War, national parks were established by legislation and were meant to be permanent. They were designed to conserve wildlife, landscapes, and later specific habitats, or ecological zones, while also making them accessible to visitors. Parks 'were designed for an age of tourism, the era of the motor car and the camera'.[3] These areas were generally small to begin with, but expanded as the twentieth century advanced and became ubiquitous in Commonwealth countries which have tended, along with the US, to provide a global model. Wildlife reserves and controlled zones now cover huge tracts, especially in former British African colonies which have relatively large areas of sparsely inhabited land. It is difficult to specify precise areas as different types of protected land are involved: for example, Botswana claims nearly 40 per cent of the country under regulation and Tanzania 24 per cent, or 36 per cent if forests are included.[4] While South Africa, more densely populated, and with a larger area of privately owned land, has over 6 per cent reserved, a great deal more is used for farming wildlife. Even in densely populated India, 4.7 per cent of the total geographical area is officially classed as protected for wildlife, and a great deal more for

    [2] Carruthers, *Kruger National Park*, 5; Rosaleen Duffy, *Killing for Conservation: Wildlife Policy in Zimbabwe* (Oxford: James Currey, 2000), 1.

    [3] McKenzie, *Empire of Nature*, 264.

    [4] Emmanuel Severre, Director of Wildlife, Republic of Tanzania, Ministry of Natural Resources and Tourism, Wildlife Division, 'Community Tourism-Wildlife Interface' (2003) at <http://www.iipt.org/conference>.

forests.[5] By 2003 the UN claimed over 100,000 protected areas globally, covering 11.5 per cent of the world's surface, more than the area permanently under arable crops—although it is by no means all secure or effectively managed.[6]

Parks became such a feature of the African landscape that the imperial prototype of park remains an African one. In 1925 the Albert National Park (later renamed Virunga) was carved out of a Volcanoes Protected Zone, spanning both Congo and Rwanda, largely to protect mountain gorillas. Carl Akeley, the American hunter-naturalist, who created the wild animal dioramas at the Museum of Natural History in New York, was a strong protagonist of this park.[7] South Africa introduced parks legislation in 1926, beginning with Kruger. Its creation was associated with the rise of Afrikaner nationalism, attempts at unifying English- and Afrikaans-speaking whites in a common purpose, and changes in white attitudes towards game as a purely economic resource.[8] By 1930, South Africa had set aside small additional parks for the preservation of rare or endangered species such as the bontebok, mountain zebra, and the Cape's only remaining elephant herd at Addo.

James Stevenson-Hamilton, the first warden of Kruger, a former soldier and hunter turned conservationist, was a staunch believer in the idea that wildlife was a heritage for the Empire as a whole, which he propagated in numerous publications.[9] Similarly, early twentieth-century 'penitent butchers' such as Edward North Buxton, President of the Society for the Preservation of the (Wild) Fauna of the Empire (SPFE), lamented the loss of wildlife because it was 'a precious inheritance of the Empire'.[10] In 1930, the SPFE sent Major Richard Hingston, a former colonial medical officer, to British-controlled territories in East and Central Africa to report upon game reserves and the potential for national parks. He reckoned that the region's wildlife was heading for extinction unless humans and wildlife separated, and submitted proposals for nine parks in five colonies. Little action was taken until after the Second World War. In Zimbabwe, areas like the Matopos,

---

[5] Figure dated 16 November 2005, the Wildlife Institute of India. See <http://www.wii.gov.in>.

[6] World Conservation Union (IUCN), World Commission on Protected Areas, UN List of Protected Areas Information Site, at <http://www.iucn.org/themes>.

[7] C. E. Akeley, *In Brightest Africa* (London: William Heinemann, 1924); Mary L. Jobe Akeley, *Carl Akeley's Africa* (New York: Dodd, Mead & Co., 1930).

[8] Jane Carruthers, 'Creating a National Park, 1910 to 1926', *Journal of Southern African Studies*, 15/2 (1989), 188–9.

[9] Carruthers, *Wildlife and Warfare*.

[10] Carruthers, *Kruger National Park*, 29, quoting E. H. Buxton, *Two African Trips* (London, 1902), 116.

site of Cecil Rhodes's grave, were called parks from the 1920s although legislation only came in 1949.[11] By 1965 protected areas covered 12 per cent of the country's land area (47,264 square km). National Parks Ordinances were passed in Kenya (1945), Tanzania (1948), and Uganda (1952).[12]

Initially, some Africans were tolerated in parks and seen as one of the attractions that drew visitors—as long as they lived in a 'traditional' way. Agricultural scientist Eric Nobbs, an early advocate of a Matopos park, suggested in 1919 that 'the presence of natives would be a feature of interest to many visitors and there is no occasion to disturb them'.[13] His 1924 *Guide to the Matopos* reiterated his view that visitors would be entranced by its few African residents' 'picturesque kraals, their costume, cattle, crops and customs'. In the 1930s, it was decreed that the man on guard at Cecil Rhodes's grave should be an Ndebele of the 'warrior class' and kitted out in war dress. But by the 1940s officials no longer regarded the African inhabitants as few or picturesque; their agricultural practices came under criticism, and they were removed en masse after 1945. This part of the imperial estate (as British prime minister Joseph Chamberlain once called it) was to be devoted to conservation, recreation, and the production of pleasure, with its original inhabitants airbrushed out—or at least removed to the periphery.

Colonial governments often provided the momentum for parks, but Maitseo Bolaane's work on the founding of Moremi reserve in the Okavango, northern Botswana, suggests that different models were possible.[14] In this case, a white British-Zimbabwean couple, June and Robert Kay, worked with Isaac Tudor, Jack Ramsden, and other local Africans to establish a protected area in 1963. The Bechuanaland Protectorate state was creating reserves at this time—Central Kalahari in 1961, followed a year later by Chobe in the far north. But it viewed the area around the Okavango swamps as a potential growth area for ranching. The local African elite, connected to the chieftaincy, began to change their views because persistent attempts by the government to eradicate tsetse and expand the cattle economy were failing. They were also concerned about destruction of wildlife, both by local commercial crocodile hunters and external, largely white South African, safari hunters.

---

[11] Ranger, *Voices from the Rocks*.

[12] McKenzie, *Empire of Nature*, 269–72. R. P. Neumann, *Imposing Wilderness: Struggles over Livelihood and Nature Preservation in Africa* (Berkeley, CA: University of California Press, 1998).

[13] Ranger, *Voices from The Rocks*, 41, 61–5.

[14] Maitseo Bolaane, 'Local Participation in Wildlife Conservation and Management: The Case of Moremi Game Reserve, Okavango Delta, northern Botswana 1960s'.

Okavango had been a hunting area under the control of chiefs, who saw wildlife as their, rather than an imperial, heritage. Moremi was founded and run by a Botswana branch of the Fauna Preservation Society, controlled by Africans, and connected to international wildlife organizations. This was a community management model, forty years before its time, and colonial officials were highly sceptical that such an experiment could work. Protagonists 'felt that wildlife conservation could be achieved if there were direct financial benefits to Africans and they worked hard to incorporate African support'.[15] This is echoed in numerous subsequent collaborative ventures.

Despite such local political control, the Basarwa (Bushmen) were removed from this unique riverine habitat in 1963 by the park authorities. Some were placed in villages near the park gates, such as Khwai, where their descendants remain. Following management difficulties, Okavango was taken over by the independent Botswana state in 1977 and proved to be a major success, both in terms of conservation and tourism revenue. But independence did not mark a break with colonial practice, and the issue of indigenous Basarwa rights remains contentious. Since 1997, communities were forcibly removed from the Central Kalahari Game Reserve into resettlement camps to make way for conservation. The government argued that this was essential for their development and incorporation as citizens—but Basarwa won the right to return to the reserve when the country's High Court ruled in their favour in December 2006.[16] In an earlier settlement on the other side of the border, facilitated by new legislation (the Restitution of Land Rights Act 1994), the South African government returned some 65,000 ha. of land in and near the Kalahari Gemsbok National Park to the Khomani San people in 1999.

Serengeti was the first national park in Tanzania, and by 1960, the year before independence, game reserves and controlled areas covered 20 per cent of the total land area.[17] In 1961 African regional leaders signed the Arusha Manifesto at a landmark wildlife conference that set the agenda for conservation policy in East Africa. President Julius Nyerere pledged to continue wildlife protection policies in independent Tanzania. Picking up on what Bernhard Grzimek (Chapter 15) and others had been urging him,

[15] Bolaane, 'Local Participation', ch. 4.

[16] For different perspectives on this issue, see Survival International, <http://www.survival-international.org>, where the 2006 court ruling is downloadable, and the Government of Botswana website, <http://www.gov.bw>, following links to 'The Relocation of Basarwa'.

[17] Neumann, *Imposing Wilderness*, ch. 4.

Nyerere spoke of Africans taking responsibility for an imperial heritage: 'In accepting the trusteeship of our wildlife we solemnly declare that we will do everything in our power to make sure that our children's grandchildren will be able to enjoy this rich and precious inheritance'.[18] The Ngamiland Fauna Conservation Society in Botswana translated Nyerere's speech into Setswana and distributed it in their campaign for Moremi.

At the same time, conservation was becoming part of post-war inter-nationalism, rather than simply an imperial enterprise. The International Union for the Protection of Nature, later renamed the International Union for the Conservation of Nature and Natural Resources (IUCN) was estab-lished in 1948; at the time, it was 'the only international organization concerned with nature protection in the round'.[19] The World Wide Fund for Nature (WWF, initially the World Wildlife Fund) was announced at the Arusha Conference in 1961. To begin with, the IUPN had virtually no money, and was seen as a more of a meeting place and facilitator rather than an operational agency, dedicated to networking and pooling information. It went on to chart the status of plant and animal species threatened with extinction; produce classifications of the world's protected areas; helped to create a body of new environmental law; and influence the drafting of international nature conservation conventions.

From the start there were tensions between the IUCN's recognition of human requirements for natural resources, especially by the poor in devel-oping countries, and its reliance on ecologists, some of whom were 'prone to be dismissive of human needs and to value most highly those ecosystems that were not disturbed by people'.[20] Again there were continuities with the colonial past and a tendency to impose conservation models on developing countries. It was not until the mid-1970s that non-Europeans (Venezuelan and Egyptian) were appointed Director-General and President respectively, and no one from a developing country became chair of any IUCN Com-mission before 1984. A landmark was reached in 1980, with the World Conservation Strategy and its commitment to sustainable development, as well as a greater voice for the developing world. Southern membership grew quickly from the late 1980s, and became a powerful influence.

The development of parks ran parallel with that of tourism. This multimillion-pound industry exploded in the post-war era as a result of

---

[18] The Arusha Declaration, quoted in Martin Holdgate, *The Green Web: A Union for World Conservation* (London: Earthscan Publications, 1999), 73.

[19] Holdgate, *The Green Web*, v.   [20] *Ibid.*, v–vii, 40, 71.

11. Promoting tourism: a Maori woman posing in traditional dress, shores of Lake Rotura, New Zealand.

Credit: Getty Images.

increased affluence and leisure, the availability of credit, the influence of film, television, and print media in advertising far-flung destinations, and above all cheaper air travel.[21] The uses of national parks and other protected areas

---

[21] Martin Mowforth and Ian Munt, *Tourism and Sustainability: Development and New Tourism in the Third World*, 2nd edn. (London: Routledge, 2003), 119 and *passim*.

changed accordingly. Wilderness was becoming managed. Some species could be encouraged, others discouraged, depending on their perceived balance. Animals were moved between areas. Waterholes were provided to facilitate viewing and also animal survival. Light aircraft, radio tracking, roads, Land Rovers and viewing vehicles shouldered their way into these preserves, making them and their animals more accessible to scientists and tourists. Immobilization techniques were used for animal management, and for film-making. Parks evolved into destinations for middle-income Western tourists. While wildlife tourism did not quite become a mass phenomenon, in the manner of the Mediterranean beach holiday, it was an increasingly fashionable and commercialized activity. More affluent domestic tourists in Australia, New Zealand, Canada, and South Africa also sought recreation in their own national parks. In Kruger, accommodation was provided in the shape of rondavels, or thatch-roofed circular bungalows, that drew on indigenous building styles.

For both foreign and domestic visitors, protected areas rich in fauna and flora were instilled with new value. This derived both from the multifaceted reworking of nature as an asset, and because visitors had learnt—and been taught—to see mountains and wildlife as objects of beauty. This idea has been especially important for the settler nations and Western visitors; it fed into national identities and suggested a moral good in the notion that parks had helped to save nature for posterity. Nature was posited as an escape from, or antidote to, the pace and pollution of urban modernity.[22]

Indian Wildlife Conservation

In India, the conceptual underpinnings of protected areas lie in colonial forest and game laws (Chapter 7). Various laws regulated access to game: the Madras Act of 1873, which aimed at curbing the killing of wild elephants; the Forest Act of 1878; and the Elephant Preservation Act of 1879. Other wildlife protection acts were passed in the early twentieth century and the Forest Department began to set up game sanctuaries. The creation of wildlife sanctuaries in India followed a different pattern to Africa, partly because the most spectacular wildlife lived in relatively inaccessible areas, especially forests, reachable only by elite hunter-sportsmen. There was no early equivalent of safari-style tourism, and most of the key game areas lay in princely states beyond British colonial control. Many Indian princes were

---

[22] Bunn, 'An Unnatural State', 208.

keen on game preservation for sport, but were not prepared to share their private space with tourist hunters; at most they welcomed an elite few.

The SPFE took a close interest in Indian wildlife by the 1920s. But with a few exceptions such as the Venugopal Wildlife Park in Mysore (1941) and the Hailey National Park in the United Provinces (1935), conservation areas did not really take off until after independence. The latter was renamed Corbett after the hunter turned conservationist Jim Corbett, who had helped to persuade the provincial government to establish the park, ironically named after a tiger-hunting governor (and author of *An African Survey*, Chapter 12). In the 1930s Corbett, together with an Indian lawyer, founded a Provincial Association for the Preservation of Wildlife, at a time when his interests were turning to wildlife photography, filming, and writing—not that he gave up shooting entirely. As the most popular writer on India's wildlife, probably best known for *The Man Eaters of Kumaon* (1944), Corbett played a major role in influencing the switch from hunting to cameras and conservation. Tiger preservation became a central motif—although, contrarily, the thrill of killing maneaters was what drew readers to his books.[23] Corbett did not stay around to contribute to post-colonial policy in India; he retired to East Africa where he died in 1955.

Under Nehru, India was committed to industrialization and rapid, state-led development. Population was expanding rapidly, rising 21.5 per cent between 1951 and 1961 from 361 to 439 million. From the 1960s, agricultural development intensified in the green revolution. Prominent naturalists, some of them Indian such as ornithologist Salim Ali, warned of the environmental risks of rapid socio-economic changes.[24] As in other developing countries, the tensions between development and conservation were not effectively resolved. But a combination of local interests and international pressure contributed to an expansion of protected areas as one important strategy.

As in Africa, companies catering for white hunters began to reorientate themselves towards international tourism. National parks legislation and new wildlife protection acts were introduced by various states in the 1950s. The urgency of tiger preservation provided momentum in post-colonial thinking and planning about conservation. In 1969 when the IUCN met in Delhi, shocked delegates were told that the total number of tigers in India had fallen from 40,000 at the turn of the century to 2,500. The tiger was declared an endangered species and the WWF (then working so closely with the

---

[23] Rangarajan, *India's Wildlife History*, ch. 7.   [24] *Ibid.*, ch. 8.

IUCN that merger seemed possible) raised about $1.8m for Operation Tiger in India, Bangladesh, Nepal, and Thailand.[25] Tiger shooting was banned the following year. The government launched Project Tiger in 1973, in an attempt to halt the falling numbers and minimize human intrusion into tiger habitats.

As an MP, Indira Gandhi went on a Kenyan safari and became sympathetic to environmentalist ideas, forging links with leading conservationists.[26] Saving the tiger became a highly symbolic national mission, with Mrs Gandhi personally chairing the Project Tiger Steering Committee. The former stomping grounds of princes—such as Ranthambore National Park, once the hunting preserve of the Maharajahs of Jaipur—were gradually opened to the public, and by the turn of the millennium India boasted twenty-seven tiger reserves containing over 1500 tigers—with a further 2,000 in the country as a whole.[27] However, Valmik Thapar noted the negative effect of political shifts since the days when Mrs Gandhi and her son Rajiv headed the Congress Party. Most of the 'Tiger States' were then ruled by the same political party, whose leaders were sympathetic to the conservation of forests and wildlife. By the late 1990s, the picture had changed. Eleven different parties ruled the Tiger States and Thapar claims 'political will has been totally dissipated'.[28]

Fortress Conservation and Tourism

People-free parks became the cornerstone of what has recently been dubbed fortress conservation, the antithesis of conservation by communities.[29] Tanzania's independent government, steering a flagship for wildlife protection in post-colonial Africa, took to fortress conservation with enthusiasm. Thousands of indigenous residents were forcibly evicted from protected areas at Mkomazi in the 1980s and from the Ngorongoro Crater, just as colonial governments had previously done at Manyara and Serengeti.[30] Brockington has described unsuccessful court battles over Mkomazi in the 1990s by

---

[25] Holdgate, *The Green Web*, 116; MacKenzie, *Empire of Nature*, 283–91.

[26] Rangarajan, *India's Wildlife History*, 98–9.

[27] For Project Tiger, see <http://www.projecttiger.com>.

[28] Valmik Thapar, 'The Tragedy of the Indian Tiger: Starting from Scratch', in John Seidensticker, Sarah Christie, and Peter Jackson (eds.), *Riding the Tiger: Tiger Conservation in Human-Dominated Landscapes* (Cambridge: Cambridge University Press, 1999), 296.

[29] D. Brockington, *Fortress Conservation: The Preservation of the Mkomazi: Game Reserve, Tanzania* (Oxford: James Currey, 2002).

[30] Neumann, *Imposing Wilderness*, 133, 138.

pastoralists who claimed the constitutional right to live on their customary lands. They were ruled to be recent immigrants who did not qualify for such rights. The flawed vision that inspires the conservation trusts behind Mkomazi Game Reserve was, he argues, part of a broader conservation drive across the continent, based on a premise that humans have harmed the environment. 'This is buttressed by scientists' interpretations of environmental change. It is powered by the emotive and mystical appeal of wilderness, stunning landscapes and the aura of extraordinary biodiversity.' The vision remains enormously powerful; but 'can be harmful, unjust and unnecessary'.[31]

Brockington does not deal fully with the longer-term impact of indigenous people and their livestock at Mkomazi.[32] And he recognizes that conservation is not merely imposed by Western interests. The Tanzanian authorities, as well as significant elements in Tanzanian society, developed their own 'environmentalisms'.[33] But he challenges the idea that this ecosystem was highly fragile, and required saving.[34] The reservation of Mkomazi shows how private individuals and trusts have laid claim to whole ecosystems in poor developing countries, by arguing that only they had the necessary knowledge and clout to save them for posterity. The Tony Fitzjohn/George Adamson Wildlife Preservation Trust that runs Mkomazi also controls the Kora National Park in Kenya—two protected areas comprising about 500,000 ha. The trust's website grandly describes how, in 1988 when Mkomazi was 'on the brink of ecological disaster due to overgrazing, burning and indiscriminate hunting and poaching, the Tanzanian government asked Tony Fitzjohn to reclaim the reserve'. Known by some as 'Boy Tarzan', Fitzjohn appears consciously to cultivate an image as a tough guy and wildlife saviour, which is apparent in the trust's publicity material. Its website emphasizes his links to the late Adamson, who is portrayed like a surrogate father; photographs of a half-naked Fitzjohn kissing and cuddling lions and other big cats are a clear reference to *Born Free* (Chapter 13).[35] The trust has created and meticulously cultivated the idea of a great

---

[31] Brockington, *Fortress Conservation*, 3.

[32] Review by Lotte Hughes, *African Affairs*, 102/407 (April 2003), 363–4.

[33] Dan Brockington, 'The Politics and Ethnography of Environmentalisms in Tanzania', *African Affairs*, 105/418 (January 2006), 97–116.

[34] Brockington, *Fortress Conservation*, 128.

[35] See <http:www.mkomazi.com>; Simon Ward, 'Boy Tarzan vs. Rambo of the Bush', *The Southern Africa Trumpet*, 2 (June 1997).

struggle by forceful British individuals to save an environment against all odds.

Such associations with wilderness and closeness to animals have long been central to advertising wildlife; together with imperial nostalgia, they have been described as a script acted out in tourism.[36] There is something of what Baudrillard calls the hyperreal about the invention of 'vanished savage naturalness' and re-creation of imagined utopia.[37] The hint of danger, echoing nineteenth-century hunting texts, has also been evident. Bunn describes early tourist advertising and tourism experiences in Kruger, where 'the campfire was a primary reference point for the white body imagining itself at risk in majority darkness'.[38] (There is a history to be written of the campfire which was a long-established pursuit amongst many South Africans and safety from wild animals was one element in its attraction. One might sensibly add, however, that a campfire was a vehicle for warm sociability, rather than the result of imagined, racialized danger.)

In Kruger, and most of the South African, Zimbabwean, and Kenyan parks, tourists were housed in fenced-off camps or lodges, so that their contact with wildlife was largely in vehicles. Botswana and some East African parks went down a rather different route. They encouraged camping in sites with no boundaries, so that the whole range of wild animals could literally come for breakfast. Tourists were also taken in makoros, or dug-out canoes, through the swamps, to experience birds and animals close at hand. This provided some opportunities for local communities, especially the BaYei who had specialized in canoe building and poling, to participate in and benefit from the wildlife enterprise.

Wildlife tourism was not only focused on viewing. Some countries permitted controlled hunting for sport. Game farming prospered, especially in South Africa and Zimbabwe, where, since the 1970s, landowners have won increasing legal powers over the ownership of wildlife.[39] (In Botswana, Zambia, and Mozambique, wildlife is still not privately owned.) Wildlife can be more profitable than livestock, especially in more marginal farming zones. Trophy and venison hunting became significant activities on some game farms and in this sense, the imperial safari was reproduced for a more diverse

---

[36] Edward M. Bruner and Barbara Kirshenblatt-Gimblett, 'Maasai on the Lawn: Tourist Realism in East Africa', *Cultural Anthropology* 9/2 (1994), 881–908.

[37] Jean Baudrillard, *Simulacra and Simulation* (Ann Arbor: University of Michigan Press, 1994), 13.

[38] Bunn, 'An Unnatural State', 200.   [39] Duffy, *Killing for Conservation*, especially ch. 4.

international hunting fraternity. Some of this tourist hunting yields bush-meat for local communities.[40] While game farming could enhance conservation on farmland, the priority was often to house valuable species, rather than encourage biodiversity *per se*, and farm employment has probably declined.

Colonial nostalgia, and the priorities of commercial companies which increasingly ran wildlife tourism, drove some of the trade upmarket from the 1980s. Whether in state reserves or private areas, small, exclusive safari lodges catered for restricted numbers of visitors who paid steeply for the privilege of being treated as guests—an experience modelled on the colonial house party. For example, Saruni Camp near the Maasai Mara Game Reserve, Kenya, restricted visitor numbers to a luxurious twelve and promised that they would be able to live 'in harmony with the Maasai warriors'.[41] The emphasis was on offering a safe, Western interior complete with such items as Persian rugs, Italian bathroom fittings, and antique furniture, while outside lay a potentially dangerous wild patrolled by protective *morans*. In cottages around a recently constructed waterhole, guests were told they could 'experience both the elegance and safety of a permanent accommodation and the thrill of sleeping in close contact with nature'.

The exclusion of people from parks did not, therefore, preclude the advertising of some African people as juxtaposed to wildlife for the purposes of attracting tourists. Karen Blixen's writings on Kenya in the interwar years were revived in the successful Hollywood film *Out of Africa* (1985), which helped to shape these images for the post-colonial world.[42] She arranged Africans in a hierarchy of attractiveness in which some ethnic groups were perceived to be beautiful, noble, endangered, and martial. In a critique, Ngugi wa Thiong'o said of Blixen: 'to her Africans are a special species of human beings endowed with great spirituality and a mystical apprehension of reality or else with the instinct and vitality of animals, qualities which "we in Europe" have lost'.[43]

A different brand of colonial nostalgia is an ingredient in tourism promotion in other post-imperial contexts. This is not confined to the promotion of

---

[40] L. Emerton and I. Mfunda, 'Making Wildlife Economically Viable for Communities Living around the Western Serengeti, Tanzania', Evaluating Eden Series, Working Paper No. 1 (London IEED, 1999), 20.

[41] See <http://www.sarunicamp.com>.

[42] First published as Karen Blixen, *Out of Africa* (London: Putnam, 1937).

[43] Ngugi wa Thiongo, *Decolonising the Mind: The Politics of Language in African Literature* (London: James Currey, 1986), 92; Kathryn Tidrick, *Empire and the English Character* (London: I.B. Tauris, 1990), 147 and ch. 5.

parks and safaris in Africa, but is for example crucial to Darjeeling's popular image as the quintessential Raj hill station, where the imperial legacy is well preserved in English architecture, the botanical garden, street signs, and visits to tea plantations. Rituals such as high tea at the Windamere [*sic*] Hotel (served in a Victorian-style parlour by a tiny Tibetan waitress in black dress and white pinafore) were reconstructed. The 'toy train' narrow-gauge Darjeeling Himalayan Railway, opened in 1881, which became a World Heritage Site, attracted thousands of foreign railway enthusiasts. Elsewhere in India, heritage tourism focused more on the 'native' princes of yesteryear than on European overlords. It was not simply Westerners who enjoyed this; by the late twentieth century thousands of South Asians flocked to Darjeeling, the princely parks, palaces of Rajasthan, Kolkata's Victoria Memorial and other virtual shrines to imperial might. Just as tourism helped to sustain African and Indian wildlife reserves, so it also played a role in preserving elements of the built environment of the colonial era.

Community Management and Ecotourism

Exclusive conservationism was never without critics; grass-roots protests have been described and unease also percolated through to international organizations. A major African mission for UNESCO in 1960 by British biologist Julian Huxley, its first Director-General, highlighted African resentment of wildlife that threatened crops, livestock, or competed for pasture. He warned that national parks and reserves were sometimes seen 'as European inventions and relics of "colonialism" which occupy land coveted by Africans'.[44] As a result the IUCN set up an Africa Special Project, chaired by former British ecologist Barton Worthington (Chapter 12); he was by no means the only former colonial official who moved into international organizations. This paved the way—through discussions with African leaders and officials—for the groundbreaking Arusha Conference in 1961. Both project and conference laid the foundation for the African Convention on the Conservation of Nature and Natural Resources, drafted by the IUCN and adopted by OAU members in 1968.

From the late 1970s much academic writing on Africa, as well as subaltern studies in South Asia explicitly took the part of the peasant and indigenous people. NGOs and radical activists articulated widespread criticism of development and conservation policies, which were seen to disadvantage

[44] Holdgate, *The Green Web*, 72–3.

poor rural communities. Against this political background, new approaches to conservationism were advocated which both directly invited participation by local communities and offered development benefits arising from it. In the sphere of forestry, advocates of agro-forestry envisaged rural communities foresting their own lands as part of mixed agrarian systems. After the Bali Declaration of 1982, at the World Congress on National Parks, international bodies such as the IUCN increasingly acknowledged that protected areas must serve human beings, too.[45] Martin Holdgate, a former Director-General of the IUCN (1988–94), admitted—after recalling Grzimek's approval of forced removals from parks (Chapter 15)—that

it was not until the late 1980s that IUCN, working in partnership with the Frankfurt Zoological Society in the Serengeti and the Tanzanian Ngorongoro Conservation Area Authority ... began to apply scientific knowledge in strategies for coexistence between local African people and wild species, to their mutual benefit.[46]

Community-based natural resource management (CBNRM) represented a conceptual revolution—the idea that successful conservation should involve communities rather than being state-centric, and that natural resources could be managed in such a way that both development and conservation goals were reached.[47] It aimed to protect biodiversity by engaging local people in conservation. In some contexts, it developed in parallel with a recognition of indigenous peoples' rights to natural resources.

In Africa, Zimbabwe's CAMPFIRE programme (Communal Areas Management Programme for Indigenous Resources), launched in 1986, provided an exemplar. The premise was that by offering local people a stake in wildlife, they would have more incentive to conserve it. Advocates of CAMPFIRE argued that wildlife would be ecologically more sustainable than livestock in fragile and hard-pressed African lands, especially in drier zones. It was hoped that community management of wildlife could become a key development tool, and that smallholders could benefit economically. The policy was developed jointly by the state parks department, the WWF, and local university researchers. By 1995, having attracted large amounts of donor funding

[45] McNeely, J. A., and Miller, K. (eds.), *National Parks, Conservation and Development: The Role of Protected Areas in Sustaining Society*, Proceedings of the World Congress on National Parks, Bali, Indonesia, 11–22 October 1982 (Washington, DC: Smithsonian Institution Press, 1984).

[46] Holdgate, *The Green Web*, 74.

[47] David Hulme and Marshall Murphree (eds.), *African Wildlife and Livelihoods: The Promise and Performance of Community Conservation* (Cape Town: David Philip, and Oxford: James Currey, 2001); Adams and Mulligan (eds.), *Decolonizing Nature*.

from USAID in particular, the scheme was working in twenty-five districts and considerable revenue was being generated from hunting, trophies, and venison sales.

Though CAMPFIRE has been enormously influential (both in debates about conservation and as a model for other projects), it has not been an unqualified success. Conservationists have become concerned that community management may not always be a reliable method of protecting rare species and biodiversity, while communities have questioned whether wildlife is compatible with agriculture income and social progress. The issue frequently arose as to who were the beneficiary communities, and who were excluded.[48] Zimbabwe's political crisis from 2000 led to sharp falls in tourism and hunting revenues, but even without this, direct income from CAMPFIRE was usually irregular or absent; Dzangirai argues that some local communities felt cheated as a result.[49] Powerful elites, officials, local politicians and expatriates still pull the strings in many cases.[50] Women struggled to make their voices heard in some of the community-based organizations that manage natural resources and tourism. Tourism has tended to remain in the hands of the private sector, which has the skills and contacts to promote it.[51]

Community-oriented rhetoric around both heritage and parks, however, opened new opportunities and changed the emphasis of some conservation strategies. The emphasis moved away from states as sole guarantors of conservation. Emerton notes of the Serengeti ecosystem in Tanzania: 'over time there has been a shift from an authoritarian, state-controlled approach to conservation based on principles of strict protection and exclusion to

[48] For example, Jim Igoe, 'National Parks and Human Ecosystems: The Challenge to Community Conservation. A Case Study from Siminjaro, Tanzania' in D. Chatty and M. Colchester (eds.), *Conservation and Mobile Indigenous Peoples: Displacement, Forced Settlement and Sustainable Development* (Oxford: Berghahn, 2002), 90; Vupenyu Dzingirai, "CAMPFIRE is not for Ndebele Migrants': The Impact of Excluding Outsiders from CAMPFIRE in the Zambezi Valley, Zimbabwe', *Journal of Southern African Studies*, 29/2 (2003), 445–59.

[49] Vupenyu Dzingirai, 'The New Scramble for the African Countryside', *Development and Change*, 34/2 (April 2003), 243–64.

[50] K. Homewood and M. Thompson, 'Elites, Entrepreneurs and Exclusion in Maasailand', *Human Ecology* 30/1 (2002), 107–38; Igoe, 'National Parks and Human Ecosystems', 78; Mara Goldman, 'Partitioned Nature, Privileged Knowledge: Community-Based Conservation in Tanzania', *Development and Change*, 34/5 (2003), 833–62.

[51] L. Cassidy and M. Madzwamuse, 'Enterprise Development and Community Based Natural Resource Management in Botswana', *Report of Workshop Proceedings, Maun, Botswana, March 9–12, 1999* (IUCN Botswana/SNV Botswana, 1999), downloadable online at <http://www.cb-nrm.bw>.

approaches which recognise and permit at least some degree of community participation and benefit in wildlife management.'[52] The philosophy of the national park has changed a great deal from that which informed the founding of imperial or settler colonial reserves, such as Kruger in the 1920s. But the declining emphasis on state control has other outcomes. Under the African National Congress government, the South African National Parks Board's subsidy declined, resulting in more commercialization. Private companies took over tourist facilities in a number of African national parks.

Ecotourism, perhaps the fastest-growing tourism sector in Africa by the 1990s, ran parallel with community management.[53] It had roots in older British movements, such as the Ramblers' Association, which campaigned for the right to roam and the National Parks and Access to the Countryside Act (1949). Some tourists had always shunned the package holiday that followed restricted routes and crammed visitors into confined areas. The growth of environmental movements from the 1970s, initiatives such as fair trade, and the desire for independent travel all played a part in sending certain tourists in search of a more ethical, responsible, and individual travel experience. Ecotourism could even be sold as helping to preserve local cultures and environments.

Ecotourism has come to influence the travel industry and conservation as a whole. Over time, tourism operators and conservationists in Kenya, for example, began to consider their social responsibility towards the local communities from whose lands parks and reserves had been hewn. Tourists were increasingly encouraged to visit dispersal areas outside the parks and policies changed to make African communities beneficiaries of conservation on their lands; at least some conservationists began to see them as partners rather than adversaries.[54] The question remains as to whether ecotourism is less interventionist, or any more sustainable than its mainstream counterpart, in that it takes people to the most fragile environments and isolated communities in increasing numbers.[55]

[52] Emerton and Mfunda, 'Making Wildlife Economically Viable', 9.

[53] Duffy, *Killing for Conservation*, 71; Donald G. Reid, *Ecotourism Development in Eastern and Southern Africa* (Harare: Weaver Press, 1999).

[54] David Western, Preface, 'The Evolution of Ecotourism in East Africa: From an Idea to an Industry', *Summary of the Proceedings of the East African Regional Conference on Ecotourism, March 2002*, IIED Wildlife and Development Series No. 15 (June 2003), 4.

[55] Mowforth and Munt, *Tourism and Sustainability*, 296–7.

Who Pays?—the Sundarbans in India

In order to evaluate how these strands of policy and practice have materialized in recent contexts, Lotte Hughes visited Sundarbans (or Sunderbans) wildlife sanctuary in India in 2003. This provides a good example of a human-wildlife conflict zone. This vast area of natural beauty and rich biodiversity in the Bay of Bengal, divided between India and Bangladesh, has a tiger reserve in a mangrove forest at its core. Established on the Indian side in 1973, tigers increased from about 60 to 245 at the last count.[56] Despite being fenced in, tigers posed a direct threat to neighbouring villages since they regularly escaped from the reserve. The core area of 1,330 square kilometres has had national park status since 1984, and became a World Heritage Site the following year. It is surrounded by a buffer zone. No one lives inside the tiger reserve, but there are more than 1,000 villages within the Sundarbans area, of which 100 are very close to the reserve.

As in other situations where protected areas are inadequately fenced, wild animals move freely into surrounding dispersal areas or zones in search of food, water, and mates. In the process they compete with domestic stock for pasture and water, trample crops, and kill people and livestock. In Sundarbans, people rely upon fishing, subsistence farming and honey collecting to make a meagre living. Tourism, despite official claims that up to 50,000 tourists visit annually, is insufficiently developed to provide much work for unskilled locals.[57] In order to fish and collect honey and wood, people have to risk their lives every day when they venture into the network of dense forests and tidal creeks. The main threat comes from amphibious Royal Bengal tigers, with crocodiles a close second. Besides swimming across to villages, tigers are also adept at silently climbing onto fishing boats and seizing their terrified occupants, especially at night. Between 1973 and 1989, tigers killed 600 people—most of them poor villagers. Two Indian ecologists captured the dilemma: 'Men die; they lose their near and dear ones to tigers, every time they go home, they decide not to come out again, and yet they come; in this saline tract, soft feelings and fear vanish; it makes a man ruthless, tough, and teaches him to fight for survival.'[58]

---

[56] See Project Tiger, <http://www.projecttiger.nic.in>.

[57] According to the official leaflet 'A Bonanza for Nature Lovers, Sundarban [sic] Tiger Reserve (India: Canning, 2000).

[58] A. B. Chaudhuri and Kalyan Chakrabarti, *Sundarbans Mangrove (Ecology and Wildlife)* (Dehra Dun: Jugal Kisthore, 1989), 65.

Niranjan Raptan, a former tiger poacher turned farmer and tourist guide, described in 2003 the ambivalence felt by local villagers towards the reserve and its 'royal' occupants.[59] 'We love the tiger, we don't want to stop preserving them, but they should be stopped from swimming across to here. The government should think about this.' He was asked whether the villagers felt that tigers—as a protected species—got more help from the government than they did. 'Our views are, no. The government is saving the lives of tigers. They are not neglecting the people, but at the same time the government cannot prevent the tiger from coming to this village.' However, the villagers have long complained about the lack of roads, clinics, and clean water and want to see some of the money spent on tiger preservation reallocated to village development. 'If the government allocates money for development we can uplift our lifestyles—which will mean there will be more jobs, and there will be no need to go to the forest for honey, wood cutting and fishing.'

These villagers of Annpur and Jamespur, named after the family of Daniel Hamilton, an East India Company trader who founded the settlements, also raised the issue of compensation for the lives of people killed by tigers. There had been seven or eight deaths in 2003, but only those with licenses, such as fishermen and honey collectors, counted officially. Ten more victims were unlicensed. Only the families of those with forest permits got compensation, and this was meagre, totalling about 1,000 rupees (under £15), or two-thirds of monthly family income. The villagers were reportedly told by government to take out life insurance—a luxury they could not afford. With little hope of government assistance, villagers (both Hindu and Muslim) relied on praying to Banbibi, goddess of the forest, for protection. Her shrines could be seen in every village and dotted along the reserve fence.[60]

A new threat is presented by plans to 'open up' Sundarbans, at present only reachable by slow boat, to more sophisticated tourism. Sahara India Pariwar, a powerful corporation with media, construction, and aviation interests, floated a £78m plan to build a helipad and resort complete with five-star hotels, golf course, and casino that will attract the kind of visitor who hasn't got the time or patience for a three-hour boat trip. Sahara, owned by billionaire Subrata Roy, has acquired 900 acres in the wetlands,

[59] Interview by Lotte Hughes, Sundarbans, September 2003.

[60] Additional information from the nature education centre at Sajnekhali, from the Project Tiger Status Report 2001 (see <http://www.sanctuaryasia.com>), and from conversations with local people and tourist guides.

on which it plans to build a series of floating 'ecotourist cities'. In late 2004 construction was delayed by campaigners who claimed the project would totally destroy the ecosystem. They included author Amitav Ghosh who set a novel, appropriately published at this time, in the Sundarbans.[61] The project posed a distinct threat to mangrove forests, which have long protected this coastline from cyclones and other storm damage. (Loss of the mangrove shield exacerbated the impact of the 2005 tsunami across Asia, scientists reported.)[62] In such fragile areas, speculation and tourist development can also drive up land prices and undermine access by poor farmers, fishermen, pastoralists and others who use natural resources for subsistence.

Tourism and Rights

By 2004 tourism was estimated to be responsible for more than 10.4 per cent of global GDP and to provide 214.7m jobs.[63] While the major tourist destinations are the US and Europe, significant eddies reach poor countries of the Commonwealth. South Africa's tourist arrivals increased from about 600,000 in 1993 to about 1.6 million in 1999.[64] In Botswana, it was the fastest-growing sector in the early twenty-first century, accounting for an estimated 20 per cent of GDP. The commodities produced from wilderness areas have changed since the imperial era. While meat and trophies are still to be had, whether from hunting for bushmeat or upmarket shooting safaris, revenues from viewing, accommodation, and transport—and the many spin-offs—are far more valuable. There are economic as well as aesthetic and scientific arguments for wildlife conservation.

National parks are a global phenomenon but a number of Commonwealth countries have been particularly successful in evolving strategies for wildlife conservation and reserved areas. The legacies of imperialism remain significant, although they have been refashioned for a post-colonial world. While the natural wealth of protected areas is no longer seen as part of an imperial resource, some environmentalists view it as a global heritage and justify the expansion of reserves on scientific grounds. The expanding number and size of national parks and sanctuaries has meant the gradual excision of large

[61] Randeep Ramesh, '£78m Tourism Plan for Indian Mangroves Mired in Protests', *The Guardian*, 12 October 2004; Amitav Ghosh, *The Hungry Tide* (London: HarperCollins, 2004).

[62] John Vidal, 'How the Mangrove Shield was Lost', *The Guardian*, 6 January 2005.

[63] World Travel and Tourism Council figures, 2004, viewable at <http:www.wttc.org>.

[64] Garth Allen and Frank Brennan, *Tourism in the New South Africa: Social Responsibility and the Tourist Experience* (London: I.B. Tauris, 2004), 20.

swathes of land from local people's use. Some local communities and indigenous peoples have reacted to displacement by developing arguments that they own, or know most about, wildlife and protected areas (Chapter 19). The question arises as to whether historic users of natural resources have rights to them, even if this leads to loss of biodiversity and other negative side effects.[65] Control and ownership of natural resources in some protected areas remains fiercely contested, all the more since their tourism and other economic values have risen.

[65] Mike Norton-Griffiths, 'Property Rights and Wildlife Conservation Options in Kenya', CSERGE Working Paper GEC 95–07 (University College London and the University of East Anglia, Norwich, 1995), 1.

18

The Post-Imperial Urban Environment

In this chapter we turn to themes of race, space, environmental justice, and indigenous reassertions in the post-colonial city. We will use as examples: services and urban planning in Singapore; riots in Sydney; and a comparative discussion of parks and public symbols. Although the location of cities had largely been fixed in the colonial period, they were undergoing rapid change by the mid-twentieth century as communities from the surrounding countryside poured into the urban areas. At the beginning of the twentieth century, one tenth of the world's population lived in cities; by its end more than half did so. In 1900 the ten largest cities were located in Europe and the US, with the exception of Tokyo at seventh. By the early twenty-first century no European urban agglomerations were in this league. The balance shifted from the West to the rest, especially after 1950. Of former colonial cities, Greater Mumbai with about 16 million people, Kolkata (13 million), and Delhi (13 million) were in this group.[1] Mumbai had housed around one million people in 1911.

Cities in non-settler states became increasingly dominated, demographically, by the descendants of rural communities from their hinterlands. While English often served as a common medium of communication, regional languages also urbanized with their speakers. Overall, urbanization was linked with rising living standards. But, especially in mega-cities, the gap increased between the rich and overwhelming numbers of urban poor, most of whom were not able to make it into formal employment. Rates of growth in former settler cities were usually less sudden, but they also became increasingly culturally diverse. Canadian cities are one example. The small migrations of indigenous people were only one reason for this.

---

[1] Figures from <http://www.citypopulation.de> which also gives other figures for 'urban agglomerations' and on this basis puts Mumbai at 20 million, Delhi at 19 million, and Kolkata, twelfth in rank at 16 million; and from <http://www.citymayors.com>, which has a different order, and includes both greater urban areas (with some gaps) and delimited municipalities, based on UN figures. New York would also qualify and, in some lists, Karachi, with Cairo coming close.

Their increasing multi-ethnicity resulted largely from new sources of global migration: for example, the movement of people from non-British parts of Europe, from the Caribbean, as well as African Americans, Indians, and East Asians. Post-colonial conflict created new diasporas: some of the 80,000 Ugandan Asians expelled by Idi Amin in 1972 went to Canada, and Toronto became home to the single largest population of expatriate Somalis.

While the entrepôt role was frequently important in the growth of colonial cities, their subsequent trajectory differed. Urban centres integrated more fully with the political economy of their countries as markets for products, centres of demand, as much as channels for commodities. Industrialization was uneven. Former settler cities and some elsewhere, such as Mumbai, Singapore, and Hong Kong, succeeded in becoming, at least in part, financial centres, 'centres of intelligence' or 'informational cities'—especially with the development of electronic technology.[2] Those in South-East Asia shared in the regional tiger economy, benefiting from rapid manufacturing development, particularly after 1985 when massive foreign investment flowed in. Economic development came to be dictated more by transnational capital than by the export of raw materials.[3] Cheap skilled labour was a major draw for corporate investors.

The outcome of conflicts over space that were so fundamental in shaping internal city boundaries, shifted.[4] In part, this was a result of demographic processes. For example, many of the communities that previously occupied specific enclaves, and gave Indian cities a cosmopolitan feel, shrank in size. The numbers of Anglo-Indians, Europeans, Parsees, Chinese, and Jewish people decreased for a variety of reasons that included migration to the West, and low birth rates. As noted previously (Chapter 9), the social geography of colonial cities reflected racial hierarchies. By the late colonial period these were already eroding; for example, in South-East Asia wealthy Chinese could purchase property in former European strongholds. In Nairobi some Asians moved out of the overcrowded six-acre bazaar into formerly whites-only suburbs.[5] Old race divisions, which had left their mark spatially, were partly replaced by class divisions. British communities,

[2] Ida Susser, *The Castells Reader on Cities and Social Theory* (Oxford: Blackwell, 2002).

[3] Fu-Chen Lo and Yue-Man Yeung (eds), *Globalization and the World of Large Cities* (Tokyo: United Nations University Press, 1998), 3–4.

[4] Alan Gilbert and Josef Gugler, *Cities, Poverty and Development: Urbanization in the Third World* (Oxford: Oxford University Press, 1997).

[5] Hake, *African Metropolis*, 173–6; Thornton White, Silberman, Anderson, *Nairobi: Master Plan for a Colonial Capital*, 14.

here and elsewhere, were to some extent replaced by enclaves of expatriates working in the cosmopolitan multinational aid and corporate sectors. But if areas of privilege were partly defended, working-class communities in many cities also burst out of the restrictive environments of compound, barrack, and *khaya* (backyard servants' quarters), moving both into city centres, and out to their peripheries. Municipalities often lost control of hawkers, informal activities, and settlements.

British cities were also transformed in the post-colonial world. It is an irony that the country with the largest modern empire, and highest number of extra-European subjects, was so successful for so long in restricting multi-ethnic immigration into its heartland. The arrival of Caribbean workers in 1948, followed by South Asian mass migration, transformed British demography so that by 2001, 9 per cent of the population or about five million people in England and Wales, were identified as ethnic minorities. New diasporas brought with them new demands. The South Asian population, and their ubiquitous restaurants catering mostly for British clientele, expanded the market for spices, basmati rice, and tropical fresh foods. Mosques and Indian restaurants refashioned the built environment. African immigrants with strong currency created a market for bushmeat, or venison, including bush rat from West Africa and a range of monkeys, largely illegally supplied, which in turn impacted directly on African environments. 'If the trends continue as at present', William Adams argued in 2004, 'the bushmeat trade will lead to the extinction of large mammals across almost all tracts of tropical forest not tightly protected'.[6]

Water and Housing—Singapore and Modernity

Cities require engineered water supplies and sewage outlets; urban environmental change can partly be mapped by following these flows. Although more than 70 per cent of the earth's surface is covered by water, only about 2.5 per cent of this is fresh. Location by the sea is useful for sewage but not—until expensive recent desalinization processes became available—for usable water. Only a limited percentage of fresh water is actually available to humans. The rest is 'locked up' in polar ice, glaciers, or sited in inaccessible places.[7] Water is heavy to move, and expensive to store and channel;

---

[6] William M. Adams, *Against Extinction: The Story of Conservation* (London: Earthscan, 2004), 216.

[7] M. Barlow and T. Clarke, *Blue Gold: The Battle Against Corporate Theft of the World's Water* (London: Earthscan, 2002), 5.

concentrations of population do not necessarily coincide with the availability of fresh water. For example, the Congo River and its tributaries account for around 30 per cent of the run-off in Africa but less than 10 per cent of Africa's population, and few cities, are within reach. Availability can be heavily dependent on season, and varies wildly from one year to the next; India gets 90 per cent of its rainfall in the summer monsoon.

As populations swelled in the colonial era, municipal managers faced the challenge of providing both clean water and sewage treatment. Simultaneously, ideas emanating from British medical circles about the links between impure water supply and diseases such as cholera were applied to the colonies.[8] Open standing water became associated with malaria. Urbanization and industrialization, and the cultural emphasis on personal cleanliness, were generally accompanied by an increase in per capita use of reticulated water. In the twentieth century, water withdrawals increased at more than twice the rate of population growth, implying a massive growth in total water usage.[9] This presented particular problems for municipal managers in cities with limited revenues and large populations of poor people.

There are stark contrasts in the effectiveness with which urban services such as water and housing were provided. Singapore largely conquered these problems. Old Singapore suffered from appalling sanitation, high rates of disease, overcrowded housing, and lack of municipal regulation.[10] Nineteenth-century Singapore was created on a gridiron layout; Stamford Raffles divided it into *kampongs* for particular racial and occupational groups, and the pattern was maintained for the first half of the twentieth century. The economically powerful Chinese dominated the city centre, and Indians were also in central locations, while Malays were not.[11]

Municipal water managers in Singapore attached water meters as early as 1899 to 'coolie' lodging houses, brothels, and other overcrowded premises in an attempt to check wastage and collect revenue. Some landlords stopped taking the supply, but most simply passed the cost on to their already poor tenants. By the mid-1920s almost all water services in the city were metered.

[8] Brenda S. A. Yeoh, *Contesting Space: Power Relations and the Urban Built Environment in Colonial Singapore* (Oxford, New York, and Kuala Lumpur: Oxford University Press, 1996), 176.

[9] M. W. Rosegrant, X. Cai, and S. A. Cline, *World Water and Food to 2025: Dealing with Scarcity* (Washington, DC: International Food Policy Research Institute), 21.

[10] Yeoh, *Contesting Space.*

[11] Lee van Grunsven, 'Singapore: The Changing Residential Landscape in a Winner City', in Peter Marcuse and Ronald van Kempen, (eds.), *Globalizing Cities: A New Spatial Order?* (Oxford: Blackwell, 2000).

This facilitated municipal investment in water. As the city expanded, taking in new docks, wharves, and suburbs with bucolic names like Orchard Road, demand for water shot up and more reservoirs had to be built, some on mainland Malaysia. New rubber factories also required a great deal of water, and shipping demands increased. By 1920 the city was being supplied with more than 9.5 million gallons a day.[12]

Modernized and municipal-run sewage disposal came in the 1920s, after a protracted battle with private Chinese syndicates who had monopolized the business of removing night soil to market gardens and plantations on the city outskirts. Europeans complained about 'vegetable horrors, reeking with decomposed excreta' that deterred people from building houses anywhere near such gardens. Environmental improvement was shot through with contending cultural values. 'From the municipal perspective, night-soil harboured disease-causing germs, exuded noxious odours, and must be systematically removed from human habitation and destroyed. From the Chinese perspective, night soil was a valuable source of manure to be accumulated in vessels and sold to farmers.'[13] Albert Howard (Chapter 12) would have applauded the Chinese.

W. J. Simpson, whom we have mentioned in connection with plague, wrote about the links between housing and disease in Singapore following an enquiry in 1906. It earned the reputation of a 'pigsty'.[14] An Improvement Trust was founded in 1927 to carry out more ambitious urban management and in the 1930s it provided public housing for lower-income families. This expanded on the shop-house model (shops combined with housing above and behind) with airwells and back lanes (Chapter 9). By the 1960s, old and new shop-houses accommodated one quarter of the total population of the city in a 1,700-acre Central Area—which had long been 'one of the most crowded slums in the world'.[15]

In the late colonial period, British colonial governments increasingly concerned themselves with creating more family-oriented and stable housing for the poor. Since city-centre land in Singapore was highly valuable, planners sought to demolish the slums and relocate people to new suburbs. Subeconomic housing, as well as high-rise concrete flats, mushroomed on

---

[12] Yeoh, *Contesting Space*, 178–9; 186.   [13] *Ibid.*, 187–99, 175, 204–5.

[14] Martin Perry, Lily Kong, and Brenda Yeoh, *Singapore: A Developmental City State* (Chichester: John Wiley, 1997), 49.

[15] Teh Cheang Wan, 'Public Housing', in Ooi Jin-Bee and Chiang Hai Ding (eds.), *Modern Singapore* (Singapore: University of Singapore, 1969), 172.

city outskirts. After independence, large areas of land (44 square km or 7.6 per cent of the city by 1990) were reclaimed from the sea to accommodate demands for roads, port and airport facilities, and expanding industry.[16] A high-rise, controlled, and compressed urban environment was created, not least through state action. Singapore's authoritarian government could enforce such regulation, and, as a city state, could focus its energies on the urban context. One argument was that this benefited employers by keeping labour costs low and helping to ensure competitiveness in a globalizing

12. Singapore, old and new, 1976.

Credit: Mary Evans Picture Library/Hubertus Kannus.

[16] Perry, Kong, and Yeoh, *Singapore*, 168, and ch. 6 generally.

market. In Hong Kong, under direct British authority, free trade was also combined with one of 'the largest public housing programmes in the non-Communist world'.[17]

New housing developments and streets were kept relatively clean, by tight environmental management—famously including a ban on chewing gum—and basic services were extended to many of the urban poor. Urbanization policy in the post-colonial world also aimed to break up racial rigidities, and emphasized multiculturalism as part of nation building. Chinese, Malays, and Indians were distributed among housing estates, and built environments intentionally 'made little or no concession to ethnic customs or religious practice'. In the process of building a new city, the old 'inherited landscape that reflected the identity of individual ethnic groups' was in large part swept away.[18]

Singapore was struggling economically at independence, with around 10 per cent unemployment (admittedly low compared to most developing countries), a heavy dependence on the entrepôt trade, and a small manufacturing base. But it enjoyed a relatively equitable distribution of wealth, accountable governance, the potential for economic diversification, and low production costs. Per capita income more than tripled between 1980 and 1995, making it the second highest after Japan in the Asia-Pacific region. The economy changed from entrepôt to low-tech manufacturing and trading, and finally to high-tech manufacturing, financial, and business services by 2000, as the government deliberately embraced foreign capital. One upshot was that Singapore became a middle-class society, and though low-income groups remained, including new immigrants, housing and services were generally available.[19] Singapore was transformed into a high-rise, intensively planned, world city.[20] With its compact design, and commitment to public transport, it could also depend less on cars. Though it was very largely dependent on imported food and natural resources, Rogers and Gumuchdjian see this kind of city as environmentally efficient with a relatively low per capita consumption of energy.[21] Tropical cities have an advantage here, at least until air-conditioning becomes ubiquitous.

---

[17] Peter Hall, *Cities of Tomorrow: An Intellectual History of Urban Planning and Design in the Twentieth Century* (Oxford: Blackwell, 1996), 356.

[18] Perry, Kong, and Yeoh, *Singapore*, 22.   [19] Van Grunsven, 'Singapore', 100–7.

[20] Anthony D. King, *Urbanism, Colonialism, and the World Economy: Cultural and Spatial Foundations of the World Urban System* (London and New York: Routledge, 1990), 26.

[21] Rogers and Gumuchdjian, *Cities for a Small Planet*.

Within the non-settler, post-colonial Commonwealth, however, Singapore was atypical. Greater Lagos, with about 11 million people, outstripped the Witwatersrand in South Africa (7 million) to become sub-Saharan Africa's largest city. Lagos sprawled as colonial planning systems eroded and public provision decayed. It was densely populated in places, but mainly with people in self-built shack housing who lacked basic services. Access to energy, water, sewerage, transportation, and housing have all been haphazard. While many people have electricity, the city—in a high rainfall region—suffers from an acute shortage of water. (In Nigeria as a whole, more than half the population has no access to safe drinking water.)[22] And due to inadequate sewerage, much of the city's rainwater and human waste is disposed of through open ditches that discharge onto tidal flats. If some cities can be viewed as efficient in using natural resources and housing dense populations, Lagos was more appropriately classified amongst those which were 'parasites on the landscape [and] relentless polluters'—although per capita energy consumption may also be relatively low.[23] South African metropolitan zones remain starkly divided in relation to housing and service provision. And other African cities such as Nairobi (with about 3 million people) have spawned major slums; Kibera is said to be the biggest in Africa. Post-colonial Commonwealth cities experienced very different trajectories that reflected their histories, their national context, and their location in global society.

Environmental Injustice and Reassertion in the City

Former settler cities in Canada, Australia, and New Zealand are ranked amongst those with the best quality of life, globally. Together with European cities, they dominate this list, to the exclusion of British, American, and Japanese conurbations.[24] Even within wealthier cities, however, there are significant pockets of poverty. Environmental and social ills have concentrated in impoverished and often racially specific areas. These include Canadian and Australian suburbs dominated by indigenous people. In Canada, the so-called hypermobility of aboriginal people moving seasonally between First Nation reserves in summer and cities in the winter has resulted in regular searches for urban accommodation, and in people falling through the

---

[22] Constance E. Hunt, *Thirsty Planet: Strategies for Sustainable Water Management* (London and New York: Zed Books, 2004), 49, citing Marq De Villiers, *Water Wars: Is the World's Water Running Out?* (London: Weidenfeld & Nicolson, 1999).

[23] Rogers and Gumuchdjian, *Cities for a Small Planet*, 27.

[24] See <http://www.citymayors.com>.

net into homelessness.[25] About 45 per cent of Canada's indigenous people live in urban areas, some 320,000 in all. When tensions in these ethnically specific neighbourhoods—arising from poverty, overcrowding, unemployment, and despair—boiled over into protest, deep historical resentments resurfaced.

Responses from white majority society in settler cities have tended to focus on race and denial of historical responsibility for social ills, as happened in 2004 in the Sydney suburb of Redfern—a flashpoint for clashes between police and Aboriginal protestors after the death in suspicious circumstances of an Aboriginal boy, Thomas 'T. J.' Hickey. Redfern may have been given a benign, nature-linked name by the city fathers, but this is belied by its social reality. The death of the teenager, who was impaled on a metal fence while fleeing police, sparked the continent's worst race riots in recent times. A BBC television documentary, *The Boy from the Block*, examined the background partly in urban environmental terms. Aboriginal residents call part of Redfern 'The Block'—a unique place, with a strong sense of community, to which generations of rural indigenous people have been gravitating since the 1940s. First, a core group came to find work in the nearby railway yards. They were joined by waves of other migrants, seeking relatives from home, or visiting friends and family in city hospitals or prisons. The Block became their base and, over time, the antithesis of the respectable, planned, overwhelmingly white, middle-class suburb. What some call this 'squalid grid' of 'near-derelict houses' became a haven for transients—involved in a pattern of to-ing and fro-ing not unlike the Canadian one.[26] In the late 1980s, during an earlier wave of street battles, police specifically blamed itinerant people for starting riots.

Until major regeneration plans were recently laid, there was little green space here. The social geography of Redfern was characterized by chronically overcrowded housing, outdoor drinking, visible drug taking in public spaces, and a high crime rate. 'This small inner-city precinct', declared the local press, 'is on the edge of the booming Sydney CBD, yet it is cursed by poverty and an epidemic of drug addiction and crime. Redfern is a microcosm for all the problems that bedevil indigenous Australia'.[27] Redfern's inhabitants saw

---

[25] Mary Ann Beavis, Nancy Klos, *et al.*, 'Literature Review: Aboriginal Peoples and Homelessness', Canada Mortgage and Housing Corporation (1997), viewable at <http://www.ginsler.com/documents/f-aborig.html>.

[26] Quotes from the *New York Times*, 17 February 2004.

[27] Editorial, *The Australian*, 18 August 2004.

it in another light and developed their own, alternative brand of civic pride. Especially from the 1970s, when the federal government bought houses in The Block for Aboriginal citizens in an attempt to alleviate homelessness and other social problems, it 'became a key launch pad for the push for indigenous self-determination'.[28] In defence of Redfern, one resident wrote: 'For me, as an Aboriginal person, Redfern is a place where one can interact with a powerful collective will to struggle against imperial forces that continue to interfere with, and endeavour to reinterpret, our history, our identity, and our future prospects from a very different colonial perspective'.[29] Some Aboriginal spokespeople still felt keenly the spatial legacies of conquest and empire.

As a rallying point for indigenous protest, linking urban and rural communities, The Block acquired a reputation for 'trouble' in the eyes of conservative white Australians—and triggered fears that social and environmental ills would spill over and pollute the city as a whole. In such situations media and other images of 'drunken Aborigines', particularly in public spaces, were used to signify an enduring object of 'European colonial contempt'. As Barry Morris has recently pointed out, this image has a long and involved history in Australia, and does not simply indicate a person who cannot hold their drink: 'The notion encodes the Australian version of the white man's burden.'[30] Michael Jackson argues further: 'so fraught is public space for many Aboriginals that they will often venture into it only when drunk', because the 'altered state of consciousness' boosts self-assertiveness.[31]

We shall return to this image when discussing contestation over parks, and their use as sites of indigenous protest. While indigenous communities sometimes lived in ghettoes, indigenous expression began to transform the post-colonial landscape in some cities formerly dominated by British setlters. Claims over land, urban space, and natural resources were linked with urban reassertion and renewed struggles for cultural identity; 'the flowering of

---

[28] Martin Chulov, 'The Block's Still Seething', *The Australian* (18 August 2004), viewable at <http://www.eniar.org>.

[29] 'Despair the Reality for a Race Lost in the Alien Space of Redfern', Ray Minniecon, director of Crossroads Aboriginal Ministries, Redfern, 17 February 2004, for Weekly Indigenous News, Cultural Survival (<http://www.culturalsurvival.org>).

[30] Barry Morris, 'A Crisis in Identity: Aborigines, Media, the Law and Politics—Civil Disobedience in an Australian Town,' *Critique of Anthropology*, 25/1 (March 2005), 65. Morris examines media coverage of a 'riot' at Brewarrina, New South Wales, in 1986.

[31] Michael Jackson, *Existential Anthropology: Events, Exigencies and Effects* (Oxford: Berghahn, 2005), 19–20, 27.

post-settlement Aboriginal history coincided with the end of the era of assimilation'.[32] Among those publicly challenging the attempted erasure of Aboriginal identity were politically engaged artists and museum curators who endeavoured to 'Aboriginalize' national heritage and urban public space—both at home and overseas. For instance a sculpture installation for the Sydney Biennale in 1988 featured 200 log coffins made by artists from Arnhem Land, each of which represented 'a year of the invasion'. Seen as one of the most important works ever assembled by Aboriginal artists, the entire collection was bought by the National Gallery, Canberra, and transported with difficulty from bush to city by barge and road.

A recent example of the export of this concept was the opening in Athens in the summer of 2004 of a major exhibition, 'Our Place: Indigenous Australia Now', which was timed to coincide with the Olympics. This included exhibits depicting the 'stolen generation' (Aboriginal children forcibly taken from their families and placed with white foster parents), protest footage from the 1972 tent embassy in Canberra (see Chapter 19), family photographs, and paintings on boab nuts showing attacks by white settlers. It focused on five themes of spirit, country, conflict, family, and cultural renewal, and it celebrated stories of loss and ultimate triumph told around a campfire. In a reversal of past triumphalism, Australian museums are attempting to re-present new forms of identity and pride, and embrace reconciliation, 'as part of their social purpose'.[33] This mirrors similar processes in Canada, where the Métis/Blackfoot architect Douglas Cardinal was commissioned to design major public buildings that included the Canadian Museum of Civilization at Hull, Quebec. His work is environmentally sensitive and is regarded as being informed by an indigenous world-view—an organic architecture marked by curvilinear lines.

In another, very public bid to bridge the social and spatial divides between black and white Australia, bodily and politically, hundreds of thousands of people walked across the bridges of the nation's cities in 2000, on the eve of the centenary of federation. This giant walkabout was seen as 'a symbol of their desire for reconciliation and the opening of a new era in our national life'.[34] But the gesture did not persuade those at the top. After the

---

[32] Robert Manne, 'Introduction', in R. Manne (ed.), *Whitewash: On Keith Windschuttle's Fabrication of Aboriginal History* (Melbourne: Black Inc. Agenda, 2003). Seen online.

[33] Victoria Kyriakopoulos, 'A Different Flame for Athens', *The Age* (5 July 2004), viewable at <http://www.eniar.org>.

[34] Manne, *Whitewash*.

most important of these walks, by 250,000 people across Sydney Harbour Bridge, Prime Minister John Howard dashed hopes of public reconciliation by refusing to issue a government apology for past wrongdoing. This was a bridge too far.

Issues around the use of urban public space have also been a focus for ongoing protest in New Zealand. Maori had become a predominantly urban people by 1960—a complete turnaround from their largely rural past, and a trend hastened by the Second World War.[35] Those incorporated in the war effort were expected to 'go home' afterwards, but many stayed on in town. Previous Maori migration tended to avoid cities, and was usually temporary and tribally organized. Post-war, big cities—particularly Auckland—became a magnet, and tribe (*iwi*) had little to do with patterns of settlement. Young single people, especially women, made up the largest category of migrant in the 1950s, and nuclear families followed. Housing was and remained poor and overcrowded compared to Pakeha (European), and 'suburbs not far short of Maori ghettoes emerged', though there were attempts by the state to encourage Maori and Pakeha to intermingle residentially.

It was urban Maori who predominantly led the wave of activism that began in the 1970s, which has focused on land and resource rights, self-determination, and cultural nationalism. Pakeha icons have been physically attacked; at least one colonial statue was beheaded, and the anniversary of the 1835 Declaration of Independence was marked by the chopping down of the solitary pine on One Tree Hill, Auckland. A large grove of native Totara trees, precious to Maori, which once grew there had been replaced by Californian pines, one of which graced the summit. For some Maori, this represented Pakeha domination; the insult was compounded by a memorial further down the hill erected by merchant and 'father' of Auckland, Logan Campbell, 'in memory of the Maori race'.[36] In 1995, Maori organized a seventy-nine-day occupation of Moutoa Gardens, a public park near the centre of Wanganui city, in protest at delays in settling Waitangi claims (Chapter 19). The park was renamed Pakaitore, the original Maori name for the area, and continues to be a site of protest, as public parks frequently are elsewhere. Maori periodically threaten to re-occupy it, over such contended environmental issues as ownership of the Whanangui River.

---

[35] James Belich, *Paradise Reforged: A History of the New Zealanders from Polynesian Settlement to the End of the Nineteenth Century* (Auckland: Penguin, 1996), 472–3.

[36] Thanks to Tom Brooking for explaining the background to this.

This focus on parks may be linked (albeit at an unconscious level) to their historical association with early settlers, who connected parks and Australasia's open spaces with English landscapes and nobility: '"parks" were a rare constant in the affections of European explorers and settlers.'[37] They were also public spaces for the poor. Significantly, the 1986 'riot' which Morris examines in a small Australian town began in a public park, after whites at a nearby hotel took exception to Aboriginal mourners using this space for a wake following the death of a young man in police custody. The publican reportedly shouted at the mourners: 'Get out of the park!' and police heavy-handedly removed them.[38] Clearly, on this occasion certain residents and police did not regard the park as part of any shared heritage, or shared public space.

As in Australia, North America, and some other former colonies, New Zealand's museums have overhauled the way they showcase the nation's past—erasing the worst excesses of imperial triumphalism while giving greater emphasis to indigenous culture. (Some Indian museums are embarrassing exceptions to this rule, whose ethnographic dioramas of tribal people depicted as happy primitives remain frozen in the early twentieth century.) The National Museum of New Zealand has been renamed Te Papa, and describes itself as a bicultural organization whose main tasks are to preserve and present the *taonga* (treasures) of New Zealand's peoples and to interpret the country's heritage in environmental and cultural terms.[39] The museum is headed up jointly by a Pakeha chief executive and a Kaikhautu (Maori leader), and the exhibits aim to give equal weight to Maori heritage and culture. This reflects the official policy of biculturalism adopted by the Labour government after 1984, but critics have accused the state of creating an illusion of partnership while ignoring the Maori community's more radical demands.[40]

New Public Symbols and Naming

In many former colonial cities indigenous assertions and colonial monuments jostle for space in a modernist environment. In India, for example, statues of Queen Victoria and other imperial figures still people the streets of

---

[37] Bonyhady, *The Colonial Earth*, 77–8.   [38] Morris, 'A Crisis in Identity', 74.

[39] All references to Te Papa are from its website, <http://www.tepapa.govt.nz>.

[40] Te Ahu, 'The Evolution of Contemporary Maori Protest', viewable at <http://www.maori-news.com/writings/papers/other/protest>.

major cities. Conversely, subaltern protest figures from the imperial past are being increasingly memorialized in both urban and rural areas in the form of monuments, paintings, and other public images. Urban monuments tend to be more overtly politicized, and include, for example, celebratory images of the 1850s Santal rebellion. Statues were erected to honour the subaltern 'freedom fighter' Birsa Mundi, an *adivasi* who led the Birsaite Rebellion in Jharkhand (formerly Bihar), eastern India, was captured by the British in 1895, and earned martyr status after dying in captivity five years later. (See Chapter 16; the new state of Jharkhand was created on the anniversary of his birthday.) His legacy and image are strongly contested, with one Indian critic decrying a 1960s image as 'shocking' because it copied colonial photographs of Birsa in chains.[41]

Many, but not all Commonwealth countries renamed towns or streets after independence. India approached the issue uncertainly, revealing contested views about urban space and divided identities. Bombay City Council renamed India's largest city Mumbai, after the Hindu goddess Mumbadevi, in 1995. Kolkata and Chennai, formerly Calcutta and Madras, followed suit. However, many Indians reportedly either did not know the new names, or refused to adopt them. Others accused regional governments and political parties—notably the Hindu nationalist Shiv Sena and the Bharathya Janatha Party—of pushing name changes as a divisive element of religious nationalism and regional pride rather than anti-colonialism.[42]

Elsewhere, new public symbols of nationhood include the totem poles now ubiquitous in Canadian cities such as Vancouver, or the large Maasai shield on Kenya's flag, which belies the actual marginalization of this community in Kenyan society. Indigenous activists in some countries, notably Australia, produced and fly their own flags as a public demonstration of their sovereignty and separate identity. The establishment of a flag-flying Aboriginal 'tent embassy' on the lawns of Parliament House, Canberra, in 1972 was an important marker that has been repeated many times since, particularly during the mass protests across Australia that marked bicentenary year (1988). Entire tent cities—which can be read as an inversion of the concrete

[41] Mahasweta Devi (1997) quoted in Daniel J. Rycroft, 'Revisioning Birsa Munda: An Afterword on *Vir Vanavasi* Constructs versus Identity-Hybridity in Jharkhand', paper presented at a conference on 'Reinterpreting Adivasi Movements in South Asia', University of Sussex, March 2005.

[42] Author Sharda Dwivedi, quoted in Ramola Talwar Badam, 'India—What's in a Name?' <http://CBSNEWS.com> (Mumbai: 11 October 2004).

jungle by transient rural–urban migrants—have sprung up from time to time, including one in Brisbane in 1982 that drew Aboriginal people from all over Australia to protest against the Commonwealth Games. Generally speaking, city planners have invented a public symbolism in which indigenous signifiers are increasingly drawn upon. Heritage is being redefined as all-inclusive, and history as lived practice—exhibited in memory, memorialization, and popular politics—is booming. However, suburbs everywhere have conspicuously tended to avoid this kind of makeover.

Immigrant as well as indigenous groups claimed urban space. Tension between the Irish and the English played a role in shaping Australian white identity and national symbolism. People of Irish descent formed about 4 per cent of the population in 1901, but were swelled by 'new' Irish to 17 per cent by 1988.[43] Whereas earlier Irishness was increasingly subsumed under white Australianism, this changed with new migrations: 'in Ireland there was no need for the vigorous affirmation—defence—of Ireland's character, demanded by the hostile situation in Australia. Under siege, under threat and attack, such Irish felt a strong need to assert the value of their culture.'[44] Gaelic street signs and memorials to Irish heroes and famine victims were among the public expressions of this. The community (by no means homogeneous) benefited during the 1990s from Australia's swing to multiculturalism, which saw government policies encouraging public expressions of ethnic identity. Such undercurrents informed the unsuccessful attempt by Irish Australian Prime Minister Paul Keating to make the country a republic in 1999.

The landscape of some streets and parks has changed by usage, as well as new memorials. No longer zones of safety for the middle classes, they have become home to the homeless, including many of indigenous descent. In Canada, indigenous homelessness was attributed partly to the fact that the federal government stopped building subsidized housing in the early 1990s. In Australia, Aboriginal runaways and street youth included more men than women; this was attributed to the high incidence of family violence and sexual abuse in Aboriginal communities.[45] In Kolkata, thousands of pavement dwellers were too poor even to live in the slums. Mostly unskilled

---

[43] Patrick O'Farrell, *The Irish in Australia: 1788 to the Present* (Kensington, NWS: University of New South Wales Press, 2001), 328, citing demographer C. A. Price.

[44] *Ibid.*, 6.

[45] Report of the Royal Commission on Aboriginal Peoples (1996); Beavis, Klos, *et al.*, 'Aboriginal Peoples and Homelessness'.

villagers, they tended to be the city's most recent migrants, concentrated in the central business district and high-income areas. A late twentieth-century survey put their number at up to 55,000 in the city and four times that in the conurbation as a whole.[46] While some impoverished communities remained ghettoized in post-colonial cities, others have broken down the old spatial boundaries.

Nairobi's city centre Uhuru Park (freedom in Swahili) and Jeevanjee Gardens (named after British East Africa's first Asian member of parliament and chief labour recruiter for the Uganda Railway) became havens for hundreds of street children and homeless persons.[47] In the daytime, because it is too dangerous to sleep there at night, unemployed men retire to Uhuru's threadbare lawns for a nap and what is locally known as an 'air burger'. Jeevanjee Gardens still feature a marble statue of Queen Victoria, erected by their creator in 1906. Inscribed 'Empress of India', the monarch—vandalized and worse for wear—is now surrounded by itinerant preachers and glue-sniffing waifs. 'Elderly Indians still know [the Gardens] as *Rani Bagh* (Queen's Garden) ... [while] there are those who, mistaking Queen Victoria for the Virgin Mary, have their own religious reasons for going there.'[48] Recent restoration of the park has included the erection of 'a sculpture of Jeevanjee on a pedestal [which] blends with the one of Queen Victoria'. Jeevanjee's granddaughter enlisted Kenyan environmentalist and Nobel Peace Prize winner Wangari Maathai in a successful campaign to save the Gardens from developers in the 1990s. In 1992, when KANU was still in power, Maathai, the leader of the Greenbelt women's movement, and later deputy environment minister, also successfully opposed government plans to build a giant $200 million skyscraper in Uhuru Park. Best known for her efforts to mobilize women to plant millions of trees across Kenya, and using trees 'as a focal point around which other environmental issues are brought to attention', she came to symbolize ordinary Kenyans' fight for urban and rural environmental justice.[49] She has long linked democracy, forest conservation, and urban as well as rural development in her rhetoric.

[46] Sanjoy Chakravorty, 'From Colonial City to Global City? The Far-from-Complete Spatial Transformation of Calcutta', in P. Marcuse and R. van Kempen (eds.) *Globalizing Cities: A New Spatial Order?* (Oxford: Blackwells, 2000), 68, 76 n.

[47] Zarina Patel, *Challenge to Colonialism: The Struggle of Alibhai Mulla Jeevanjee for Equal Rights in Kenya* (Nairobi: Zand Graphics, 1997), 45.

[48] Patel, *Challenge to Colonialism*, ch. 23, 213 ('The Story of the Public Park').

[49] John Vidal, 'Rooting for Peace', environment section, *The Guardian*, 13 October 2004.

Environmental Protest

In many cities in the developing world the struggle for housing and land was led by squatter movements, for 'the most conspicuous political action of the urban masses is the illegal occupation of land'.[50] In some cases it was organized on such a large scale that the authorities have no option but to accept it, and eventually grant legal title. Water, or lack of it, has also been the focus of much protest.[51] As apartheid controls over African urbanization broke down in South Africa from the late 1970s, millions flocked to the cities.[52] Informal settlers successfully challenged the apartheid's state control of peri-urban space. Urban black South Africans also became keenly aware of environmental injustice in the apartheid era, because of the conditions under which they lived and worked. Taking Engels's early observations one step further, Peter Lukey notes: 'they bore (and indeed most still bear) a double burden, facing environmental hazards in their workplaces and environmental hazards where they live.'[53] Globalized 'red-green' action on a broader front brought, for example, Greenpeace and the International Transport Workers' Federation together with South African trade unionists to stop ships carrying toxic waste from docking in Durban in 1992. However, concerns about job losses that might result from higher environmental standards were raised by both management and trade unionists, and hampered alliances between unions and environmental groups.

Activists were, however, able to make significant gains in particular fields such as compensation for asbestos workers.[54] Under apartheid, it was relatively easy to keep information from African employees, while regulatory bodies were sympathetic to the demands of capital. The decade from 1955 to 1965 was both the time when the link between asbestos and mesothelioma was established, and when British companies in South Africa invested heavily in new mines and mills. Asbestos mining did not stop until 1996 and workers paid with their lives for a commodity whose dangers had long been known. It

---

[50] Gilbert and Gugler, *Cities, Poverty and Development*, 192.

[51] V. Shiva, *Water Wars: Privatization, Pollution and Profit* (London: Pluto Press, 2002), xi.

[52] William Beinart, *Twentieth-Century South Africa* (Oxford, Oxford University Press, 2001), chs. 8 and 10.

[53] David A. McDonald (ed.), *Environmental Justice in South Africa* (Athens: Ohio University Press; Cape Town: University of Cape Town Press, 2002), 275, 277–9, 282.

[54] Jock McCulloch, *Asbestos Blues: Labour, Capital, Physicians and the State in South Africa* (Oxford: James Currey, 2002), 199 and conclusion.

causes three diseases: asbestosis, lung cancer, and mesothelioma. The last, in particular, affected women, children, and stevedores at ports who had never worked in a mine, but who had been exposed to fibres through polluted items such as clothes and leaking hessian bags. Rather like bubonic plague's port-by-port trajectory (Chapter 10), thousands of workers in more than fifty countries who handled South African asbestos were also placed at risk. The industry and the state had simply refused to accept that the 'miraculous mineral' was hazardous and the industry had no future; it generated too much wealth.

Nearly forty years later, in 2001, trade unionists and legal activists combined with a British law firm to win £21m damages for asbestos victims from British-owned Cape Plc. It was the first time that a claim against the overseas operations of a British parent company was heard in Britain. Though they got much less than they had asked for, the award raised hopes that multinational companies would in future be held responsible for the behaviour of their subsidiaries in the developing world, and demonstrated what a globalized environmental justice movement could achieve. In effect it challenged the 'rigid separation of production and consumption' that characterized the extraction of raw materials in the colonial and apartheid era.[55]

While the ANC under Nelson Mandela (1994–9) and Thabo Mbeki developed some redistributive policies, it faced enormous problems in making affordable services available, and in addressing the legacy of urban poverty and shack settlements. Although drinkable water was made available to millions after 1994, millions also remained without access to piped water. Many could not afford the costs of metered water. The government introduced a policy of providing a limited amount of free water to each household, calculated on the basis of twenty-five litres per person per day.[56] But this was insufficient for most poor households, and those that ran up debts were threatened with disconnection. The ANC's cautious financial policy, its difficulties in delivering to the urban poor, and its preparedness to incorporate the private sector in service provision, triggered new social movements in the late 1990s.[57] Groups such as the Anti-Privatization Forum, Soweto Electricity Crisis Committee, and Concerned Citizen's Forum have

[55] Ibid., 10–12.
[56] D. A. McDonald and J. Pape (eds.), *Cost Recovery and the Crisis of Service Delivery in South Africa* (Pretoria: HSRC, 2002); D. A. McDonald and G. Ruiters (eds.), *The Age of Commodity: Water Privatisation in Southern Africa* (London: Earthscan, 2005).
[57] McDonald (ed.), *Environmental Justice*, 2–5.

drawn on, and made links with, anti-globalization movements more generally, and begun to throw up a new populist leadership. They have succeeded in framing urban politics partly around environmental injustice.

To conclude, post-colonial Commonwealth cities bear numerous imprints of the imperial past—spatially, culturally, ethnically, and industrially. The raw materials that once visibly flowed through them to the wider world are less evident. There is a greater preponderance of service industries, including specialized informational ones; especially in developing countries, the informal sector has visibly helped to shape the modern city.[58] Indigenization is evident in de-racialization and the use of space, place names, architecture, museums, the arts, and other public creativity. Their multiculturalism is qualitatively different, not least evident in globalized cuisine, music, and dress. Tourism, including business tourism, offers opportunities to urban as well as wildlife entrepreneurs; its promotion increasingly borrows images from the indigenous past in order to suggest a certain exoticism, and a shared heritage which may not necessarily be felt.

---

[58] Saskia Sassen, 'Rebuilding the Global City: Economy, Ethnicity and Space' in Anthony D. King, (ed.), *Re-Presenting the City: Ethnicity, Capital and Culture in the 21st Century Metropolis* (Basingstoke: Macmillan, 1996), 33.

19

Reassertion of Indigenous Environmental Rights and Knowledge

Indigenous peoples have always asserted their territorial, resource and other rights when threatened by encroachment, not least in the settlement colonies covered in this chapter—Canada, New Zealand, and Australia, where they were most dramatically displaced. But in the second half of the twentieth century, the aboriginal inhabitants of these countries reasserted themselves with considerable force and success, using methods very different from those of the earlier actions—including judicial channels unwittingly provided by the colonizers. In the process, displaced and dislocated communities have attempted to repossess 'stolen' space—physically, intellectually, and judicially.

Reassertion in the United States and these three Commonwealth countries has had global ideological ripples, which is partly why we have chosen to examine them. They also share British-based legal systems and political traditions that indigenous groups have used to good effect. We are focusing here on indigenous communities in the narrower sense, in countries where whites remained the demographic majority. Their challenge was to predominantly anglophone societies, the descendants of British settlers and immigrants who arrived mostly over the last two hundred years. The discussion is limited largely to the environmental aspects of reassertion rather than legal and other ramifications; we will mention important court cases, but not cover all landmark events on the timeline of indigenous struggle.

The exploration of patterns of resistance in Chapter 16 covered South Asia and Africa where colonized people remained in the demographic majority and regained political power. Though the reassertions discussed here have strategies and aims in common, they are qualitatively different. They were not so much an attempt, by force if necessary, to repel incomers and the controls they impose (it is far too late for that), or to win overall power in an anti-colonial struggle, as a highly articulate call from the heart for justice, land, and a form of self-determination. Moreover, new movements are increasingly ideological and transnational, involving organized networks that use globalized discourses of discontent. The media, internet, NGOs, and UN fora are their tools of choice, which enable activists to influence the behaviour of states and corporations. Reassertion is the opposite of retreat, one aboriginal response to conquest, and suggests that this modern phenomenon is partly about renewed confidence.[1]

The rise of anglophone settler nationalisms in the first half of the twentieth century challenged hegemonic British imperial sovereignty. But these challenges did not directly involve minority indigenous peoples, and their rights were acutely threatened by colonial and post-colonial state formation.[2] This applied also to many anti-colonial nationalist movements elsewhere, such as India. Some indigenous people themselves adopted the language of sovereignty, though this did not always mean that they pitted themselves against the state. For example, in 1917 when the US declared war on Germany, the Iroquois Confederacy Council (a political union of Native American and Canadian First Nations) also declared war as an allied nation. Iroquois chief Deskahe unsuccessfully appealed their case for sovereignty before the League of Nations in Geneva in 1923, and other pleas were later made in London, in the belief that Britain had recognized their status when the Crown signed treaties with Iroquois leaders. Britain rebuffed them, saying this was an internal Canadian matter.[3] Sovereignty and treaty questions remain live issues for many indigenous communities.

Earlier chapters have described the many forms of struggle over natural resources throughout the Empire. Indigenous peoples in settler-dominated states had often tried to preserve access to land. They came increasingly to realize—in an era of decolonization—that reclaiming elements of what they considered to be their resource base could form an effective basis for political struggle. These claims became central to their reassertion as communities and nations. In addition to decolonization, the growth of civil society and social movements, the rise of the United Nations, and the proliferation of environmental and human rights-focused NGOs

[1] Henry Reynolds, *The Other Side of the Frontier: Aboriginal Resistance to the European Invasion of Australia* (Ringwood and Harmondsworth: Penguin, 1981).

[2] Richard Howitt (ed.), with John Connell and Philip Hirsch, *Resources, Nations and Indigenous Peoples: Case Studies from Australasia, Melanesia and Southeast Asia* (Melbourne and Oxford: Oxford University Press, 1996).

[3] Frederick E. Hoxie (ed.), *Encyclopaedia of North American Indians* (Boston and New York: Houghton Mifflin, 1996), 298–9, 12, 219–20.

have all influenced the process. The British Anti-Slavery and Aborigines Protection Society (now Anti-Slavery International), with roots in the late eighteenth century, has long promoted the rights of minority and indigenous groups. Groups championing indigenous rights multiplied after the Second World War when they became a 'kind of entity almost tailor-made for international indigenous politics'.[4] There were around 1,000 formal NGOs in the 1950s, 5,000 by the early 1990s, and 15,000 by 2000.[5] Two international NGOs committed to indigenous rights, Survival and Cultural Survival, were founded in Britain and the US in 1969 and 1972 respectively, and Minority Rights Group International in 1965. Most importantly, the last twenty years has seen a proliferation of indigenous NGOs in the south, run by grass-roots activists, some of whom challenge the top-down nature of many northern-based operations. They have also successfully inserted themselves into environmental networks and international congresses on environmental global issues.

Other social changes have had important impacts. Church and mission, often unintentionally, provided a route to secular enlightenment. Literacy brought with it a new critical understanding of colonial history. Newfound knowledge and contacts were used to agitate for rights and freedom, and establish independent churches and political parties. Since the 1930s, urbanization and greater mobility offered new opportunities for learning, earning, and networking. Aboriginal soldiers went to fight in two world wars and came back decorated and chastened, wondering about the disparity between how they were treated as equals on foreign battlefields yet as inferiors at home on 'civvy street'. The rise of aboriginal print and broadcast media gave this population a public voice; in particular radio, and later electronic media, united far-flung and isolated communities.[6]

Demographics changed, with Maori for example trebling in number between 1960 and 2000, which gave them greater visibility and social

---

[4] Colette Chabbott, 'Development INGOs', in John Boli and George M. Thomas (eds.), *Constructing World Culture: International Nongovernmental Organizations since 1875* (Stanford: Stanford University Press, 1999), 228.

[5] Ronald Niezen, *The Origins of Indigenism: Human Rights and the Politics of Identity* (Berkeley, CA: University of California Press, 2003), 42–3.

[6] Valerie Alia, *Un/Covering the North: News, Media and Aboriginal People* (Vancouver: UBC Press, 1999).

centrality.[7] More people of mixed descent self-identified as indigenous, which swelled numbers considerably.[8] Indigenous populations began producing their own lawyers, teachers, and politicians, who took up the cudgels on behalf of their communities, sometimes in collaboration with non-indigenous academics and activists. By various means, people became better equipped to engage in legal and political challenges.

By the 1980s the indigenous rights movement was learning new tactics, from earlier social movements led by women, blacks, gays, and greens, to organize, mobilize, and voice its defiance. A decade later it was routinely using the UN system to do so, facilitated by moves within the UN to address indigenous rights. Indigenous peoples demanded the right to self-determination above all, though not always in separate states; this continues to be fiercely contended by those who claim only states, not peoples, can be self-determining in international law.[9] They also increasingly rejected ethnographic classifications, linked as they were with colonial attempts to control and assimilate 'natives', and demanded the right to define themselves as a prerequisite to identifying their collective needs and rights.

By the mid-1990s, this loose global alliance was able to take advantage of a crisis of confidence in Western scientific, anthropological, and environmental knowledge, concerns about the breakdown of planetary ecological health, and new ways of looking at nature and culture. Indigenes made claims about their capacity to live in harmony with nature that struck a chord with Western sympathizers, environmentalists, and anti-globalization campaigners, some of whom saw in it a romantic possibility for socio-environmental renewal. However, today's indigenous movement is itself partly a product of globalization, and the globalization of environmental ideas, in so far as it uses new technology and ideas to network and campaign across borders. Many indigenous nations and pressure groups now have their own websites.[10]

[7] Belich, *Paradise Reforged*, 464. There were twelve times more Maori in 2000 than in 1900, 471.

[8] In Australia, for example, the recorded number of Aboriginal and Torres Strait Islanders rose by 35 per cent from 1966 to 1971 because the official distinction between full-blood Aboriginal and 'half-caste' had changed and more people began identifying as Aboriginal; Max Griffiths, *Aboriginal Affairs: A Short History* (Kenthurst, NSW: Kangaroo Press, 1995), 113.

[9] Peter Poynton, 'Dream Lovers: Indigenous People and the Inalienable Right to Self-Determination' in Howitt, Connell, and Hirsch (eds.), *Resources*, 42–56.

[10] See 'Indigenous Peoples and Information Technology', *Indigenous Affairs* 2/03 [sic] (Copenhagen: IWGIA, spring 2003).

Reassertion in Canada

The first Canadian national umbrella organization, the National Indian Council, was formed in the 1960s, as well as dozens of provincial groups.[11] As in Australia, indigenous activists were inspired at this time by the American civil rights movement and both Black and Red (Native American) Power, as well as local heroes such as Louis Riel, leader of the Red River Rebellion of 1869, whose memory continued to fire Métis aspirations.[12] There was an increasing backlash against the Indian Act, dating back to 1876, and the government's assimilation policies. These attempted to suppress indigenous culture by removing successive generations of children from their homes into residential schools. While these gave access to literacy and education, they severed cultural chains and were remembered as sites of sexual or physical abuse. Protest was coupled with growing pride in indigenous culture, while an articulate, better-educated leadership increasingly used their partial assimilation to advance indigenous rights from within the system.[13] Aspects of the indigenous as well as colonial past were contested. Women such as Mary Two-Axe Farley and Nellie Carlson protested in the 1950s at the way the Indian Act made a woman's status dependent on that of her husband, and a group called Indian Rights for Indian Women fought sexual discrimination in band membership.[14]

The main focus then and since was on land and treaty rights, self-determination and self-government, socio-economic development, and education. Processes were established from 1969 for hearing claims to land and resources. The 1970s and early 1980s saw a harder push for aboriginal land rights—including delegations sent to London—and demands for control over natural resources on aboriginal land. Some were successful; in 1971, the Enoch Indians of Alberta—who had been earning large sums from oil since the 1950s, but lacked the power to do what they chose with

[11] Canada's Constitution recognizes three groups of aboriginal peoples: First Nations (often referred to as Indians), Métis (people of mixed descent), and Inuit.

[12] The Métis people resisted government plans to transfer lands from the Hudson's Bay Company to the new dominion, and formed a breakaway government with Riel as president. They were granted 1.4m acres in a new province, Manitoba. Riel was hung for high treason in 1885, but Métis rights were written into the 1982 Constitution alongside those of Indians and Inuit.

[13] James Wilson, *Canada's Indians*, Minority Rights Group Report No. 21 (London: Minority Rights International, 1982).

[14] Olive Patricia Dickason, *Canada's First Nations: A History of Founding Peoples from Earliest Times*, 3rd edn. (Oxford: Oxford University Press, 2002), 313–14.

it—won control over their capital budget and planning.[15] Many bands have since entered into joint ventures with commercial companies to drill for oil and gas on their reserves. Indian cultural colleges were set up to teach traditional knowledge and beliefs, paving the way for the First Nations University of Canada, Saskatchewan, the only aboriginal-run university in North America, which opened in 2003. 'Education is our buffalo of the year 2003 and beyond', was how one First Nations leader hailed this.[16]

From the 1950s and 1960s, the Canadian government persuaded groups such as the Innu people of the Labrador–Quebec peninsula to abandon their nomadic hunting lifestyle and live in government-built villages in northern Quebec and off the Labrador Coast, where they languished in poverty. The fundamental cause of this decline, say Innu and outside researchers, was sedentarization: 'the very source of Innu well-being, *Nitassinan*, the land of the interior of the Labrador–Quebec peninsula, has gradually become a separate sphere rather than ... the centre of their activities.'[17] Inextricably linked to this lifestyle and connectivity with land was 'a particular way of understanding the world', the integrity of which was shattered. Hugh Brody, anthropologist and activist, has argued similarly: 'The losses to the outer and inner world feed each other, making recovery intensely difficult and breakdown—of society, family and self—overwhelming realities.'[18] Innu reassertion has included using 'pan-Native' methods of healing the community, maintaining their language and links to the land, and producing defiant documentaries such as *Ntapueu* (1997). Other reassertion has been more overtly political, including civil disobedience, treaty negotiations with the state, and protests over mining, hydroelectric projects, and NATO bomber flights which they say harm caribou, other wildlife, and humans.[19]

Also in the 1950s, the government forcibly relocated Inuit families from Port Harrison (now Inukjuak) on Quebec's Ungava peninsula, and others from North Baffin, more than 2000 km north to Ellesmere and Cornwallis Islands in the High Arctic. Officials decided that Inuit living in areas that

---

[15] Wilson, *Canada's Indians*, 14–19.

[16] Perry Bellegarde, chief of the Federation of Saskatchewan Indian Nations, quoted by CBC News, 21 June 2003.

[17] Colin Sansom, *A Way of Life That Does Not Exist: Canada and the Extinguishment of the Innu* (London: Verso, 2003).

[18] Hugh Brody, *Maps and Dreams* (London: Faber & Faber, 2002), xiv.

[19] Brody's film *Hunters and Bombers* (1990) focused on problems caused by military flights. Also see Roger Moody (ed.), *The Indigenous Voice: Visions & Realities*, vol. 1 (London and New Jersey: IWGIA and Zed Books, 1988), 124–5.

could not continue to support them should be moved to a place with greater natural resources—yet they chose to shift the most destitute and welfare-dependent of families, who were not the best-equipped hunters and had difficulty coping with the severe climate. Most benefits were cut off. People were expected to give up other livelihoods and start hunting. Though campaigning began in 1978 it was not until the 1990s that this led to official inquiries into suffering and neglect. Inuit won compensation and resettlement packages for families who wanted to return home. Their protest also involved challenging the myth of the happy, self-reliant 'Eskimo' as portrayed in the 1922 film *Nanook of the North*, which had strongly influenced official thinking. Oral testimony from relocation survivors made headlines and forced an official about-turn.[20] As in New Zealand and Australia, achieving official recognition of the value and credibility of oral testimony has been of major significance.

Indigenous groups made good use of the courts—notably in the Calder and Delgamuukw actions of 1973 and 1997.[21] The latter decision was a milestone, because the Supreme Court ruled for the first time that aboriginal title existed and oral history could be used to prove it. However, it did not grant title to any First Nation; it just created a test for proving it.[22] Tribal groups or bands have also intensified their efforts to renegotiate the treaties through which Indians gave up their lands and hunting rights and were moved onto reserves, where they faced isolation and poverty. More than seventy treaties were negotiated between 1701 and 1923. They could not be legally challenged until 1951, when the government lifted a 1927 ban on indigenous groups hiring lawyers to bring a claim against the Crown. This, and the Calder decision, opened a floodgate of claims. As in New Zealand, colonial treaties have proved useful bargaining tools with government, enabling bands to stake claims to land and resources they used

---

[20] Alan R. Marcus, 'Out in the Cold: The Legacy of Canada's Inuit Relocation Experiment in the High Arctic', IWGIA Document 71 (Copenhagen: IWGIA, 1992); Dickason, *Canada's First Nations*, 389.

[21] Dickason, *Canada's First Nations*, 332–3, 337–8. For Calder, see Kathleen Lickers, 'Looking Forward, Looking Back: Canada's Response to Land Claims', *Cultural Survival Quarterly*, 28.2 [sic] (15 June 2004); Garth Nettheim, *Indigenous Rights, Human Rights and Australia*, Working Paper No. 15 (Institute of Commonwealth Studies, University of London, 1987); Kenneth Maddock, *Your Land is Our Land: Aboriginal Land Rights* (Harmondsworth: Penguin Books Australia, 1983), 18–19.

[22] *Delgamuukw* v. *British Columbia*. To prove aboriginal title groups must prove pre-sovereignty occupancy, continuity between present-day and pre-sovereignty occupation, and exclusive possession of traditional lands. See <http://www.delgamuukw.org>.

before Europeans arrived. But many more claims have been lodged than resolved, and some have also led to land rights being extinguished.[23]

Some bands enlisted anthropological help in mapping territory in order to prove their long occupation and historical use of it, and to oppose projects such as the Alaska Highway pipeline. This 'catalysed and galvanized the Indian people's insistence on their rights', because it threatened to cut their lands in two, and blatantly represented the subordination of local livelihoods and environmental concerns to distant American interests.[24] When the Cross Lake Crees campaigned against hydroelectric development and the export of energy from their territory to Minnesota, they emphasized how Cree culture—once allegedly in harmony with the environment—had been destroyed by environmental abuses caused by this industry. They told the citizens of Minnesota that the energy they received was responsible for human rights violations—'there is blood in that power that turns on the lights'. Crees linked up with non-indigenous opponents, who were concerned about threats to farmlands and wildlife habitats, to improve the grid between Minnesota and Wisconsin. A media blitz followed. It was a powerful example of collaboration between indigenous and environmental lobby groups, using the media to promote 'the politics of shame'.[25]

Other successful actions by Cree people—former middlemen in the fur trade—have employed powerful symbols from their fur-trading past, such as the use of canoes as protest vehicles. In 1990 James Bay Cree elders paddled down the Hudson River to a press conference in New York to oppose plans for a giant hydroelectric scheme. The use of canoes echoed the way in which bands once marked the start of each fur-trading season by paddling downriver in a flotilla to a trading ceremony with Europeans. There was massive publicity; New York State cancelled plans to buy electricity from the company concerned; it was obliged to make an environmental impact assessment, and the whole project was suspended. Two years later, canoes were used again on the canals of Amsterdam, in a protest about water rights before the International Water Tribunal.[26]

The inherent right to aboriginal self-government is included in the 1982 Constitution. This has allowed groups like the Cree, Naskapi, Sechelt,

---

[23] For details of the treaties see <http://www.ainc-inac.cg.ca>.

[24] Brody, *Maps and Dreams*, 133.   [25] Niezen, *Origins of Indigenism*, 180–4.

[26] *Ibid.*, 185–6; Harvey Feit, 'Negotiating Recognition of Aboriginal Rights: History, Strategies and Reactions to the James Bay and Northern Quebec Agreement', in N. Peterson and M. Langton, *Aborigines, Land and Land Rights* (Canberra: Australian Institute of Aboriginal Studies, 1983), 416–38.

and Nisga'a to take control of their own affairs. The Cree nation reached an historic agreement in 2002 with the government of Quebec that gave them control over their lands, development, and economy. 'Unusually, this agreement was not based on damages but made the Cree part of the official development process', commented lawyer and Cree spokesman Romeo Saganash.[27] But the best example of self-determination is Nunavut, a self-governing, 2.1 million square km territory created in 1999 after decades of negotiation. It is the largest private landholding in North America; the word means 'our land'.[28] The Inuit (Nunavummiut to be exact) won controls over more than one fifth of Canada's land mass, extensive mineral rights, recognition of their legal rights to harvest wildlife, a leading role in all aspects of wildlife management (though the government retained ultimate responsibility for this), and more than Can\$1.17 billion in funding. In return, they surrendered aboriginal title. Though Inuit see traditional harvesting practices—fishing, trapping, and hunting—as aboriginal rights, they now talk of using these as the backbone of Nunavut's economic growth: 'The future of the Inuit is no longer based simply on the success of the hunt; but more importantly depends upon the success of understanding the nuances of a developing economy in relation to global markets'.[29] If education is today's buffalo for Saskatchewan bands, global marketing may be today's seal for Inuit.

Community control can in some cases intensify commodification, and— just as science has become more diverse in its sites (Chapter 12)—so natural resource management by indigenous people can draw on a pool of wider knowledge and technical expertise. Caribou meat from Nunavut is selling well in Europe, while research is being done on the commercial potential of musk-ox wool. Hunters and trappers supplement their income by making arts and crafts, using antler, bone, sealskin and leather, that raises several million Canadian dollars per year. Inuit are pressing for bigger fishing quotas, especially for shrimp, and have ambitious plans for mining diamonds, gold, and base metals, reviving the oil and gas industry, and developing heritage and wildlife tourism—in the hope that 'the real money

[27] From a talk by Romeo Saganash at Queen Elizabeth House, Oxford, October 2002.

[28] The Nunavut Agreement, the largest single land-claim settlement in Canadian history, is viewable at <http://www.tunngavik.com>. Also see J. Dahl, J. Hicks, and P. Jull (eds.), *Nunavut: Inuit Regain Control of their Lands and their Lives* (Copenhagen: IWGIA, 2000).

[29] 'Nunavut: Flexing its Economic Muscle', *Aboriginal Times*, Vol. 8/1 (Alberta: Niche Publishing, Nov.–Dec. 2003), 23.

lies with active travellers travelling the globe looking for pristine, untouched, natural beauty'.[30]

While these initiatives draw on global and hybrid knowledge they are, in the minds of their protagonists, reinforcing local identity and power. The promotional language of ecotourism is combined with advocacy for Inuit and Nunavut. The potential for Canadian wilderness recreation was recognized more than a century ago, with canoe trips particularly popular with vacationers and sportsmen, but aboriginal control of it is something new.[31] The Nunavut government is striving to make Inuktitut its official working language, while wildlife laws incorporate concepts from Inuit traditional knowledge. All in all, the Inuit are building on their major resource gains by marketing the natural world in such a way that their view of 'respect for the land' is maintained while profits are maximized, and their environmental knowledge is both privileged and consolidated.

New Zealand and the Maori Renaissance

The Maori renaissance in the second half of the twentieth century has been put down largely to demographics, industrialization, and urbanization. In the 1930s more than 80 per cent of Maori were rural dwellers, but by 2000, 83 per cent lived in towns and cities. The broader context was the great changes taking place in New Zealand society as a whole from 1960–2000 as part of a 'domestic process of decolonisation—a "coming-out" of difference and dissent, and a "coming-in" of new influences and new migrations'.[32]

In the 1970s, Maori activists rallied to oppose assimilation policies, and land laws introduced in 1967 that were dubbed 'the last land grab'. The economic downturn that cast a shadow nationwide from the mid-1970s hit Maori particularly hard, because they worked in vulnerable sectors. Unemployment rates were about four times higher than those of Pakeha by the late 1980s. In 1970 the first protest group was spawned, Nga Tamatoa, which led the push for Maori language teaching in schools. Black Power was a major inspiration, but there were also uneasy alliances with Pakeha movements in this era, including feminist, gay, socialist, anti-nuclear, and

---

[30] Ibid., 24–6.

[31] Bruce W. Hodgins and Jamie Benidickson, *The Temagami Experience: Recreation, Resources, and Aboriginal Rights in the Northern Ontario Wilderness* (Toronto: University of Toronto Press, 1989), 63–5.

[32] Belich, *Paradise Reforged*, 466–9, 464.

anti-Vietnam War. Dissent came to a head in a 1975 Land March (*hikoi*) on parliament, the first large national Maori protest. Led by octogenarian Whina Cooper, the marchers' aim was to protest against land losses and raise public awareness. Their choice of means was itself historical: rebel leader Titokowaru had used a *hikoi* in 1867 during the Land Wars.[33] The march succeeded in putting Maori grievances on the map, and led directly that year to the creation of the Waitangi Tribunal, a permanent commission of enquiry into breaches of Treaty of Waitangi principles.[34]

What are these? The situation facing Maori vis-à-vis the Crown is significantly different from that of Australian Aboriginal people in two key respects: unlike Australia, New Zealand was never regarded as *terra nullius*. The Crown recognized from the start that the entire country was owned by Maori, and until it was sold, land continued to belong to them. Maori customary land is defined as a category of property, which the courts have assumed continues to exist unless extinguished.[35] Second, the British never made a treaty with Aborigines but did do so with Maori. The signing of the Treaty of Waitangi in 1840 between the Crown and Maori chiefs was a major turning point, whose repercussions shape Maori-European relations to this day. The British thought the treaty had given them control over New Zealand, while Maori leaders did not believe they had granted any such thing. The Maori version of the treaty (there were at least five)[36] only conceded governorship (*kawanatanga*) to the British, while Maori retained resources, chieftainship, and sovereignty (*taonga, rangatiratanga,* and *mana*). In the English version, however, Maori sovereignty was ceded to the Crown, and chieftainship wasn't even mentioned. Early unease with the treaty gave way to protests that intensified in the 1880s, when Maori sent hundreds of petitions to government and two deputations to London.[37] Since 1975, with the establishment of the tribunal, Maori have been able to use the treaty to reassert their collective rights to land and other natural resources, for it specifically acknowledged and guaranteed their ownership of lands, forests,

---

[33] A hikoi is 'a communal march or walk in support of a cause', H. W. Orsman (ed.), *Oxford New Zealand Dictionary* (Auckland and Oxford: Oxford University Press, 1997), 347.

[34] Belich, *Paradise Reforged*, 474–8 and ch. 17.

[35] Court of Appeal, judgement in the Marlborough Sounds case (*Ngati Apa and Others* vs *Attorney-General and Others*, 19 June 2003, paragraphs 37, 47).

[36] James Belich, *Making Peoples: A History of the New Zealanders from Polynesian Settlement to the End of the Nineteenth Century* (Auckland: Penguin Books, 1996), 194.

[37] Claudia Orange, *The Treaty of Waitangi* (Wellington: Allen & Unwin with Port Nicholson Press, 1987), 4.

fisheries, and other property. Though some activists view it as fraudulent, the treaty has proved its greater worth to Maori as a binding contract between them and the Crown.[38] It has given them enormous leverage.

In some ways the Maori reconstruction and contemporary assertion of traditional knowledge has been produced in relation to the treaty, in ways that are similar to the processes and positioning around treaty renegotiations in Canada.[39] The treaty and Waitangi Tribunal have enabled Maori to frame and voice their knowledge in the public arena vis-à-vis a formerly hegemonic knowledge system, and make *taha* Maori—the Maori view of things—a cornerstone of New Zealand's socio-political order and consciousness. (Canada, by contrast, has not gone that far.) Their rights and knowledge have become publicly institutionalized, and their authority officially recognized, because the tribunal is simultaneously a state institution and an indigenous platform. Stories and song are key repositories of folklore, knowledge, and belief, and they are being used in legal processes to prove connectivity to land and resources.

Maori initiated a great national debate, which still rages, on what the treaty means in the modern world. Before 1985, when the tribunal's jurisdiction was extended back to 1840, customary land rights were not recognized in local courts unless supported by European documents.[40] The establishment of the Waitangi claims process has given Maori a distinct advantage over indigenous communities in other parts of the world, and enabled them to broaden their domestic influence in environmental management and commercial resource extraction. Maori now exercise considerable power in, for example, the tourism, energy, water, and fisheries sectors, and have benefited financially as a result. A recent landmark decision acknowledged that Maori groups (not individuals) still have the right to claim customary title to the foreshore and seabed, which is enormously significant in terms of marine farming licences, management of coastal marine resources, and the protection of customary and commercial fisheries. Maori are now major stakeholders in the country's fishing industry, with assets valued at about NZ$1 billion. They make up the Treaty of Waitangi Fisheries Commission, which manages these assets on behalf of the tribes (*iwi*) and

---

[38] Belich, *Making Peoples*, 193; Belich, *Paradise Reforged*, 478.

[39] See, for example, 'Implementing Delgamuuk'w Conference Transcripts', March 1999, viewable at <http://www.ubcic.bc.ca/docs>.

[40] Robert Macdonald, *The Maori of Aotearoa-New Zealand*, Minority Rights Group Report (London: Minority Rights Group, 1990).

which is developing mechanisms for distributing half of these assets to *iwi*.[41]

There is, however, growing opposition to Maori rights and claims. In 2004 a draft bill proposed to vest ownership of all foreshore and seabed in the Crown. Maori allege that the Act (enacted Novermber) breaches the treaty (the Waitangi Tribunal agrees) and is intended to extinguish (existing) Maori customary property rights.[42] Some 50,000 people joined a (two-week) cross-country march on parliament, which the BBC dubbed a 'Maori march to defend beaches'.[43] Other New Zealanders reacted angrily to what they saw as Maori attempts to take over the beaches, places of great cultural significance. The beach—along with the boat, bach or holiday home, and barbecue—is one of the key sites of Pakeha folk culture, according to Belich: 'They represent a modern populist engagement with the New Zealand landscape.'[44] More broadly the beach has come to represent, for all antipodeans, the outdoors, open accessible space, family relaxation and teenage adventure, free fish, escape from urban confinement, national pride, and nature itself, bathed by the seas that define a nation's shape yet constantly and quietly erode it. This first frontier, crossed by European invaders and Maori traders/resisters, is again a site of struggle.

Right-wing politicians seem determined to use the 'beach' issue to claw back Pakeha rights and end positive discrimination towards Maori, although many Maori say they have no desire to restrict public access to the foreshore. Activism has crystallized around the organization Te Ope Mana a Tai ('the group that has responsibility for the coast'), an informal network of tribes that produces information on the foreshore issue and advocates for Maori. The speed and sophistication with which Te Ope and its website were launched is symptomatic of indigenous activism on environmental issues today.[45] But this crisis has highlighted an inherent contradiction—common to many indigenous communities—between the way in which ancestral links to specific land and other resources are declared to be central to

---

[41] P. Ali Memon and R. C. Cullen, 'Rehabilitation of Indigenous Fisheries in New Zealand', in Howitt, Connell, and Hirsch (eds.), *Resources*, 252–3. Also information supplied by lawyer Maui Solomon.

[42] The Tribunal's Report on the Crown's Foreshore and Seabed Policy, WAI 1071, is viewable at <http://www.waitangi-tribunal.govt.nz/reports/generic/wai1071foreshore/>. For an update on the Foreshore and Seabed Act, see <http://www.justice.govt.ns/foreshore/>

[43] BBC News World Edition, 5 May 2004, <http://news.bbc.co.uk/2/hi/asia-pacific/3684953.stm>.

[44] Belich, *Paradise Reforged*, 527.   [45] See <http://www.teope.co.nz>.

indigenous identity, yet so many people are long urbanized and racially intermarried and cannot easily prove their roots in land or tribe. This is a particularly touchy subject in New Zealand, sparking disagreements between urban and rural Maori groups who have found themselves pitted against each other over certain claims. Some urban dwellers declare they no longer affiliate primarily with their traditional tribe, but rather with urban-based Maori organizations.

Without Maori reassertion the country's political map would have been very different, though the liberalization of government in the 1970s and later 1980s (as the Labour Party successively won and lost power) also provided a space and opening for Maori demands. The reassertion of Maori rights and knowledge in the last twenty years is termed a renaissance. Maori-ization has led to massive Maori language gains in education and other sectors, which will ensure its survival, and the renaming of the country as Aotearoa/New Zealand.

Australia

On 26 January 1988, Australia and Bicentenary Day, Aboriginal activist Burnum Burnum parodied the arrival of the British fleet at Botany Bay by planting an Aboriginal flag on the white cliffs of Dover and claiming sovereignty over Britain. Beads and trinkets were given to a bemused passer-by, who turned out to be an Australian tourist.[46] In the late 1960s, this activist had led a movement to reclaim the remains of Truganini, among the 'last' Aborigines in Tasmania, from a Tasmanian museum for burial.[47] In 1972 he was among the organizers of the Aboriginal Tent Embassy, set up outside Parliament House in Canberra to demonstrate Aboriginal isolation in their own country. Media and public interest was intense, and the 'Embassy' and its flag (red, black, and yellow to symbolize earth, people, and sun) became the focus for mass protest and political controversy.[48] More than thirty years later the Tent Embassy team was still going strong, and returned in 2001 to Dover beach to perform a traditional fire ceremony to 'let the land know we are here'.[49]

[46] Nettheim, *Indigenous Rights*, 1–2.

[47] Truganini is often described as the last Aboriginal Tasmanian, a claim denied by Aboriginal writers like Anne Pattel-Gray, *Through Aboriginal Eyes: The Cry from the Wilderness* (Geneva: WCC Publications, 1991), 49.

[48] Keith D. Suter and Kaye Stearman, *Aboriginal Australians* (London: MRG, 1994 update).

[49] European Network for Indigenous Australian Rights, <http://www.eniar.org/news>, 21 August 2001.

An insistence on self-determination linked to reclamation and assertion of culture is a feature of these and numerous other protests, whose spiritual underpinning is rooted in land. A major focal point for spiritual expression is Dreaming sites, where Aboriginal people believe they draw upon the power of ancestral spirit beings who created the features of the landscape during the Dreaming. To keep this life force active, people must protect and stay in contact with the sites; at death, one's spirit is believed to return to the site from which it came. Some legislation specifically acknowledges this connectivity, in defining Aboriginal landowners as local descent groups that 'have common spiritual affiliations to a site on the land, being affiliations that place the group under a primary spiritual responsibility for that site and for the land'.[50] Songs, believed to have been created by the Dreaming ancestors, are sung during ceremonies which invoke how the spirit beings named rocks, rivers, trees, and other parts of landscape. Richard Moyle notes that since Dreaming myths link to 'precise areas of land which are still recognised today, they embody information about land ownership'. And because the myths are kept alive in song lyrics, they 'themselves represent the earliest statements about land ownership—a kind of original land claim'. Like the curricula in traditional Maori schools of learning, these song texts are depositories of knowledge that is believed to be inviolate.[51]

Aboriginal resurgence in the last three decades has been driven largely by urban communities. Rural action included the 'outstation movement' that involved Aboriginal people on reserves leaving mission and government stations to live in small tribal bands and pursue as much of a traditional lifestyle as was possible.[52] Activists tried using legal challenges to regain land and other rights from the 1960s. In the Gove (also known as Milirrpum) land rights case, launched in 1963 but not settled until 1971, Yirrkala clans from the Northern Territory challenged a mining company and the federal government over leases that allowed the company, Nabalco, to mine bauxite on their land. The court ruled that the land was in fact not theirs; it had allegedly ceased to be Aboriginal-owned in 1788, when the imposition of British sovereignty effectively extinguished Aboriginal land title. The

---

[50] The Aboriginal Land Rights (Northern Territory) Act 1976, section 3, paragraph 3; Robert Layton, 'Ambilineal Descent and Traditional Pitjantjutjara Rights to Land', and other chapters in N. Peterson and M. Langton (eds.), *Aborigines, Land and Land Rights* (Canberra: Australian Institute of Aboriginal Studies, 1983), 15–32.

[51] Richard Moyle, 'Songs, Ceremonies and Sites: The Agharringa Case', in Peterson and Langton, *Aborigines*, 91–2.

[52] Suter and Stearman, *Aboriginal Australians,* 14.

argument rested upon the notion that Australia was *terra nullius* or 'no man's land', and therefore available.[53]

Other landmark events included the Gurindji Walk-Off of 1966, when striking stockhands left a sheep station in the Northern Territory in protest at low wages and appalling working conditions. The strike developed into a broader call for the return of sacred ancestral lands at Wattie Creek (Daguragu), and is seen to mark the start of the land-rights movement.[54] Indigenous lobbying, coupled with changes in government—particularly the pro-Aboriginal Labour administration from 1972–5—led to various changes in the law as well as limited restitutions. Another Labour government passed the Aboriginal and Torres Strait Islander Heritage Act in 1984, to protect sacred sites nationwide. By the 1980s Aboriginal lobbyists were increasingly using international protocols, global fora, and the AGMs of multinational oil and mining giants to make their case, partly because there was still a fairly weak legal base for their claims within Australia.

In 1981, under a Land Rights Act, the Pitjantjatjara people of South Australia were given freehold title to 102,000 square km in the Great Central Reserve; this was the first settlement of its kind negotiated between a government and an indigenous community, and included the right to negotiate terms and royalties with mining companies. Three years later Pitjantjatjara from Maralinga and Emu Fields—who had lost their lands to British atomic testing in the 1950s and 1960s—had 76,000 square km returned; the rest was contaminated and unfit for habitation. Much of the land available for Aboriginal reclaim is arid, marginal, and relatively unsuitable for pastoralism and agriculture. But it has been found to be high value in other respects—largely for mining and tourism. As in other British colonies, mineral rights were retained by the Crown, but some Aboriginal communities have been able to negotiate royalties from minerals and other extraction.

Mining has presented global indigenous peoples with a particular challenge because it is an 'ambivalent phenomenon' that offers to produce fabulous wealth from land that is otherwise relatively worthless in material terms, while also threatening to destroy those lands 'and the social fabric woven from them'.[55] Though environmental impact assessments are supposed to

---

[53] *Milirrpum and Others v. Nabalco Pty Ltd.*, 17 FLR 141, cited in Nettheim, *Indigenous Rights*; Griffiths, *Aboriginal Affairs*, and by numerous other authors.

[54] Suter and Stearman, *Aboriginal Australians*, 7.

[55] John Connell and Richard Howitt (eds.), *Mining and Indigenous Peoples in Australasia* (Sydney: Sydney University Press, 1991), 4, 9.

13. Aboriginal protestors, New South Wales Parliament House, 2004.

Credit: Getty Images.

be made, no state requires a thorough Social Impact Assessment before giving mining companies the green light. More than a third of the world's diamonds are produced at Argyle, in the East Kimberley region, where mining began in 1981. Though the mine was established on pastoral land leased from the Crown by non-Aboriginals, three sacred sites lay on or next to the diamond deposits, fifty-five more lay nearby, and it was discovered that exploration work had been carried out without the necessary permission. Legal action—alleging a breach of the Aboriginal Heritage Act—was launched soon afterwards but had to be dropped.[56] Conflict then tore the community apart when some people accepted compensation in return for agreeing not to oppose the mine; they thought it better than nothing at all, while others felt they had been sold short. The state amended the Act and refused to protect the main sacred site. The upshot was that some local Aboriginal communities enjoyed indirect economic benefits, others reacted by joining the outstation movement, but sacred sites were desecrated and hopes dashed that traditional ownership would be recognized.

Aboriginal arguments at Argyle hinged upon the idea that mining would—by wrecking sacred sites—destroy indigenous relationships to the land and consequently indigenous identity and culture, too. The government suggested the claims were not genuine; the communities were 'detribalized' and allegedly no longer regarded the sites as very significant. Opposing world-views could not be reconciled. However, an alternative analysis suggests that 'it is arguable that the mining, far from destroying Aboriginal relationships to land, might actually reinforce and uphold Aboriginal cosmology and law', and that those who made the agreement with the miners saw it in terms of a customary exchange called *winan*.[57]

Tourism presents a similar dilemma. Aboriginal players were able in some cases to influence regional tourist development so that it benefited their communities, and partly redressed their marginalization by getting more involved in planning processes.[58] Joint management of national parks is a model developed in Australia, where the first such park on Aboriginal land was established at Kakadu in 1978. To begin with, the traditional owners

---

[56] John Connell and Richard Howitt (eds.), *Mining and Indigenous Peoples in Australasia* (Sydney: Sydney University Press, 1991), 141.

[57] Michael Dillon, 'Interpreting Argyle: Aborigines and Diamond Mining in Northwest Australia', in Connell and Howitt, *Mining*, 147.

[58] Jocelyn Davies and Elspeth Young, 'Taking Centre Stage: Aboriginal Strategies for Redressing Marginalisation', in Howitt, Connell, and Hirsch, *Resources*, 154–5.

only had an advisory role in its management, but from 1989 an Aboriginal majority was formally established on the board.[59] The Anangu community notably fought a long battle for the return of the Uluru-Kata Tjuta National Park which they finally achieved in 1985. When a management board was created the following year, six Aboriginals were among its ten members. Anangu jointly owned and managed the park—hugely symbolic as a national and international environmental and cultural icon—and received annual rent and 25 per cent of park entrance fees.[60] Aboriginal knowledge shaped the management plan, which draws upon Tjukurpa—a reference both to the creation period and the orally transmitted law, religion, and morals that govern Anangu society. However, Anangu only secured title to Uluru on condition that they immediately leased it back to the national parks directorate for ninety-nine years.

British cinema advertisements for Australian tourism in summer 2004 showed Aboriginal women walking through this landscape, against a backdrop of Uluru—all mention of the former Ayers Rock or any other symbols of European-derived Aussie-ness firmly erased. Uluru is 'the most readily identified image of Australia', and this semiotic twinning of Uluru with Aboriginals indicates how far white Australia has come to accept indigenous rights—although many would argue this is merely surface spin for profit motives.[61] Anangu used Commonwealth legislation to stake their claim to the park, and ultimately overcame arguments that Aboriginal ownership would deter tourists and lower the park's conservation value. In fact, tourists flock to Uluru partly because they are drawn by Aboriginal culture. Unlike African protected areas, indigenous people are allowed to live here—though there is also a difference in that Australia does not have large predators.

The park authority provides the community with most services and employment. But the downside includes growing pressures on limited natural resources, caused both by the rise in tourist numbers and Aboriginal

[59] M. A. Hill and J. A. Press, 'Kakadu National Park: An Australian Experience in Co-Management', in D. Western, R. M. Wright, and S. C. Strum (eds.), *Natural Connections: Perspectives in Community-based Conservation* (Washington, DC: Island Press, 1994), 135–57; Hannah Reid, David Fig, Hector Magome, and Nigel Leader-Williams, 'Co-Management of Contractual National Parks in South Africa: Lessons from Australia', *Conservation and Society*, 2/2 (2004), 377–409.

[60] Graham Griffin, 'Welcome to Aboriginal Land: Anangu Ownership and Management of the Uluru-Kata Tjuta National Park', in Chatty and Colchester (eds.), *Conservation and Mobile Indigenous Peoples*, 362–76.

[61] Quote is Griffin, 'Welcome', 364, citing other sources.

population, since the park has acted as a magnet for other Anangu. Firewood collection and off-road driving has increased soil erosion. There are also issues around bio-prospecting, privacy, and demands by some Anangu to limit tourist access to their culture, images, and most sacred sites. Tourists want to meet indigenes, but few indigenes want to meet them, or have the professional skills to deal with large numbers of visitors. The conundrum is: how can a community tap into tourist dollars while maintaining its privacy, dignity, and cultural integrity?[62]

Carruthers, writing comparatively on South Africa and Australia (whose contractual parks model has heavily influenced that of South Africa), points out that 'national parks are currently favoured spaces for reclaiming, perhaps even reinventing, the cultures of formerly disadvantaged peoples as well as for publicising aspects of indigenous knowledge among a broader public'. She warns of the dangers of using parks to 'spearhead campaigns for native title' and as shrines to ethnic nationalism, and the paradoxes inherent in declaring indigenous knowledge and ceremonies private while simultaneously displaying them for tourists in an act of 'voluntary primitivism'.[63] However, it can also be said that Aboriginal values have played a key role in the transformation of Australian attitudes to land, resources, and the protection of cultural heritage. Unlike South Africa, contractual national parks are viewed as living cultural landscapes and mechanisms are in place to ensure that indigenous communities play a meaningful role in joint management.

A major turning point came in 1992 with the Mabo Decision in Australia's High Court, in a case brought by five Meriam elders from Murray Island. Eddie Mabo and his fellow plaintiffs offered detailed evidence about their community's customs and traditions in order to prove their intimate connection to the island, drawing on history, anthropology, administrative records, and land, constitutional, and international law. In so doing, they had to prove what the land *meant* to them in the past and present—largely without the benefit of written evidence. The Mabo judgement recognized that native land title had largely not been extinguished, that native title rights were enforceable under the common law, and Aboriginal people could assert these rights if they could prove a 'traditional connection' with a specific tract of Crown land. These rulings became law the following year

---

[62] Griffin, 'Welcome', 369–71 in particular.

[63] Carruthers, 'Past and Future Landscape Ideology: The Kalahari Gemsbok National Park', in Beinart and McGregor (eds.), *Social History and African Environments*, 255, 266.

in the Native Title Act, which also recognized that Aborigines had a right to negotiate mining and other proposed developments on claimed lands. This might appear a sensational success, but many have questioned how much of a victory Mabo and the Act actually were. If title has already passed to a third party there is little chance of reclaiming it, even if it can be shown to have been taken illegally. Native title is confined to areas called 'vacant Crown lands' that have never been settled; despite inflammatory talk of Australian backyards being at risk of takeover there is actually precious little left to claim.[64] Activist Gary Foley has declared that, in view of this narrow definition, 'to defend native title is to defend the most extensive single act of dispossession since 1788'.[65]

Aboriginal claimants see land as the key to culture, identity, history, the sacred, and sustenance; it represents life itself and an umbilical cord to the ancestors. Therefore it is logical that rights and reassertion have revolved around the land question, and been shaped by it. Yet as in New Zealand, long-urbanized communities no longer live off the land, have no real wish to, and cannot readily prove their links to specific territory. In the rhetoric, driven now by judicial imperatives, emphasis is laid upon continuity of connections with land and traditional law since native title is lost if it can be shown that these have been severed; it is only through these links that the common law recognized native title. There are many problems with the legislation, few successful outcomes, and fights over multiple claims to the same piece of land.[66] Indigenous women have struggled to get their voices heard, in the face of pressures from both Aboriginal men and white male officials. Women, whose Dreaming is distinct from men's, use their traditional land-based knowledge to bring claims, but it has not been easy to prove female legitimacy to do so. Nevertheless, in the process of registering sacred sites women have been able to assert the significance and uniqueness of their own sites.

Apart from the successes mentioned, Aboriginal groups have won important recognition of the right to hunt, gather, fish, and burn in traditional ways. Fire is 'simultaneously an expression and a means of demonstrating

---

[64] Michael Bachelard, *The Great Land Grab: What Every Australian Should Know About Wik, Mabo and the Ten-Point Plan* (Melbourne: Hyland House, 1997), 10; Diane Fields, *The Fight for Black Rights* (Sydney South, NSW: Bookmarks Australia, 1995), 14. The 1996 Wik Decision was a major victory for the Wik peoples of Queensland; it said aboriginal title was not extinguished by pastoral leases.

[65] Gary Foley, 'Native Title is not Land Rights' (1997), <http://www.kooriweb.org/foley/essays>.

[66] Bachelard, *The Great Land Grab*, 16–17.

continued links between people and their country'.[67] The right to burn has become an integral part of native title, and is protected by law. Renaming—of individuals, communities, and places—has played a crucial role in demonstrating the uniqueness of Aboriginal identity, as is the case in New Zealand. Instead of the colonizers' blanket label there are now Koori (New South Wales), Murri (Queensland), and Noongar (Western and South Australia). The replacement of European place names with their indigenous originals has enormous symbolic potency in reasserting the traditional Dreaming creation stories that tell how spirit ancestors mapped out the land in the first place, the collective knowledge these enshrine, and the customary law that was established in this way.[68]

However, Australian activists keenly felt the lack of colonial treaty rights, which enabled Maori in particular to achieve a relatively strong bargaining position. Since the 1980s, the idea of making a treaty with government began to gain ground. Both sympathetic whites and Aboriginal activists have called on successive prime ministers to sign a treaty that acknowledges prior Aboriginal ownership of the continent, and to write indigenous rights into the constitution. The government—no doubt terrified of going down the Waitangi route—preferred to talk of reconciliation between black and white.

To Conclude

The social and geographical marginality of indigenous peoples once rendered them inaudible and invisible, particularly in the late nineteenth and first half of the twentieth centuries. The Empire has struck back, reasserting aboriginal knowledge systems in order to challenge hegemonic ones, reasserting rights in order to redress past wrongs. Indigenous peoples, archaeologists, anthropologists, and other scholars have sought to re-insert indigenous peoples back into history—a history previously dominated by Europeans which began with the arrival of the British. White Australians, New Zealanders, and Canadians have had to confront a past they might have preferred to forget, or gloss over. Since the late 1960s, these older narratives, newly written, have been absorbed into general histories of continents and cultures.

---

[67] Lesley Head and Camilla Hughes, 'One Land, Which Law? Fire in the Northern Territory' in Howitt, Connell, and Hirsch (eds.), *Resources*, 278, 285–6.

[68] Rosemary Hunter, 'Aboriginal Histories, Australian Histories, and the Law', in Bain Attwood, (ed.), *In the Age of Mabo: History, Aborigines and Australia* (NSW: Allen & Unwin, 1996), 1–16.

Assertion of custodianship over land has extended to ideas, memory, and knowledge. The emergence of indigenous media has enabled aboriginal people to become 'national and global newsmakers in their own right, instead of colonized peoples primarily represented to the outside world by others'.[69] However, it is unlikely that colonized people in these countries will gain overall political power as they have in South Africa, where whites are a dwindling minority.

From the mid-1970s, it became clear that natural resource management had to take account of aboriginal rights and claims. Governments were shocked to realize they were wrong in assuming that resources such as minerals, fisheries, forests, and water were vested in the Crown. The exploitation of environmental wealth, we have argued, laid down deep structures in the architecture of empire, and helped to shape the social geography of colonial territories. Lawsuits have challenged the very bedrock on which nations and constitutions were made.[70] But alongside aboriginal gains, many problems remain. An obsession with heritage and authenticity can result in a distorted sense of self and a tendency for communities to represent 'their past in ways which are patently false in historical terms', never mind present themselves as static, bounded entities instead of ever-changing, fluid ones.[71] There is a question mark for some over whether indigenous groups have an innate right to environmental stewardship, and necessarily make the best stewards. Those in Canada and New Zealand seem keener than their Australian counterparts on asserting the right to exploit resources, sometimes on an industrial scale. As a result of the land-claims process and new legislation, new elites have arisen and wealth has divided communities. Indigenous groups are not homogeneous, but can be treated as such in claims and other political processes that tend to disadvantage certain group members, particularly women.

While some communities such as the Inuit of Greenland have achieved home rule, and groups elsewhere have reclaimed land and achieved jurisdiction over resources and industries, others have found that the only land to which they are likely to be entitled is marginal. Descendants of the long-term displaced and dispossessed tend not to have gained from territorially based approaches to self-determination and sovereignty.

---

[69] Alia, *Un/Covering the North*, 160.

[70] Paul McHugh, 'The Legal and Constitutional Position of the Crown in Resource Management', in Howitt, Connell, and Hirsch (eds.), 300 and passim.

[71] Attwood, *Age of Mabo*, xxxvi–vii.

SELECT BIBLIOGRAPHY

ABROL, DINESH, ' "Colonised Minds" or Progressive Nationalist Scientists: The Science and Culture Group' in MacLeod and Kumar, *Technology and the Raj*, 265–88.

ACHOLA, MILCAH AMOLO, 'Colonial Policy and Urban Health: The Case of Colonial Nairobi', *Azania*, 36–7 (2001–2), 119–37.

ADAMS, WILLIAM M. and MULLIGAN, M., *Decolonizing Nature: Strategies for Conservation in a Post-Colonial Era* (London: Earthscan, 2003).

ADAS, MICHAEL, *Machines as the Measure of Men: Science, Technology, and Ideologies of Western Dominance* (Ithaca, NY: Cornell University Press, 1989).

AGARWAL, A., CHOPRA, R., and SHARMA, K. (eds.), *The First Citizens' Report: State of India's Environment* (Delhi: Centre for Science and Environment, 1982, 1996).

—— and NARAIN, S. (eds.), *Dying Wisdom: Rise, Fall and Potential of India's Traditional Water Harvesting Systems* (Delhi: Centre for Science and Environment, 1997).

AKELEY, C. E., *In Brightest Africa* (London: William Heinemann, 1924).

ALIA, VALERIE, *Un/Covering the North: News, Media and Aboriginal People* (Vancouver: UBC Press, 1999).

ALIER, JUAN MARTINEZ, 'The Andean Case', paper presented to a conference on 'The Environmental Dimensions of European Colonialism: A Comparative Perspective', Centre for Brazilian Studies and Centre for African Studies, St Antony's College, University of Oxford (2004).

ALLEAUME, GHISLAINE, 'An Industrial Revolution in Agriculture? Some Observations on the Evolution of Rural Egypt in the Nineteenth Century', in A. K. Bowman and E. Rogan, *Agriculture in Egypt from Pharaonic to Modern Times* (Oxford: Oxford University Press, 1999), 331–45.

ALLEN, GARTH, and BRENNAN, FRANK, *Tourism in the New South Africa: Social Responsibility and the Tourist Experience* (London: I.B. Tauris, 2004).

ALLINGHAM, ANNE, *Taming the Wilderness: The First Decade of Pastoral Settlement in the Kennedy District* (Townsville: James Cook University of Northern Queensland, 1977).

ALPERS, EDWARD A., *The East African Slave Trade* (Nairobi: East African Publishing House, 1967).

—— *Ivory and Slaves in East Central Africa: Changing Patterns of International Trade to the Later Nineteenth Century* (London: Heinemann, 1975).

AL-SABAH, Y. S. F., *The Oil Economy of Kuwait* (London: Kegan Paul, 1980).

ANDERSON, DAVID M., 'Managing the Forest: The Conservation History of Lembus' in Anderson and Grove (eds.), *Conservation in Africa.*, 249–68.

—— *Eroding the Commons: The Politics of Ecology in Baringo, Kenya, 1890–1963* (Oxford: James Currey, 2002).

ANDERSON, DAVID M. and GROVE, RICHARD (eds.), *Conservation in Africa: People, Policies and Practice* (Cambridge: Cambridge University Press, 1987).

—— and RATHBONE, RICHARD (eds.), *Africa's Urban Past* (Oxford: James Currey, 2000).

ANKER, PEDER, 'The Ecology of Nations: British Imperial Sciences of Nature, 1895–1945', unpublished Ph.D., Harvard University (1999).

—— *Imperial Ecology: Environmental Order in the British Empire, 1895–1945* (Cambridge, MA: Harvard University Press, 2001).

ARNOLD, DAVID, *Colonizing the Body: State Medicine and Epidemic Disease in Nineteenth Century India* (Stanford, CA: University of California Press, 1993).

—— 'Rebellious Hillmen: The Gudem-Rampa Risings 1839–1924' in Ranajit Guha (ed.), *Subaltern Studies I*, 88–142.

—— 'Touching the Body: Perspectives on the Indian Plague, 1896–1900', in Ranajit Guha (ed.), *Subaltern Studies V*, 55–90.

—— (ed.), *Imperial Medicine and Indigenous Societies* (Manchester: Manchester University Press, 1988).

—— and GUHA, RAMACHANDRA (eds.), *Nature, Culture, Imperialism: Essays on the Environmental History of South Asia* (Delhi: Oxford University Press, 1996).

—— (ed.), *Science, Technology and Medicine in Colonial India: The New Cambridge History of India III: 5* (Cambridge: Cambridge University Press, 2000).

ATTWOOD, BAIN (ed.), *In the Age of Mabo: History, Aborigines and Australia* (St Leonards, NSW: Allen & Unwin, 1996).

BACHELARD, MICHAEL, *The Great Land Grab: What Every Australian Should Know About Wik, Mabo and the Ten-Point Plan* (Melbourne: Hyland House, 1997).

BADEN-POWELL, B. H., *Hand-Book of the Economic Products of the Punjab*, 2 vols. (Roorkee: Thomason Civil Engineering College Press, 1868–72).

BAHR, GABRIEL, *A History of Land Ownership in Modern Egypt, 1800–1950* (London: Oxford University Press, 1962).

BAINES, EDWARD, 'On the Woollen Manufacture of England, with Special Reference to Leeds Clothing District', *Report of the Proceedings of the British Association for the Advancement of Science, Transactions of the Sections* (London, 1858).

BAKER, D. E. U., *Colonialism in an Indian Hinterland: The Central Provinces, 1820–1920* (Delhi: Oxford University Press, 1993).

BARLOW, M., and CLARKE, T., *Blue Gold: The Battle Against Corporate Theft of the World's Water* (London: Earthscan, 2002).

BARNARD, ALAN, *The Australian Wool Market, 1840–1900* (Carlton, Victoria: Melbourne University Press, 1958).

BARR, NEIL, and CARY, JOHN, *Greening a Brown Land: The Australian Search for Sustainable Land Use* (Melbourne: Macmillan, 1992).

BARTON, GREGORY A., *Empire Forestry and the Origins of Environmentalism* (Cambridge: Cambridge University Press, 2002).

BAUDRILLARD, JEAN, *Simulacra and Simulation* (Ann Arbor: University of Michigan Press, 1994).

BAYLY, C. A. (ed.) *Indian Society and the Making of the British Empire, The New Cambridge History of India II: 1* (Cambridge: Cambridge University Press, 1988).

—— *Empire and Information: Intelligence Gathering and Social Communication in India, 1780–1870* (Cambridge: Cambridge University Press, 1996).

BEINART, WILLIAM, 'Production and the Material Basis of Chieftainship in Pondoland, c.1830–1880', in S. Marks and A. Atmore (eds.), *Economy and Society in Pre-Industrial South Africa* (London: Longman, 1980), 120–47.

—— 'The Renaturing of African Animals: Film and Literature in the 1950s and 1960s', *Kronos: Journal of Cape History*, 29 (2003), 201–26.

—— and COATES, PETER, *Environment and History: The Taming of Nature in the United States and South Africa* (London: Routledge, 1995).

—— —— 'Men, Science, Travel and Nature in the Eighteenth and Nineteenth-Century Cape', *Journal of Southern African Studies*, 24/4 (December 1998), 775–99.

—— —— 'African History and Environmental History', *African Affairs*, 99/395 (2000), 169–302.

—— —— *The Rise of Conservation in South Africa: Settlers, Livestock and the Environment, 1770–1950* (Oxford: Oxford University Press, 2003).

BEINART, WILLIAM, and McGREGOR, JoANN (eds.), *Social History and African Environments* (Oxford: James Currey, 2003).

BEINART, WILLIAM, and MIDDLETON, KAREN, 'Plant Transfers in Historical Perspective: A Review Article', *Environment and History*, 10/1 (2004), 3–29.

BELICH, JAMES, *Making Peoples: A History of the New Zealanders from Polynesian Settlement to the End of the Nineteenth Century* (Auckland: Penguin Books, 1996).

—— *Paradise Reforged: A History of the New Zealanders from the 1880s to the Year 2000* (Auckland: Allen Lane, Penguin Press, 2001).

BENEDICT, CAROL, *Bubonic Plague in Nineteenth-Century China* (Stanford, CA: Stanford University Press, 1996).

BENIDICKSON, JAMIE, *Idleness, Water, and a Canoe: Reflections on Paddling for Pleasure* (Toronto: University of Toronto Press, 1997).

BERG, MAXINE, 'In Pursuit of Luxury: Global History and British Consumer Goods in the Eighteenth Century', *Past and Present*, 182 (2004), 85–142.

BHATIA, B. M., *Famines in India, 1850–1945* (London: Asia Publishing House, 1963).

BLAINEY, G., *The Tyranny of Distance: How Distance Shaped Australia's History* (London: Macmillan, 1975).

BOLAANE, MAITSEO, 'Local Participation in Wildlife Conservation and Management: The Case of Moremi Game Reserve, Okavango Delta, Northern Botswana 1960s', unpublished D.Phil. dissertation, University of Oxford (2004).

BOLTON, GEOFFREY, *Spoils and Spoilers: A History of Australians Shaping their Environment* (Sydney: Allan & Unwin, 1992).

BONNER, PHIL, and LEKGOATHI, PETER, *Rand Water: A Century of Excellence* (Johannesburg: Rand Water Publications, 2004).

BONYHADY, TIM, *Australian Colonial Paintings in the Australian National Gallery* (Melbourne: Australian National Gallery, 1986).

—— *The Colonial Earth* (Carlton, Victoria: Miegunyah Press, Melbourne University Press, 2000).

BOSERUP, ESTHER, *The Conditions of Agricultural Growth* (London: Faber, 1965).

BOURN, DAVID, REID, ROBIN, ROGERS, DAVID, SNOW, BILL, and WINT, WILLIAM, *Environmental Change and the Autonomous Control of Tsetse and Trypanosomosis in Sub-Saharan Africa* (Oxford: Oxford Environment Research Group, 2001).

BOWMAN, ALAN K., and ROGAN, EUGENE, 'Agriculture in Egypt from Pharaonic to Modern Times', in A. K. Bowman and E. Rogan (eds.), *Agriculture in Egypt from Pharaonic to Modern Times* (Oxford: Oxford University Press, 1999), 1–32.

BOYD, JOHN MORTON (ed.), *Fraser Darling in Africa: A Rhino in the Whistling Thorn* (Edinburgh: Edinburgh University Press, 1992).

BRANDIS, D., *Memorandum on the Demarcation of the Public Forests in the Madras Presidency* (Simla, 1878).

—— *Progress of Forestry in India* (1884, reprinted from Transactions of the Scottish Arboricultural Society).

—— *Forestry in India* repr. (1897; repr. Dehra Dun: Natraj Publishers, 1994).

BRAUDEL, FERNAND, *The Mediterranean and the Mediterranean World in the Age of Philip II*, vol. 1 (London: Fontana/Collins, 1975).

BREWER, J. and PORTER, R. (eds.), *Consumption and the World of Goods* (London: Routledge, 1994).

BROCKINGTON, DAN, *Fortress Conservation: The Preservation of the Mkomazi Game Reserve, Tanzania* (Oxford: James Currey, 2002).

—— 'The Politics and Ethnography of Environmentalisms in Tanzania', *African Affairs* 105/418 (2006), 97–116.

BROCKWAY, L. H., *Science and Colonial Expansion: The Role of the British Royal Botanical Gardens* (New York: Academic Press, 1979).

BRODY, HUGH, *Maps and Dreams* (London: Faber & Faber, 2002).

BROOKS, SHIRLEY, 'Playing the Game: The Struggle for Wildlife Protection in Zululand, 1910–1930', unpublished MA thesis, Queen's University, Kingston (1990).

BROWN, JENNIFER S. H., and VIBERT, ELIZABETH (eds.), *Reading Beyond Words: Contexts for Native History* (Peterborough, Ontario: Broadview Press, 1996).

BROWN, KAREN, 'Cultural Constructions of the Wild: The Rhetoric and Practice of Wildlife Conservation in the Cape Colony at the Turn of the Twentieth Century', *South African Historical Journal*, 47 (2002), 75–95.

—— 'uNakane: The Ecological and Chemical Campaign against Livestock Trypanosomiasis in KwaZulu Natal, 1894–2004', unpublished paper, Wellcome Unit for the History of Medicine, Oxford (2004).

BRUNER, EDWARD M., and KIRSHENBLATT-GIMBLETT, BARBARA, 'Maasai on the Lawn: Tourist Realism in East Africa', *Cultural Anthropology* 9/2 (1994), 881–908.

BRYANT, RAYMOND L., and BAILEY, SINEAD, *Third World Political Ecology* (London: Routledge, 1997).

BUCKLEY, ROBERT BURTON, *Irrigation Works in India and Egypt* (London and New York: E. & F. N. Spon, 1893).

BUCKNER, PHILLIP A., and REID, JOHN G., *The Atlantic Region to Confederation: A History* (Toronto: University of Toronto Press, 1994).

BUNDY, COLIN, *The Rise and Fall of the South African Peasantry* (London: Heinemann, 1979).

BUNN, DAVID, 'An Unnatural State: Tourism, Water and Wildlife Photography in the Early Kruger National Park', in Beinart and McGregor (eds.), *Social History and African Environments*, 199–218.

BURCHELL, WILLIAM J., *Travels in the Interior of Southern Africa* (1822–4; repr. London: Batchworth Press, 1953).

BUSVINE, JAMES R., *Disease Transmission by Insects: Its Discovery and 90 Years of Effort to Prevent It* (Berlin and London: Springer-Verlag, 1993).

BUTLIN, N. G., *Australian Domestic Product, Investment and Foreign Borrowing, 1861–1938/39* (Cambridge: Cambridge University Press, 1962).

CAIN, P. J., and HOPKINS, A. G., *British Imperialism: Innovation and Expansion, 1688–1914* (London: Longman, 1993).

CAMPBELL, JUDY, *Invisible Invaders: Smallpox and Other Diseases in Aboriginal Australia, 1780–1880* (Carlton, Victoria: Melbourne University Press, 2002).

CARRUTHERS, JANE, 'Game Protection in the Transvaal 1846 to 1926', unpublished Ph.D. dissertation, University of Cape Town (1988).

CARRUTHERS, JANE, 'Creating a National Park, 1910 to 1926', *Journal of Southern African Studies*, 15/2 (1989), 188–216.

—— *The Kruger National Park: A Social and Political History* (Pietermaritzburg: University of Natal Press, 1995).

—— *Wildlife and Warfare: The Life of James Stevenson-Hamilton* (Pietermaritzburg: University of Natal Press, 2001).

—— 'Past and Future Landscape Ideology: The Kalahari Gemsbok National Park', in Beinart and McGregor (eds.), *Social History and African Environments*, 255–66.

CARSWELL, GRACE, 'Soil Conservation Policies in Colonial Kigezi, Uganda', in Beinart and McGregor (eds.), *Social History and African Environments*, 131–54.

CASSIDY, L., and MADZWAMUSE, M., 'Enterprise Development and Community Based Natural Resource Management in Botswana', *Report of Workshop Proceedings, Maun, Botswana, March 9–12, 1999* (IUCN Botswana/SNV Botswana, 1999), downloadable at <http://www.cbnrm.bw>.

CATANACH, I. J., 'Plague and the Indian Village, 1896–1914', in Peter Robb (ed.), *Rural India: Land, Power and Society under British Rule* (London and Dublin: Curzon Press, 1983), 216–43.

CHABBOTT, COLETTE, 'Development INGOs', in John Boli and George M. Thomas (eds.), *Constructing World Culture: International Nongovernmental Organizations since 1875* (Stanford: Stanford University Press, 1999).

CHAKRAVARTI, RANABIR, 'The Creation and Expansion of Settlements and Management of Hydraulic Resources in Ancient India', in Grove, Damodaran, and Sangwan (eds.), *Nature and the Orient*, 87–105.

CHAKRAVORTY, SANJOY, 'From Colonial City to Global City? The Far-from-Complete Spatial Transformation of Calcutta', in P. Marcuse and R. van Kempen (eds.), *Globalizing Cities: A New Spatial Order?* (Oxford: Blackwells, 2000), 56–77.

CHANDAVARKAR, RAJNARAYAN, 'Plague Panic and Epidemic Politics in India, 1896–1914', in T. Ranger and R. Slack (eds.), *Epidemics and Ideas: Essays on the Historical Perception of Pestilence* (Cambridge: Cambridge University Press, 1999), 203–40.

CHAUDHURI, A. B., and CHAKRABARTI, KALYAN, *Sundarbans Mangrove (Ecology and Wildlife)*, (Dehra Dun: Jugal Kisthore, 1989).

CHATTY, DAWN, 'The Bedouin of Central Oman: Adaptation or Fossilization?', in P. Salzman (ed.), *Contemporary Nomadic and Pastoral Peoples: Asia and the North* (Virginia, US: Department of Anthropology, College of William and Mary, 1981), 13–32.

—— *From Camel to Truck: The Bedouin in the Modern World* (New York: Vantage Press, 1986).

—— 'Petroleum Exploitation and the Displacement of Pastoral Nomadic House-holds in Oman', in Seteney Shami, *Population Displacement and Resettlement: Development and Conflict in the Middle East* (New York: Center for Migration Studies, 1994), 89–106.

—— 'Animal Reintroduction Projects in the Middle East: Conservation without a Human Face', in Chatty and Colchester (eds.), *Conservation and Mobile Indigenous Peoples*, 227–43.

—— and COLCHESTER, MARCUS (eds.) *Conservation and Mobile Indigenous Peoples: Displacement, Forced Settlement, and Sustainable Development* (Oxford: Berghahn, 2002).

CHRIWA, WISEMAN CHIJERE, 'Fishing Rights, Ecology and Conservation along Southern Lake Malawi, 1920–1960', *African Affairs*, 95/380 (1996), 351–77.

CHURCHILL, WINSTON, *The River War* (London: Eyre & Spottiswood, 1933).

CLAYTON, ANTHONY, and SAVAGE, DONALD C., *Government and Labour in Kenya, 1895–1963* (London: Frank Cass, 1974).

CLEGHORN, HUGH, *The Forests and Gardens of South India* (London: W. H. Allen, 1861).

COE, SOPHIE D., and COE, MICHAEL D., *The True History of Chocolate* (London: Thames & Hudson, 2000).

COLE, DONALD P., 'Bedouin and Social Change in Saudi Arabia', in J. Galaty and P. C. Salzman (eds.), *Change and Development in Nomadic and Pastoral Societies* (Leiden: Brill, 1981), 128–49.

—— 'The Enmeshment of Nomads in Sa'udi Arabian Society: The case of Al Murrah', in Nelson (ed.), *The Desert and the Sown*, 113–28.

COLLETT, DAVID, 'Pastoralists and Wildlife: Image and Reality in Kenya Maa-sailand', in Anderson and Grove (eds.), *Conservation in Africa*, 129–48.

COLLINS, R. O., and TIGNOR, R. L., *Egypt & The Sudan* (New Jersey: Prentice-Hall, 1967).

COLLINS, R. O., and DENG, FRANCIS M., (eds.), *The British in the Sudan, 1898–1956* (London: Macmillan, 1984).

CONNELL, JOHN, and HOWITT, RICHARD (eds.), *Mining and Indigenous Peoples in Australasia* (Sydney: Sydney University Press, 1991).

CONNOR, JOHN, *The Australian Frontier Wars, 1788–1838* (Sydney: University of New South Wales Press, 2002).

CONRAD, MARGARET, FINKEL, ALVIN, and JAENEN, CORNELIUS, *History of the Canadian Peoples: Beginnings to 1867* (London: Copp Clark Pitman, 1993).

CONSTANTINE, STEPHEN, *Buy and Build: The Advertising Posters of the Empire Marketing Board* (London: HMSO, 1986).

COUPER-JOHNSON, ROSS, *El Nino: The Weather Phenomenon that Changed the World* (London: Hodder & Stoughton, 2000).

COX, E. W., *The Evolution of the Australian Merino* (Sydney: Angus & Robertson, 1936).

CRESSEY, DAVID, 'Literacy in Context: Meaning and Measurement in Early Modern England', in Brewer and Porter (eds.), *Consumption and the World of Goods*, 305–19.

CRONON, WILLIAM, *Nature's Metropolis: Chicago and the Great West* (New York: W. W. Norton, 1991).

CROSBY, ALFRED, *Ecological Imperialism: The Biological Expansion of Europe, 900–1900* (Cambridge: Cambridge University Press, 1986).

CROUCHLEY, A. E., *The Economic Development of Modern Egypt* (London: Longmans, Green & Co., 1938).

CRUMMEY, DONALD (ed.), *Banditry, Rebellion and Social Protest in Africa* (London: James Currey, 1986).

CRYSTAL, JILL, *Oil and Politics in the Gulf: Rulers and Merchants in Kuwait and Qatar* (Cambridge: Cambridge University Press, 1990).

CURSON, P. H., *Times of Crisis: Epidemics in Sydney, 1788–1900* (Sydney: Sydney University Press, 1985).

CURTIN, PHILIP D., 'Epidemiology and the Slave Trade', *Political Science Quarterly*, 83 (1967), 190–216.

—— *Death by Migration: Europe's Encounter with the Tropical World in the Nineteenth Century* (Cambridge: Cambridge University Press, 1989).

—— *The Rise and Fall of the Plantation Complex: Essays in Atlantic History* (Cambridge: Cambridge University Press, 1990).

——FEIERMAN, S., THOMPSON, L., and VANSINA, J., *African History* (London: Longman, 1978).

DAHL, J., HICKS, J., and JULL, P. (eds.), *Nunavut: Inuit Regain Control of their Lands and their Lives* (Copenhagen: IWGIA, 2000).

DARLING, F. FRASER, *A Herd of Red Deer* (London: Oxford University Press, 1937).

DARWIN, JOHN, *Britain, Egypt and the Middle East: Imperial Policy in the Aftermath of War, 1918–1922* (London: Macmillan, 1981).

DASMANN, RAYMOND, *African Game Ranching* (Oxford: Pergamon Press, 1964).

DAVIES, JOCELYN, and YOUNG, ELSPETH, 'Taking Centre Stage: Aboriginal Strategies for Redressing Marginalisation', in Howitt, Connell, and Hirsch (eds.), *Resources, Nations and Indigenous Peoples*, 152–71.

DAVIES, K. G., *The Royal African Company* (New York: Atheneum, 1970).

DAVIS, MIKE, *Late Victorian Holocausts: El Nino Famines and the Making of the Third World* (London: Verso, 2001).

DAY, DAVID, *Claiming a Continent: A New History of Australia* (Sydney: Harper Collins, 2001).

DELIUS, PETER, *The Land Belongs to Us: The Pedi Polity under Sekwati and Sekhukhune* (Johannesburg: Ravan Press, 1983).

—— *A Lion Amongst the Cattle: Reconstruction and Resistance in the Northern Transvaal* (Oxford: James Currey, 1996).

—— and SCHIRMER, S., 'Soil Conservation in a Racially Ordered Society: South Africa, 1930–1970', *Journal of Southern African Studies*, 26/4 (December 2000), 719–41.

DIAMOND, JARED, *Guns, Germs and Steel: A Short History of Everybody for the Last 13,000 Years* (London: Vintage, 1998).

DICKASON, OLIVE PATRICIA, *Canada's First Nations: A History of Founding Peoples from Earliest Times*, 3rd edn. (Don Mills and Oxford: Oxford University Press, 2002).

DICKSON, H. R. P., *Kuwait and her Neighbours* (London: George Allen & Unwin, 1956).

DICKSON, VIOLA, *The Wildflowers of Kuwait and Bahrein* (London: George Allen & Unwin, 1955).

DILLON, MICHAEL, 'Interpreting Argyle: Aborigines and Diamond Mining in Northwest Australia', in Connell and Howitt (eds.) *Mining and Indigenous Peoples in Australasia*, 139–52.

DRAYTON, RICHARD, *Nature's Government: Science, Imperial Britain, and the 'Improvement' of the World* (New Haven: Yale University Press, 2000).

DRESCHER, SEYMOUR, *Econocide: British Slavery in the Era of Abolition* (Pittsburgh, PA: University of Pittsburgh Press, 1977).

DRIVER, FELIX, and GILBERT, DAVID, (eds.), *Imperial Cities: Landscape, Display and Identity* (Manchester: Manchester University Press, 1999).

DUFFY, ROSALEEN, *Killing for Conservation: Wildlife Policy in Zimbabwe* (Oxford: James Currey, 2000).

DUNLAP, THOMAS, *Nature and the English Diaspora: Environment and History in the United States, Canada, Australia, and New Zealand* (Cambridge: Cambridge University Press, 1999).

DZINGIRAI, VUPENYU, "CAMPFIRE is not for Ndebele Migrants': The Impact of Excluding Outsiders from CAMPFIRE in the Zambezi Valley, Zimbabwe', *Journal of Southern African Studies*, 29/2 (2003), 445–59.

—— 'The New Scramble for the African Countryside', *Development and Change*, 34/2 (April 2003), 243–64.

EARDLEY-WILMOT, SAINTHILL, *Forest Life and Sport in India* (London: Edward Arnold, 1910).

ECHENBERG, MYRON, 'Pestis Redux: The Initial Years of the Third Bubonic Plague Pandemic, 1894–1901', *Journal of World History*, 13/2 (2002), 429–49.

—— *Plague Ports* (New York: New York University Press, 2007).

ELTIS, DAVID, *The Rise of African Slavery in the Americas* (Cambridge: Cambridge University Press, 2000).

ELTON, CHARLES, *Animal Ecology* (first pub. 1927: Chicago: University of Chicago Press, 2002).

—— *The Ecology of Invasions by Animals and Plants* (London: Methuen, 1958).

EMERTON, LUCY, and MFUNDA, IDDI, 'Making Wildlife Economically Viable for Communities Living around the Western Serengeti, Tanzania', Evaluating Eden Series, Working Paper No. 1 (London: IEED, 1999).

FABIAN, JOHANNES, *Out of Our Minds: Reason and Madness in the Exploration of Central Africa* (Berkeley, LA: University of California Press, 2000).

FAIRHEAD, JAMES, and LEACH, MELISSA, *Misreading the African Landscape: Society and Ecology in a Forest–Savanna Mosaic* (Cambridge: Cambridge University Press, 1996).

FERNANDEZ-ARMESTO, FELIPE, *The Canary Islands after the Conquest: The Making of a Colonial Society in the Early Sixteenth Century* (Oxford: Clarendon Press, 1982).

FIELDS, DIANE, *The Fight for Black Rights* (Sydney South, NSW: Bookmarks Australia, 1995).

FINNIE, DAVID H., *Shifting Lines in the Sand: Kuwait's Elusive Frontier with Iraq* (London: I.B. Tauris, 1992).

FLANNERY, TIMOTHY F., *The Future Eaters: An Ecological History of the Australian Lands and People* (London: Secker & Warburg, 1996).

—— 'The Fate of Empire in Low- and High-Energy Ecosystems' in Griffiths and Robin (eds.), *Ecology and Empire*, 46–59.

FORBES, R. J., *Studies in Early Petroleum History* (Leiden: E. J. Brill, 1958).

FORD, JOHN, *The Role of the Trypanosomiases in African Ecology: A Study of the Tsetse Fly Problem* (London: Oxford University Press, 1971).

FRASER, MARYNA (ed.), *Johannesburg Pioneer Journals, 1888–1909* (Cape Town: Van Riebeeck Society, 1986).

FROST, WARWICK, 'Australia Unlimited? Environmental Debate in the Age of Catastrophe, 1910–1939', *Environment and History*, 10/3 (2004), 285–303.

GADGIL, MADHAV, and GUHA, RAMACHANDRA, *This Fissured Land: An Ecological History of India* (Delhi and Oxford: Oxford University Press, 1992).

—— —— 'State Forestry and Social Conflict in British India', in Hardiman, *Peasant Resistance in India*, 259–95.

GALLAGHER, NANCY E., *Egypt's Other Wars: Epidemics and the Politics of Public Health* (New York: Syracuse University Press, 1990).

GATACRE, W. F., *Report on the Bubonic Plague in Bombay, 1896–97* (Bombay: Times of India, 1897).

GEMERY, HENRY A., and HOGENDORN, JAN S., 'Comparative Disadvantage: The Case of Sugar Cultivation in West Africa', *Journal of Interdisciplinary History*, 9 (1979), 429–49.

GEORGANO, N. *et al.*, *Britain's Motor Industry: The First Hundred Years* (Sparkford: G. T. Foulis, 1995).

GIBLIN, JAMES, 'Trypanosomiasis Control in African History: An Evaded Issue?', *Journal of African History*, 31 (1990), 59–80.

GILBERT, ALAN, and GUGLER, JOSEF, *Cities, Poverty and Development: Urbanization in the Third World* (Oxford: Oxford University Press, 1997).

GILMARTIN, DAVID, 'Models of the Hydraulic Environment: Colonial Irrigation, State Power and Community in the Indus Basin', in Arnold and Guha (eds.), *Nature, Culture, Imperialism*, 210–36.

GOLDMAN, MARA, 'Partitioned Nature, Privileged Knowledge: Community-based Conservation in Tanzania', *Development and Change*, 34/5 (2003), 833–62.

GOLDSCHMIDT, TIJS, *Darwin's Dreampond: Drama in Lake Victoria* (Cambridge, MA: MIT Press, 1996).

GOODY, JACK, *Technology, Tradition, and the State in Africa* (London: Oxford University Press, 1971).

GORDON-CUMMING, R. *Five Years' Adventures in the Far Interior of South Africa* (London: John Murray, 1856).

GRIFFIN, GRAHAM, 'Welcome to Aboriginal Land: Anangu Ownership and Management of the Uluṟu-Kata Tjuṯa National Park', in Chatty and Colchester (eds.), *Conservation and Mobile Indigenous Peoples*, 362–76.

GRIFFITHS, MAX, *Aboriginal Affairs: A Short History* (Kenthurst, NSW: Kangaroo Press, 1995).

GRIFFITHS, TOM, and ROBIN, LIBBY (eds.), *Ecology and Empire: Environmental History of Settler Societies* (Edinburgh: Keele University Press, 1997).

GROVE, RICHARD H., *Green Imperialism: Colonial Expansion, Tropical Island Edens and the Origins of Environmentalism* (Cambridge: Cambridge University Press, 1995).

—— *Ecology, Climate and Empire: Colonialism and Global Environmental History 1400–1940* (Cambridge: White Horse Press, 1997).

—— DAMODARAN, V., and SANGWAN, S. (eds.), *Nature and the Orient: The Environmental History of South and South East Asia* (Delhi: Oxford University Press, 1998).

GRUNSVEN, LEE VAN, 'Singapore: The Changing Residential Landscape in a Winner City', in Peter Marcuse and Ronald van Kempen, (eds.), *Globalizing Cities: A New Spatial Order?* (Oxford: Blackwell, 2000).

GRZIMEK, B. and M., *Serengeti Shall Not Die* (London: Collins, 1965).

—— MESSNER, R., RIEFENSTAHL, L., and TICHY, H., *Visions of Paradise* (London: Hodder & Stoughton, 1981).

GUHA, RAMACHANDRA, 'Forestry and Social Protest in British Kumaun, c. 1893–1921', in Ranajit Guha (ed.), *Subaltern Studies IV*, 54–100.

—— *The Unquiet Woods: Ecological Change and Peasant Resistance in the Himalaya* (Delhi: Oxford University Press, 1989).

—— 'The Authoritarian Biologist and the Arrogance of Anti-humanism: Wildlife Conservation in the Third World', in Saberwal and Rangarajan, *Battles Over Nature*, 139–57.

—— 'An Early Environmental Debate: The Making of the 1878 Forest Act', *Indian Economic and Social History Review*, 27 (1990), 65–84.

—— 'The Malign Encounter: The Chipko Movement and Compelling Visions of Nature', in T. Banuri and F. Apfell Marglin (eds.), *Who Will Save the Forests?* (London: Zed Books, 1993), 80–113.

GUHA, RANAJIT (ed.), *Subaltern Studies I, III, IV, V: Writings on South Asian History and Society* (Delhi and Oxford: Oxford University Press, 1982, 1984, 1985, 1987).

—— *Elementary Aspects of Peasant Insurgency in Colonial India* (Delhi: Oxford University Press, 1992).

HAILEY, LORD, *An African Survey: A Study of the Problems Arising in Africa South of the Sahara* (London: Oxford University Press, 1938).

HAINSWORTH, D. R., *The Sydney Traders: Simon Lord and his Contemporaries, 1788–1821* (Melbourne: Cassell, 1971).

HAKANSSON, THOMAS, 'The Human Ecology of World Systems in East Africa: The Impact of the Ivory Trade', *Human Ecology*, 32/5 (2004), 561–91.

HAKE, ANDREW, *African Metropolis: Nairobi's Self-Help City* (London: Chatto & Windus for Sussex University Press, 1977).

HALL, PETER, *Cities of Tomorrow: An Intellectual History of Urban Planning and Design in the Twentieth Century* (Oxford: Blackwell, 1996).

—— *Cities in Civilization* (London: Weidenfeld & Nicolson, 1998).

HALL-MATTHEWS, DAVID, 'Historical Roots of Famine Relief Paradigms: Ideas on Dependency and Free Trade in India in the 1870s', *Disasters: The Journal of Disaster Studies, Policy and Management*, 20/3 (1996), 216–30.

HANCOCK, W. K., *Australia* (London: Ernest Benn, 1930).

—— *Survey of British Commonwealth Affairs, Volume II, Problems of Economic Policy, 1918–1939, Part 1* (London: Oxford University Press, 1940).

A Handbook of Arabia, Admiralty Naval Intelligence Division, vol. 1 (London: HMSO, 1916).

HARDIMAN, D. (ed.), *Peasant Resistance in India, 1858–1914* (Delhi: Oxford University Press, 1992).

—— 'Small-Dam Systems of the Sahyadris', in Arnold and Guha (eds.), *Nature, Culture, Imperialism*, 185–209.

HARRIS, COLE, *The Resettlement of British Columbia: Essays on Colonialism and Geographic Change* (Vancouver: UBC Press, 1998).

HARTSHORN, J. E., *Oil Companies and Governments: An Account of the International Oil Industry and its Political Environment* (London: Faber & Faber, 1962).

HAVINDEN, MARK, and MEREDITH, DAVID, *Colonialism and Development: Britain and its Tropical Colonies, 1850–1960* (London: Routledge, 1993).

HEAD, LESLEY, and HUGHES, CAMILLA, 'One Land, Which Law? Fire in the Northern Territory', in Howitt, Connell, and Hirsch (eds.), *Resources, Nations and Indigenous Peoples*, 278–88.

HEADRICK, DANIEL R., *The Tools of Empire: Technology and European Imperialism in the Nineteenth Century* (New York: Oxford University Press, 1981).

—— *The Tentacles of Progress: Technology Transfer in the Age of Imperialism, 1850–1940* (New York: Oxford University Press, 1988).

HERBERT, EUGENIA, 'Smallpox Inoculation in Africa', *Journal of African History*, 16 (1975), 539–59.

HILL, M. A., and PRESS, J. A., 'Kakadu National Park: An Australian Experience in Co-management', in D. Western, R. M. Wright, and S. C. Strum (eds.), *Natural Connections: Perspectives in Community-based Conservation* (Washington, DC: Island Press, 1994), 135–57.

HIRST, L. FABIAN, *The Conquest of Plague* (Oxford: Clarendon Press, 1953).

HODGINS, BRUCE W., and BENIDICKSON, JAMIE, *The Temagami Experience: Recreation, Resources, and Aboriginal Rights in the Northern Ontario Wilderness* (Toronto: University of Toronto Press, 1989).

HOLDGATE, MARTIN, *The Green Web: A Union for World Conservation* (London: Earthscan Publications, 1999).

HOME, ROBERT, *Of Planting and Planning: The Making of British Colonial Cities* (London: E. and F. N. Spon, Chapman & Hall, 1997).

HOMEWOOD, K. M., and RODGERS, W. A., *Maasailand Ecology: Pastoralist Development and Wildlife Conservation in Ngorongoro, Tanzania* (Cambridge: Cambridge University Press, 1991).

—— and THOMPSON, M., 'Elites, Entrepreneurs and Exclusion in Maasailand', *Human Ecology* 30/1 (2002), 107–38.

HOPPE, KIRK, 'Lords of the Fly: Colonial Visions and Revisions of African Sleeping Sickness Environments on Ugandan Lake Victoria, 1906–1961', *Africa*, 67 (1997), 86–105.

—— *Lords of the Fly: Sleeping Sickness Control in British East Africa, 1900–1960* (Westport, CT: Praeger, 2003).

HOWARD, ALBERT, *An Agricultural Testament* (London and New York: Oxford University Press, 1940).

HOWARD, LOUISE E., *Sir Albert Howard in India* (London: Faber & Faber, 1953).

HOWITT, RICHARD (ed.), with Connell, John, and Hirsch, Philip, *Resources, Nations and Indigenous Peoples: Case Studies from Australasia, Melanesia, and Southeast Asia* (Melbourne and Oxford: Oxford University Press, 1996).

HOXIE, FREDERICK E. (ed.), *Encyclopaedia of North American Indians* (Boston and New York: Houghton Mifflin, 1996).

HUGHES, LOTTE, 'Moving the Maasai: A Colonial Misadventure', D.Phil. dissertation, University of Oxford (2002).

—— *Moving the Maasai: A Colonial Misadventure* (Basingstoke: Palgrave Macmillan, 2006).

HUGHES, ROBERT, *The Fatal Shore: The Epic of Australia's Founding* (New York: Knopf, 1986).

HULME, DAVID, and MURPHREE, MARSHALL W. (eds.), *African Wildlife and Livelihoods: The Promise and Performance of Community Conservation* (Cape Town: David Philip, and Oxford: James Currey, 2001).

HUMAN, JOE, and PATTANAIK, MANOJ, *Community Forest Management: A Casebook from India* (Oxford: Oxfam, 2000).

HUNT, CONSTANCE E., *Thirsty Planet: Strategies for Sustainable Water Management* (London and New York: Zed Books, 2004).

HUNT, JOHN M., *Petroleum Geochemistry and Geology*, 2nd edn. (New York: W. H. Freeman, 1996).

HUNTER, ROSEMARY, 'Aboriginal Histories, Australian Histories, and the Law', in Bain Attwood (ed.), *In the Age of Mabo: History, Aborigines and Australia* (NSW, Australia: Allen & Unwin, 1996), 1–16.

IGOE, JIM, 'National Parks and Human Ecosystems: The Challenge to Community Conservation. A Case Study from Siminjaro, Tanzania, in Chatty and Colchester (eds.), *Conservation and Mobile Indigenous Peoples*, 77–96.

ILIFFE, JOHN, *A Modern History of Tanganyika* (Cambridge: Cambridge University Press, 1979).

INGRAM, BRUCE, *Bedouin of Northern Arabia: Traditions of the Al-Dhafir* (London and New York: KPI, 1986).

INIKORI, JOSEPH (ed.), *Forced Migration: The Impact of the Export Slave Trade on African Societies* (London: Hutchinson, 1982).

—— and ENGERMAN, STANLEY L. (eds.), *The Atlantic Slave Trade: Effects on Economies, Societies, and Peoples in Africa, the Americas, and Europe* (Durham, NC: Duke University Press, 1992).

INNIS, HAROLD A., *Problems of Staple Production in* Canada (Toronto: Ryerson Press, 1933).

—— *The Cod Fisheries: The History of an International Economy* (New Haven: Yale University Press, 1940).

—— *The Fur Trade in Canada: An Introduction to Canadian Economic History* (1930; Toronto: University of Toronto Press, 1999).

ISENBERG, ANDREW, *The Destruction of the Bison: An Environmental History* (Cambridge: Cambridge University Press, 2000).

ISSAWI, CHARLES, *Egypt: An Economic and Social Analysis* (London: Oxford University Press, 1947).

JACKSON, MICHAEL, *Existential Anthropology: Events, Exigencies and Effects* (Oxford: Berghahn, 2005).

JACOBS, N., *Environment, Power and Injustice: A South African History* (Cambridge: Cambridge University Press, 2003).

JENISH, D'ARCY, *Epic Wanderer: David Thompson and the Mapping of the Canadian West* (Toronto: Anchor Canada, 2004).

JENKINS, D. T., and PONTING, K. G., *The British Wool Textile Industry, 1770–1914* (London: Heinemann, 1982).

JOHNSON, DOUGLAS L., *The Nature of Nomadism; A Comparative Study of Pastoral Migrations in Southwestern Asia and Northern Africa* (Chicago: University of Chicago, 1969).

JOHNSON, DOUGLAS, and ANDERSON, DAVID (eds.), *The Ecology of Survival: Case Studies from Northeast African History* (London: Croom Helm, 1988).

JOHNSON, NELS, 'Ahmad: A Kuwaiti Pearl Diver', in Edmund Burke III (ed.), *Struggle and Survival in the Modern Middle East* (London: I.B. Tauris, 1993), 91–9.

JORDAN, A. M., *Trypanosomiasis Control and African Rural Development* (Harlow: Longman, 1986).

KARLSSON, BENGT G., 'A Matter of Rights: Forest Reservations, Legal Activism and the Sangma Movement in 20th Century Garo Hills', paper presented at the International Conference on the Forest and Environmental History of the British Empire and Commonwealth (University of Sussex, March 2003).

KAY, STEPHEN, *Travels and Researches in Caffraria* (New York: Harper, 1834).

KEDOURIE, ELIE, *England and the Middle East: The Destruction of the Ottoman Empire, 1914–1921* (London: Bowes & Bowes, 1956).

KENT, MARIAN, *Oil, and Empire: British Policy and Mesopotamian Oil, 1900–1920* (London: Macmillan, 1976).

KHALAF, SULAYMAN, 'Continuity and Change in Camel Racing in the UAE', *Anthropos*, (1999), 85–106, viewable online at <http://www.enhg.org/articles/camelrac>.

KHAN, M. A. Waheed, 'Dr Cleghorn's Role in Indian Forestry', *The Indian Forester*, 88/6 (1962), 391–5.

KING, ANTHONY D., *Colonial Urban Development: Culture, Social Power and Environment* (London: Routledge & Kegan Paul, 1976).

—— *Urbanism, Colonialism, and the World Economy: Cultural and Spatial Foundations of the World Urban System* (London and New York: Routledge, 1990).

—— *The Bungalow: The Production of a Global Culture* (New York: Oxford University Press, 1995).

KIPLE, KENNETH F., *The Caribbean Slave: A Biological History* (Cambridge: Cambridge University Press, 1984).

KJEKSHUS, HELGE, *Ecology Control and Economic Development in East African History* (London: Heinemann, 1977).

KLEIN, HERBERT S., *The Atlantic Slave Trade* (Cambridge: Cambridge University Press, 1999).

KLEIN, IRA, 'Urban Development and Death: Bombay City, 1870–1914', *Modern Asian Studies*, 20 (1986), 725–54.

KLUNZINGER, C. B., *Upper Egypt: Its People and Products* (London: Blackie & Son, 1878).

KOPONEN, JUHANI, *People and Production in Late Precolonial Tanzania: History and Structures* (Helsinki: Monographs of the Finnish Society for Development Studies, No. 2, 1988).

KURLANSKY, MARK, *Cod: A Biography of the Fish that Changed the World* (London: Jonathan Cape, 1998).

LAMB, H. H., *Climate, History and the Modern World* (London: Routledge, 1997).

LANCASTER, WILLIAM, and LANCASTER, FIDELITY, 'Desert Devices: The Pastoral System of the Rwala Bedu', in J. G. Galaty and D. L. Johnson (eds.), *The World of Pastoralism: Herding Systems in Comparative Perspective* (Belhaven: Guilford Press, 1990), 177–94.

LANDAU, PAUL S., and KASPIN, Deborah D. (eds.), *Images and Empires: Visuality in Colonial and Postcolonial Africa* (Berkeley, CA: University of California Press, 2002).

LAYTON, ROBERT, 'Ambilineal Descent and Traditional Pitjantjatjara Rights to Land', in Peterson and Langton (eds.), *Aborigines, Land and Land Rights*, 15–32.

LEE, RICHARD B., *The !Kung San: Men, Women, and Work in a Foraging Society* (Cambridge: Cambridge University Press, 1979).

LEWCOCK, RONALD, *Early Nineteenth Century Architecture in South Africa: A Study in the Interaction of Two Cultures, 1795–1837* (Cape Town: A. A. Balkema, 1963).

LICKERS, KATHLEEN, 'Looking Forward, Looking Back: Canada's Response to Land Claims', *Cultural Survival Quarterly*, 28.2 [*sic*], 15 June 2004.

LIENHARDT, PETER, *Disorientations—A Society in Flux: Kuwait in the 1950s*, ed. A. Al-Shahi (Reading: Ithaca Press, 1993).

LINDSAY, W. K., 'Integrating Parks and Pastoralists: Some Lessons from Amboseli', in Anderson and Grove (eds.), *Conservation in Africa*, 149–67.

LINES, WILLIAM J., *Taming the Great South Land: A History of the Conquest of Nature in Australia* (Berkeley, CA: University of California Press, 1991).

LO, FU-CHEN, and YEUNG, YUE-MAN (eds.), *Globalization and the World of Large Cities* (Tokyo, New York: United Nations University Press, 1998).

LOEWENSTEIN, ANDREW B., 'The Veiled Protectorate of Kowait', *Middle Eastern Studies*, 36/2 (April 2000), 103–23.

LONGHURST, HENRY, *Adventure in Oil: The Story of British Petroleum* (London: Sidgwick & Jackson, 1959).

LONGRIGG, S. T., *Oil in the Middle East: Its Discovery and Development*, 3rd edn. (London: Oxford University Press, 1968).

LOVEJOY, PAUL, *Transformations in Slavery: A History of Slavery in Africa* (Cambridge: Cambridge University Press, 2000).

LUDDEN, DAVID, *An Agrarian History of South Asia, The New Cambridge History of India IV: 4* (Cambridge: Cambridge University Press, 1999).

LUNA, R. K., *Plantation Forestry in India* (Dehra Dun, 1989).

LYONS, Maryinez, *The Colonial Disease: A Social History of Sleeping Sickness in Northern Zaire, 1900–1940* (Cambridge: Cambridge University Press, 1992).

—— 'Sleeping Sickness Epidemics and Public Health in the Belgian Congo', in Arnold (ed.), *Imperial Medicine and Indigenous Societies*, 105–24.

MCCRACKEN, JOHN, 'Experts and Expertise in Colonial Malawi', *African Affairs*, 81/322 (1982), 101–16.

—— 'Colonialism, Capitalism and Ecological Crisis in Malawi: A Reassessment', in Anderson and Grove (eds.), *Conservation in Africa*, 63–77.

—— 'Planters, Peasants and the Colonial State: the Impact of the Native Tobacco Board in the Central Province of Malawi', *Journal of Southern African Studies*, 9/2 (1983), 172–92.

MCCULLOCH, JOCK, *Asbestos Blues: Labour, Capital, Physicians and the State in South Africa* (Oxford: James Currey, 2002).

MCDONALD, DAVID A. (ed.), *Environmental Justice in South Africa* (Athens: Ohio University Press; Cape Town: University of Cape Town Press, 2002).

MACDONALD, ROBERT, *The Maori of Aotearoa-New Zealand*, Minority Rights Group Report (London: Minority Rights Group, 1990).

MCEWAN, CHERYL, 'Representing West African Forests in British Imperial Discourse c. 1830–1900', in R. A. Cline-Cole and C. Madge (eds.), *Contesting Forestry in West Africa* (Aldershot, VT: Ashgate, 2000), 16–35.

MCGREGOR, RUSSELL, *Imagined Destinies: Aboriginal Australians and the Doomed Race Theory, 1880–1939* (Carlton, Victoria: Melbourne University Press, 1997).

MCHUGH, PAUL, 'The Legal and Constitutional Position of the Crown in Resource Management', in Howitt, Connell and Hirsch (eds.), *Resources*, 300–16.

MACKENZIE, A. FIONA D., *Land, Ecology and Resistance in Kenya, 1880–1952* (Edinburgh: Edinburgh University Press, 1998).

—— 'Contested Ground: Colonial Narratives and the Kenyan Environment, 1920–1945', *Journal of Southern African Studies*, 26/4 (2000), 679–718.

MacKenzie, John M., *The Empire of Nature: Hunting, Conservation and British Imperialism* (Manchester: Manchester University Press, 1988).

—— 'Empire and the Ecological Apocalypse: The Historiography of the Imperial Environment', in Griffiths and Robin (eds.), *Ecology and Empire*, 215–28.

—— 'Chivalry, Social Darwinism and Ritualised Killing: The Hunting Ethos in Central Africa up to 1914', in Anderson and Grove (eds.), *Conservation in Africa*, 41–62.

—— '"The Second City of the Empire": Glasgow—Imperial Municipality', in Driver and Gilbert (eds.), *Imperial Cities*, 215–37.

MacKenzie, John M., *Propaganda and Empire: The Manipulation of British Public Opinion 1880–1960* (Manchester: Manchester University Press, 1984).

MacLeod, Roy, and Kumar, Deepak (eds.), *Technology and the Raj: Western Technology and Technical Transfers to India, 1700–1947* (New Delhi: Sage Publications, 1995).

McNeely, J. A., and Miller, K. (eds.), *National Parks, Conservation and Development: The Role of Protected Areas in Sustaining Society, Proceedings of the World Congress on National Parks, Bali, Indonesia, 11–22 October 1982* (Washington, DC: Smithsonian Institution Press, 1984).

McNeill, John, *Something New Under the Sun: An Environmental History of the Twentieth Century* (London: Allen Lane, 2000).

—— 'Ecology, Epidemics and Empires: Environmental Change and the Geopolitics of Tropical America, 1600–1825', *Environment and History*, 5 (1999), 175–84.

McNeill, William H., *Plagues and Peoples* (New York: Anchor Press/Doubleday, 1976).

Maddock, Kenneth, *Your Land is Our Land: Aboriginal Land Rights* (Harmondsworth: Penguin Books Australia, 1983).

Makoloo, Maurice Odhiambo, *Kenya: Minorities, Indigenous Peoples and Ethnic Diversity* (London: Minority Rights Group International, 2005).

Manne, Robert (ed.), *Whitewash: On Keith Windschuttle's Fabrication of Aboriginal History* (Melbourne: Black Inc. Agenda, 2003).

Marcus, Alan R., 'Out in the Cold: The Legacy of Canada's Inuit Relocation Experiment in the High Arctic', IWGIA Document 71 (Copenhagen: IWGIA, 1992).

Markus, Thomas A., *Buildings and Power: Freedom and Control in the Origins of Modern Building Types* (London: Routledge, 1993).

Marnham, Patrick, *Fantastic Invasion: Dispatches from Africa* (London: Abacus, 1981).

Matthai, Duleep, 'Report of the Committee on the Ecological Role of Forests, Forest Protection and Meeting the Development Aspirations of the People in and around Forests' (unpublished, commissioned by Government of India: 1990).

MEMON, P. ALI, and CULLEN, R. C., 'Rehabilitation of Indigenous Fisheries in New Zealand', in Howitt, Connell, and Hirsch (eds.), *Resources*, 252–64.

MELVILLE, ELINOR G. K., *A Plague of Sheep: Environmental Consequences of the Conquest of Mexico* (Cambridge: Cambridge University Press, 1994).

MERCHANT, CAROLYN, *The Death of Nature: Women, Ecology, and the Scientific Revolution* (San Francisco, CA: Harper & Row, 1990).

METCALF, THOMAS R., 'Architecture in the British Empire', in Robin W. Winks (ed.), *Oxford History of the British Empire: Historiography*, vol. V (Oxford: Oxford University Press, 1999), 584–95.

MILES, S. B., *The Countries and Tribes of the Persian Gulf*, 2nd edn. (1919; London: Frank Cass, 1966).

MILLER, JIM R., *Skyscrapers Hide the Heavens: A History of Indian-White Relations in Canada* (Toronto: University of Toronto Press, 2000).

MILLER, LEE (ed.), *From the Heart: Voices of the American Indian* (New York: Pimlico, 1997).

MINTZ, SIDNEY W., *Sweetness and Power: The Place of Sugar in Modern History* (Harmondsworth: Penguin, 1985).

—— 'The Changing Roles of Food in the Study of Consumption', in Brewer and Porter, *Consumption and the World of Goods*, 261–73.

MITCHELL, B. R., *International Historical Statistics: Africa, Asia and Oceania, 1750–2000* (Basingstoke: Palgrave Macmillan, 2003).

MOODY, ROGER (ed.), *The Indigenous Voice: Visions & Realities*, vol. 1 (London and New Jersey: IWGIA and Zed Books, 1988).

MOORE, JASON W., 'Sugar and the Expansion of the Early Modern World-Economy: Commodity Frontiers, Ecological Transformation', *Review*, 23/3 (2000), 409–33.

MORRIS, BARRY, 'A Crisis in Identity: Aborigines, Media, the Law and Politics—Civil Disobedience in an Australian Town', *Critique of Anthropology*, 25/1 (March 2005), 59–85.

MORRIS, JAMES, *Farewell the Trumpets: An Imperial Retreat* (Harmondsworth: Penguin, 1982).

MOWFORTH, MARTIN, and MUNT, IAN, *Tourism and Sustainability: Development and New Tourism in the Third World*, 2nd edn. (London: Routledge, 2003).

MOYLE, RICHARD, 'Songs, Ceremonies and Sites: The Agharringa Case', in Peterson and Langton, *Aborigines, Land and Land Rights*, 66–93.

MUMFORD, LEWIS, *The City in History: Its Origins, its Transformations, and its Prospects* (London: Secker & Warburg, 1961).

MUNDA, R. D., and MULLICK, S. BOSU, (eds.), *The Jharkhand Movement* (Copenhagen: IWGIA, 2003).

MUTWIRA, ROBEN, 'A Question of Condoning Game Slaughter: Southern Rhodesian Wildlife Policy (1890–1953)', *Journal of Southern African Studies*, 15/2 (1989), 250–62.

MYLREA, S. G., 'Before Oil Came to Kuwait: Memoirs of C. Stanley G. Mylrea, Pioneer Physician in Bahrein and Kuwait, 1907–1947'. Unpublished papers in the Middle East Centre Archives, St Antony's College, University of Oxford.

NASUTION, KHOO SALMA, and WADE, MALCOLM, *Penang Postcard Collection, 1899–1930s* (Penang: Janus, 2003).

NELL, DAWN, 'Ecology, Agriculture and Wildlife Utilization in South Africa and Kenya, c.1950–1990', unpublished D.Phil dissertation, University of Oxford (2003).

NELSON, CYNTHIA (ed.), *The Desert and the Sown: Nomads in Wider Society* (Berkeley, CA: University of California, 1973).

NETTHEIM, GARTH, *Indigenous Rights, Human Rights and Australia*, Working Paper No. 15 (Institute of Commonwealth Studies, University of London, 1987).

NEUMANN, R. P., *Imposing Wilderness: Struggles over Livelihood and Nature Preservation in Africa* (Berkeley, CA: University of California Press, 1998).

NEWMAN, PETER C., *Company of Adventurers*, vol. 1 (Toronto: Penguin, 1986).
—— *Caesars of the Wilderness* (Toronto: Penguin, 1988).

NIEZEN, RONALD, *The Origins of Indigenism: Human Rights and the Politics of Identity* (Berkeley, CA: University of California Press, 2003).

NIGAM, SANJAY, 'Disciplining and Policing the "Criminals by Birth", Part 1: The Making of a Colonial Stereotype—The Criminal Tribes and Castes of North India', *Indian Economic and Social History Review*, 27/2 (1990), 131–64.

NORTH, MARIANNE, *Recollections of a Happy Life: Being the Autobiography of Marianne North Edited by her Sister Mrs J. A. Symonds* (London: Macmillan, 1892).
—— and BATEMAN, GRAHAM, *A Vision of Eden: The Life and Work of Marianne North* (Exeter: Webb & Bower, 1980).

NORTON-GRIFFITHS, MIKE, 'Property Rights and Wildlife Conservation Options in Kenya', CSERGE Working Paper GEC 95–07 (University College London and the University of East Anglia, Norwich, 1995).

O'FARRELL, PATRICK, *The Irish in Australia: 1788 to the Present* (Kensington, NWS: University of New South Wales Press, 2001).

OPIE, ROBERT, *Rule Britannia: Trading on the British Image* (Harmondsworth: Viking, Penguin, 1985).

ORANGE, CLAUDIA, *The Treaty of Waitangi* (Wellington: Allen & Unwin with Port Nicholson Press, 1987).

OSMASTON, B. B., *Wild Life and Adventures in Indian Forests* (Ulverston, Cumbria: pub. and edited by Henry Osmaston, 1977, 1999).

OWEN, ROGER, 'A Long Look at Nearly Two Centuries of Long Staple Cotton', in Bowman and Rogan, *Agriculture in Egypt from Pharaonic to Modern Times*, 347–65.

PACKARD, RANDALL M., *White Plague, Black Labor: Tuberculosis and the Political Economy of Health and Disease in South Africa* (Pietermaritzburg: University of Natal Press, 1989).

PALLADINO, PAULO, *Entomology, Ecology and Agriculture: The Making of Scientific Careers in North America, 1885–1985* (Amsterdam: Harwood Academic, 1996).

PARKER, IAN, *What I Tell You Three Times Is True: Conservation, Ivory, History and Politics* (Librario Publishing, 2004).

PATEL, ZARINA, *Challenge to Colonialism: The Struggle of Alibhai Mulla Jeevanjee for Equal Rights in Kenya* (Nairobi: Zand Graphics, 1997).

—— *Alibhai Mulla Jeevanjee* (Nairobi: East African Educational Publishers, 2002).

PATTEL-GRAY, ANNE, *Through Aboriginal Eyes: The Cry from the Wilderness* (Geneva: WCC Publications, 1991).

PELLY, LOUIS, *Report on a Journey to Riyadh* (Bombay: 1866; Cambridge and New York: Oleander Press, 1978).

PERRY, MARTIN, KONG, LILY, and YEOH, BRENDA, *Singapore: A Developmental City State* (Chichester: John Wiley & Sons, 1997).

PETERSON, N., and LANGTON, M., *Aborigines, Land and Land Rights* (Canberra: Australian Institute of Aboriginal Studies, 1983).

PINNEY, C., *Camera Indica: The Social Life of Indian Photographs* (London: Reaktion Books, 1997).

PORTER, A. N. (ed.), *Atlas of British Overseas Expansion* (London: Routledge, 1991).

—— (ed.), *Oxford History of the British Empire, vol. III: The Nineteenth Century* (Oxford: Oxford University Press, 1999).

POWELL, J. M., *An Historical Geography of Modern Australia: The Restive Fringe* (Cambridge: Cambridge University Press, 1988).

—— *The Emergence of Bioregionalism in the Murray-Darling Basin* (Canberra: Murray Darling Basin Commission, 1993).

PRATAP, AJAY, *The Hoe and the Axe: An Ethnohistory of Shifting Cultivation in Eastern India* (Delhi: Oxford University Press, 2000).

PRATT, MARY LOUISE, *Imperial Eyes: Travel Writing and Transculturation* (London: Routledge, 1992).

PRINGLE, T., *Narrative of a Residence in South Africa*, Vol. 1 (first published 1834; repr. Brentwood, Essex: Empire Book Association, 1986).

PURI, SUNITA, ' "Catching" the Plague: Visual Narratives of the Indian Body, Colonial Power, and Infectious Disease in Bombay, 1896–1897', unpublished M.St. thesis, University of Oxford (2003).

PYNE, STEPHEN J., *Burning Bush: A Fire History of Australia* (New York: Holt, 1991).

RABAN, JONATHAN, *Bad Land: An American Romance* (New York: Vintage, 1997).

RABY, PETER, *Alfred Russel Wallace: A Life* (London: Pimlico, 2003).

RAJAN, RAVI, 'Imperial Environmentalism or Environmental Imperialism? European Forestry, Colonial Foresters and the Agendas of Forest Management in British India, 1800–1900', in Grove, Damodaran, and Sangwan (eds.), *Nature and the Orient*, 324–71.

RANGARAJAN, MAHESH, 'Imperial Agendas and India's Forests: The Early History of Indian Forestry, 1800–1878', *The Indian Economic and Social History Review* 31/2 (1994), 147–67.

—— *Fencing the Forest: Conservation and Ecological Change in India's Central Provinces 1860–1914* (New Delhi and Oxford: Oxford University Press, 1996).

—— (ed.), *The Oxford Anthology of Indian Wildlife Vol. 1: Hunting and Shooting* (Delhi: Oxford University Press, 1999).

—— *India's Wildlife History: An Introduction* (Delhi: Permanent Black, 2001).

RANGER, T., *Voices from the Rocks: Nature, Culture and History in the Matopos Hills of Zimbabwe* (Oxford: James Currey, 1999).

RATCLIFFE, FRANCES, *Flying Fox and Drifting Sand: The Adventures of a Biologist in Australia* (London: Chatto & Windus, 1938).

RAUNKIAER, BARCLAY, *Through Wahhabiland on Camelback* (London: Routledge & Kegan Paul, 1969).

RAWAT, AJAY S., 'Brandis: The Father of Organised Forestry in India', in A. S. Rawat (ed.), *Indian Forestry: A Perspective* (Delhi: Indus Publishing, 1993).

RAY, ARTHUR J., *Indians in the Fur Trade: Their Role as Trappers, Hunters and Middlemen in the Lands Southwest of the Hudson Bay, 1660–1870* (Toronto: University of Toronto Press, 1974).

—— and FREEMAN, DONALD B., *'Give Us Good Measure': An Economic Analysis of Relations between the Indians and the Hudson's Bay Company before 1763* (Toronto: University of Toronto Press, 1978).

REID, HANNAH, FIG, DAVID, MAGOME, HECTOR, and LEADER-WILLIAMS, NIGEL, 'Co-management of Contractual National Parks in South Africa: Lessons from Australia', *Conservation and Society*, 2/2 (2004), 377–409.

REYNOLDS, HENRY, *The Other Side of the Frontier: Aboriginal Resistance to the European Invasion of Australia* (Ringwood and Harmondsworth: Penguin Books, 1981).

RIBBENTROP, B., *Forestry in British India* (Calcutta: Government Printer, 1900).

RICHARDS, AUDREY I., *Land, Labour and Diet in Northern Rhodesia: An Economic Study of the Bemba Tribe* (1939; Oxford University Press: International African Institute, London, 1995).

RICHARDS, JOHN, *The Unending Frontier: An Environmental History of the Early Modern World* (Berkeley, CA: University of California Press, 2003).

RICHARDSON, BONHAM C., *The Caribbean in the Wider World, 1492–1992: A Regional Geography* (Cambridge: Cambridge University Press, 1992).

—— *Economy and Environment in the Caribbean: Barbados and the Windwards in the late 1800s* (Barbados: University of the West Indies Press, 1997).

RITVO, HARRIET, *The Animal Estate: The English and Other Creatures in the Victorian Age* (Harmondsworth: Penguin Books, 1990).

ROBERTS, STEPHEN, *History of Australian Land Settlement, 1788–1920* (Melbourne: Macmillan, 1924).

—— *The Squatting Age in Australia, 1835–1847* (Melbourne: Melbourne University Press, 1935; repr. Cambridge University Press, 1964).

ROBIN, LIBBY, 'Ecology: A Science of Empire', in Griffiths and Robin (eds.), *Ecology and Empire*, 63–75.

ROCHE, CHRIS, '"Ornaments of the Desert": Springbok Treks in the Cape Colony, 1774–1908', unpublished MA thesis, University of Cape Town (2004).

RODNEY, WALTER, *How Europe Underdeveloped Africa* (London: Bogle L'Ouverture Publications, 1972).

ROGERS, RICHARD, and GUMUCHDJIAN, PHILIP, *Cities for a Small Planet* (London: Faber & Faber, 1997).

ROLLS, ERIC, *They All Ran Wild: The Story of Pests on the Land in Australia* (Sydney: Angus & Robertson, 1969).

—— 'The Nature of Australia', in Griffiths and Robin (eds.), *Ecology and Empire*, 35–45.

ROSEGRANT, M. W., CAI, X., and CLINE, S. A., *World Water and Food to 2025: Dealing with Scarcity* (Washington, DC: International Food Policy Research Institute).

ROTBERG, ROBERT I., *Joseph Thomson and the Exploration of Africa* (London: Chatto & Windus, 1971).

ROY, AMIT, 'Second Phase of Jharkhand Movement', in R. D. Munda and S. Bosu Mullick, (eds.), *The Jharkhand Movement* (Copenhagen: IWGIA, 2003), 73–7.

RYAN, JAMES R., *Picturing Empire: Photography and the Visualization of the British Empire* (London: Reaktion Books, 1997).

RYCROFT, DANIEL J., 'Revisioning Birsa Munda: An Afterword on Vir Vanavasi Constructs versus Identity-Hybridity in Jharkhand', paper presented at a conference on Reinterpreting Adivasi Movements in South Asia, University of Sussex, 2005.

RYDER, M. L., *Sheep and Man* (London: Duckworth, London, 1983).

SABERWAL, V., and KOTHARI, A., *People, Parks and Wildlife: Towards Coexistence* (New Delhi: Longman, 2000).

SABERWAL, V., and RANGARAJAN, M. (eds.), *Battles Over Nature: Science and the Politics of Conservation* (Delhi: Permanent Black, 2003).

SALDANHA, INDRA MUNSHI, 'Colonial Forest Regulations and Collective Resistance: Nineteenth-century Thana District', in Grove, Damodaran, and Sangwan (eds.), *Nature and the Orient*, 708–33.

SANGER, R. H., *The Arabian Peninsula* (Ithaca, NY: Cornell University Press, 1954).

SANGWAN, SATPAL, *Science, Technology and Colonisation: An Indian Experience, 1757–1857* (Delhi: Anamika Prakashan, 1991).

SANSOM, COLIN, *A Way of Life That Does Not Exist: Canada and the Extinguishment of the Innu* (London: Verso, 2003).

SARKAR, SUMIT, 'Primitive Rebellion and Modern Nationalism: A Note on Forest Satyagraha in the Non-Cooperation and Civil Disobedience Movements', in K. N. Panikkar (ed.), *National and Left Movements in India* (Delhi: Vikas, 1980), 14–26.

SASSEN, SASKIA, 'Rebuilding the Global City: Economy, Ethnicity and Space', in Anthony D. King, (ed.), *Re-Presenting the City: Ethnicity, Capital and Culture in the 21st Century Metropolis* (Basingstoke: Macmillan, 1996), 23–42.

SCHAMA, SIMON, *The Embarrassment of Riches: An Interpretation of Dutch Culture in the Golden Age* (Berkeley, CA: University of California Press, 1987).

SCHIEBINGER, LONDA, *Plants and Empire: Colonial Bioprospecting in the Atlantic World* (Cambridge, MA: Harvard University Press, 2004).

SCOTT, JAMES, *Seeing Like a State: How Certain Schemes to Improve the Human Condition Have Failed* (New Haven: Yale University Press, 1998).

SCULLY, WILLIAM CHARLES, *The Ridge of the White Waters* (London: Stanley Paul, 1913).

SEARLE, GEOFFREY, *The Golden Age: A History of the Colony of Victoria, 1851–1861* (Melbourne: Melbourne University Press, 1963).

SEN, SUNIL, *Peasant Movements in India: Mid-Nineteenth and Twentieth Centuries* (Calcutta and Delhi: K. P. Bagchi, 1982).

SELOUS, FREDERICK COURTENEY, *A Hunter's Wanderings in Africa* (first published 1881; London: Macmillan, 1928).

SEVERIN, TIM, *The Spice Islands Voyage: In Search of Wallace* (London: Abacus, 1998).

SHAMMAS, CAROLE, 'Changes in English and Anglo-American Consumption from 1550 to 1800', in Brewer and Porter (eds.), *Consumption and the World of Goods*, 177–205.

SHERMER, MICHAEL, *In Darwin's Shadow: The Life and Science of Alfred Russel Wallace* (Oxford: Oxford University Press, 2002).

SHIVA, VANDANA, *Staying Alive: Women, Ecology and Development* (London: Zed, 1988).

—— *Water Wars: Privatization, Pollution and Profit* (London: Pluto Press, 2002).

SIM, T. R., *The Forests and Forest Flora of the Colony of the Cape of Good Hope* (Cape Town: Government of the Cape of Good Hope, 1907).

SIMON, NOEL, *Between the Sunlight and the Thunder: The Wild Life of Kenya* (London: Collins, 1962).

SIMPSON, W. J., *A Treatise on Plague* (Cambridge: Cambridge University Press, 1905).

—— *Report on Sanitary Matters in the East Africa Protectorate, Uganda, and Zanzibar*, African No. 1025 (London: Colonial Office, 1915).

SINGH, SATYAJIT, *Taming the Waters: The Political Economy of Large Dams in India* (Delhi: Oxford University Press, 1997).

SIVARAMAKRISHNAN, K., 'Colonialism and Forestry in India: Imagining the Past in Present Politics', *Comparative Studies in Society and History*, 37 (1995), 3–40.

—— *Modern Forests: Statemaking and Environmental Change in Colonial Eastern India* (Stanford: Stanford University Press, 1999).

SKEAD, C. J., *Historical Mammal Incidence in the Cape Province, vol. 2, The Eastern Half of the Cape Province, including the Ciskei, Transkei and East Griqualand* (Cape Town: Provincial Administration of the Cape of Good Hope, 1987).

SLOTTEN, R. A., *The Heretic in Darwin's Court: The Life of Alfred Russel Wallace* (New York and Chichester: Columbia University Press, 2004).

SLUGLETT, PETER, *Britain in Iraq, 1914–1932* (London: Ithaca Press, 1976).

SMOUT, T. C., *Nature Contested: Environmental History in Scotland and Northern England since 1600* (Edinburgh: Edinburgh University Press, 2000).

—— 'Review Article: Problems for Global Environmental Historians', *Environment and History*, 8 (2002), 107–16.

SOUTHALL, AIDAN, *The City in Time and Space* (Cambridge: Cambridge University Press, 1998).

STEBBING, E. P., *The Forests of India*, vol. 1 (London: John Lane, 1922).

STEVENS, S., *Conservation through Cultural Survival: Indigenous Peoples and Protected Areas* (Washington, DC: Island Press, 1997).

STEVENSON-HAMILTON, JAMES, *South African Eden: The Kruger National Park, 1902–1946* (first published 1937; Cape Town: Struik, 1993).

STOCKING, GEORGE W., *Middle East Oil: A Study in Political and Economic Controversy* (London: Allen Lane, Penguin Books, 1971).

STOKES, ERIC, *The Peasant Armed: The Indian Revolt of 1857*, ed. C. A. Bayly (Oxford: Clarendon Press, 1986).

SUNDAR, NANDINI, *Subalterns and Sovereigns: An Anthropological History of Bastar, 1854–1996* (Delhi: Oxford University Press, 1997).

SUSSER, IDA, *The Castells Reader on Cities and Social Theory* (Oxford: Blackwell, 2002).

SUTER, KEITH D., and STEARMAN, KAYE, *Aboriginal Australians* (London: Minority Rights Group, 1994 update).

SWANSON, MAYNARD W., 'The Sanitation Syndrome: Bubonic Plague and Urban Native Policy in the Cape Colony, 1900–09', *Journal of African History*, 18 (1977), 387–410.

SWART, SANDRA, 'The Ant of the White Soul: Popular Natural History, the Politics of Afrikaner Identity, and the Entomological Writings of Eugene Marais', in Beinart and McGregor, (eds.) *Social History and African Environments*, 219–39.

SWEET, LOUISE, 'Camel Raiding of North Arabian Bedouin: A Mechanism of Ecological Adaptation', in Louise Sweet (ed.), *Peoples and Cultures of the Middle East: An Anthropologial Reader, Vol. I, Cultural Depth and Diversity* (Garden City, New York: Natural History Press, 1970), 265–89.

TAYLOR, STEPHEN, *The Mighty Nimrod: A Life of Frederick Courteney Selous, African Hunter and Adventurer, 1851–1917* (London: Collins, 1989).

The Indian Problem Solved: Undeveloped Wealth in India and State Reproductive Works, etc., preface 1874 (London: Virtue, Spalding & Co.).

The Indigenous World 2005 (Copenhagen: IWGIA, 2005).

THAPAR, VALMIK, 'The Tragedy of the Indian Tiger: Starting from Scratch', in John Seidensticker, Sarah Christie, and Peter Jackson (eds.), *Riding the Tiger: Tiger Conservation in Human-Dominated Landscapes* (Cambridge: Cambridge University Press, 1999), 296–306.

THIONGO, NGUGI WA, *Decolonising the Mind: The Politics of Language in African Literature* (London: James Currey, 1986).

THOMAS, KEITH, *Man and the Natural World: Changing Attitudes in England 1500–1800* (Harmondsworth: Penguin Books, 1984).

THOMSON, JOSEPH, *Through Masai Land* (London: Sampson Low, Marston, Searle & Rivington, 1885).

—— and HARRIS-SMITH, E., *Ulu: An African Romance* (London: Sampson Low, Marston & Co., 1888).

THOMSON, J. B., *Joseph Thomson, African Explorer: A Biography by his Brother* (London: Sampson Low, Marston & Co., 1896).

THORNTON, E. N., *A Report on an Investigation into Plague in the Protectorate of Uganda* (Entebbe: Government Printer, 1930).

THORNTON, JOHN, *Africa and Africans in the Making of the Atlantic World, 1400–1600* (Cambridge: Cambridge University Press, 1992).

THORNTON WHITE, L.W., SILBERMAN, L., and ANDERSON, P. R., *Nairobi: Master Plan for a Colonial Capital* (London: HMSO, 1948).

THROUP, D. W., 'The Origins of Mau Mau', *African Affairs*, 84/336 (1985), 399–433.

TIDRICK, KATHRYN, *Empire and the English Character* (London: I.B. Tauris, 1990).

TIFFEN, MARY, MORTIMORE, MICHAEL, and GICHUKI, FRANCIS, *More People, Less Erosion: Environmental Recovery in Kenya* (Chichester: Wiley, 1994).

TILLEY, HELEN, 'Africa as a "Living Laboratory": The African Research Survey and British Colonial Empire: Consolidating Environmental, Medical, and Anthropological Debates, 1920–1940', unpublished D.Phil. thesis, University of Oxford (2001).

TOMLINSON, B. R., 'Empire of the Dandelion: Ecological Imperialism and Economic Expansion, 1860–1914', *Journal of Imperial and Commonwealth History*, 26/2 (1998), 84–99.

TOOVEY, JACQUELINE (ed.), *Tigers of the Raj: Pages from the Shikar Diaries, 1884 to 1949, of Col. Burton, Sportsman and Conservationist* (Gloucester: Alan Sutton Publishing, 1987).

TROLLOPE, ANTHONY, *Australia and New Zealand,* vol. 2 (London: Chapman & Hall, 1873).

TROTTER, H., *The Common Commercial Timbers of India and their Uses* (Calcutta: Government Printer, 1929).

TROUP, R. S., *Colonial Forest Administration* (London: Oxford University Press, 1940).

TUCKEY, J. H., *Narrative of an Expedition to Explore the River Zaire, Usually Called the Congo, in South Africa in 1816* (London: John Murray, 1818).

TURNBULL, C. M., *The Straits Settlements, 1826–67: Indian Presidency to Crown Colony* (London: Athlone Press, 1972).

TYRRELL, IAN, *True Gardens of the Gods: Californian-Australian Environmental Reform, 1860–1930* (Berkeley, CA: University of California Press, 1999).

VAIL, LEROY, 'Ecology and History: The Example of Eastern Zambia', *Journal of Southern African Studies*, 3 (1977), 129–55.

VANDERHAEGHE, GUY, *The Englishman's Boy* (London: Anchor, 1998).

van HEYNINGEN, ELIZABETH, 'Cape Town and the Plague of 1901', in Christopher Saunders, Howard Phillips, and E. van Heyningen (eds.), *Studies in the History of Cape Town*, vol. 4 (Cape Town: University of Cape Town, 1984), 66–107.

—— *The Last Crossing* (London: Abacus, 2005).

VAN KIRK, SYLVIA, *Many Tender Ties: Women in Fur-Trade Society, 1670–1870* (Norman: University of Oklahoma Press, 1983).

van ONSELEN, CHARLES, *Studies in the Social and Economic History of the Witwatersrand, 1886–1914*, vols. 1 and 2 (Harlow: Longman, 1982).

VAUGHAN, MEGAN, *Curing their Ills: Colonial Power and African Illness* (Cambridge: Polity Press, 1991).

VENN, FIONA, *Oil Diplomacy in the Twentieth Century* (Basingstoke: Macmillan, 1986).

VILLE, SIMON, *The Rural Entrepreneurs: A History of the Stock and Station Agent Industry in Australia and New Zealand* (Cambridge: Cambridge University Press, 2000).

VILLIERS, ALAN, 'Some Aspects of the Arab Dhow Trade', in Louise Sweet (ed.), *Peoples and Cultures of the Middle East: An Anthropological Reader*, vol. I, *Cultural Depth and Diversity* (Garden City, New York: Natural History Press, 1970), 155–72.

VINCENT, D., *Literacy and Popular Culture: England, 1750–1914* (Cambridge: Cambridge University Press, 1989).

VISARIA, LEELA and PRAVIN, 'Population (1757–1947)', in Dharma Kumar and Tapan Raychaudhuri (eds.), *Cambridge Economic History of India*, vol. 2, *c. 1757–1970* (Cambridge: Cambridge University Press, 1983), 463–532.

WAGNER, ROGER, 'Zoutpansberg: The Dynamics of a Hunting Frontier, 1848–1867', in Marks and Atmore (eds.), *Economy and Society*, 313–49.

WAKIL, A. W., *The Third Pandemic of Plague in Egypt* (Cairo: The Egyptian University, 1932).

WALLACE, A. R., *The Malay Archipelago: The Land of the Orang-utan, and the Bird of Paradise: A Narrative of Travels with Studies of Man and Nature* (London: Macmillan, 1869).

WALLER, RICHARD, 'Tsetse Fly in Western Narok, Kenya', *Journal of African History*, 31/1 (1990), 81–101.

WALVIN, JAMES, *Black Ivory: Slavery in the British Empire* (Oxford: Blackwell, 2001).

WAN, TEH CHEANG, 'Public Housing', in Ooi Jin-Bee and Chiang Hai Ding (eds.), *Modern Singapore* (Singapore: University of Singapore, 1969).

WARKENTIN, GERMAINE, 'Discovering Radisson: A Renaissance Adventurer between Two Worlds', in Brown and Vibert, *Reading Beyond Words*, 43–70.

WATTS, DAVID, *The West Indies: Patterns of Development, Culture and Environmental Change since 1492* (Cambridge: Cambridge University Press, 1987).

The Wealth of India: A Dictionary of Indian Raw Materials and Indian Products, 10, (Delhi: Council of Science and Industrial Research, 1976).

WEBBER, THOMAS W., *The Forests of Upper India and their Inhabitants* (London: Edward Arnold, 1902).

WESTERN, DAVID, 'Amboseli National Park: Enlisting Landowners to Conserve Migratory Wildlife', *Ambio*, 11/5 (1982), 302–8.

—— Preface: 'The Evolution of Ecotourism in East Africa: From an Idea to an Industry', *Summary of the Proceedings of the East African Regional Conference on Ecotourism, March 2002*, IIED Wildlife and Development Series No. 15 (June 2003).

WHITCOMBE, ELIZABETH, 'Irrigation', in D. Kumar and T. Raychaudhuri (eds.), *The Cambridge Economic History of India*, vol. 2, *c.1757–1970* (Cambridge: Cambridge University Press, 1983), ch. 8.

—— 'The Environmental Costs of Irrigation in British India: Waterlogging,

Salinity, Malaria', in Arnold and Guha (eds.), *Nature, Culture, Imperialism*, 237–59.

WHITE, RICHARD, *The Middle Ground: Indians, Empires, and Republics in the Great Lakes Region, 1650–1815* (Cambridge: Cambridge University Press, 1991).

WILKS, IVOR, *Asante in the Nineteenth Century: The Structure and Evolution of a Political Order* (Cambridge: Cambridge University Press, 1975).

WILLCOCKS, WILLIAM, *Lectures on the Ancient System of Irrigation in Bengal and its Application to Modern Problems* (Calcutta: University of Calcutta Press, 1930).

—— *Sixty Years in the East* (Edinburgh and London: William Blackwood & Sons, 1935).

—— and CRAIG, J. I., *Egyptian Irrigation*, 3rd edn. (London: E. & F. N. Spon; New York: Spon & Chamberlain, 1913).

WILLIAMS, ERIC, *Capitalism and Slavery* (London: Andre Deutsch, 1944).

WILLIAMS, MICHAEL, *Deforesting the Earth: From Prehistory to Global Crisis* (Chicago and London: University of Chicago Press, 2003).

WILLIAMSON, W., *In a Persian Oil Field: A Study in Scientific and Industrial Development*, 2nd edn. (1927; London: Ernest Benn, 1930).

WILLS, Jr., JOHN E, 'European Consumption and Asian Production in the Seventeenth and Eighteenth Centuries', in Brewer and Porter, *Consumption and the World of Goods*, 133–47.

WILSON, JAMES, *Canada's Indians*, Minority Rights Group Report No. 21 (London: Minority Rights Group International, 1982).

WINCHESTER, SIMON, *Krakatoa: The Day the World Exploded, 27 August 1883* (London: Viking, 2003).

WINKS, ROBIN W. (ed.), *Oxford History of the British Empire*, vol., V, *Historiography* (Oxford: Oxford University Press, 1999).

WITTFOGEL, KARL A., *Oriental Despotism: A Comparative Study of Total Power* (New Haven: Yale University Press, 1957).

WORSTER, DONALD, *Dust Bowl: The Southern Plains in the 1930s* (New York: Oxford University Press, 1979).

—— *Rivers of Empire: Water, Aridity, and the Growth of the American West* (New York, Oxford: Oxford University Press, 1985).

—— 'Appendix: Doing Environmental History', in Donald Worster (ed.), *The Ends of the Earth* (New York: Cambridge University Press, 1989).

WORTHINGTON, E. B., *Science in Africa* (London: Oxford University Press, 1938).

—— *The Ecological Century: A Personal Appraisal* (Oxford: Oxford University Press, 1983).

WRIGLEY, E. A., 'Meeting Human Energy Needs: Constraints, Opportunities, and Effects', in Paul Slack (ed.), *Environments and Historical Change: The Linacre Lectures* (Oxford: Oxford University Press, 1999).

WYNN, GRAEME, *Remaking the Land God Gave to Cain: A Brief Environmental History of Canada*, lecture series no. 62 (London: Canada House, 1998).

YEOH, BRENDA S. A., *Contesting Space: Power Relations and the Urban Built Environment in Colonial Singapore* (Oxford, New York, and Kuala Lumpur: Oxford University Press, 1996).

YERGIN, DANIEL, *The Prize: The Epic Quest for Oil, Money and Power* (London and New York: Simon & Schuster, 1991).

YOUNG, ANN R. M., *Environmental Change in Australia since 1788* (Melbourne: Oxford University Press, 1996).

ZAHEDIEH, NUALA, 'Overseas Expansion and Trade in the Seventeenth Century', in Nicholas Canny (ed.), *Oxford History of the British Empire*, vol. 1 *The Origins of Empire*, (Oxford: Oxford University Press, 1998), 398–422.

INDEX

Note: Page numbers in *italics* indicate illustrations